Shared Cognition in Organizations

The Management of Knowledge

LEA's Organization and Management Series
Arthur Brief and James Walsh, Series Editors

Beach • Image Theory: Theoretical and Empirical Foundations

Thompson/Levine/Messick • Shared Cognition in Organizations: The Management of Knowledge

Shared Cognition in Organizations

The Management of Knowledge

Leigh L. Thompson
Northwestern University

John M. Levine
University of Pittsburgh

David M. Messick
Northwestern University

 LAWRENCE ERLBAUM ASSOCIATES, PUBLISHERS
1999   Mahwah, NJ   London

 # 40 83030 1

Lawrence Erlbaum Associates, Inc., Publishers
10 Industrial Avenue
Mahwah, NJ 07430

Cover design by Kathryn Houghtaling Lacey

Library of Congress Cataloging-in-Publication Data
Thompson, Leigh.
Shared cognition in organizations: the management of knowl-
edge / Leigh L. Thompson, John M. Levine, David M. Messick.
    p.   cm.
Includes bibliographical references and index.
ISBN 0-8058-2890-7 (alk. paper). — ISBN 0-8058-2891-5 (pbk. :
alk. paper)
1. Knowledge management. 2. Organization. I. Levine, John
M. II. Messick, David M. III. Title.
HD30.2.T495   1999
658.4'038—dc21
                            99-20558
                                CIP

Books published by Lawrence Erlbaum Associates are printed on
acid-free paper, and their bindings are chosen for strength and
durability.

Printed in the United States of America
10 9 8 7 6 5 4 3 2 1

Contents

Part II   Emotional and Motivational Systems

Part III   Communication and Behavioral Systems

About the Editors

Leigh L. Thompson was named the John L. and Helen Kellogg Distinguished Professor of Organization Behavior at the Kellogg Graduate School of Management in 1995. She was a fellow at the center for Advanced Study in the Behavioral Sciences in 1994–1995, and received a Presidential Young Investigator Award from the National Science Foundation in 1991. She is also the director of the AT&T Behavioral Research Laboratory, the Kellogg Team Building for Managers Executive Program, and the Kellogg Teams and Groups Center (KTAG) at Northwestern University. Dr. Thompson's research focuses on negotiation, group decision making, judgment, and team performance. Her book, *The Mind and Heart of the Negotiator* (Prentice-Hall, 1998), integrates negotiation and group decision making with social psychological processes.

Dr. Thompson is a member of the editorial boards of *Organization Behavior and Human Decision Processes*, *Journal of Experimental Social Psychology*, *Journal of Behavioral Decision Making*, *International Journal of Conflict Management*, and *Group Decision and Negotiation*. She was named a fellow of the American Psychological Society and is a member of the Academy of Management, American Psychological Association, Judgment and Decision Making Society, and the Society for Experimental Social Psychologists.

BA 1982, Communication Studies, Northwestern University; MA 1984, Education, University of California, Santa Barbara; PhD 1988, Psychology, Northwestern University.

John M. Levine is Professor of Psychology and Senior Scientist in the Learning Research and Development Center at the University of Pittsburgh. Dr. Levine's research focuses on small group processes, particularly group socialization, majority and minority influence, and team performance. He has authored or coauthored more than 70 journal articles and chapters.

Dr. Levine is currently editor of the *Journal of Experimental Social Psychology*. He has served as associate editor of the *Journal of Research in Personality* and the *Journal of Experimental Social Psychology*, and has been a member of several editorial boards, including *Social Psychology Quarterly, Journal of Personality and Social Psychology, Review of Personality and Social Psychology, Basic and Applied Social Psychology, Personality and Social Psychology Bulletin, Social Cognition*, and *Group Processes and Intergroup Relations*. Dr. Levine has also been a member of the NSF Advisory Panel for Social and Developmental Psychology and the NIMH Social and Group Processes Review Committee. He is a fellow of the American Psychological Association and the American Psychological Society and a member of the Society of Experimental Social Psychology and the European Association of Experimental Social Psychology.

BA 1965, Psychology, Northwestern University; MS 1967, PhD 1969, Psychology, University of Wisconsin–Madison.

David M. Messick was named the Morris and Alice Kaplan Professor of Ethics and Decision in Management at the Kellogg Graduate School of Management in 1991. Dr. Messick's teaching and research interests are in the ethical and social aspects of decision making and information processing. The author of more than 100 articles and chapters, his scholarly work has been published in prominent academic journals.

Dr. Messick is a past editor of the *Journal of Experimental Social Psychology* and a member of the editorial boards of the *Journal of Behavioral Decision Making, Journal of Experimental and Social Psychology, Social Justice Research*, and the *European Review of Social Psychology*. He received the Distinguished Alumnus award from the Department of Psychology at the University of North Carolina in 1986, and was an Eastern European Exchange Fellow of the National Academy of Science in 1990. He is a member of the American Psychological Society, Society for Experimental Social Psychology, Society for Personality and Social Psychology, and the Society for Business Ethics.

BA 1961, Psychology, University of Delaware; MA 1964, PhD 1965, Psychology, University of North Carolina.

Contributors

Linda Argote	*Carnegie Mellon University*
Renee J. Bator	*State University of New York at Plattsburgh*
Terry L. Boles	*University of Iowa*
Ronald S. Burt	*University of Chicago*
Robert B. Cialdini	*Arizona State University*
Elliott T. Fan	*Northwestern University*
Deborah H. Gruenfeld	*Northwestern University*
Rosanna E. Guadagno	*Arizona State University*
E. Tory Higgins	*Columbia University*
John T. Jost	*Stanford University*
Peter H. Kim	*University of Southern California*
Roderick M. Kramer	*Stanford University*
Arie W. Kruglanski	*University of Maryland at College Park*
Richard L. Moreland	*University of Pittsburgh*
Janice Nadler	*University of Illinois at Urbana–Champaign*
Fernando Olivera	*Carnegie Mellon University*
Linda Simon	*University of Maryland at College Park*
Garold Stasser	*Miami University*
Philip E. Tetlock	*The Ohio State University*

Series Editors' Foreword

Arthur P. Brief
Tulane University

James P. Walsh
University of Michigan

The term "organizational learning" has come into common usage among managers and scholars alike. Its familiarity belies the fact that how knowledge is created, stored, retrieved, and diffused in organizations remains poorly understood. Leigh Thompson, John Levine, and David Messick's collection of essays are aimed at remedying this state of affairs. Their book richly details a variety of processes that explain the effective management of knowledge in organizations.

The contributors to Thompson et al.'s collection, although focusing on a common problem, approach it in highly distinctive ways. Not only does level of analysis (individual, group, and organization) and discipline orientation (psychology and sociology) vary between essays; how the problem of knowledge management is interpreted also is not a constant. Some authors see the problem in terms of managing uncertainty, distrust, and dirty secrets, whereas others view it as being concerned with socializing newcomers, treating collective paranoia, and constructing social realities. Because of this diversity, the reader, no matter what he or she brings to the book, will walk away from it having been challenged and stimulated.

Shared Cognition in Organizations: The Management of Knowledge truly charts new territory in the organizational sciences. For this reason, we are proud to include it in the LEA Series in Organization and Management. The series is intended to provide an outlet for scholarly works that create promising new avenues of investigation or meaningfully alter the course of existing ones. Thompson, Levine, and Messick's book fits this mold of discovery perfectly.

Preface

The chapters in this book were presented at a conference titled "Shared Cognition in Organizations: The Management of Knowledge," held at the J. L. Allen Center at Northwestern University in November of 1996. The conference was designed to bring together behavioral scientists who were interested in the creation, conservation, distribution, and protection of knowledge in organizations.

The Dispute Resolution Research Center and Dean Donald Jacobs of the J. L. Kellogg Graduate School of Management (of Northwestern University) were the cosponsors of this event. We are grateful for their support on this project and the subsequent development of this book. Assistance with the coordination of the conference and preparation of this volume was provided initially by Claire Buisseret, whose management and organizational skills proved invaluable. Subsequent administrative and editing assistance was provided by Katie Shonk and Rachel Claff. Rachel Claff is the person who is truly responsible for bringing this book to fruition. We are deeply indebted to her for organizing the review process, editing the manuscripts, and putting all of the pieces together.

—Leigh L. Thompson
—John M. Levine
—David M. Messick

Introduction

Leigh L. Thompson
Northwestern University

John M. Levine
University of Pittsburgh

David M. Messick
Northwestern University

The idea for a conference on shared cognition in organizations came about several years ago, when we decided to bring together a group of eminent scholars interested in how people in organizations create, distribute, and act on knowledge. Our goal was to explore new directions in social cognition research that shed light on how organizational members think and reason.

In recent years, increasing attention has been devoted to the social bases of cognition (for example, see Higgins, 1992; Hinsz, Tindale, & Vollrath, 1997; Levine, Resnick, & Higgins, 1993; Nye & Brower, 1996; Resnick, Levine, & Teasley, 1991; Thompson, 1998). Using such rubrics as socially shared cognition, distributed cognition, and contextualized cognition, investigators are focusing on cognition as an interpersonal as well as an intrapersonal process. Without negating the importance of information processing at the individual level, social psychologists (as well as developmental and organizational psychologists, anthropologists, sociologists, and educational researchers) are exploring the implications of viewing cognition as a fundamentally social activity. This new way of thinking about social cognition was a major impetus for organizing our conference and preparing this volume of conference papers.

At about the same time the area of socially shared cognition was beginning to develop, an interesting intellectual migration was occurring with social psychologists, both newly minted and well-established, moving from psychology departments in colleges of arts and sciences to organization behavior departments in business schools. This migration has resulted in two important developments.

First, social psychologists who enter business schools find themselves barraged with interesting questions about how knowledge is used by teams and collectives. These questions do not come only from MBA students demanding that professors present a clear take-home point. In addition, they are frequently asked by business school colleagues trained in different areas, such as sociology and economics. These questions have forced social psychologists to think more deeply about issues of persuasion, motivation, and group interaction in organizational contexts and this thinking has often led to new research questions concerning how socially shared knowledge is developed and used. Second, social psychologists who enter business schools often change their research methodologies. Controlled laboratory experiments with college sophomores often lose their appeal, whereas observations of work teams on shop floors, archival analyses of CEO decisions, and questionnaires distributed in MBA classrooms become more attractive. These new methodologies often produce information about socially shared knowledge that is difficult if not impossible to obtain using traditional social psychological methods.

A third factor that inspired the conference and resulting volume is our belief that social psychologists interested in social cognition have much to learn from organizational theorists. Those of us who observe events in organizations are gratified to learn that our theories about such phenomena as proximity and liking, mere exposure, and thought-induced affect are applicable there. However, in many instances, what we consider to be uniquely social psychological phenomena have been analyzed in other terms. For example, talk to educated executives about social cognition, schemas, and heuristics, and they will tell you about March and Simon's theory of the firm. Mention biases, and they will cite escalation of commitment and Shubik's dollar auction. Talk about polarization and the formation of group-level norms, and they will bring up clique networks and information brokers. We believe that social psychologists have much to offer to the field of organizational behavior, but our contributions depend on our openness to the theoretical contributions of organizational scholars.

We can think of no organizational phenomenon more relevant to social cognition than knowledge. In fact, as we prepared this volume, we were introduced to a new title in many organizational charts: CKO, or chief knowledge officer. In this volume, we brought together a distinguished group of social psychologists who have made important contributions to social cognition and group processes. We cast a wide net in terms of the topics covered and we challenged authors to think about how their research applies to the management (or mismanagement) of knowledge in organizations. We divided the volume into three sections: the first focusing on knowledge systems, the second focusing on emotional and motivational systems, and the third focusing on communication and behavioral systems. A final conclusion chapter discusses and integrates the various contributions.

The first section deals with how knowledge and information are created, stored, and acted on within organizations. Moreland focuses on transactive memory systems in groups, which are shared mental representations for encoding and acting on knowledge. In a programmatic series of experiments, he finds that group members who train together perform better, even holding constant the training that each member has. Thus, team training allows group members to develop implicit, shared understandings of the task and each person's knowledge base. Higgins examines how the mere act of transferring knowledge can affect actors' beliefs about the knowledge. Specifically, people naturally tune their message to suit the perceived needs and interests of their audience. The very act of tuning introduces a bias in the communicator's subsequent use of the message as a source of knowledge and evaluations, yet the communicator does not realize this. Stasser examines how the distribution of knowledge among group members affects the likelihood of its use, independent of its actual value. Small groups tend to mention disproportionate amounts of shared, relative to unshared, information at the expense of pooling unshared information. This tendency to discuss common information is not easily remedied. Finally, Messick examines organizations in which knowledge places the originator in a position of risk. *Dirty secrets* are secrets about real or potential wrongdoing that are concealed from competitors, governmental and regulatory agencies, the press, and the public. Messick focuses on the tobacco industry as a case in point and argues that concealing knowledge is a strategic decision.

The second section focuses on emotional and motivational aspects of knowledge within organizations. Jost, Kruglanski, and Simon examine how social actors' motivations affect how they use knowledge. In a series of experiments, the authors demonstrate that individual needs for cognitive closure are more satisfied by the emergence and maintenance of shared knowledge that is politically conservative, socially intolerant, antidemocratic, and system-justifying than by knowledge that poses a challenge to the status quo. Tetlock examines how accountability affects the utilization of knowledge. In this approach, people are viewed as intuitive politicians whose key goal is to protect their identity in the eyes of key constituencies. A theory of accountability is proposed in which several predictions are made about social actors' behavior. Thompson, Nadler, and Kim focus on how organizational actors use emotions to gain resources when negotiating. In contrast to the traditional view of emotion as a detriment to effective negotiation, The authors suggest that negotiators can capitalize on emotion at the bargaining table. Strategies involve both perceiving emotion in others and experiencing emotion for oneself. Finally, Kramer examines how paranoia can develop in organizational knowledge communities. Kramer demonstrates how trust-related judgments may be conceptualized as a dilemma game, in which social actors are uncertain about others' motives, intentions, and behavior.

The last section focuses on communication and behavioral aspects of knowledge. Cialdini, Bator, and Guadagno discuss the formation of norms within organizations as a consequence of behaviors and context. The Triple Tumor of Dishonesty model is used to argue that organizations that establish dishonest business practices as a socially acceptable behavioral norm lose far more than they gain. The authors suggest how organizations may benefit by taking advantage of descriptive and injunctive norms. Burt examines how social networks influence the dissemination and treatment of knowledge. Burt highlights the tension between the network theory of structural holes defining entrepreneurial opportunity versus the network theory of cohesion defining security and trust. Burt presents an alternative to cohesion: A network theory of trust emerging from third-party gossip. Gruenfeld and Fan examine how groups communicate norms and highlight the discontinuity between what newcomers see and what oldtimers say. Gruenfeld and Fan present the results of an empirical study in which newcomers to intact groups display greater integrative complexity after, rather than before, their group membership, suggesting that newcomers experience cognitive growth in response to their new environment. Levine and Moreland focus on knowledge transmission and newcomer socialization in work groups. They argue that a critical task for newcomers entering workgroups is learning the shared mental models that oldtimers possess. Levine and Moreland point out that shared mental models can inhibit as well as enhance group performance. Finally, Olivera and Argote examine how organizations learn and develop new products as a result of knowledge acquisition and transfer. They present a CORE framework (Construction, Operation, Reconstruction, and External relations) that identifies tradeoffs in the product development process.

In a concluding chapter, Boles summarizes and integrates the various contributions and suggests some interesting directions for future research.

REFERENCES

Higgins, E. T. (1992). Achieving "shared reality" in the communication game: A social action that creates meaning. *Journal of Language and Social Psychology, 11*, 107–131.

Hinsz, V. B., Tindale, R. S., & Vollrath, D. A. (1997). The emerging conceptualization of groups as information processors. *Psychological Bulletin, 121*, 43–64.

Levine, J. M., Resnick, L. B., & Higgins, E. T. (1993). Social foundations of cognition. *Annual Review of Psychology, 44*, 585–612.

Nye, J. L., & Brower, A. M. (1996). *What's social about social cognition?* Thousand Oaks, CA: Sage.

Resnick, L., Levine, J., & Teasley, S. (Eds.). (1991). *Perspectives on socially shared cognition.* Washington, DC: American Psychological Association.

Thompson, L. (1998). *The mind and heart of the negotiator.* Upper Saddle River, NJ: Prentice-Hall.

KNOWLEDGE SYSTEMS

1

Transactive Memory: Learning Who Knows What in Work Groups and Organizations

Richard L. Moreland
University of Pittsburgh

In many organizations, work that was once done by individuals is now done by groups. These groups include top management teams, cross-functional teams, self-managed work teams, and special task forces. The trend toward group work in organizations has generated a parallel trend toward group research among many social scientists, especially organizational psychologists (see Levine & Moreland, 1990; Sanna & Parks, 1997). Much of that research focuses on work group performance. Organizations often use groups to improve worker productivity and the available evidence suggests that this goal is often achieved (see Carr, 1992; Hoerr, 1989; Katzenbach & Smith, 1993; Montebello & Buzzota, 1993; Wellins, Byham, & Dixon, 1994). However, work groups sometimes fail (see Dubnicki & Limburg, 1991; Dumaine, 1994; Hackman, 1998; Vogt & Hunt, 1988) and even when they seem to succeed, further improvements in worker productivity may still be possible. A careful theoretical analysis of work group performance, investigating causal factors that could be managed by an organization, is thus potentially valuable (Dunphy & Bryant, 1996).

IMPROVING THE PERFORMANCE OF WORK GROUPS BY MANAGING THEIR COMPOSITION

Several theoretical models of work group performance have been offered (e.g., Cohen, 1994; Gladstein, 1984; Hackman, 1987). These models differ from one another in various ways, but most of them identify group composition as an important factor. Composition refers to the number and types of workers who belong to the group (Moreland & Levine, 1992a). Many individual characteristics, including not only the workers' abilities but also their demographic characteristics, opinions, and personality traits, might be relevant to a group's tasks. The group's performance of such tasks could thus be improved by altering its composition for those characteristics. Changes in both the central tendency and the variability of group members might be helpful. For example, the group's central tendency could be improved by (a) hiring workers with desirable characteristics or firing workers with undesirable characteristics, (b) training workers in ways that strengthen desirable characteristics or weaken undesirable characteristics, or (c) linking the group to outsiders with desirable characteristics (see Ancona & Caldwell, 1988). Changes in group variability could also be made, using similar tactics, but such changes can influence performance in more complex ways (Moreland, Levine, & Wingert, 1996). Although diversity can improve a group's performance, such gains are often offset by losses arising from conflict among group members.

Altering a work group's composition is an appealing strategy, but it may not always be practical. Fortunately, another strategy is usually possible (see Hackman & Morris, 1975), namely making better use of whatever characteristics a group's members already possess. This requires that someone know not only which worker characteristics are relevant to the group's tasks, but also how those characteristics are distributed among group members. Traditionally, a manager was always assumed to have and use such knowledge. But in many organizations, work groups are now becoming self-managed (Lawler, Mohrman, & Ledford, 1992; Manz & Sims, 1993; *Training and Development*, 1994). In these groups, which may not have a leader, who is responsible for identifying task-relevant characteristics and evaluating their distribution among group members (see Kozlowski, Gully, Salas, & Cannon-Bowers, 1996; Saavedra & Kwun, 1993)? The latter task can be especially difficult in an era when the activities of many work groups are rapidly changing (Herr, 1993; Parker, Wall, & Jackson, 1997; Waller, 1997), temporary employees come and go more often (Barsness, 1996; Feldman, 1995; Mantel, 1994), and regular group members are likely to be diverse (Jackson & Alvarez, 1993).

Perhaps the performance of some work groups, especially self-managed teams, could be improved by helping members learn more about one another so that they could make better use of the group's human resources. Among those resources, the task knowledge of group members, often referred to as the group's "intellectual capital" or "knowledge assets" (Marquardt, 1996; Stewart, 1995a), seems especially important. An analysis of how group members could share task knowledge with one another can be found in Wegner's work on transactive memory (see Wegner, 1987, 1995; Wegner, Giuliano, & Hertel, 1985).

TRANSACTIVE MEMORY AND WORK GROUP PERFORMANCE

Wegner was the first to analyze transactive memory, especially as it occurs in couples. He noted that people often supplement their own memories, which are limited and can be unreliable, with various external aids. These include objects (e.g., address or appointment books) and other people (e.g., friends or coworkers). Wegner was especially interested in the use of people as memory aids. He speculated that a transactive memory system may develop in many groups to ensure that important information is remembered. This system combines the knowledge possessed by individual group members with a shared awareness of who knows what. So when group members need information, but cannot remember it themselves or doubt that their memories are accurate, they can turn to each other for help. A transactive memory system can thus provide a group's members with more and better information than any of them could remember alone.

The potential benefits of transactive memory for a work group's performance are clear. When group members know more about each other, they can plan their work more sensibly, assigning tasks to the people who will perform them best. Coordination ought to improve as well because workers can anticipate rather than simply react to each other's behavior (see Murnighan & Conlon, 1991; Wittenbaum, Vaughan, & Stasser, 1998). As a result, they can work together more efficiently, even if task assignments are unclear. Finally, problems should be solved more quickly and easily when workers know more about one another because they can then match problems with the people most likely to solve them (see Moreland & Levine, 1992b). Once those people are identified, they can be asked for help or the problems can simply be given to them to solve.

If these claims seem unconvincing, then just imagine a work group (e.g., subjects in most laboratory experiments on group performance) whose members are ignorant about who knows what. In such a group, sensible planning would not be possible. Tasks might be assigned to people at random, or maybe on the basis of such irrelevant cues as appearance or demeanor. The group might fail to plan its work at all, allowing people to work at whatever tasks they liked best (see Weingart, 1992). It would be surprising if either of these options led to an optimal use of the group's resources. Coordination would probably suffer as well, as confused members struggled to make sense of each other's behavior, and problems might become more troublesome, as unqualified members tried to solve them.

Do work groups really perform better when their members know who is good at what? Unfortunately, research on transactive memory is scarce. Most of that research involves couples rather than groups (see Hollingshead, 1998; Wegner, Erber, & Raymond, 1991), and tasks that are not much like those faced by most workers. There is, however, some indirect evidence that transactive memory can improve a group's performance. It comes from research on group decision making that investigates whether the quality of a group's decisions is related to how well its members can recognize expertise (see Libby, Trotman, & Zimmer, 1987; Stasser, Stewart, & Wittenbaum, 1995; Yetton & Bottger, 1982). Expertise recognition is clearly an important part of transactive memory because it not only guides group, members to those individuals who have useful information, but also allows members to evaluate whatever information they obtain by considering its sources. And decision making clearly plays an important role in many of the tasks that work groups perform (Guzzo & Salas, 1995).

In general, groups make wiser decisions when their members are better at recognizing expertise. Some of the most interesting work in this area is done by Henry (see Henry, 1993, 1995a, 1995b; Henry, Strickland, Yorges, & Ladd, 1996), and by Littlepage and his colleagues (Littlepage, Schmidt, Whisler, & Frost, 1995; Littlepage & Silbiger, 1992; Littlepage, Robison, & Reddington, 1997). In Henry's research, subjects are usually asked to answer trivia questions (e.g., When was the safety pin invented?), first alone and then in small groups. Afterwards, they evaluate one another's expertise. The ability of group members to recognize expertise is assessed by comparing those evaluations with measures of actual expertise. Henry has been especially interested in discovering ways to improve the recognition of expertise by groups. I will consider that issue later on, but for now, two general findings from Henry's research seem noteworthy. First, a group's members can form (without discussion) shared beliefs about their relative expertise, and those beliefs are often accurate. Second, groups make better decisions when their members' beliefs about relative expertise are more accurate.

Littlepage and his colleagues usually ask subjects in their research to solve problems posed by hypothetical scenarios (e.g., Desert Survival) involving the survival of a group in a dangerous environment after a traumatic event. Subjects solve these problems alone at first, then in groups. Afterwards they evaluate one another's expertise. The ability of group members to recognize expertise is again assessed by comparing these evaluations with measures of real expertise. Like Henry, Littlepage and his colleagues find that group members form shared beliefs about their relative expertise. Those beliefs are not always accurate, however, perhaps because the decision-making task in these studies is relatively complex. Nevertheless, Littlepage and his colleagues do find, like Henry, that groups make better decisions when their members' beliefs about relative expertise are more accurate.

These and other findings suggest that transactive memory systems, which reflect the ability of group members to recognize expertise, may indeed be valuable for work groups. But how do such systems develop, and can they be managed? In most work groups, the development of transactive memory systems is probably a slow and gradual process. As workers spend time together, performing the same or similar tasks, they become familiar with one another. Each person's strengths and weaknesses are noted and then taken into account as group members learn to work together productively. Although no one has yet studied this process directly, many studies have shown that groups perform better if their members are more familiar with one another (see Argote, 1993; Barsness, 1996; Goodman & Shah, 1992; Gruenfeld, Mannix, Williams, & Neale, 1996; Jehn & Shah, 1997; Kanki & Foushee, 1989; Larson, Foster-Fishman, & Keys, 1994; Murnighan & Conlon, 1991; Watson, Kumar, & Michaelsen, 1993; Watson, Michaelsen, & Sharp, 1991). Kanki and Foushee (1989), for example, found that the performance benefits of keeping an aircrew's members together across simulated flights were strong enough to overcome such dangers as boredom and fatigue. Goodman and his colleagues (see Goodman & Shah, 1992) found in several studies that coal mining crews whose members worked together more often were more productive and had fewer accidents. Finally, Murnighan and Conlon (1991) found that the best string quartets in Britain, as measured by such criteria as album sales, concert bookings, and newspaper or magazine reviews, were those whose members had played together longest.

There are, of course, several reasons why familiarity among its members might help a group to perform better. Familiarity often strengthens group cohesion, for example, which can improve group performance (Mullen & Copper, 1994). None of the studies I just cited actually showed that familiarity was helpful because it helped group members to recognize one another's expertise. Moreover, familiarity is sometimes harmful rather than helpful for group performance (see Katz, 1982; Kim, 1997; Leedom & Simon, 1995) and it does not always improve the recognition of expertise among group members (see Libby, Trotman, & Zimmer, 1987; Littlepage, Schmidt, Whisler, & Frost, 1995). Findings such as these may be anomalies, but they can also provide valuable evidence about boundary conditions for the effects of familiarity on expertise recognition (and transactive memory systems).

Let us suppose, for a moment, that transactive memory systems do develop in work groups as their members become more familiar with each other and that the performance of such groups improves as a result. What are the implications of all this for managers? One clear implication is that work groups should be kept intact as much as possible. Efforts should be made to minimize turnover in existing groups, for example, because the arrival of new members and the departure of old members can disrupt transactive memory systems by changing the distribution of task-relevant knowledge within a group. It is impossible to eliminate turnover, so efforts should also be made to improve group socialization processes in ways that help newcomers and oldtimers become familiar with one another, thereby restoring the transactive memory systems in their groups. Suggestions for such changes are offered by Levine and Moreland, in chapter 12 of this volume. Finally, when new work groups are formed, their members should be trained together rather than apart (Moreland, Argote, & Krishnan, 1998) so that transactive memory systems develop more quickly. If the members of a new group are trained separately or in special groups created solely for training purposes, they will know less about one another and thus have more trouble working together productively.

TRANSACTIVE MEMORY THROUGH GROUP TRAINING

My own research over the past few years has focused on transactive memory systems in newly formed work groups. Linda Argote, from Carnegie Mellon University, has been my collaborator in all this research, and several graduate students have helped with it as well (see Liang, Moreland, & Argote, 1995; Moreland, Argote, & Krishnan, 1996, 1998). We were intrigued by the fact that many organizations ask employees to work in groups, yet few organizations provide training for such work. Moreover, the group training that is provided often seems misguided because it is based on two dubious assumptions, namely that employees can be taught a generic set of social skills that will allow them to adapt to any work group, and that adapting to a work group is unrelated to learning how that group's tasks are performed. If these assumptions are indeed wrong, then group work requires a different kind of training—employees should learn to perform tasks in the same groups where they will be working. We have explored this issue in several laboratory experiments on small groups whose members were trained to perform a complex task. In these experiments, various versions of group and individual training were provided and their effects on group performance were compared. Our two general predictions were that work groups would perform better if their members were trained together rather than apart and that the performance benefits of such training would depend on the development of transactive memory systems.

Experiment One

The subjects in our first experiment (Liang, Moreland, & Argote, 1995) were 90 students from undergraduate business courses at Carnegie Mellon University. These students were randomly assigned to small work groups, each containing three persons of the same sex. Each group was asked to assemble the AM portion of an AM–FM radio, using materials from a radio kit. That kit included a circuit board and dozens of electronic components. The subjects were asked to insert each component into its proper place on the circuit board and then to wire all of the components together.

Two types of training were provided. Half of the groups were randomly assigned to an individual training condition and the other half were assigned to a group training condition. In the individual training condition, group members were trained separately, whereas in the group training condition, they were trained together. The content of training was exactly the same in both conditions.

The experiment was carried out in two hour-long sessions held a week apart. The first session focused on training and the second session focused on testing. In the individual training condition, each subject participated in a personal training session, but later worked with other subjects in a group for the testing session. In the group training condition, the members of each group participated in both sessions together.

At the start of the experiment, subjects were told that the purpose of our research was to examine how training affects work group performance. Everyone knew that they would return later to perform the task as a group. Subjects in the individual training condition did not know who the members of that group would be, whereas subjects in the group training conditions expected to remain in the same group.

Each training session began with the experimenter demonstrating how to assemble the radio. Subjects were allowed to ask questions during this demonstration, which lasted for about 15 minutes. They were then given up to 30 minutes to practice assembling a radio themselves. In the group training condition, subjects worked together on one radio. After subjects completed their practice radios, the experimenter evaluated those radios, identifying any assembly errors and explaining how to correct them.

The testing session began with a memory test. Each group was given 7 minutes to recall how to assemble the radio. Group members collaborated on this task, recording what they remembered on a single sheet of paper. We then asked each group to actually assemble a radio. Thirty minutes were allotted for this task; subjects were told to work as quickly as possible, but also to minimize assembly errors. While assembling their radios, groups were not allowed to review their recall sheets or consult with the experimenter. Cash prizes were offered as incentives for good task performance. Finally, every subject completed a brief questionnaire that provided background information and assessed beliefs about the group and its task.

Three measures of group performance were collected and analyzed, namely (a) how well each group recalled the procedure for assembling a radio, (b) how quickly each group assembled its radio, and (c) how many assembly errors each group made. We found no differences between training conditions in how quickly the groups assembled their radios, but there were significant differences in both procedural recall and assembly errors.

As expected, groups whose members were trained together recalled more about how to assemble a radio, and made fewer assembly errors, than did groups whose members were trained apart.

Videotapes of the groups working on their radios allowed us to explore several factors that could have produced these performance effects. We were most interested in three factors associated with the operation of transactive memory systems. The first of these factors was *memory differentiation*, or the tendency for group members to specialize in remembering different aspects of the assembly process. For example, one person might remember where radio components should be inserted in the circuit board, while another person remembers how those components should be wired together. The second factor was *task coordination*, or the ability of group members to work together efficiently on the radio. There should be less confusion, fewer misunderstandings, and greater cooperation in groups with stronger transactive memory systems. The final factor was *task credibility*, or the level of trust among group members in one another's radio knowledge. In groups with stronger transactive memory systems, members should make fewer public claims of expertise, be more open to one another's suggestions, and criticize one another's work less often.

Three other factors that seemed relevant to group performance and might have varied across training conditions were also coded from the videotapes. The first factor was *task motivation*, or how eager group members were to win the prizes we offered by assembling their radio quickly and accurately. The second factor was *group cohesion*, or the level of attraction among group members. The final factor was *social identity,* or the tendency for subjects to think about themselves as group members rather than individuals.

Two judges (one blind to both our hypotheses and the training conditions), were given a list of behaviors exemplifying these six factors. With those behaviors in mind, the judges watched each videotape and made an overall rating of the group on each factor. The only exception was social identity, which was evaluated by counting how often personal versus collective pronouns (e.g., "I" vs. "We") were used by group members while they assembled their radio. The ratio of collective pronouns to all pronouns was computed and used as a measure of social identity (see Cialdini et al., 1976; Veroff, Sutherland, Chadiha, & Ortega, 1993). The coding reliability for all six factors was assessed by computing intraclass correlations. Those correlations indicated good reliability in the judges' evaluations. Scores on the three transactive memory factors were strongly correlated, so they were made into a composite index by averaging them together for each group. We did not assume that the other three factors were related, nor did they prove to be correlated with each other, so they were examined separately in our analyses.

Did training affect how group members behaved while they assembled their radios? As we expected, scores on all three of the transactive memory factors, and on the transactive memory index, were significantly higher in the group training condition. Among the other three factors, only social identity differed significantly across training conditions. Higher social identity scores were found for groups whose members were trained together rather than apart.

These findings suggested that the effects of group training on performance may indeed have been mediated by transactive memory. To explore that issue, we performed a series of multiple regression analyses (see Baron & Kenny, 1986) in which training methods were represented by a dummy variable, transactive memory was measured using the composite index, and group performance was measured by assembly errors. We began by regressing first assembly errors and then transactive memory index scores on training methods. Training methods had significant effects in both analyses, as the results described earlier suggest. Assembly errors were then regressed on training methods and transactive memory index scores simultaneously. The effects of transactive memory on assembly errors remained significant, but the effects of training methods became nonsignificant, indicating that the effects of training methods on group performance were mediated by transactive memory. In other words, training methods no longer mattered when variability among groups in transactive memory was taken into account. Analogous regression analyses involving the social identity factor were also performed, but their results provided no evidence of mediation.

This experiment provided direct evidence that a group's performance can be improved by training its members together rather than apart. As we expected, groups remembered more about how to assemble the radios, and produced radios with fewer flaws, when their members were trained together. We also expected and found stronger transactive memory systems in groups whose members were trained together. The members of those groups were more likely to specialize at remembering different aspects of their task, coordinate their work activities better, and show greater trust in one another's expertise. Finally, transactive memory systems were responsible for the positive effects of group training on group performance, just as we expected.

Experiment Two

Our second experiment was designed with three goals in mind. First, it was important to replicate the results of our initial experiment, so we recreated the same individual and group training conditions and reexamined their effects on group performance.

A second goal was to evaluate alternative explanations for our results. Newly formed groups often experience special problems, such as anxiety about acceptance, interpersonal conflicts, and uncertainty about group norms (LaCoursiere, 1980; Tuckman, 1965), that can limit their performance. Training the members of a work group together provides more time for them to resolve these problems. This suggests that enhanced development might contribute to the performance advantages of group training. Another alternative explanation for our results involves strategic learning. Working in groups creates a variety of coordination problems (see Wittenbaum, Vaughan, & Stasser, 1998). Some of those problems can be solved through simple strategies that are relevant to almost any group (see, for example, Johnson & Johnson, 1998). These generic strategies, which include building commitment to the group and organizing its activities, require little knowledge about any specific group. Training the members of a work group together provides them with more opportunities to employ such strategies. This suggests that strategic learning might contribute as well to the performance advantages of group training.

To evaluate these alternative explanations, two new training conditions were developed for the second experiment. One of these was identical to the individual training condition except that a brief team-building exercise was conducted after the training session. This exercise (see McGrath, 1993) was meant to foster group development. Group members were asked to create a quiz that the university could use to evaluate students who wanted to serve as mentors for freshmen during their fall orientation. Another new condition was identical to the group training condition except that each group was scrambled between its training and testing sessions—subjects who were trained together were separated by reassigning everyone to new groups. This change was not announced until the end of the training session.

The team-building condition was meant to encourage group development without providing the kinds of information group members needed to develop transactive memory systems. The reassignment condition was meant to disable whatever transactive memory systems group members had already developed by making such systems irrelevant, leaving strategic learning as the only major benefit of group training. If group development and/or strategic learning are indeed responsible for the performance advantages of group training, then the performance of groups in these two new conditions should be good. But if the performance advantages of group training depend on transactive memory systems, then the performance of those groups should be poor. Groups lacked transactive memory systems in the team-building condition, and in the reassignment condition, those systems were no longer relevant.

The third goal for this experiment was to explore the impact of turnover on transactive memory systems. One benefit of such systems is that each member of a work group can rely on the others for information about various aspects of the task. But what if someone leaves the group, taking with him or her valuable knowledge that nobody else possesses? This problem could have arisen in the reassignment condition, where groups experienced sudden and dramatic turnover after their training sessions. By analyzing how those groups reacted to that challenge, we hoped to learn something about the effects of turnover on group training and performance.

The subjects for this experiment were 186 students enrolled in introductory psychology courses at the University of Pittsburgh. Many of the procedures were the same as those in our first experiment. Once again, subjects were randomly assigned to small, same-sex work groups. The task and materials were the same and each group again participated in both training and testing sessions. However, the training sessions in this experiment were modified slightly for groups in the individual training conditions. Rather than participating in separate sessions, the members of these groups were trained in the same room at the same time, but could not observe or interact with one another while they practiced assembling their radios. This made the experiences of subjects in the individual and group training conditions more comparable. Another minor procedural modification involved the testing sessions. At the beginning of each session, before working on their recall sheets, all subjects were asked to complete a brief questionnaire. Aside from these two changes, the training and testing sessions (including time limits) were carried out just as they were before.

Our initial analyses focused on evaluating the two new training conditions. On their questionnaires, the subjects made ratings indicating their agreement or disagreement with the answers to various questions about their groups. Some of those questions involved feelings about group development (e.g., "Does this work group seem more like one group or three separate individuals?"), whereas others involved thoughts about transactive memory systems (e.g., "How much do you think the other members of this work group know about your skills at assembling the radio?"). The ratings in each of these categories were strongly correlated, so they were averaged together (first within subjects and then within groups) to create indices of group development and transactive memory for each group. Scores on the group development index were significantly higher in the group training and the team-building conditions than in the individual training or the reassignment conditions. And scores on the transactive memory index were significantly higher in the group training condition than in the individual training, team-building, or reassignment conditions. These two new conditions thus seemed to affect groups in the ways that we hoped. The team-building condition encouraged group development without producing transactive memory systems, whereas the reassignment condition disabled transactive memory systems by making them irrelevant.

Our next set of analyses focused on group performance. Once again, no differences were found in how quickly groups in different training conditions assembled their radios. There were, however, significant differences in procedural recall and assembly errors. As we expected, group training led to better performance on both of these measures than did any of the other training methods, which did not differ from one another.

Videotapes of the groups were again rated by two judges, using the same procedures as before. Intraclass correlations again indicated that these ratings were made reliably. Because scores on the three transactive memory factors were again correlated strongly, they were again averaged together to create a composite index for each group. As we expected, scores on that index were significantly higher in the group training condition than in the other three conditions, which did not differ from one another. As for the other three factors, only social identity differed significantly across training conditions. Scores on that factor were higher in the group training and team-building conditions than in the individual training or reassignment conditions.

Were the effects of training methods on group performance mediated by transactive memory? Multiple regression analyses were again used to explore that issue. Once again, group performance was measured by assembly errors and the composite index served to measure transactive memory. But in these analyses, training methods were represented by three dummy variables, using a coding scheme (Cohen & Cohen, 1983) that contrasted the group training condition with the other three training conditions. As before, we began by using training methods to predict assembly errors, and then transactive memory index scores, in separate analyses. Training methods had significant effects in both analyses. We then used training methods and transactive memory index scores to predict assembly errors simultaneously. The effects of transactive memory were significant, but the effects of training methods became nonsignificant. Analogous regression analyses involving the social identity factor were also performed, but produced no evidence of mediation by that factor. So, once again, differences in group performance across training conditions were mediated by the operation of transactive memory systems, just as we expected.

The first goal for this experiment, to replicate the results of our first experiment, was thus achieved. Once again, groups whose members were trained (and remained) together outperformed groups whose members were trained in other ways, and this performance advantage depended on the operation of transactive memory systems. Another goal for this experiment was to evaluate the contributions of group development and generic learning to the performance advantages of group training. Those contributions appeared to be minimal. Groups in both the new training conditions (where transactive memory systems were either missing or disabled) performed much worse than those in the group training condition and no better than those in the individual training condition. The weak performance of groups in the reassignment condition can be taken as evidence that generic training programs, which assume that experiential learning about work groups will transfer from one group to another, are unlikely to succeed. Finally, this experiment gave us a glimpse of how turnover can affect the operation of transactive memory systems. Groups in the reassignment condition experienced sudden and dramatic turnover, disabling their transactive memory systems and thereby harming their performance. But the damage was less severe than it might have been. Although these groups performed worse than groups in the group training condition, they performed about as well as groups in the individual and team-building conditions.

Experiment Three

Our first two experiments suggested that group training really can help workers to learn who knows what about a task. But no direct measures of such knowledge were collected in either experiment. Instead, we measured several behaviors related to the operation of transactive memory systems and then *inferred* that such systems were stronger in groups where such behaviors were more common. The primary goal for our third experiment was thus to measure more directly what the members of a work group actually know about one another. We expected to find, as our earlier results suggested, that group members would know more about one another if they were trained together rather than apart. We also expected such knowledge to be *shared* more often if group members were trained together. Shared knowledge is a key feature of transactive memory systems (see Wegner, 1987, 1995). A secondary goal for this experiment was to see what role social loafing (see Karau & Williams, 1993) might play in group training and performance. Training a work group's members together could encourage some of them to take advantage of the others by learning only those aspects of a task that seem most interesting. Because such workers never expect to perform the whole task on their own, they may hope that other members of the group will compensate for their ignorance by performing whatever aspects of the task they failed to learn.

The subjects for this experiment were 78 students enrolled in introductory psychology courses at the University of Pittsburgh. Many of the procedures were identical to those in our first two experiments. The subjects were again assigned randomly to small, same-sex work groups. The task and materials were the same and every group participated in both training and testing sessions. During the first session, each group received either individual or group training, and training sessions were conducted in the same manner as our second experiment. But a week later, when the testing sessions were held, important procedural changes were made. We began these sessions by asking every subject to complete a brief questionnaire. Up to 10 minutes were allotted for this task. Then, as usual, the subjects were asked first to complete a recall sheet and then to assemble a radio as quickly and accurately as possible. The standard time limits were imposed on both tasks. But in this experiment, the subjects were asked to perform those tasks *individually*. In fact, they were not allowed to observe or talk with one another while working at either task. This was an unpleasant surprise for the subjects, who were told during their training sessions that they would later be working on the radios in groups.

The questionnaire measured in various ways what each group's members knew about one another's radio expertise. The first question simply asked subjects to describe, in their own words, each person's strengths and weaknesses at building radios. Responses to this question were later rated by two judges (one blind to training conditions) for their overall level of detail. Intraclass correlations indicated that these ratings were made reliably. In the next part of the questionnaire, subjects were asked to rate how skillful each member of their group was at different aspects of building a radio. These ratings included how much each person could remember about the procedure for assembling radios, how quickly that person could assemble a radio, and how many errors such a radio would contain. The third part of the questionnaire was similar except that subjects were asked to rank each member of their group (from best to worst) for those same skills. The questionnaire ended with two unusual questions regarding the distribution of expertise among group members. One question asked subjects to guess what percentage of the knowledge needed to build a radio well was possessed by everyone in their group (shared knowledge), rather than by just some members (unshared knowledge). The other question asked subjects to rate how similar the errors would be in radios built by different members of their group.

Responses from the questionnaires were used to produce three indices for each group. These measured (a) the *complexity* of group members' beliefs about one another's radio expertise, (b) the *accuracy* of those beliefs, and (c) the level of *agreement* about the distribution of expertise. The complexity index was produced using the first question and the last two questions on the questionnaire. Subjects' responses on each question were first averaged within groups, then standardized (because the questions used different response formats), and finally (because they were strongly correlated) averaged together to produce a complexity index. As we expected, complexity was significantly greater in groups whose members were trained together rather than apart. When group members were trained together, they wrote more detailed analyses of one another's strengths and weaknesses at building radios, guessed that less of the information needed to build radios was known by everyone in their group, and expected more dissimilar errors to occur if the members of their group built radios alone. The accuracy index was produced using the various rating and ranking questions on the questionnaire. The rating questions involved such radio-building skills as procedural recall, speed of assembly, and assembly errors. Subjects' answers to those questions revealed their *beliefs* about how strong those skills were in each group member. Because each of the subjects later completed a recall sheet and built a radio alone, objective information was available about how strong those skills really were. This made it possible to measure the accuracy of subjects' beliefs about one another. For a given skill, we first correlated a subject's ratings of the group's members with their actual performance. This yielded three correlations for each subject, reflecting that person's accuracy at perceiving the skills of every group member. Next, the subject's correlations were transformed (using Fisher's r-to-Z procedure) and averaged together. The resulting figures were then averaged within groups to produce a single score for each group. Subjects' responses to the ranking questions on the questionnaire were processed in much the same way. The result of these computations was a set of six accuracy scores for each group, derived from its members' ratings or rankings of three radio-building skills. Those scores were strongly correlated, so they were averaged together to yield an accuracy index for each group. As we expected, significantly greater accuracy was found in groups whose members were trained together rather than apart.

The agreement index was produced in a similar way. Once again, we used the rating and ranking questions, but this time each subject's responses were correlated with those of the other group members rather than with any actual performance information. This produced three correlations for each subject, reflecting that person's agreement with other members about the distribution of skills within the group. These scores were processed in the same way as before, creating a set of six agreement scores for each group. Those scores were also strongly correlated, so once again we averaged them together to produce an agreement index for each group. Significantly greater agreement was found in groups whose members were trained together rather than apart, as we expected.

These results show that training a work group's members together rather than apart can indeed help to produce a transactive memory system. When group members were trained together, they had more complex beliefs about the distribution of radio-building skills within their group. In particular, they were more likely to see one another as unique individuals, each with special skills that other group members might not possess. Beliefs about the distribution of radio-building skills were also more accurate, and more likely to be shared, in groups whose members were trained together. The advantages of creating a work group whose members share complex, yet accurate beliefs about who is good at what are easy to imagine. Such a group should perform very well.

An assumption underlying our earlier experiments was that indirect and direct measures of transactive memory systems would be strongly correlated. That is, behaviors involving memory differentiation, task coordination, and task credibility should occur more often in groups whose members have complex, accurate, and shared beliefs about one another's expertise. Was that assumption correct? All the subjects in our third experiment worked alone during their testing sessions, so no videotapes of group performance were made. However, we did make videotapes of the training sessions in that experiment. Videotapes of groups whose members were trained together were thus evaluated by two judges, one blind to the research hypotheses. These judges rated the same three behavioral factors as in our earlier experiments, using the same procedures. Once again, intraclass correlations indicated that these evaluations were made reliably. Because scores on the three factors were strongly correlated, each group's scores were averaged to create a composite index. That index was then correlated with the questionnaire indices of complexity, accuracy, and agreement for each group. All these correlations were positive and significant, suggesting that indirect, behavioral measures of transactive memory systems (like those used in our earlier experiments) can detect their operation in work groups.

Finally, this experiment also provided some information about how social loafing might affect group training and performance. As noted earlier, the usual performance measures (procedural recall, speed of assembly, assembly errors) were collected from every subject during the testing sessions. Although performance on these measures was a bit worse in groups whose members were trained together rather than apart, none of those differences was significant, whether individuals or groups were used as the units of analysis. We should not dismiss the problem of social loafing, but these results suggest that it is not severe. Apparently, group members learn their task about as thoroughly whether they are trained together or apart.

ALTERNATE ROUTES TO TRANSACTIVE MEMORY

Our first three experiments showed that a transactive memory system can substantially improve a work group's performance, and that training the group's members together is a reliable way to produce such a system. Given those findings, we considered several directions for future research. The impact of turnover among workers on transactive memory systems, for example, seemed worth exploring in more detail. As time passes, turnover is inevitable for most work groups, and as we noted earlier, turnover can be harmful when a group's performance depends on its transactive memory system. As members come and go, that system must be modified to reflect changes in the distribution of expertise within the group. When turnover is frequent and/or unexpected, such modifications may be difficult to make, raising doubts among group members about who really knows what. A group that relied on such knowledge to perform its tasks might thus have more trouble coping with turnover than a group whose members never knew much about one another's expertise. Of course, when turnover is infrequent and/or expected, a group with a transactive memory system may be able to use that system to its advantage. For example, if someone is expected to leave the group, then a transactive memory system should help the group to identify what task knowledge is about to be lost and respond in ways that will limit the harmful effects of that loss. One tactic might be to arrange for the person who is leaving to transfer his or her task knowledge to other group members. Another tactic might be to seek a new member whose task knowledge resembles that of the person who is leaving. In either case, a transactive memory system would be helpful to the group, both for identifying what kinds of knowledge are relevant and for generating consensus about which tactic to use.

Thoughts about turnover, however, put us in a pragmatic frame of mind and led us to consider other ways in which transactive memory systems might develop in work groups. Training a group's members together and then keeping them together seems appealing in principle, but may be difficult or impossible in practice. What are the alternatives? Why not, for example, try to provide the members of a newly formed group the same kinds of information about one another that they would have acquired through group training? One approach is to simply inform everyone in the group about what role each member should play when the group's task is performed. Stasser, Stewart, and Wittenbaum (1995) used this approach in an experiment on information sharing. Groups of college students were given clues about a hypothetical murder and then asked to use that information to discover who (among several suspects) committed the crime. Within each group, some clues were distributed to everyone, whereas other clues were distributed in ways that provided each member with expertise on a different suspect. The latter clues were critical for solving the crime. Every group was informed that its members might receive different sets of clues. Information about exactly who knew what, however, varied from one group to another. In some groups, but not others, each member was privately informed about his or her own area of expertise. And in some groups, but not others, everyone's area of expertise was publicly announced. Simply informing everyone about their own expertise had little impact on group performance, but announcing everyone's expertise helped group members to talk about more of the critical clues and thereby solve the crime. In other words, providing the kind of information found in transactive memory systems improved group performance.

While planning our fourth experiment, we chose a subtler approach, namely to provide groups with information that could be used to identify the distribution of expertise among their members. But that information was not organized or summarized in any simple way, forcing each group to draw its own conclusions about who knew what. This experiment is still in progress, but should be completed soon, with help from Sean Fitzgerald and Larissa Myaskovsky. Some preliminary findings are worth reporting here, however, if only to clarify the issues that concern us.

At present, 120 subjects (about two thirds of our target sample) have taken part in the experiment. All of the subjects are students enrolled in introductory psychology classes at the University of Pittsburgh. Many of the procedures are identical to those in our earlier experiments. Subjects are again randomly assigned to small, same-sex work groups. The task and materials are the same and every group participates in both training and testing sessions. During its first session, each group receives either individual or group training, and training sessions are conducted in the same manner as our second experiment. But a week later, during the testing sessions, some procedural changes are made. Half of the groups that received individual training, and all of the groups that received group training, are treated just as before. But the other half of the individual training groups are given feedback about the skills of their members. This feedback takes the form of a chart that shows how well group members built radios during the training session. Five skills (resistors, capacitors, transistors, other components, wiring) form the chart's rows and three rankings (first place, second place, third place) form its columns. Every cell in the chart contains the name of a group member, along with (in parentheses) a score revealing how well that person performed that aspect of radio building. These scores are calculated by subtracting the number of errors that person made from the number of points that could have been earned. Higher scores thus indicate better performance.

Groups in the feedback condition have 5 minutes to review their charts. We were not sure whether or how the information on those charts would be used, but as it turns out, most groups seem very interested in that information, reviewing and discussing the chart's contents as long as they can. And we have the impression (confirmed in the debriefing sessions) that many groups summarize their charts by simply identifying who is best at each aspect of the task.

From this point on, the procedure is similar to that in our second experiment. Each group is asked first to complete a recall sheet and then to assemble a radio as quickly and accurately as possible. The standard time limits are imposed on both tasks. Afterwards, all subjects are given 5 minutes to complete a brief questionnaire. That questionnaire is similar to the one in our second experiment, but also contains two new questions. One question asks subjects to rate how much the experimenter wanted their group to succeed. This question was included because we feared that groups in the feedback condition might perform well because the experimenter, who provided them with a potentially useful chart, seemed to be helping them succeed. The other question asks subjects how difficult it was to communicate with one another about the task. We included this question because one of our colleagues, Sara Kiesler at Carnegie Mellon University, suggested that an important advantage of training group members together may be the development of *jargon*—special ways of talking about the task that help workers to perform it more quickly and easily (see Lyon, 1974).

As in our earlier experiments, each group is videotaped while it works on its radio. The three behaviors related to transactive memory are being rated again, by judges blind to the research hypotheses and/or training conditions, along with three behaviors related to how subjects talk about the task. Those behaviors are (a) the overall level of task, rather than socioemotional, communication in the group; (b) apparent miscommunication among group members about the task; and (c) the use of task jargon. We are interested in whether any performance advantages remain significant even when these three behaviors are taken into account.

This experiment is not yet complete, but one important finding is emerging: Groups in the feedback condition build radios nearly as well as groups whose members were trained together, and groups in both of those conditions build radios much better than do groups whose members were trained apart. This finding suggests that there is indeed more than one way for transactive memory systems to develop in work groups. It also suggests some interesting questions about what kinds of feedback groups need for such systems to arise. Does everyone need to receive the kind of feedback contained in our charts, or would it be sufficient to provide that feedback to just one group member? Does it matter who that person is? Could the feedback in our charts be simplified? It may be sufficient to simply identify the person who is best at each aspect of the task, or even just the person whose task performance is best overall.

This last option reminded us of Henry's research on the recognition of expertise. As I noted earlier, much of that research involves a standard paradigm. Subjects are asked to answer a series of trivia questions, first alone and then in small groups. Afterwards, they evaluate one another's expertise. Comparisons between these evaluations and measures of actual expertise are then made to see how well groups can recognize expertise among their members. Using this paradigm, Henry has studied several interventions, some rather subtle, that might help groups to better recognize expertise. For example, Henry (1995b) studied two interventions involving changes in subjects' behavior during group discussions. In the first intervention, subjects were asked to develop several possible answers for each trivia question, then evaluate the likely accuracy of each answer, and finally share those evaluations with other members during group discussions. Henry believed that evaluating the relative merits of their own answers might help subjects to evaluate the relative merits of answers proposed by others. In a second intervention, subjects were asked to evaluate the answers proposed by other group members for each trivia question, and then choose (as part of the group discussion) which person seemed to have the best answer. Finally, subjects in a control condition received no instructions about how to behave, either alone or in their groups. Were the interventions helpful? The results were mixed. The second intervention produced high levels of expertise recognition, but did not surpass the control condition in that regard. The first intervention was less helpful, but still produced levels of expertise recognition that were higher than would be expected by chance.

Other interventions that Henry has studied, such as providing subjects with continuous feedback about the correct answers to the trivia questions (Henry, Strickland, Yorges, & Ladd, 1996; see also Blickensderfer, Cannon-Bowers, & Salas, 1997), or asking subjects to share, during their group discussions, any information they possess that seems relevant to those questions (Henry, 1995a), also appear to be helpful. These findings imply that there are several ways to help work groups develop transactive memory systems and thereby improve their performance. If providing a group's members direct access to information about who knows what is impossible, or seems likely to produce harmful side-effects (e.g., destabilizing group structure or causing conflict among group members), then more subtle and indirect means of fostering transactive memory systems are apparently available.

TRANSACTIVE MEMORY SYSTEMS IN ORGANIZATIONS

Before closing the chapter, it seems worthwhile to speculate about transactive memory systems in organizations. Do such systems develop within organizations, and if so, is it possible to manage them? Many organizations are investing considerable time, energy, and money in efforts to answer these questions (see Stewart, 1995a, 1995b, 1997). Some speculation, supported by any relevant theory or research that can be found, may thus be warranted.

If transactive memory systems can develop in organizations, then they may well differ from the transactive memory systems of work groups.

Organizations are obviously larger than work groups, for example, so their transactive memory systems should contain more (and more varied) sources of task knowledge. As a result, workers are likely to have more trouble identifying who knows what in organizations than in work groups. Organizations are less cohesive than work groups as well and tend to evoke weaker commitment from their members (Moreland & Levine, in press). People who work for the same organization, but belong to different work groups, may thus be less willing to share their task knowledge (Constant, Sproull, & Kiesler, 1996). Finally, transactive memory systems in organizations have an educational quality that is rarely found in the transactive memory systems of work groups. Once knowledge about a task has been transferred from one worker to another in an organization, the latter person is usually expected to use that knowledge independently, without returning to its source. But in a work group, someone may repeatedly ask for the same task knowledge from the same source. Transactive memory systems are thus used by work group members to make their tasks easier, rather than to learn more about those tasks.

How do transactive memory systems operate in organizations? There are several ways in which a worker, seeking knowledge about a task, might proceed. These options can be divided into two broad categories, reflecting two different approaches to the problem (see Marquardt, 1996; Robinson & Weldon, 1993). The general goal of the *interpersonal approach* is to locate a specific person (or persons) in the organization and then obtain whatever information is needed from him or her. The general goal of the *technological approach* is to obtain whatever information is needed through the use of computers. These two approaches overlap to some extent, of course. For instance, a worker who takes an interpersonal approach may sometimes rely on computers to reach his or her goal, whereas a worker who takes a technological approach may sometimes rely on people. But even if the distinction between these two approaches is rough, it may still be helpful, given how little is known about transactive memory systems in organizations.

Interpersonal Approaches

When someone is searching for task knowledge in an organization, how might the interpersonal approach be implemented? That person could start with the members of his or her own work group, asking not what they know themselves, but rather whether they know of anyone outside the group who might be helpful. Ancona and her colleagues (see Ancona, 1990; Ancona & Caldwell, 1988, 1992) have shown that successful work groups try to manage the flow of information and other resources across their boundaries by developing special activities and roles. In a study of new product development teams, for example, Ancona and Caldwell (1988) found that scout, ambassador, sentry, and guard activities occurred more often in successful teams, and that workers in those teams were more likely to play immigrant, captive, and emigrant roles. Many of these activities and roles, especially scouting and immigration, could generate information about an organization that would help work group members to enter its transactive memory system. Organizations should thus consider how to foster such activities and roles because of the benefits they can yield for work groups.

There are, of course, many other ways in which a work group's members could obtain information about their organization's transactive memory system (see Marquardt, 1996). Most organizations, for example, keep workers informed about recent events by publishing (perhaps electronically) periodic newsletters that everyone receives. Those newsletters often contain information about the accomplishments of various work groups or workers, thereby revealing who knows what in the organization. Presenting such information in the form of stories, which people appear to process more readily (see Martin, 1982), could draw more attention to that information and help workers to remember it better. Special events, such as parties, picnics, or colloquia, and certain activities, such as training exercises, can also help workers in an organization learn to more about each other, thereby strengthening the organization's transactive memory system. Sutton and Hargadon (1996), for example, studied a product design firm in which brainstorming sessions were often held. Although the major purpose of those sessions was to produce ideas, the researchers found that brainstorming produced other benefits as well, including the development and maintenance of organizational memories. Some of those memories focused on who knew what in the organization. Finally, the transactive memory systems of some organizations are easier for workers to use because of structural features (e.g., linking arrangements, matrix organization) or practices (e.g., job rotation, cross-functional teams) that bring people from different segments of those organizations into contact with one another more often.

Finally, some people may have broader knowledge than others about what is going on in their organizations. Such knowledge often includes information about who knows what. In his chapter for this volume, for example, Burt focuses on workers who occupy structural holes in the social networks of their organizations. These workers have many weak ties (see Granovetter, 1973) with people or groups who might not otherwise come into contact with one another. As a result, they can provide valuable guidance for anyone seeking task knowledge within their organizational domains. Some organizations have formalized such activities by creating special roles, such as an ombudsman (Marquardt, 1996), whose duty is to help knowledge seekers reach someone who can provide the necessary information. In other organizations, special units (see Stewart's, 1995a, description of the PPO division at Hewlett-Packard) have been created for the same purpose. In all these organizations, workers know just where to go for information about who knows what.

My analysis of the interpersonal approach has focused so far on the identification of people in an organization who may possess the task knowledge that a worker needs. But once those people have been identified, will that worker ask them for help? Maybe he or she is too shy, would feel embarrassed to admit ignorance about the task, or is worried about becoming indebted to others for their help. And if such help is requested, are the people who can provide it willing to do so? In many organizations, those who seek task knowledge and those who can provide it are strangers who have little in common besides their employer. Task knowledge can also become a source of power (Eisenberg & Phillips, 1991; Krackhardt, 1990), something to keep rather than give away. Some workers may also keep task knowledge to themselves because they worry about how others might use it. Finally, unless they are actually rewarded by the organization for sharing their task knowledge with others, workers who do so must behave altruistically. Given all these potential problems, is knowledge about tasks ever shared? There is some evidence that it is (see Constant, Sproull, & Kiesler, 1996), especially when those who are asked to share what they know are strongly committed to the organization (Organ, 1988). There can also be several intangible rewards for workers who share their task knowledge. These rewards include personal growth (when questions from others lead to new insights), stronger self-esteem, greater prestige in the organization, and the expectation that favors will someday be repaid.

Technological Approaches

Computers have changed almost every aspect of organizations, including how workers seek and find information about their tasks. The technological approach to organizational systems of transactive memory can be implemented in several ways. First, ordinary e-mail is often used by workers seeking task knowledge (see Constant, Sproull, & Kiesler, 1996). Someone can send out a request for information to everyone in the organization, or just to people on relevant distribution lists. Once the request has gone out, all that remains is to await replies. Variations on this approach (see Stewart, 1995b) include using a private forum created for the organization by a commercial Internet provider, such as Compu-Serve, or posting and reading messages of many kinds (e.g., news, gossip, war stories, or descriptions of best practices) using software designed for information sharing, such as Lotus Notes. Once replies to a message are received, they must be sorted for helpfulness, credibility of source, and so on. The person who requested help may then recontact some of the people who replied to his or her message, seeking clarification or elaboration of the information that was provided. In this way, a technological approach may slowly become more interpersonal. But note that such a transformation is not inevitable; people who seek and provide task information in this way need never meet and may never exchange further messages with one another. In some cases, they may even remain anonymous.

Another technological approach, one that seems a bit more sophisticated, is the use of electronic Yellow Pages. Several organizations (see Stewart, 1995a) have worked hard at developing these information resources, again using Lotus Notes or similar software. Many kinds of information, ranging from personal resumes to instructions or guidelines, and from frequently asked questions to news items, can be found in an organization's Yellow Pages. An important advantage, however, is that all of this information has been organized using keywords, so that when a specific kind of task knowledge is required, someone can enter the relevant keywords into his or her computer and either find that knowledge directly or identify other people within the organization who may possess it (note that only the latter process actually involves transactive memory). Of course, this approach works best when the information in the organization's Yellow Pages is both comprehensive and accurate, an optimal set of keywords was used to organize that information, and the worker who needs information uses the proper keywords to search for it. One can become confused by it all, so some organizations now supplement their Yellow Pages by offering personalized assistance to users (see Stewart's, 1995a, description of the Knowledge Coordinators at NatWest Markets).

Finally, several organizations (especially large consulting firms) have recently developed complex software designed to help workers learn everything that anyone in their organization knows about various tasks (see Stewart, 1997). An organizational intranet is incorporated into many of these programs so that users can jump quickly from one web page to another on their computers, following associational links among people or work groups, tasks, procedures, equipment, and so on. Again, not all web page chains involve transactive memory—some workers find the information that they need on the intranet itself, whereas others use the intranet to discover where such information can be found. Only the latter workers have learned who knows what in their organization.

What Works Best?

At this point, it is impossible to tell whether interpersonal or technological approaches are more effective for workers who are seeking task knowledge through the transactive memory systems of their organizations. Evidence regarding the effectiveness of either approach is scarce and seldom very convincing. For example, organizations favoring the technological approach often praise it highly, but that praise may reflect their concerns about the costs associated with that approach rather than its actual value. It is not necessary, of course, to "choose" one approach over the other, except that organizations with limited resources may want to know how those resources could be used most wisely. In that spirit, a brief summary of the major strengths and weaknesses of each approach seems worthwhile.

A major strength of the interpersonal approach is that knowledge about a task can be shared in ways that are tailored to a worker's specific needs. In other words, the transfer of knowledge is customized, so that the person who requested information learns exactly what he or she wanted to know. Misunderstandings can also be detected and corrected relatively quickly. A major disadvantage of this approach is that task knowledge may not be shared at all. The person who needs information may not know who to ask for it, and even when an information source can be identified, problems may still arise if the person who needs the information is afraid to request it, or the person who has the information declines to provide it. The thoughts and feelings of workers about their jobs, themselves, and one another are notoriously difficult to manage, yet they can play a vital role in the interpersonal approach to transactive memory systems. As for the technological approach, a major strength is how much knowledge about tasks it can provide. In principle, there is no limit to the amount of information that can be stored in an organization's intranet. That information is standardized, rather than customized, and readily available to anyone who has computer access, regardless of the relationship (if any) between that person and whoever stored the information. A major disadvantage of this approach is that it can be very costly (see Stewart, 1995b), both to store all the information initially and then to update that information as time passes.

There is a clear need for more and better evidence regarding these (and perhaps other) approaches to transactive memory systems in organizations. Gathering such evidence may be difficult, but the rewards are likely to be high, well worth the effort required.

REFERENCES

Ancona, D. G. (1990). Outward bound: Strategies for team survival in an organization. *Academy of Management Journal, 33,* 334–365.

Ancona, D. G., & Caldwell, D. F. (1988). Beyond task and maintenance: Defining external functions in groups. *Group and Organizational Studies, 13,* 468–494.

Ancona, D. G., & Caldwell, D. F. (1992). Bridging the boundary: External activity and performance in organizational teams. *Administrative Science Quarterly, 37,* 634–665.

Argote, L. (1993). Group and organizational learning curves: Individual, system, and environmental components. *British Journal of Social Psychology, 32,* 31–51.

28   MORELAND

Baron, R. M., & Kenny, D. A. (1986). The moderator-mediator variable distinction in social psychological research: Conceptual, strategic, and statistical considerations. *Journal of Personality and Social Psychology, 51,* 1173–1182.

Barsness, Z. I. (1996). *The impact of contingent workers on work group effectiveness: A process model of the relationship between group composition and group effectiveness.* Unpublished doctoral dissertation, Northwestern University, Evanston, IL.

Blickensderfer, E., Cannon-Bowers, J. A., & Salas, E. (1997). Theoretical bases for team self-correction: Fostering shared mental models. In M. Beyerlein (Ed.), *Advances in interdisciplinary studies of work teams* (pp. 249–279). Greenwich, CT: JAI.

Carr, C. (1992). *Teampower: Lessons from America's top companies in putting teampower to work.* Englewood Cliffs, NJ: Prentice-Hall.

Cialdini, R. B., Borden, R. J., Thorne, A., Walker, M. R., Freeman, S., & Sloan, L. R. (1976). Basking in reflected glory: Three (football) field studies. *Journal of Personality and Social Psychology, 34,* 366–375.

Cohen, J., & Cohen, P. (1983). *Applied multiple regression/correlation analyses for the behavioral sciences.* Hillsdale, NJ: Lawrence Erlbaum Associates.

Cohen, S. G. (1994). Designing effective self-managing work teams. In M. Beyerlein (Ed.), *Advances in interdisciplinary studies of work teams* (Vol. 1, pp. 67–102). Greenwich, CT: JAI.

Constant, D., Sproull, L., & Kiesler, S. (1996). The kindness of strangers: The usefulness of electronic weak ties for technical advice. *Organization Science, 7,* 119–135.

Dubnicki, C., & Limburg, W. J. (1991, September/October). How do healthcare teams measure up? *Healthcare Forum, 34,* 10–11.

Dumaine, B. (1994, September 5). The trouble with teams. *Fortune, 130,* 86–92.

Dunphy, D., & Bryant, B. (1996). Teams: Panaceas or prescriptions for improved performance? *Human Relations, 49,* 677–699.

Eisenberg, E. M., & Phillips, S. R. (1991). Miscommunications in organizations. In N. Coupland, H. Giles, & J. M. Wiemann (Eds.), *Miscommunications and problematic talk* (pp. 244–258). Newbury Park, CA: Sage.

Feldman, D. C. (1995). Managing part-time and temporary employment relationships: Individual needs and organizational demands. In M. Landon (Ed.), *Employees, careers, and job creation: Developing growth-oriented human resource strategies and programs* (pp. 121–141). San Francisco: Jossey-Bass.

Gladstein, D. (1984). Groups in context: A model of task group effectiveness. *Administrative Science Quarterly, 29,* 499–517.

Goodman, P. S., & Shah, S. (1992). Familiarity and work group outcomes. In S. Worchel, W. Wood, & J. A. Simpson (Eds.), *Group process and productivity* (pp. 276–298). Newbury Park, CA: Sage.

Granovetter, M. S. (1973). The strength of weak ties. *American Journal of Sociology, 78,* 1360–1380.

Gruenfeld, D. H., Mannix, E. A., Williams, K. Y., & Neale, M. A. (1996). Group composition and decision making: How member familiarity and information distribution affect process and performance. *Organizational Behavior and Human Decision Processes, 67,* 1–15.

Guzzo, R. A., & Salas, E. (1995). *Team effectiveness and decision making in organizations.* San Francisco, CA: Jossey-Bass.

Hackman, J. R. (1987). The design of work teams. In J. W. Lorsch (Ed.), *Handbook of organizational behavior* (pp. 315–342). Englewood Cliffs, NJ: Prentice-Hall.

Hackman, J. R. (1998). Why teams don't work. In R. S. Tindale, L. Heath, J. Edwards, E. Posavac, F. B. Bryant, Y. Suarez-Balcazar, E. Henderson-King, & J. Myers (Eds.), *Theory and research on small groups* (pp. 245–267). New York: Plenum.

Hackman, J. R., & Morris, C. G. (1975). Group tasks, group interaction process, and group performance effectiveness: A review and proposed integration. In L. Berkowitz (Ed.), *Advances in experimental social psychology* (Vol. 8, pp. 45–99). New York: Academic Press.

Henry, R. A. (1993). Group judgment accuracy: Reliability and validity of post-discussion confidence judgments. *Organizational Behavior and Human Decision Processes, 56,* 11–27.

Henry, R. A. (1995a). Improving group judgment accuracy: Information sharing and determining the best member. *Organizational Behavior and Human Decision Processes, 62,* 190–197.

Henry, R. A. (1995b). Using relative confidence judgments to evaluate group effectiveness. *Basic and Applied Social Psychology, 16,* 333–350.

Henry, R. A., Strickland, O. J., Yorges, S. L., & Ladd, D. (1996). Helping groups determine their most accurate member: The role of outcome feedback. *Journal of Applied Social Psychology, 26,* 1153–1170.

Herr, E. L. (1993). Contests and influences on the need for personal flexibility for the 21st century. *Canadian Journal of Counseling, 27,* 219–235.

Hoerr, J. (1989, July 10). The payoff from teamwork. *Newsweek,* 56–62.

Hollingshead, A. B. (1998). Retrieval processes in transactive memory systems. *Journal of Personality and Social Psychology, 74,* 659–671.

Jackson, S. E., & Alvarez, E. B. (1993). Working through diversity as a strategic imperative. In S. E. Jackson (Ed.), *Diversity in the workplace: Human resource initiatives* (pp. 13–29). New York: Guilford.

Jehn, K. A., & Shah, P. P. (1997). Interpersonal relationships and task performance: An examination of mediating processes in friendship and acquaintance groups. *Journal of Personality and Social Psychology, 72,* 775–790.

Johnson, W., & Johnson, R. T. (1998). Cooperative learning and social interdependence theory. In R. S. Tindale, L. Heath, J. Edwards, E. Posavac, F. B. Bryant, Y. Suarez-Balcazar, E. Henderson-King, & J. Myers (Eds.), *Theory and research on small groups* (pp. 9–35). New York: Plenum.

Kanki, B. G., & Foushee, H. C. (1989). Communication as group process mediator of aircrew performance. *Aviation, Space, and Environmental Medicine, 4,* 402–410.

Karau, S. J., & Williams, K. D. (1993). Social loafing: A meta-analytic review and theoretical integration. *Journal of Personality and Social Psychology, 65,* 681–706.

Katz, R. (1982). The effects of group longevity on project communication and performance. *Administrative Science Quarterly, 27,* 81–104.

Katzenbach, J. R., & Smith, D. K. (1993). *The wisdom of teams: Creating the high-performance organization.* Cambridge, MA: Harvard Business School Press.

Kim, P. H. (1997). When what you know can hurt you: A study of experiential effects on group discussion and performance. *Organizational Behavior and Human Decision Processes, 69,* 165–177.

Kozlowski, S. W. J., Gully, S. M., Salas, E., & Cannon-Bowers, J. A. (1996). Team leadership and development: Theory, principles, and guidelines for training leaders and teams. In M. Beyerlein (Ed.), *Advances in interdisciplinary studies of work teams* (Vol. 3, pp. 253–291). Greenwich, CT: JAI.

Krackhardt, D. (1990). Assessing the political landscape: Structure, cognition, and power in organizations. *Administrative Science Quarterly, 35,* 342–369.

LaCoursiere, R. (1980). *The life cycle of groups: Group developmental stage theory.* New York: Human Sciences.

Larson, J. R., Jr., Foster-Fishman, P. G., & Keys, C. B. (1994). Discussion of shared and unshared information in decision-making groups. *Journal of Personality and Social Psychology, 67,* 446–461.

Lawler, E. E., Mohrman, S. A., & Ledford, G. E. (1992). *Employee involvement and total quality management.* San Francisco: Jossey-Bass.

Leedom, D. K., & Simon, R. (1995). Improving team coordination: A case for behavior-based training. *Military Psychology, 7,* 109–122.

Levine, J. M., & Moreland, R. L. (1990). Progress in small group research. *Annual Review of Psychology, 41,* 585–634.

Liang, D. W., Moreland, R. L., & Argote, L. (1995). Group versus individual training and group performance: The mediating role of transactive memory. *Personality and Social Psychology Bulletin, 21,* 384–393.

Libby, R., Trotman, K. T., & Zimmer, I. (1987). Member variation, recognition of expertise, and group performance. *Journal of Applied Psychology, 72*, 81–87.

Littlepage, G. E., Robison, W., & Reddington, K. (1997). Effects of task experience and group experience on group performance, member ability, and recognition of expertise. *Organizational Behavior and Human Decision Processes, 69*, 133–147.

Littlepage, G. E., Schmidt, G. W., Whisler, E. W., & Frost, A. G. (1995). An input-process-output analysis of influence and performance in problem-solving groups. *Journal of Personality and Social Psychology, 69*, 877–889.

Littlepage, G. E., & Silbiger, H. (1992). Recognition of expertise in decision-making groups: Effects of group size and participation patterns. *Small Group Research, 23*, 344–355.

Lyon, E. (1974). Work and play: Resource constraints in a small theater. *Urban Life and Culture, 3*, 71–97.

Mantel, B. (1994, September 5). Workplace issues for temporary workers. In E. Weiss (Executive Producer), *All things considered*. Washington, DC: National Public Radio.

Manz, C. C., & Sims, H. P. (1993). *Business without bosses: How self-managing teams are building high-performance companies*. New York: Wiley.

Marquardt, M. J. (1996). *Building the learning organization: A systems approach to quantum improvement and global success*. New York: McGraw-Hill.

Martin, J. (1982). Stories and scripts in organizational settings. In A. Hastorf & I. Isen (Eds.), *Cognitive social psychology* (pp. 255–305). New York: Elsevier.

McGrath, J. E. (1993). The JEMCO Workshop: Description of a longitudinal study. *Small Group Research, 24*, 285–306.

Montebello, A. R., & Buzzotta, V. R. (1993, March). Work teams that work. *Training and Development*, 59–64.

Moreland, R. L., Argote, L., & Krishnan, R. (1996). Socially shared cognition at work: Transactive memory and group performance. In J. L. Nye & A. M. Brower (Eds.), *What's social about social cognition? Research on socially shared cognition in small groups* (pp. 57–84). Thousand Oaks, CA: Sage.

Moreland, R. L., Argote, L., & Krishnan, R. (1998). Training people to work in groups. In R. S. Tindale, L. Heath, J. Edwards, E. Posavac, F. B. Bryant, Y. Suarez-Balcazar, E. Henderson-King, & J. Myers (Eds.), *Theory and research on small groups* (pp. 36–60). New York: Plenum.

Moreland, R. L., & Levine, J. M. (1992a). The composition of small groups. In E. J. Lawler, B. Markovsky, C. Ridgeway, & H. A. Walker (Eds.), *Advances in group processes* (Vol. 9, pp. 237–280). Greenwich, CT: JAI.

Moreland, R. L., & Levine, J. M. (1992b). Problem identification by groups. In S. Worchel, W. Wood, & J. A. Simpson (Eds.), *Group process and productivity* (pp. 17–47). Newbury Park, CA: Sage.

Moreland, R. L., & Levine, J. M. (in press). Socialization in organizations and work groups. In M. Turner (Ed.), *Groups at work: Advances in theory and research*. Mahwah, NJ: Lawrence Erlbaum Associates.

Moreland, R. L., Levine, J. M., & Wingert, M. L. (1996). Creating the ideal group: Group composition effects at work. In E. H. Witte & J. H. Davis (Eds.), *Understanding group behavior: Small group processes and interpersonal relations* (pp. 11–35). Mahwah, NJ: Lawrence Erlbaum Associates.

Mullen, B., & Copper, C. (1994). The relation between group cohesiveness and performance: An integration. *Psychological Bulletin, 115*, 210–227.

Murnighan, J. K., & Conlon, D. E. (1991). The dynamics of intense work groups: A study of British string quartets. *Administrative Science Quarterly, 36*, 165–186.

Organ, D. W. (1988). *Organizational citizenship behavior: The good soldier syndrome*. Lexington, MA: Lexington.

Parker, S. K., Wall, T. D., & Jackson, P. R. (1997). "That's not my job": Developing flexible employee work orientations. *Academy of Management Journal, 40*, 899–929.

Robinson, S., & Weldon, E. (1993). Feedback seeking in groups: A theoretical perspective. *British Journal of Social Psychology, 32,* 71–86.

Saavedra, R., & Kwun, S. K. (1993). Peer evaluation in self-managing work groups. *Journal of Applied Psychology, 78,* 450–462.

Sanna, L. J., & Parks, C. D. (1997). Group research trends in social and organizational psychology: Whatever happened to intragroup research? *Psychological Science, 8,* 261–267.

Stasser, G., Stewart, D., & Wittenbaum, G. M. (1995). Expert roles and information exchange during discussion: The importance of knowing who knows what. *Journal of Experimental Social Psychology, 31,* 244–265.

Stewart, T. A. (1995a, Nov. 27). Getting real about brainpower. *Fortune, 132,* 201–203.

Stewart, T. A. (1995b, Oct. 30). Mapping corporate brainpower. *Fortune, 132,* 209–212.

Stewart, T. A. (1997, Sep. 29). Does anyone around here know . . . ? *Fortune, 136,* 279–280.

Sutton, R. J., & Hargadon, A. (1996). Brainstorming groups in context: Effectiveness in a produce design firm. *Administrative Science Quarterly, 41,* 685–718.

Trends that will influence workplace learning and performance in the next five years. (1994, May). *Training and Development, 48,* 29–32.

Tuckman, B. W. (1965). Developmental sequence in small groups. *Psychological Bulletin, 63,* 384–399.

Veroff, J., Sutherland, L., Chadiha, L., & Ortega, R. M. (1993). Newlyweds tell their stories: A narrative method for assessing marital experiences. *Journal of Social and Personal Relationships, 10,* 437–457.

Vogt, J. F., & Hunt, B. D. (1988, May). What *really* goes wrong with participative work groups? *Training and Development Journal,* 96–100.

Waller, M. J. (1997). Keeping the pins in the air: How work groups juggle multiple tasks. In M. Beyerlein (Ed.), *Interdisciplinary studies of work teams* (Vol. 4, pp, 217–247). Greenwich, CT: JAI.

Watson, W. E., Kumar, K., & Michaelsen, L. K. (1993). Cultural diversity's impact on interaction process and performance: Comparing homogeneous and diverse task groups. *Academy of Management Journal, 36,* 590–602.

Watson, W. E., Michaelsen, L. K., & Sharp, W. (1991). Member competence, group interaction, and group decision making: A longitudinal study. *Journal of Applied Psychology, 76,* 803–809.

Wegner, D. M. (1987). Transactive memory: A contemporary analysis of the group mind. In B. Mullen & G. R. Goethals (Eds.), *Theories of group behavior* (pp. 185–208). New York: Springer-Verlag.

Wegner, D. M. (1995). A computer network model of human transactive memory. *Social Cognition, 13,* 319–339.

Wegner, D. M., Erber, R., & Raymond, P. (1991). Transactive memory in close relationships. *Journal of Personality and Social Psychology, 61,* 923–929.

Wegner, D. M., Giuliano, T., & Hertel, P. T. (1985). Cognitive interdependence in close relationships. In W. J. Ickes (Ed.), *Compatible and incompatible relationships* (pp. 253–276). New York: Springer-Verlag.

Weingart, L. R. (1992). Impact of group goals, task component complexity, effort, and planning on group performance. *Journal of Applied Psychology, 77,* 682–693.

Wellins, R. S., Byham, W. C., & Dixon, G. R. (1994). *Inside teams: How 20 world-class organizations are winning through teamwork.* San Francisco: Jossey-Bass.

Wittenbaum, G. M., Vaughan, S. I., & Stasser, G. (1998). Coordination in task-performing groups. In R. S. Tindale, L. Heath, J. Edwards, E. Posavac, F. B. Bryant, Y. Suarez-Balcazar, E. Henderson-King, & J. Myers (Eds.), *Theory and research on small groups* (pp. 177–204). New York: Plenum.

Yetton, P. W., & Bottger, P. C. (1982). Individual versus group problem solving: An empirical test of a best-member strategy. *Organizational Behavior and Human Performance, 29,* 307–321.

2

"Saying Is Believing" Effects: When Sharing Reality About Something Biases Knowledge and Evaluations

E. Tory Higgins
Columbia University

Your boss asks your opinion on some issue. You already have some idea about your boss's own opinion on this issue. What do you do? If you are like most people, you take your boss's opinion into account when communicating your opinion. Such tailoring and tuning of messages to suit one's audience is common in interpersonal communication. Indeed, several models of communication suggest that audience tuning is not only common but is a principle of good communication (for reviews, see Higgins, 1981, 1992; Krauss & Fussell, 1996). A question that has continued to fascinate me is: "What happens to our own knowledge or evaluations of a topic when we tune our message to suit the audience?" The goal of this chapter is to provide one answer to this question by considering the interrelations among three psychological principles—audience tuning, aboutness, and shared reality.

I am certainly not the first psychologist to be fascinated with what happens to communicators when they modify their message to suit their audience. Both the classic role-playing and cognitive dissonance literatures, for example, describe how people's own attitudes on some topic can be influenced by their producing messages to suit their audience (e.g., Festinger, 1957; Janis & King, 1954). The typical study in these literatures involves the experimenter as the audience who requests a message advocacy that is counter to the communicator's initial attitude. The effect of the communicator's advocacy on changing his or her own attitude is measured. These earlier studies have had an enormous impact on our understanding of self-persuasion. Regarding the larger question of how audience tuning influences communicators' own knowledge on a topic, however, these kinds of studies provide only limited information for a variety of reasons.

To begin with, it is important to recognize that people do not have to be induced by others to tailor their messages in a particular direction. They do so spontaneously. As mentioned earlier, a good communicator takes his or her audience into account when constructing the message. Indeed, this is true even at the basic level of assuring that the communicator and the audience have the same reference or topic in mind for the communication. Communication cannot proceed without there being at least this amount of common ground (e.g., Clark & Brennan, 1991). But beyond common reference for the communication, communicators also take the audience's background knowledge and opinions into account and spontaneously tune their messages to be congruent with them (for reviews, see Higgins, 1992; Krauss & Fussell, 1996). Moreover, such spontaneous tuning is not limited to audiences who are high in power or status, such as an experimenter in a study or a boss at work. People tune to all sorts of audiences, including coworkers and even young children.

The effects of audience tuning on the communicator also do not depend on the message being counterattitudinal. A communicator can develop a position on an issue for the first time during the communication itself. In such cases, the effects of audience tuning cannot be measured by comparing post-message opinions with pre-message opinions as in the cognitive dissonance and role-playing studies. Instead, the post-message opinions of people who communicated to different audiences are compared (see, for example, Higgins, 1992).

Audience tuning, moreover, does not change only the attitudes of communicators. It can change their judgments and knowledge as well. Most significant is the change that can occur in the communicators' own memory for the original information that was the basis for the message (see Higgins, 1992). Thus, even if communicators wanted later to check whether their post-message attitude or judgment was supported by the background information, they could not do so accurately because their memory of the information itself would have changed. Evidence for such effects on knowledge is reviewed later in this chapter.

My approach to understanding how audience tuning influences communicators' own knowledge and evaluations of a topic is to examine the interrelations among audience tuning, aboutness, and shared reality. This chapter begins by reviewing some examples of audience tuning and its biasing effects on subsequent knowledge and evaluations. Next, the aboutness principle is described and is used to understand why audience tuning introduces biases. The final section considers the principle of shared reality and discusses how tuning about some topic to an audience creates a shared reality with them. It is this shared reality that transforms audience-tuned messages into seemingly objective and accurate statements on the topic.

AUDIENCE TUNING

It has long been observed that social interaction requires taking others into account (e.g., Mead, 1934; Stryker & Statham, 1985; Weber, 1971), and that perspective-taking is basic to communication (e.g., Clark & Brennan, 1991; Higgins, 1981; Krauss & Fussell, 1996; Mead, 1934; Rommetveit, 1974). Communicators take into account both personal characteristics of their audience, such as their background knowledge or attitudes, and momentary situational factors such as their audience's vantage point or current state of comprehension (Krauss & Fussell, 1996).

One rudimentary form of audience tuning involves communicators modifying their message to suit the immediate informational needs of their partner. Even young children will vary their messages to suit the immediate needs of their communication partners. Children's messages about identical stimuli will vary, for example, depending on whether they are addressed to adults versus children their own age, someone who is or is not blindfolded, or partners who do or do not have information in common with them (see, for example, Higgins, 1977). There is strong evidence that communicators' messages take into account what their audience knows, feels, thinks, and believes (e.g., Manis, Cornell, & Moore, 1974).

It is important to note that communicators not only attempt to take their audience into account when constructing their message but they do so successfully. Even young children decrease their use of local names when communicating to a stranger in their community as compared to a neighbor (Higgins, 1977). In a classic study, Krauss, Vivekanathan, and Weinheimer (1968) asked subjects to describe color chips for their own later use or for the later use of another person and found that the chips were more accurately identified by others from descriptions that were originally intended for another person (see also Krauss & Fussell, 1996).

In a series of studies, my colleagues and I have found that communicators also tune their message about a target person to suit the attitude of their audience toward that person (for a review, see Higgins, 1992). The basic paradigm of these studies was quite similar. Undergraduate communicators were provided with behavioral descriptions about a male target person and were asked to transmit their knowledge about him to an audience who they believed already knew him and either liked or disliked him. The communicators in every study described the target person in relatively positive terms to the audience who supposedly liked him and in relatively negative terms to the audience who supposedly disliked him. There was also evidence that this basic tuning effect could either increase (supertuning) or decrease (anti-tuning) depending on whether the motivation to take the audience into account was stronger or weaker. Higgins and McCann (1984), for example, found that the amount of tuning to a high status audience's attitude was greater than normal for high authoritarian communicators and was smaller than normal for low authoritarian communicators (where normal basic tuning was found for both high and low authoritarians when they communicated to an equal status audience).

What is the effect of audience tuning? Several studies have found that the communicators' own knowledge and evaluations of the target person are influenced by the messages they produce. The attitudes, impressions, and recollections of communicators are more positive after they positively tune their message for an audience who they think likes the target person than after they negatively tune their message for an audience they think dislikes the target person. It is notable that these effects were not found when communicators expected to communicate to an audience they believed liked or disliked the target person but did not actually communicate (see Higgins & Rholes, 1978). Thus, simply knowing that the audience likes or dislikes the target person is not enough to influence attitudes, impressions, and memory. Path analyses performed in other studies also indicate that the effects of the audience's attitude on communicators' own knowledge and evaluations of the target person are mediated by the message modifications from audience tuning. Moreover, these saying-is-believing effects have been found to persist, or even increase, weeks after the original message is produced (see Higgins, 1992).

In summary, communicators spontaneously tune their messages to suit their audience's knowledge or evaluation of the message topic, and this audience tuning has significant effects on communicators' own subsequent knowledge and evaluation of the message topic. Thus, simply following the standard communication rule to take one's audience into account has unintended consequences of biasing communicators' own knowledge and evaluations of the message topic. To understand why this happens, let me turn next to the aboutness principle as a general source of bias in social cognition.

THE ABOUTNESS PRINCIPLE

Imagine that you watch a debate and observe a debater's strong advocacy of a position. Even though you know that the debating coach assigned each position to be advocated, you decide that the position advocated was the debater's true personal opinion. Now imagine that shortly after exercising you meet a guy who bothered you earlier in the day. You feel more angry at him than you did when the incident happened. Such experiences exemplify two well-known social cognitive biases—correspondence bias and misattribution. What do these biases have in common with the saying-is-believing effects described earlier? Might there be a single psychological principle that underlies each of these disparate biases? Recently, I have proposed one possibility—the aboutness principle (see also Higgins, 1997).

The *aboutness principle* refers to the following tendency: When people perceive a response (their own or another person's), they represent it as being about some thing and this thing that the response is about is inferred to be the source of the response.

I propose that people generally share a set of natural assumptions about psychological processes that together yield the aboutness principle. People's first assumption is, "When a response occurs, it is about something." That is, responses do not simply occur all by themselves, randomly, with no relation to anything. They do not just happen. Rather, responses are to something, they are about something. People ask themselves, "Where did that come from?" and believe that there is some source of the response. This assumption is both reasonable and adaptive.

When a response occurs, whether one's own or another person's, it potentially provides the observer with information to take action. But in order to serve this function, it is necessary for the observer to represent what the response is about. A person's own fear response to an input, for example, provides information to avoid something. But avoid what? It is necessary to represent that the fear response is about X in order to take action to avoid X. Similarly, to take action on observing the response of another person, it is necessary to represent what that person's response is about. Simply categorizing another person's facial expression as frowning, for example, provides insufficient information to take action. In order to take action, this person's expression must be represented as being about the circumstances surrounding its production or the emotional tendencies of the person who produced it. Perceiving the responses of self or others in the world can only serve their self-regulatory function of facilitating action if they are represented as being about something. It is natural, then, for people to assume that the responses they observe are responses to something and thus to represent them as being about something.

I propose that people's second assumption is, "A response is about a particular thing." It would be natural for people to provide one answer to the question, "Where did that come from?" It would be natural to assign one meaning to the event, to represent the response as being about something. This assumption is also reasonable and adaptive. After all, people's early and everyday experiences in life concern their own responses to a particular thing, such as their mother or a favorite toy, and others' responses to them as a particular thing. Moreover, it is economical to represent responses as being about a single thing. It is natural, then, for people to assume that an observed response is in relation to a particular thing and thus to represent each response as being about some thing.

I propose that people's third assumption is, "Whatever thing a response is about is the source of the response." Once again, this is a reasonable and useful assumption. Common everyday experiences involve responses to objects that are the source of the experience. When smelling a rose, one perceives the rose as the source of the fragrance one experiences. When a baby girl feels happy when hugged by her mother, the emotional response is in relation to the mother's hug and the mother's hug is the source of the response. When a boy throws a snowball, the response of the snowball is in relation to the boy's throw and the boy's throw is the source of the snowball's movement. It is natural, then, for people to assume that the thing they represent the response as being about is the source of the response.

These three assumptions together yield the aboutness principle. I have described each of these assumptions as being quite natural and, in addition, as being reasonable and adaptive. It would be natural, then, for people to combine them in the aboutness principle. There are problems, however, in using the aboutness principle despite its generally adaptive benefits. There are three basic problems, as follows:

1. People can represent a response as being about something that it is not actually about. People, for example, can possess psychological theories that are simply wrong, just as scientists historically have held theories that were wrong. If a person applies a mistaken theory to represent what a response is about, then the wrong something will be represented as what the response is about. It should be noted, moreover, that people's mistaken theories can be constructed on the spot or situationally induced as well as being chronic, previously established beliefs.

2. People can mistakenly infer that what they represent their response as being about is a source of the response. Although what people represent their response as being about is typically a source of the response, this is not always the case. It will certainly not be the case if, as just mentioned, a mistaken theory is used to represent what the response is about. But even if the theory that is applied in representing what the response is about is not mistaken, the inference that what the response is about is a source of the response can be wrong. For example, it is not mistaken to believe that the categorization of a target is about the target. But there are cases, such as the extremely vague target information used in a study by Higgins and Brendl (1995), where the source of the category used to judge the target is the accessibility of the category. The target contributes little, if anything, to category selection.

3. People can mistakenly infer that what they represent their response as being about is the source of the response. This is the most common mistake. The basic problem here is that a response typically has multiple sources rather than a single source. A student's performance on an exam, for example, might be represented as being about his or her knowledge of the course material, but knowledge of the course material is only one source of exam performance. Motivation while taking the exam and exam difficulty are additional sources of exam performance. In this case, as in others, the inference that what a response is about is the source of the response fails to sufficiently take into account the fact that there are likely to be other sources of the response.

Let us now return to the two social-cognitive biases mentioned at the beginning of this section to illustrate how people's use of the aboutness principle can create problems in human inference.

Correspondence Bias. Observing another person's behavior can involve rather complex input including the behavior, the person who produced the behavior, some entity to which the behavior was directed, and the surrounding circumstances of the behavior. Consider the input in the classic study by Jones and Harris (1967), for example. Each participant in the study was shown an essay that either supported or opposed Fidel Castro, the Communist Cuban President, and was told either that the author had freely chosen to advocate the position taken in the essay or that the author was a member of a debating team and had been assigned the position by the debating coach. In one key condition of the study, then, the input involved an essayist who produced a supportive behavior directed toward Castro after being told to do so by the debating coach.

The surprising finding of the study was that the participants in this condition tended to judge the essayist as personally having a favorable attitude toward Castro despite the fact that the essayist was told to take a favorable position toward Castro by the debating coach. This tendency for people to infer that the source of an observed behavior is a disposition in the actor that corresponds to the behavior he or she produced rather than the situation in which the behavior took place (i.e., either the entity toward which the behavior was directed or the surrounding circumstances) has been called the *observer bias* (Jones & Nisbett, 1972), the *fundamental attribution error* (Ross, 1977) or the *correspondence bias* (Gilbert & Jones, 1986; see also Jones, 1979).

This specific tendency may appear to be ubiquitous because in many studies, the participants believe that the study is about an individual who has performed a certain behavior and the procedures of the studies typically promote this perception (see Quattrone, 1982). Thus, the participants are likely to represent the behavior as being about the actor. According to the aboutness principle, then, the participants will emphasize the actor as being the source of the behavior rather than the situation in which the behavior occurred.

The aboutness principle, however, does not assume that there is some general or fundamental tendency to infer a particular kind of source for perceived responses, such as a fundamental tendency to infer that the source of another person's behavior is a disposition corresponding to that behavior. Depending on additional qualities of the input (e.g., Quattrone, 1982), or even the explanatory predispositions of the perceiver (e.g., Miller, 1984), perceivers will represent an actor's behavior as being about either the actor or the situation and infer that the source of the behavior was either the actor's disposition or situational forces, respectively (see Higgins & Bargh, 1987).

Misattribution. In Schachter and Singer's (1962) classic study on emotion, students participated in a supposed study on the effects of vitamin supplements on vision. The participants were injected with epinephrine or a placebo and were or were not told that the drug had specific side effects. The participants in one condition were injected with epinephrine and were misinformed about the side effects of the drug (e.g., "you will have an itching sensation over parts of your body"). While waiting for the supposed vision drug to take full effect, these participants were more likely than those in control conditions to express either anger or euphoria depending on whether a stooge in the waiting room with them acted in an angry or euphoric manner, respectively. Schachter and Singer (1962) suggested that the participants in this condition could not attribute their epinephrine-induced arousal experience to the drug because they had been told that it had different side effects and thus they attributed their experience to the emotional state defined by the behavior of their waiting room partner. Because perceivers attribute their response to an emotional state rather than to the drug that actually produced it, this phenomenon has been called *misattribution*.

The misattribution phenomenon was extended in research on excitation transfer (see Zillmann, 1982). In a study by Zillmann, Johnson, and Day (1974), for example, the participants were first provoked by another person, next engaged in strenuous physical exercise, and then were given the opportunity to retaliate against the person who had provoked them earlier. The study found that the participants were more likely to retaliate when given the opportunity several minutes after their exercise than immediately after. Immediately after exercise, there are many clear cues that one's arousal is due to the exercise but as time goes by, it becomes less clear that one's remaining arousal is due to the exercise. It becomes more likely, then, that whatever arousal (or excitation) remains from the exercise will be misattributed (or transferred) to one's anger when meeting the provoker again, thus increasing the likelihood of retaliation.

This phenomenon can be understood as compelling cases of people applying the aboutness principle to their own responses. The participants in the "epinephrine–misinformed" condition of the Schachter and Singer (1962) study could not represent their response to epinephrine as being about the drug and thus represented it as being about the emotional situation defined by their partner in the waiting room. They then inferred that the source of their response was the emotion corresponding to the emotional situation, without taking the drug into account as a source of their response. In the Zillmann et al. (1974) study, those participants who had some time to recover from their exercise before remeeting their provoker quite naturally represented all of their arousal, including the arousal remaining from the exercise, as being about their anger at the provoker. They then inferred that the source of their response was their anger at the provoker's prior behavior to them, producing retaliation, without taking their exercise into account as a source of their response.

Let us return now to the saying-is-believing effect and consider how use of the aboutness principle might underlie this phenomenon as well.

Saying-Is-Believing Effect. There are various kinds of social influence that will induce people to express ideas that are not their own. Across a variety of literature, including role-playing, cognitive dissonance, and social cognition, the striking finding is that communicators often end up believing what they say (e.g., Festinger & Carlsmith, 1959; Higgins & Rholes, 1978; Janis & King, 1954). The Higgins and Rholes study is one example of this phenomenon. Participants read an essay describing the behaviors of a target person, Donald, and then communicated about him to an audience they believed liked or disliked him. The study found that the audience's attitude influenced how the communicators described Donald and these messages, in turn, influenced the communicators' own subsequent evaluations and recollections of Donald.

Let us now consider this phenomenon in terms of the aboutness principle. When communicators produce a message on some topic, it would be natural for them to represent their message responses as being about the topic. It would be natural for communicators in the Higgins and Rholes (1978) study, for example, to represent their summaries of Donald's behaviors as being about Donald. According to the aboutness principle, these communicators would then infer that the source of their summaries was Donald's characteristics as reflected in his behaviors. As these perceivers become less able over time to remember the specific details of the stimulus information, they are likely to rely increasingly on their prior message summaries to decide what they saw and how they feel about it. This would not be a problem if the source of the summaries was just Donald's characteristics as reflected in his behaviors. But this was not the case. The audience to whom the message was directed was another important source of the message summaries. By not taking this additional source of the message summaries into account sufficiently, communicators who read exactly the same information about Donald, but communicated to different audiences, had very different recollections and evaluations of him 2 weeks later.

One reason, then, that audience tuning has significant effects on communicators' own knowledge and evaluation of the message topic is the operation of the aboutness principle. But this is not the only underlying factor. A second important factor is shared reality, which is considered next.

SHARED REALITY

Without social verification, our experiences as individuals are transitory, random, and ephemeral. Once our experiences are recognized and shared by others, however, they are no longer subjective but instead achieve the phenomenological status of objective reality. In brief, our individual experiences are established as valid and reliable to the extent that they are shared with others. This notion that social verification is crucially involved in the construction of individual experience has a long history in social psychology (e.g., Asch, 1952; Cooley, 1902/1964; Durkheim, 1897/1951; Festinger, 1950; Lewin, 1931; Mead, 1934; Rommetveit, 1974; Sherif, 1936; Weber, 1971), a tradition that has recently been reviewed and extended by Hardin and Higgins (1996).

Hardin and Higgins (1996) contrasted their formulation of shared reality from its best known precursor, the theory of social comparison (Festinger, 1950, 1954). As Festinger (1950) summarized this theory, "where the dependence upon physical reality is low, the dependence upon social reality is correspondingly high" (p. 272). Hardin and Higgins' (1996) "shared reality" notion assumes no distinction between physical and social realities. Instead, they postulated that any experience—ranging from the immediate tactile sensation of a stone to the abstract understanding of a philosophical concept—survives as a reliable, valid, and predictable state of the world to the extent that it is socially verified. In addition, the notion of shared reality does not emphasize self-assessment functions to the extent that social comparison theory does.

Hardin and Higgins (1996) adopted a statistical metaphor to summarize the functions of consensual social verification in the establishment and maintenance of individual experience. When an experience is recognized and shared with others in the process of social interaction, it achieves reliability, validity, generality, and predictability.

Shared reality functions to establish the reliability of an experience, just as repeated observation of a phenomenon gives it statistical reliability. When an experience is shared, it is demonstrably reliable by virtue of its repeated recognition by members of the community who share the perception or belief. As one's experience is recognized by others, one learns that it is reproducible in others and therefore not random or capricious. Validity is predicated on reliability. As in the scientific experiment, a basic function of shared reality is to establish that a given phenomenon is valid—that it corresponds to some objectively real aspect of the world. Reliably shared experience is demonstrably validated experience.

A goal of any scientific theory is to establish some level of generality. Generality is established to the degree that understanding is broader than a particular datum. The process of sharing one's experience with others demonstrates directly that the experience is not one of a kind or unique but that it has a reality that is broader and more general than the immediate moment. It exists across people, time, and particular situations. As it does for good scientific theories and statistical analyses, predictability follows from the reliability, validity, and generality that is achieved through shared reality. Hence, shared reality serves the fundamental epistemic function of facilitating the prediction and control of oneself and one's environment.

Interestingly, the very etiology of the words *subjective* and *objective* reflects a long-standing appreciation for the role of social verification in the status of experience. According to the *Oxford English Dictionary*, both words are rooted in the late Latin and have come to signify an elementary distinction between kinds of knowledge. Whereas *subjective* refers to solipsistic experience known only to the individual mind, *objective* refers to things or realities that are known to exist independently of the individual and can be observed by others. More recent, in the history of science, *objective* is used to refer to phenomena that can be verified by other scientists. Therefore, even the common English lexicon reflects the recognition of the distinction between experience that is shared and unshared.

An excellent example of how shared reality creates and maintains individual experience is found in Sherif's (1936) classic "autokinetic" experiments. The basic paradigm of these studies involves exposing subjects to a fixed point of light in a completely darkened room, telling them that the light may appear to move, and then asking them to judge the direction and magnitude of any movement. Typically the light does appear to move with an erratic quality because of the subjects' own saccadic eye movement.

Sherif compared the autokinetic effect as it manifested for subjects alone versus in groups of other subjects. He found that there were individual differences in the judgments of subjects working alone but when they subsequently performed the task with others, their individual judgments converged to form a group norm. When subjects began the task in a group, convergence was even greater and the number of trials necessary for the norm to be established was smaller. Follow-up studies demonstrated that the shared reality created by the groups survives across generations of subjects, indicating that once a shared reality is achieved, it can be maintained with stability long after the originators of the norm have gone (e.g., Jacobs & Campbell, 1961).

Importantly, the group norms of the different groups in a study were often different. The shared reality established by the groups in these studies had a relatively arbitrary relation to the external physical stimulus and thus the norm of any one group was no more accurate than the norm of any other group, just as the English word "dog" no better represents a slobbering four-legged creature wagging its tail than the French word "chien." Yet consensus was established within each group in these studies and was passed on to subsequent generations. It should also be noted that subjects do not understand their experience in terms of conformity but rather describe their judgments as reflecting their actual perception of reality. Subjects deny that they are merely going along with their colleagues but instead insist that they are expressing their true experience. Most important, all evidence suggests that individual experience was transformed by being shared with others.

A corollary of Hardin and Higgins' (1996) statistical metaphor is that shared reality will be regularly realized in ongoing social regulation. Just as statistical models (or scientific theories) regulate the hypotheses addressed, tested, and pursued, the basic functions of shared reality would suggest that its achievement should be a dominant regulatory goal of social interaction. That is, to the extent shared reality is required for establishing the reliability, validity, predictability, and generality of experience, efforts to establish shared reality should be ubiquitous in social interaction and not limited to special circumstances involving highly ambiguous stimuli. Efforts to establish shared reality should dominate social interaction, guiding its course and consequences (see Asch, 1952; Higgins, 1981; Rommetveit, 1974; Watzlawick, Beavin, & Jackson, 1967).

The proposal that the individual's grasp of reality is determined by the extent to which it is socially shared implies an essential role of communication in human cognition. Indeed, it implies that it would be impossible to fully understand individual cognition outside the context of ongoing communicative activity (see Higgins, 1981; Krauss & Fussell, 1996). In an earlier discussion of the importance of shared reality, the communication game approach described the irreducibly social sharing character of communication (Higgins, 1981, 1992; Higgins & McCann, 1984). In particular, communication is known to: (a) involve shared, rule-governed conventions concerning social roles and behavior (e.g., Rommetveit, 1974; Watzlawick et al., 1967); (b) require cooperative co-orientation and mutual perspective-taking (e.g., Grice, 1975; Mead, 1934; Rommetveit, 1974); (c) function not only to transmit information but also to create and define social relationships, with the content and relationship being interdependent (e.g., Garfinkel, 1967; Watzlawick et al., 1967); and (d) be a socially interdependent process in which the purpose and very meaning of the interchange is collaboratively determined (e.g., Garfinkel, 1967; Krauss & Fussell, 1996; Rommetveit, 1974; Watzlawick et al., 1967).

In sum, interpersonal communication inherently involves sharing reality with others. Communicators are motivated to establish a shared reality with their partner and, when they do so, the shared reality is experienced as objective truth. It is not only that communicators consider their audience-tuned messages to be about the topic of the message rather than about the audience. They also consider their audience-tuned message to provide objective, accurate information on the message topic because it was shared with the audience. It is the combination of the aboutness principle and shared reality that makes communicators treat their audience-tuned message as if they were simple statements of fact.

Although interpersonal communication inherently involves sharing reality with others, this does not imply that communicators are equally motivated to share reality with all audiences. One would expect, for example, that communicators are not equally motivated to share reality with their in-group members than with out-group members. This might mean that they would tune their messages more to the attitudes of in-group than out-group members. But independent of the amount of audience tuning, the messages produced for an in-group (versus out-group) member should have a greater impact on the communicators' subsequent evaluations and knowledge if these messages are experienced more as a shared reality in this condition.

This possibility was tested recently in a study by Chen (1997). Female undergraduates at Columbia College communicated to audiences who were either members of their in-group (other Columbia College females) or members of an out-group with whom they had a mild rivalry (Barnard College females). Using the same basic paradigm described earlier, the communicators believed that their audience either liked or disliked the target female who was the topic of the message. The study replicated the basic audience-tuning effect for both in-group and out-group audiences. Thus, group membership did not influence the extent to which the communicators followed the communication rule of taking the audience's perspective into account.

Group membership, however, did influence the extent to which audience-tuned messages later influenced the communicators. The messages functioned as a mediator between audience attitude and the communicators' own subsequent attitudes, impressions, and memory of the target person only when the audience tuning was for in-group members! Thus, only the messages shaped for and shared with in-group members played a significant role in communicators' own later knowledge and evaluations of the target person. This result is consistent with the notion that only when the message is experienced as a shared reality is it treated as an objective and accurate source of information.

One other aspect of Chen's (1997) study should be noted. The communicators in this study spontaneously distorted their description of a target person to be consistent with their audience's attitude. To the extent that the communicators were aware that their message was not consistent with the facts about the target person, one might want to explain the message effects on attitudes in terms of the communicators resolving cognitive dissonance. But one would expect, if anything, greater dissonance, and thus a stronger attitude effect, when tailoring information to suit an out-group member than an in-group member. The results were opposite to this prediction.

CONCLUDING REMARKS

This chapter began with the observation that when we communicate on some topic, most of us take our audience's attitude into account. This observation raised the question, "What happens to our own knowledge or evaluations of a topic when we tune our message to suit the audience?" I proposed in this chapter that the interrelation among audience tuning, aboutness, and shared reality provides an answer to this question.

Good communication requires taking the audience's characteristics into account, including the audience's attitude on some topic. Thus, audience tuning is performed spontaneously. The aboutness principle suggests that the message produced will be considered to be about the message topic rather than about the audience for whom it was tuned. Thus, the information contained in the message will be treated as if it only reflected whatever topic information was originally available. But because the information contained in the message was, in fact, also influenced by the audience tuning, audience tuning introduces a bias in the subsequent use of the message as a source of knowledge and evaluations. This problem is compounded when the message is experienced as a shared reality with the audience because shared reality makes the message seem objective and accurate. Therefore, a process that begins naturally ends with bias, and the benefits of sharing produce the cost of treating bias as if it were truth.

REFERENCES

Asch, S. E. (1952). *Social psychology.* Englewood Cliffs, NJ: Prentice-Hall.
Chen, Y. (1997). *Effects of group membership and audience's attitude on communication.* Unpublished doctoral dissertation, Columbia University, New York.

Clark, H. H., & Brennan, S. E. (1991). Grounding in communication. In L. B. Resnick, J. M. Levine, & S. D. Teasley (Eds.), *Perspectives on socially shared cognition* (pp. 127–149). Washington, DC: American Psychological Association.

Cooley, C. H. (1964). *Human nature and the social order.* New York: Schocken Books. (Original work published 1902.)

Durkheim, E. (1951). *Suicide: A study in sociology.* New York: The Free Press. (Original work published 1897.)

Festinger, L. (1950). Informal social communication. *Psychological Review, 57,* 271–282.

Festinger, L. (1954). A theory of social comparison processes. *Human Relations, 1,* 117–140.

Festinger, L. (1957). *A theory of cognitive dissonance.* Evanston, IL: Row, Peterson.

Festinger, L., & Carlsmith, J. M. (1959). Cognitive consequences of forced compliance. *Journal of Abnormal and Social Psychology, 58,* 203–211.

Garfinkel, H. (1967). *Studies in ethnomethodology.* Englewood Cliffs, NJ: Prentice-Hall.

Gilbert, D. T., & Jones, E. E. (1986). Perceiver-induced constraint: Interpretations of self-generated reality. *Journal of Personality and Social Psychology, 50,* 269–280.

Grice, H. P. (1975). Logic and conversation. In P. Cole & J. L. Morgan (Eds.), *Syntax and semantics: Speech acts* (Vol. 3, pp. 365–372). New York: Seminar Press.

Hardin, C., & Higgins, E. T. (1996). Shared reality: How social verification makes the subjective objective. In R. M. Sorrentino & E. T. Higgins (Eds.), *Handbook of motivation and cognition, Volume 3: The interpersonal context* (pp. 28–84). New York: Guilford Press.

Higgins, E. T. (1977). Communication development as related to channel, incentive, and social class. *Genetic Psychology Monographs, 96*(1), 75–141.

Higgins, E. T. (1981). The "communication game": Implications for social cognition and persuasion. In E. T. Higgins, C. P. Herman, & M. P. Zanna (Eds.), *Social cognition: The Ontario Symposium* (pp. 343–392). Hillsdale, NJ: Lawrence Erlbaum Associates.

Higgins, E. T. (1992). Achieving "shared reality" in the communication game: A social action that creates meaning. *Journal of Language and Social Psychology, 11,* 107–131.

Higgins, E. T. (1997). Biases in social cognition: "Aboutness" as a general principle. In C. McGarty & S. A. Haslam (Eds.), *The message of social psychology* (pp. 182–199). Oxford, England: Blackwell.

Higgins, E. T., & Bargh, J. A. (1987). Social cognition and social perception. *Annual Review of Psychology, 38,* 369–425.

Higgins, E. T., & Brendl, M. (1995). Accessibility and applicability: Some "activation rules" influencing judgment. *Journal of Experimental Social Psychology, 31,* 218–243.

Higgins, E. T., & McCann, C. D. (1984). Social encoding and subsequent attitudes, impressions, and memory: "Context-driven" and motivational aspects of processing. *Journal of Personality and Social Psychology, 47,* 26–39.

Higgins, E. T., & Rholes, W. S. (1978). "Saying is believing": Effects of message modification on memory and liking for the person described. *Journal of Experimental Social Psychology, 14,* 363–378.

Jacobs, R. C., & Campbell, D. T. (1961). The perpetuation of an arbitrary tradition through several generations of a laboratory microculture. *Journal of Abnormal and Social Psychology, 62,* 649–658.

Janis, I. L., & King, B. T. (1954). The influence of role-playing on opinion change. *Journal of Abnormal and Social Psychology, 49,* 211–218.

Jones, E. E. (1979). The rocky road from acts to dispositions. *American Psychologist, 34,* 107–117.

Jones, E. E., & Harris, V. A. (1967). The attribution of attitudes. *Journal of Experimental Social Psychology, 3,* 1–24.

Jones, E. E., & Nisbett, R. E. (1972). The actor and the observer: Divergent perceptions of the causes of behavior. In E. E. Jones, D. Kanouse, H. H. Kelley, R. E. Nisbett, S. Valins, & B. Weiner (Eds.), *Attribution: Perceiving the causes of behavior* (pp. 79–94). Hillsdale, NJ: Lawrence Erlbaum Associates.

Krauss, R. M., & Fussell, S. R. (1996). Social psychological models of interpersonal communication. In E. T. Higgins & A. W. Kruglanski (Eds.), *Social Psychology: Handbook of basic principles* (pp. 655–701). New York: Guilford Press.

Krauss, R. M., Vivekanathan, P. S., & Weinheimer (1968). "Inner Speech" and "External Speech": Characteristics and communicative effectiveness of socially and non-socially encoded messages. *Journal of Personality and Social Psychology, 9*, 295–300.

Lewin, K. (1931). Environmental forces in child behavior and development. In C. Murchison (Ed.), *A handbook of child psychology* (pp. 590–625). Worcester, MA: Clark University Press.

Manis, M., Cornell, S. D., & Moore, J. C. (1974). Transmission of attitude-relevant information through a communication chain. *Journal of Personality and Social Psychology, 30*, 81–94.

Mead, G. H., (1934). *Mind, self, and society.* Chicago: University of Chicago Press.

Miller, J. G. (1984). Culture and the development of everyday social explanation. *Journal of Personality and Social Psychology, 46*, 961–978.

Quattrone, G. A. (1982). Overattribution and unit formation: When behavior engulfs the person. *Journal of Personality and Social Psychology, 42*, 593–607.

Rommetveit, R. (1974). *On message structure: A framework for the study of language and communication.* New York: Wiley.

Ross, L. (1977). The intuitive psychologist and his shortcomings: Distortions in the attribution process. In L. Berkowitz (Ed.), *Advances in experimental social psychology* (Vol. 10, pp. 173–220). New York: Academic Press.

Schachter, S., & Singer, J. E. (1962). Cognitive, social, and physiological determinants of emotional state. *Psychological Review, 69*, 379–399.

Sherif, M. (1936). *The psychology of social norms.* New York: Harper.

Stryker, S., & Statham, A. (1985). Symbolic interaction and role theory. In G. Lindzey & E. Aronson (Eds.), *Handbook of social psychology* (Vol. 1, pp. 311–318). New York: Random House.

Watzlawick, P., Beavin, J. H., & Jackson, D. D. (1967). *Pragmatics of human communication.* New York: Norton.

Weber, M. (1971). *Max Weber: The interpretation of social reality,* J. E. T. Eldridge (Ed.). New York: Scribner's.

Zillmann, D. (1978). Attribution and misattribution of excitatory reactions. In J. H. Harvey, W. J. Ickes, & R. F. Kidd (Eds.), *New directions in attribution research* (Vol. 2, pp. 335–368). Hillsdale, NJ: Lawrence Erlbaum Associates.

Zillmann, D., Johnson, R. C., & Day, K. D. (1974). Attribution of apparent arousal and proficiency of recovery from sympathetic activation affecting excitation transfer to aggressive behavior. *Journal of Experimental Social Psychology, 10*, 503–515.

3

The Uncertain Role of Unshared Information in Collective Choice

Garold Stasser
Miami University

Intuitively, it seems that unique information is valuable. Rehashing commonly known information and stating the obvious are not recommended strategies for bolstering one's image. In contrast, novel insights and new information are hard currency in social exchange. The presumed value of unique information is not overlooked in the group performance literature. General models of team performance state simply that potential productivity is enhanced when team members bring unique knowledge and ideas to the group (Shiflett, 1979; Steiner, 1972). In the social influence literature, novel arguments are ascribed more persuasive potential than are common arguments (e.g., Burnstein & Vinokur, 1977). From these perspectives, messages that add new information to the shared pool of knowledge are more valuable than messages that restate already shared knowledge.

However, the potential impact of unique information on collective action may be more imagined than real in many settings. Recent findings suggest that unshared knowledge does not emerge readily in group communication and faces an uncertain fate if it is aired. Gigone and Hastie (1993, 1996) noted that common information shapes individual opinions which in turn shape collective judgments (*common knowledge effect*). Stasser, Taylor, and Hanna (1989) demonstrated that decision-making groups are more likely to discuss shared than unshared information (*collective sampling*; see also Larson et al., 1994, 1996; Stasser & Stewart, 1992; Wittenbaum, 1998). Moreover, when unshared information does surface in group discussion, its impact seems muted. Other things being equal, groups are less likely to repeat unshared than shared information after it is first mentioned (Larson et al., 1994; Stasser et al., 1989). Similarly, group members tend to recall proportionately more of the shared than the unshared information that is mentioned during group discussion (Stewart & Stasser, 1995).

This chapter explores some of the social and psychological barriers to communicating and using effectively unique knowledge. Most of the work discussed focuses on face-to-face communication in small groups. Additionally, the focus is on groups that are task-oriented, having the production of something (e.g., a decision or a report) as one of their primary goals.

COLLECTIVE INFORMATION SAMPLING

Elementary probability theory asserts that, as the opportunities for an event to occur increase, the probability of it occurring at least once also increases. For example, the probability of obtaining a heart when drawing a card from a full deck of standard playing cards is .25, but the probability of obtaining at least one heart in three successive selections is about .58 (if sampling is with replacement; slightly more if without replacement). Steiner (1972) applied a sampling metaphor to understanding potential perform-ance on unitary and disjunctive group tasks. A *unitary* task is one that cannot be easily divided into subtasks and thus does not afford division of labor and a *disjunctive* task is one that the group can successfully complete if at least one of its members can complete it. To illustrate, suppose that three-person groups are composed from a population individuals of whom 25% can solve a math problem. If a group solves the problem if and only if at least one member can solve the problem, then about 58% of groups would solve the problem (following the logic in the previous card sampling exam-ple; the formal statement of this reasoning is dubbed the Lorge-Solomon Model A, Lorge & Solomon, 1962; see Davis, 1969, or Steiner, 1972, for further discussion of this and related models of group productivity).

Stasser and Titus (1985, 1987) applied similar reasoning to explain why unshared information seemingly had little impact on the decisions of groups in their studies. Consider two items of equally memorable information, "Joan is a Young Republican" and "Jack is a member of the Debate Club." Suppose that all three members of a scholarship selection committee were aware of Joan's Republican affiliation but only one knew of Jack's club membership. If each member of the selection committee mentioned 25% of what they knew about Joan and Jack en route to their selecting one of them to receive a scholarship, Jack's club membership would have only 25% chance of entering discussion, but Joan's Republican affiliation would have more than a 50% chance of entering discussion (because any one of the three could mention it). This analysis assumes that all items are equally memorable, equally likely to be selected for discussion if remembered, and what one member recalls is independent of what others recall. These assumptions are rarely, if ever, met during group discussion, but even marked violations of these simplifying assumptions do not invalidate the conclusion that information has better chance of being discussed if everyone or many know it before discussion than if one or only a few know it.

Stasser and Titus (1987) expressed these ideas more formally in Equation 3.1 below by defining the level of discussion recall, $p(R)$, as the probability that an individual will recall and contribute a given item of information to discussion. Then the probability, $p(D)$, that the item will be discussed by the group is given by:

$$p(D) = 1 - [1 - p(R)]^n, \qquad (3.1)$$

where n is the number of members who can potentially recall the item. Thus, in the foregoing example about Joan and Jack, $p(R)$ is .25. The fact that Jack belongs to Debate Club can only be recalled and mentioned by one member; therefore, n equals 1 and $p(D) = 1 - [1 - .25]^1 = .25$. In contrast, all three members can potentially recall and mention Joan's Republican affiliation; therefore, $n = 3$ and $p(D) = 1 - [1 - .25]^3 = .58$.

Stasser, Taylor, and Hanna (1989) tested some of the predictions of the Collective Information Sampling (CIS) model as expressed in Equation 3.1. For example, the model predicts that the difference in sampling rates for shared and unshared information increases as the size of the group increases. Returning to the selection of Joan and Jack for a scholarship, suppose the committee grew to six members and all had prior knowledge of Joan's political affiliation. In this case, the probability that at least one of them would bring it up during discussion would be given by $p(D) = 1 - [1 - .25]^6 = .82$ (as compared to .58 for the three-person committee).

Stasser et al. (1989) distributed information about three candidates for student body president such that some of the information was read by all members of a group (*shared* information), whereas other items were read by only one member (*unshared* information). Groups of either three or six students discussed the candidates and selected a preferred one. In their discussions, three-person groups mentioned about 18% of unshared items and 37% of shared items. This difference was greater for six-person groups, who also discussed about 18% of unshared items but 58% of shared items. (See also Stewart & Stasser, 1995, for another application of the CIS model as expressed in the previous equation.)

TEMPORAL DYNAMICS OF CIS

Larson, Foster-Fishman and Keys (1994) proposed an extension of the logic of collective information sampling. They noted that Equation 3.1 fails to capture the sequential dependencies of sampling without replacement from a finite pool of information. Even though Equation 3.1 may provide an approximation to the overall rates of sampling shared versus unshared information, it obscures important temporal patterns in the mix of shared and unshared items as discussion unfolds. Larson et al. (1994) framed the problem in the following way. Suppose that a group has three members, all of whom possess 12 items of shared information and each of whom has an additional four items of unshared information (resulting in a total of 12 unshared items). Then, at the onset of discussion, there are 36 opportunities for shared items to be mentioned (i.e., 12 items times the 3 persons who can mention each item) and 12 opportunities for unshared items to be mentioned (i.e., each member can mention one of his or her four unshared items). All other things being equal, the probability that the first item mentioned is a shared item is .75 because, of the 48 possibilities, 36 involve one of the members mentioning a shared item. However, the likelihood of the second item discussed being shared or unshared depends partly on what happened initially. For example, if the group samples a shared item initially (the more likely event), then the opportunities for sampling a shared item next are reduced because the members now have only 11 shared items remaining for consideration. This reduces the opportunities for sampling a shared item to $3 \times 11 = 33$ and the probability of sampling a shared item to $33/45 = .73$. Although the sequential dependency may seem slight in this example, the effect can be substantial as the number of sampled items increases. Moreover, note that in this process, the pool of shared items will tend to be depleted more rapidly than the pool of unshared items during the early stages of discussion and eventually the opportunties for mentioning unshared items will become greater than the opportunities for mentioning shared items.

Based on this construction of the collective sampling process, Larson et al. (1994) argued that shared information would be overrepresented in the early phases of discussions but, if discussions continued sufficiently long, unshared information would become increasingly likely to surface. Larson, Christensen, Abbott, and Franz (1996) tracked the discussions of medical teams while they discussed the diagnosis of two hypothetical cases. Each team was composed of a resident physician, an intern, and a third-year medical student. Before their discussion of a case, each member of the team viewed a videotape of the patient being interviewed in an emergency room setting. These tapes were edited so that about half of the presenting symptoms were viewed by single members of the team (unshared) whereas the remaining half were viewed by all three members (shared). The first symptoms discussed by teams were almost always ones that all three members had heard and over 70% of the symptoms discussed second were likewise shared items. However, this dominance of shared information decreased as more information was introduced into discussion. For example, the tenth item introduced into discussion was about equally likely to be a shared or an unshared item and, from then on, unshared information was mentioned more frequently than shared information. Larson, Foster-Fishman, and Franz (1998) obtained similar patterns for student groups choosing the best of three professors to teach an advanced psychology class.

To summarize briefly, in face-to-face discussions, small groups tend to mention disproportionate amounts of shared relative to unshared information. This collective sampling advantage to shared information occurs even when individual members are equally likely to mention shared and unshared items. Moreover, this sampling advantage tends to be pronounced in the early phases of discussion and to dissipate as the number of items discussed increases. Although prolonged discussions may eventually pool substantial amounts of information, early consensus, time pressures, and other diversions frequently foreshorten discussions and thus prevent them from moving to the point where the sampling advantage shifts to unshared information. In short, collective sampling dynamics in unstructured, face-to-face discussions promote the rehashing of shared information at the expense of pooling unshared information.

PROCEDURAL INTERVENTIONS

Procedural interventions can affect who talks, when they talk, and what they say. Such interventions can dramatically change how easily unshared information is disseminated. For example, suppose that a small group were engaged in a round-robin information dump. That is, one member starts by recalling everything that seems pertinent to the task at hand and the next and subsequent speakers simply add items that are not already mentioned. Under such a procedure, the flow of unshared items into discussion would be distinctly different than the patterns observed in unstructured conversations or predicted by the CIS model. To illustrate, assume that individual members had no reason to favor shared over unshared information (or had no way of telling what items were shared or unshared). Then, the first speaker in this round-robin procedure would be equally likely to mention shared and unshared items. And the contributions of subsequent speakers would become increasingly tilted toward unshared information because of the procedural injunction to avoid repeating already mentioned information. Note that even under this procedure, a shared item would be less likely to be omitted entirely because every speaker would have a chance of mentioning it if foregoing speakers failed to recall it. Nonetheless, one would expect this procedure to reduce the disparity in sampling rates of shared and unshared information particularly in the early phases of the interaction.

The procedural interventions that have been examined empirically are more subtle than a round-robin information dump. Interventions may change either the information-processing demands of the task or the allocation of information-processing responsibilities within the group.

INFORMATIONAL-PROCESSING DEMANDS TASK

Hollingshead (1996) argued that having to rank order alternatives, rather than simply choose the best, would promote a more thorough discussion of the alternatives and facilitate the exchange of unshared information. She asked three-person groups to consider three companies as potential investments under two different decision procedures. Some of the groups were instructed to choose the best investment, whereas the remaining were told to rank the companies from the best to the worst investment. Before the groups convened, each member received six items of shared information and two items of unshared information about each company. Thus, there was a total of 18 items of shared and 18 items of unshared items of information. Hollingshead created a hidden profile by designating many of the items that favored the normatively best investment to be unshared. That is, any one member knew only part of the information that supported the best choice and, as a result, fewer than 20% of members favored the best option at the onset of discussion. However, once members met, they could exchange the unshared information that supported the best option and this pooling of unshared information could lead groups to identify the best choice even though members individually could not. Of course, if discussion focused on already shared information to the exclusion of unshared information, groups would unwittingly fail in their search for the best option.

As Hollingshead (1996) predicted, groups who ranked the options were more likely to select the normatively best option as number one than were groups who simply choose the best. Moreover, groups mentioned more unshared information en route to ranking the options that they did when deciding which was best. Interestingly, these beneficial effects of the ranking procedure were obtained in face-to-face but not in computer-mediated interaction. Hollingshead (1996) attributed the poor performance in computer-mediated communication to overall low rates of information transmission regardless of decision procedure.

Whereas Hollingshead (1996) directly manipulated the informational demands of generating the response required by the task, Stasser and Stewart (1992) manipulated members' perceptions of the task in a way that changed the apparent informational demands. In matters of judgment, one does not expect self-affirming answers to emerge even if one were to consider all of the available information. Matters of judgment are often decided as much by social consensus as they are by reasoned consideration of information (Festinger, 1954; Goethals & Darley, 1977; Laughlin & Ellis, 1986). If a task is judgmental, members may be disinclined to search for further information once they agree on a solution. However, if members expect that information may lead to a logically defensible decision, they may continue their information search until they find the necessary information to identify the correct solution.

Stasser and Stewart (1992) framed a decision task in two different ways to induce either a solve or judge set. All groups read and picked a guilty suspect in a murder mystery. Half of the groups were told that the mystery had a demonstrably correct answer if all clues were considered (*solve* set), whereas the remaining half were told that they may not have enough information to determine definitely the guilty suspect (*judge* set). Groups deliberating under the judge set were asked to identify the suspect who was most likely to have committed the crime. When critical clues were unshared before discussion, groups who believed that the mystery had a demonstrably correct answer discussed more unshared clues and were more likely to identify the correct suspect than groups who had the judge set.

Whereas such procedural interventions can increase the amount of unshared information exchanged, it is important to note that the benefits may be slight under certain conditions. For example, Stasser et al. (1989) instructed some decision-making groups to engage in a structured exchange of information without stating preferences for 15 minutes and then to chose one of three decision alternatives. Whereas these groups discussed more information than groups who did not have a structured information exchange, most of the additional information discussed was shared rather than unshared information. For example, six-person groups whose discussion was unstructured exchanged 13% of their unshared information while mentioning 45% of their already shared information. By comparison, six-person groups whose discussions were structured discussed 23% of their unshared and 67% of their shared information. In this case, facilitating information exchange actually shifted the focus of discussion even more toward shared information.

COORDINATED COLLECTIVE RECALL

The collective sampling advantage to shared information stems from the fact that shared information has more opportunities to be mentioned than does unshared. The more widely disseminated information is before discussion, the more likely that at least one person will recall and mention it during discussion. This collective sampling dynamic undermines the opportunity for group members to pool their diverse knowledge. However, if members can coordinate information processing in order to avoid duplication of effort, the sampling advantage to shared information can theoretically be reduced or eliminated.

Consider, for example, the distribution of information among three people that is depicted in the top panel of Fig. 3.1, where U and S stand for an items of unshared and shared information, respectively. The subscripts a, b, and c denote salient categories of information or natural ways of dividing information given the task or context (e.g., in a decision task, subscripts might represent decision alternatives). In the case depicted in Fig. 3.1, there are nine pieces of shared and nine pieces of unshared information. Person X possesses three items of information from category a that others do not have (viz., the items represented by U_a). Likewise, persons Y and Z possess unique information in categories b and c, respectively. By virtue of their unique knowledge, we might say that X is an expert in a, Y in b, and Z in c. Nonetheless, everyone knows at least little bit about a, b, and c.

If X, Y, and Z do not recognize their expertise, then the shared items have a sampling advantage because all can recall and mention them. Suppose, however, that X was clearly identified as the knowledgeable person about a-things, Y about b-things, and Z about c-things. Furthermore, suppose that all members let their domain of recognized expertise determine what they contributed to the conversation such that X would say a-things but not b- and c-things. Under this strict division of labor, the collective sampling advantage to shared information would disappear. As illustrated in the lower panel of Fig. 3.1, such a division of labor partitions the responsibility

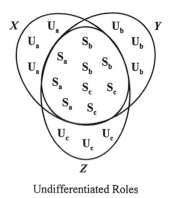

Undifferentiated Roles

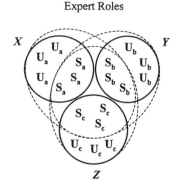

Expert Roles

FIG. 3.1. Partially distributed information systems and division of labor.

for information in a way that makes each item functionally unshared. That is, even though all could potentially mention an item, S_a, expert roles dictate that only X mention such an item.

There are many ways that such divisions of labor might arise in practice. Transactive memory theory (Moreland, Argote, & Krishnan, 1996; Wegner, 1986; Wegner, Erber, & Raymond, 1991) suggests that responsibility for domains of information might be assigned on the basis of social stereotypes, relative ease of access, or past behavior. Person X might be implicitly assigned responsibility for items in a because she always talks about a-things when X, Y, and Z converse or because she is lawyer and a-things are matters of civil law. Wegner, Erber, and Raymond (1991) showed that couples used knowledge of their partners' expertise to allocate processing in a collective recall task. Wittenbaum, Stasser, and Merry (1996) showed that members of task-oriented groups not only use social cues but also consider the informational demands of the task in allocating their attention to categories of information in preparation for collective action. Thus, implicit divisions of labor among group members can arise in subtle ways based on social cues or past experience.

Stewart and Stasser (1995) examined the effects of divisions of labor on collective information sampling when groups were performing either a collective choice or a collective recall task. During collective recall, three-person groups recalled as much as possible about three hypothetical candidates for student body president and produced a consensually endorsed written summary of the recalled information. During the choice task, they discussed the candidates and decided as a group which one was best. Some information about the candidates was shared before group interaction, whereas the remaining information was unshared. To induce a division of labor, some groups were told which members had more information about particular candidates, whereas others did not receive this expert role assignment.

Figure 3.2 displays the percentage of shared and unshared information mentioned during the collective recall and the collective choice tasks. Three things are readily apparent in the nonexpert panels of the figure (i.e., when members were not explicitly told of their relative expertise). First, shared information was more likely to be mentioned than unshared information (the basic collective sampling result predicted by equation 3.1). Second, groups mentioned more of both shared and unshared information during collective recall than during collective choice. This result underscores the earlier point that task demands can alter sampling patterns. Third, the increase in information sampled in the recall as compared to the choice task was disproportionately due to more shared information being mentioned during recall. This finding underscores the aforementioned point that simply increasing the amount of information discussed may actually shift the focus of discussion even more toward shared information.

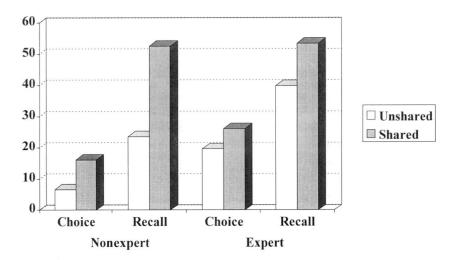

FIG. 3.2. Percentage of information mentioned during collective choice and collective recall tasks. Data from Stewart and Stasser (1995).

In contrast, assignment of expert roles facilitated the sampling of un-shared information during both collective recall and collective choice. Whereas expert roles substantially increased the likelihood that groups would mention unshared information, shared information still maintained a slight edge, especially for the recall task.

Stasser, Stewart, and Wittenbaum (1995) used a similar role assignment manipulation for groups who were working on a murder mystery task. When critical clues were unshared, groups were more likely to identify the correct suspect if members knew who among them had additional clues about each suspect. It is important to note, however, that simply forewarning members individually that they would get additional clues about a particular suspect was not sufficient to improve performance. The benefit accrued only when members were told in the presence of each other who had received additional clues about each of the suspects.

The implication is that clearly defined and mutually recognized divisions of labor in processing information may reduce the sampling advantage due to information being widely available before a group convenes. However, Stasser et al. (1995) emphasized the necessity for every one in the group to understand and accept the division of labor:

> Collective information sampling dynamics . . . suggest that a cognitive division of labor is a potentially powerful way to attenuate the sampling advantage to shared information. However, the coordination necessary for implementing such a division of labor entails both the acceptance and the assignment of responsibility in a complementary way. In other words, the road to coordi-

nated group interaction . . . in recruiting information . . . is a two-way street
. . . (F)or coordination to emerge implicitly, all members must share, and perhaps know they share, the same map for guiding traffic along this two-way
street. (pp. 264–265)

Larson and Christensen (1993) used the term *meta-knowledge* to denote
knowledge about how task-relevant resources are distributed among members (see also Moreland, Argote, & Krishnan, 1996; Wegner, 1986). In order
to pool effectively unshared knowledge, members of a group need to have
the same meta-knowledge about how access to informational resources are
distributed among members. Implicit in this statement but important
enough to state: The meta-knowledge must also be reasonably accurate.
The division of labor that emerges must assign responsibility to domains
where members do indeed possess unique knowledge. Mismatches between
members' domains of expertise and their assigned responsibilities will almost certainly exclude pockets of unshared information. Suppose that Andy
knows some unique *a* things, but the group expects him to know, and thus
implicitly assigns him responsibility for, *b* things. If Andy accepts this definition of himself as a *b* expert, his unique *a* knowledge will have little chance
to emerge.

THE IMPACT OF UNSHARED INFORMATION

The theme thus far has been that face-to-face discussions are not social
systems that facilitate the airing of unshared information. However, getting
groups to mention unshared information is but part of the battle. Getting
unshared information on the table does not insure that it will be fully
considered by the group. On the one hand, groups are not always responsive to discussion content when forming a collective choice or judgment
but simply aggregate their priori, individual opinions to produce a group
response (Davis, 1973; Kerr, 1981). In this vein, Gigone and Hastie (1993,
1996) demonstrated the *common knowledge effect*: Members' prior opinions
are shaped predominantly by shared information and group judgments
(choices) are determined predominantly by members' prior opinions. Under this construction of events, unshared information that does emerge
during discussion would have little effect on the group decision.

On the other hand, groups may be responsive to discussion content but
give unshared, as compared to shared, information relatively little weight
in their deliberations. They may question the validity of unshared items or
avoid the cognitive effort to fully consider the implications of novel information when it is mentioned (Larson et al., 1996; Stewart & Stasser, 1995).
When unshared information counters an emerging consensus, groups may

ignore it because it impedes what members experience as progress toward a group goal.

COMMON KNOWLEDGE EFFECT

Gigone and Hastie (1993) asked three-person groups to predict the introductory psychology grades of 32 students based on six cues (e.g., ACT score, GPA, workload, etc.). Before the discussion of each case, cues were distributed so that two cues were given to all members (shared information), two cues were given to two members (partially shared information), and two cues were given to only one member (unshared information). Results supported the *common knowledge* hypothesis: The influence of an item of information on group judgment is directly and positively related to the number of members who had the item before discussion. Moreover, Gigone and Hastie (1993) found that the influence of common knowledge did not depend on its being mentioned during discussion. Indeed, there was little evidence that group judgments were affected by what groups discussed.

Gigone and Hastie (1996) extended this work to a collective choice task by having groups consider 32 pairs of students and, for each pair, choose the one they thought would receive the highest grade. As in the earlier study, team members received six cues for each student. Supporting the common knowledge hypotheses, the impact of a cue on group choice was directly related to the number of members who had the cue before discussion. Only under one cue distribution plan (out of three) did the discussion of unshared cues modify this overall finding, and only rarely was an initial majority opinion reversed by discussion. In sum, when making repeated choices, these groups made decisions that were largely based on members' initial opinions, which in turn were largely determined by shared cues.

REPETITION OF INFORMATION
DURING DISCUSSION

In other cases, group decisions are affected to some degree by the contents of discussion (Stasser & Stewart, 1992; Winquist & Larson, 1998). However, unshared information often does not receive the attention that it seemingly deserves. One indication of the attention that groups are giving to information is the airtime devoted to it. Of particular interest is whether and how often items are repeated once they are mentioned during discussion. Stasser, Taylor, and Hanna (1989) recorded how much of the shared and unshared information mentioned once during a discussion was repeated later. They anticipated that, when unshared information was mentioned, it would capture the attention of the group because it was new information to all but one member. Contrary to their expectation, shared information was more likely to be repeated than was unshared information. Perversely, the implication is that shared information not only has a sampling advantage, it also has a repetition advantage over unshared information.

Because this repetition result was unexpected, Stasser et al. (1989) could only speculate about the reasons why groups would be more likely to reconsider shared then unshared information. What is clear is that their groups did not give novel information the attention that would seemingly be necessary if they were considering its implications for the decision at hand. In retrospect, there may be several reasons for this apparent disregard for novel information. First, it may have been a simple *rehearsal* effect. When shared information was mentioned during the discussion, it was at least a second exposure for all members. However, when unshared information was mentioned, it was the first exposure for all except the messenger. Thus, according to the rehearsal explanation, repetition of items during discussion is a resampling process in which better-learned information has an advantage. A second explanation is based on the notion of *social validation*. This line of reasoning suggests that groups either implicitly or explicitly assess the validity of information by seeking independent confirmation that it is correct when mentioned during discussion. Ordinarily, such confirmation from another member may be quite subtle (e.g., a nod of the head), but no affirming response from another may be sufficient to raise doubts about the validity of information. Because unshared information is new to all but the messenger, there is no one to provide such affirmation. A third explanation (i.e., groupthink, Janis, 1972) is that novel information may be threatening, particularly when members sense that they are progressing toward a mutually valued goal and fear that new information may impede their progress.

Both the consensus-disruption and social validation notions suggest that unshared information is a commodity whose social value is volatile (Wittenbaum & Stasser, 1996). On the one hand, if unshared information is accepted as valid and actively considered by the group, it has more potential to shape and reshape opinions than does already shared information. On the other hand, the bearer of novel information may accept certain social costs associated with selling the information as valid, relevant, and worthy of the attention of the group.

SOCIAL VALIDATION

Social validation occurs when others confirm that one's behaviors or opinions are correct or appropriate. Confirmation by others may be particularly important when one is uncertain or is not viewed as an expert or authority. For example, Hinsz (1990) found that groups were unlikely to adopt the correct recall of a team member unless the correct member was certain or another team member also correctly recalled the item. How certainty compensated for lack of social validation in this study is not clear. However, one suspects that members were more tenacious in promoting their recollections when they were certain and that they communicated their certainty to others, either explicitly or implicitly by their manner of presentation.

As already noted, the recall of unshared information during group discussion cannot benefit from social validation. Thus, if the messenger has no compensatory credentials, unshared information may be treated with skepticism by the group. Stewart and Stasser (1995) tracked the fate of unshared items during a collective recall task. Their groups attempted to recall accurately as much they could about three candidates for student body president. As described earlier, Stewart and Stasser distributed unshared information in this study so that each member received more information about one of the candidates. In the expert-assigned conditions, members were apprised of the distribution of expertise (i.e., more information) across group members, whereas in the nonexpert conditions, members were not told that each received more information about a particular candidate.

Stewart and Stasser (1995) evaluated a social validation hypothesis in two ways. First, they assessed how much of the shared and the unshared information mentioned during discussion was retained on the collectively endorsed, written protocol. Second, after groups finished their collective tasks, members individually completed a recognition memory test.

Figure 3.3 displays the percentage of shared and unshared items that groups mentioned during the recall task (oral) and the percentage that they

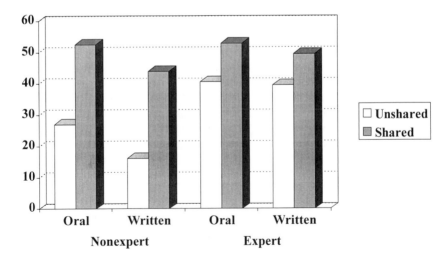

FIG. 3.3. Percentage of information mentioned during discussion (oral) and included on written protocol. Data from Stewart and Stasser (1995).

retained on the written protocol. For groups that were not aware of their expert roles (left-hand panel in Fig. 3.3), it is apparent that a substantial amount of information, particularly unshared information, was not included on the written record even though it was correctly mentioned during discussion. Making members aware of their expertise not only increased the likelihood that they would mention unshared items but also insured (with few exceptions) that the group would include in their written recall the unshared items that were mentioned during discussion.

Figure 3.4 displays a parallel finding for postdiscussion recall. The recall task was a recognition task with half of the items correctly stating information from the candidate profiles and half of the items containing incorrect information. Thus, getting 50% right was chance performance and the ordinate of Fig. 3.4 is scaled accordingly. It is apparent in Fig. 3.4 that, overall, shared information was correctly recalled more often than was unshared information. This finding is trivial for information that was not mentioned. If an unshared item was not mentioned, only one member of each group had an opportunity to remember it. However, for items that were correctly mentioned during discussion, all members had been exposed to correct versions of both shared and unshared items. Nonetheless, when expertise was not assigned, the recall for unshared items was substantially poorer than the recall for shared items. Importantly, however, this difference was wiped out when expertise was assigned; when unshared items were mentioned by designated experts, they were as likely as shared items to be recalled correctly later.

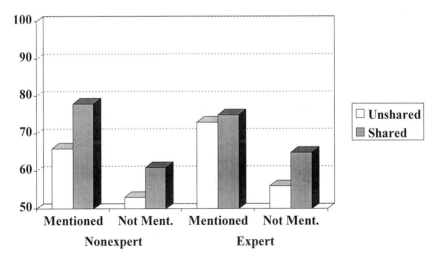

FIG. 3.4. Percentage of information correctly recognized by members after discussion as a function of its being mentioned or not mentioned. Data from Stewart and Stasser (1995).

Notice that the recall findings for the nonexpert conditions could be explained either by a lack of social validation for unshared items or by a rehearsal effect. Consider two items of information, one shared and one unshared, that were mentioned during discussion. The mentioning of the shared item would have been the second exposure for all members. However, the mentioning of the unshared item would have been the first exposure for all but the speaker. Whereas such a rehearsal effect could account for the poorer recall of unshared items when expertise was not assigned, it seems that assignment of expertise would not have negated the impact of rehearsal. Thus, the complete pattern of findings is more consistent with the conclusion that new information gained from a nonexpert is treated with some skepticism or perhaps simply given less attention than when the messenger is an expert.

These findings suggest that recognized expertise reduces the need for independent confirmation of new information and is similar to the aforementioned finding by Hinsz (1990) that groups are more likely to adopt the recall of a lone, correct member when he or she is certain rather than uncertain. As with the confidence effect, it is not clear whether the designated-expert effect is due to how the expert acts or to how others react to the expert. When members are designated as experts, they may communicate items in their domain of expertise more confidently. Or, others may be less prone to question the validity of information when it is conveyed by an expert. One suspects that both processes are involved to some degree.

STATUS: LICENSE TO KEEP COMPANY WITH UNSHARED INFORMATION?

If unshared information is greeted with a touch of skepticism or apparent indifference, group members may be reluctant to mention it unless their social standing within the group provides some "idiosyncrasy credits" (Hollander, 1958). That is, members who have high status, task competence, or leadership roles may feel less vulnerable and be less affected by the lack of affirming reactions when they mention unshared information.

The work of Larson and his colleagues (Larson et al., 1996, 1998) has demonstrated the role of leaders and high-status members in the promotion of unshared information in task-oriented teams. In a study described earlier, Larson et al. (1996) had medical teams diagnose two cases after viewing videotapes of the patients being screened in an emergency room. Recall that each team was composed of a resident physician, an intern, and a third-year medical student. Recall that team members viewed different versions of the tapes so that some of the presenting symptoms were unshared and others were not. Replicating the repetition finding of Stasser et al.

(1989), these teams were much more likely to repeat a symptom if it was shared than if it was unshared. More pertinent to the present discussion is who repeated symptoms. The resident physician was much more likely than the others to repeat information overall. Particularly interesting was the trend for repeating unshared items as the discussion progressed. Near the beginning of discussion, the resident physician accounted for about 45% of the repeat mentions of unshared items. During the later stages, this percentage increased to over 60%. Thus, to the degree that unshared items were repeated, the high status member was disproportionately responsible.

Larson et al. (1998) pursued the idea that leaders play an important role in the management of information flow during discussion and in determining the fate of unshared information. They trained designated leaders to adopt either a participative or directive style. Both types of leaders were more likely to repeat unshared than shared information. Moreover, directive leaders were more likely than participative leaders to repeat unshared items, particularly unshared items that they themselves originally received. In implementing their style of leadership, directive leaders took a very active approach to managing the flow of unshared information. In this study, Larson et al. created a hidden profile in their distribution of unshared information and groups working under a directive, as opposed to a participative, leader were more likely to identify the normatively best option.

Likewise, Wittenbaum (1998) found that task experience affected the communication of unshared information. She gave two members of four-person groups prior experience on a personnel selection task, whereas the remaining two members received experience working on an unrelated task. Then, the group members individually read brief resumes for two applicants for a faculty position; each member also received as unshared information an expanded version of one section of the resumes. When the group convened, members who were relatively inexperienced on the personnel selection task were less likely to mention and repeat unshared information, replicating the typical findings in the collective sampling literature. However, experienced members behaved more like the directive leaders in Larson et al. (1998). They were equally likely to mention shared and unshared information and more likely to repeat unshared than shared information.

The pattern emerging from these recent findings is that members who are leaders, have higher status (like the medical residents in the medical teams), or have more task experience are less likely to shy away from unshared items than are their lower status or less experienced companions. I hinted that these results may be due in part to the riskiness of keeping company with unshared information (Wittenbaum & Stasser, 1996) and that higher status or competence may insulate one, at least to some degree, from this risk. Because the validity or usefulness of unshared knowledge may frequently be questioned, the bearer of new information risks having to promote, or even defend, the content of the message. However, the current state of findings is only suggestive and does not rule out other mechanisms. For example, it could be that the critical consideration is not so much the threat of having one's message challenged or ignored but more so the relative ease that working with already shared knowledge affords. That is, laziness, not uneasiness, may be the reason for favoring shared over unshared information. If so, designation as a leader, an expert, or a pro may make one feel obligated to do the hard work of communicating and recirculating unique knowledge.

COGNITIVE CENTRALITY

Recent work by Kameda, Ohtsubo, and Takezawa (1997) emphasizes the social benefits of having shared knowledge. They proposed that a person's location in a sociocognitive network is an informative component of their social status. Location is represented as *cognitive centrality*—the amount of information or knowledge shared with other members of a group. Kameda et al. (1997) argued that a cognitively central member is regarded as competent and knowledgeable because he or she can frequently validate others' knowledge and, in turn, his or her contributions can be validated by others. They found, for example, that cognitive centrality and participation in group discussion were positively related and that the most cognitively central members changed their opinions very little regardless of whether they were in the majority or minority in their decision-making groups. Similarly, a cognitively central minority exerted more influence on others than a cognitively peripheral minority.

Although the empirical findings are sparse at this time, the concept of cognitive centrality is theoretically intriguing. One claim is that people who are well connected in the sociocognitive network are viewed as experts. Playing off Chaiken and Stangor's (1987) consensus heuristic (consensus implies correctness), Kameda et al. (1997) suggested a *cognitive centrality heuristic:* Cognitive centrality implies expertise. Somewhat perversely, this view suggests that contributing unique knowledge to discussion does not establish one's reputation as an expert. Quite the contrary; having shared knowledge permits one to be a major player in the social validation market and the concurrent processes of confirming others' contributions and having one's own contributions confirmed lead to an impression of being competent and knowledgeable. Another interesting implication is that a true expert must be careful lest he or she communicate too much unshared knowledge (or too little shared knowledge) and, by doing so, undermine the group's recognition of the expert's expertise.

INFORMATION POOLING:
THE ASSEMBLY EFFECT BONUS REVISITED

Collins and Guetzkow (1964), in their classic treatise on small group decision making, noted that groups are often capable of producing better decisions than even the best member can if acting alone. That is, the group can benefit from assembling the diverse inputs of its members. The promise of such an assembly bonus is frequently cited as a reason to entrust important social decisions to groups. Notwithstanding the promise, the evidence reviewed in this chapter suggests that groups, particularly those meeting face-to-face to exchange information, may frequently fail to deliver on this promise.

First, collective information sampling dynamics promote the exchange of shared over unshared information. As the work of Larson and his colleagues shows, this bias is particularly pronounced during the early phases of discussion—a time that is critical to the formation of a group consensus (Kerr, 1981). Second, recent evidence suggests that groups do not give unshared information the attention or consideration that it would seemingly demand. They are less likely to repeat unshared than shared information, members have a relatively poor memory for unshared items that surface during discussion, and groups are likely to omit correctly recalled unshared items from a collectively endorsed record of recall.

If the messenger is a leader or an expert, the group is less likely to ignore contributions of unique information. However, the work of Kameda and his colleagues (1997) on cognitive centrality suggests that the interplay between perceptions of expertise and communication of unshared information may be more complex than previously thought. Whereas an expert source imparts credibility to information that others cannot consensually validate, communicating and confirming shared information bolsters one's standing as an expert.

The emerging picture is that groups are better at articulating widely shared information and acting on what is commonly known than they are at pooling diverse information. Interestingly, this view of discussion groups has already emerged in the focus group literature. McQuarrie and McIntyre (1988) argued that focus groups are useful tools for understanding consumer phenomenology precisely because they filter out idiosyncratic views and help identify popular perspectives in a population. Rather than producing assembly bonuses, unstructured group discussion is much better at identifying the core of shared knowledge. The cumulative evidence suggests that a group must be carefully composed of members with mutually recognized and complementary domains of expertise to realize an assembly bonus.

ACKNOWLEDGMENT

Preparation of this chapter was supported by National Science Foundation Grant (SBR-9410584).

REFERENCES

Burnstein, E., & Vinokur, A. (1977). Persuasive argumentation and social comparison as determinants of attitude polarization. *Journal of Experimental Social Psychology, 13*, 315–332.

Chaiken, S., & Stangor, C. (1987). Attitudes and attitude change. *Annual Review of Psychology, 38*, 575–630.

Collins, B. E., & Guetzkow, H. (1964). *A social psychology of group processes for decision-making.* New York: Wiley.

Davis, J. H. (1969). *Group performance.* Reading, MA: Addison-Wesley.

Davis, J. H. (1973). Group decisions and social interaction: A theory of social decision schemes. *Psychological Review, 80*, 97–125.

Festinger, L. (1954). A theory of social comparison. *Human Relations, 7*, 117–140.

Gigone, D., & Hastie, R. (1993). The common knowledge effect: Information sampling and group judgment. *Journal of Personality and Social Psychology, 65*, 959–974.

Gigone, D., & Hastie, R. (1996). The impact of information on small group choice. *Journal of Personality and Social Psychology, 72*, 132–140.

Goethals, G. R., & Darley, J. (1977). Social comparison theory: An attribution approach. In J. Suls & R. Miller (Eds.), *Social comparison processes: Theoretical and empirical perspectives* (pp. 259–279). Washington, DC: Hemisphere.

Hinsz, V. B. (1990). Cognitive and consensus processes in group recognition memory performance. *Journal of Personality and Social Psychology, 59*, 705–718.

Hollander, E. P. (1958). Conformity, status, and idiosyncrasy credit. *Psychological Review, 65*, 117–127.

Hollingshead, A. B. (1996). The rank order effect in group decision making. *Organizational Behavior and Human Decision Processes, 68*, 181–193.

Janis, I. L. (1972). *Victims of groupthink.* Boston: Houghton Mifflin.

Kameda, T., Ohtsubo, Y., & Takezawa, M. (1997). Centrality in sociocognitive networks and social influence: An illustration in a group decision making context. *Journal of Personality and Social Psychology, 73*, 296–309.

Kerr, N. L. (1981). Social transition schemes: Charting the road to agreement. *Journal of Personality and Social Psychology, 41*, 684–702.

Larson, J. R., Jr., & Christensen, C. (1993). Groups as problem-solving units: Toward a new meaning of social cognition. *British Journal of Social Psychology, 32*, 5–30.

Larson, J. R., Jr., Christensen, C., Abbott, A. S., & Franz, T. M. (1996). Diagnosing groups: Charting the flow of information in medical decision making teams. *Journal of Personality and Social Psychology, 71*, 315–330.

Larson, J. R., Jr., Foster-Fishman, P. G., & Franz, T. M. (1998). Leadership style and the discussion of shared and unshared information in decision-making groups. *Personality and Social Psychology Bulletin, 24*(5), 482–495.

Larson, J. R., Jr., Foster-Fishman, P. G., & Keys, C. B. (1994). Discussion of shared and unshared information in decision-making groups. *Journal of Personality and Social Psychology, 67*, 446–461.

Laughlin, P. R., & Ellis, A. L. (1986). Demonstrability and social combination processes on mathematical intellective tasks. *Journal of Experimental Social Psychology, 22*, 177–189.

Lorge, I., & Solomon, H. (1962). Group and individual behavior in free-recall verbal learning. In J. H. Criswell, H. Solomon, & P. Suppes (Eds.), *Mathematical methods in small group processes* (pp. 221–231). Stanford, CA: Stanford University Press.

McQuarrie, E. F., & McIntyre, S. H. (1988). Conceptual underpinnings for the use of group interviews in consumer research. *Advances in Consumer Research, 15,* 580–586.

Moreland, R. L., Argote, L., & Krishnan, R. (1996). Socially shared cognition at work: Transactive memory and group performance. In J. L. Nye & A. M. Bower (Eds.), *What's new about social cognition? Research on socially shared cognition in small groups* (pp. 57–84). Thousand Oaks, CA: Sage.

Shiflett, S. C. (1979). Toward a general model of small group productivity. *Psychological Bulletin, 86,* 67–79.

Stasser, G., & Stewart, D. D. (1992). Discovery of hidden profiles by decision-making groups: Solving a problem versus making a judgment. *Journal of Personality and Social Psychology, 63,* 426–434.

Stasser, G., Stewart, D. D., & Wittenbaum, G. M. (1995). Expert roles and information exchange during discussion: The importance of knowing who knows what. *Journal of Experimental Social Psychology, 31,* 244–265.

Stasser, G., Taylor, L. A., & Hanna, C. (1989). Information sampling in structured and unstructured discussions of three- and six-person groups. *Journal of Personality and Social Psychology, 57,* 67–78.

Stasser, G., & Titus, W. (1985). Pooling of unshared information in group decision making: Biased information sampling during discussion. *Journal of Personality and Social Psychology, 48,* 1467–1478.

Stasser, G., & Titus, W. (1987). Effects of information load and percentage of shared information on the dissemination of unshared information during group discussion. *Journal of Personality and Social Psychology, 53,* 81–93.

Steiner, I. D. (1972). *Group process and productivity.* New York: Academic Press.

Stewart, D. D., & Stasser, G. (1995). Expert role assignment and information sampling during collective recall and decision making. *Journal of Personality and Social Psychology, 69,* 619–628.

Wegner, D. M. (1986). Transactive memory: A contemporary analysis of the group mind. In B. Mullen & G. Goethals (Eds.), *Theories of group behavior* (pp. 185–208). New York: Springer-Verlag.

Wegner, D. M., Erber, R., & Raymond, P. (1991). Transactive memory in close relationships. *Journal of Personality and Social Psychology, 61,* 923–929.

Winquist, J. R. & Larson, J. R., Jr. (1998). Information pooling: When it impacts group decision making. *Journal of Personality and Social Psychology, 74*(2), 371–377.

Wittenbaum, G. M. (1998). Information sampling in decision-making groups: The impact of members' task-relevant status. *Small Group Research, 29*(1), 57–84.

Wittenbaum, G. M., & Stasser, G. (1996). Management of information in small groups. In J. L. Nye & A. M. Bower (Eds.), *What's new about social cognition? Research on socially shared cognition in small groups* (pp. 3–28). Thousand Oaks, CA: Sage.

Wittenbaum, G. M., Stasser, G., & Merry, C. J. (1996). Tacit coordination in anticipation of small group task completion. *Journal of Experimental Social Psychology, 32,* 129–152.

4

Dirty Secrets: Strategic Uses of Ignorance and Uncertainty

David M. Messick
Northwestern University

It is appropriate, perhaps even necessary, in a book dealing with the sharing of knowledge in organizations, to include a chapter that focuses on circumstances in which knowledge, expertise, data, and facts are not shared but rather intentionally concealed, obscured, altered, or otherwise distorted. Organizations can benefit from a shared vision and purpose (Collins & Porras, 1994) and they can become more efficient if they can discover ways to move information about successful strategies from places where the innovations evolved to places where the innovations are needed. However, organizations also often have a stake in concealing information about their operations, and the focus of this chapter is on strategies and tactics of a particular type of concealment.

Bok (1982) has written eloquently about the ethics of concealment in business and in public agencies. In this chapter, I want to write about some of the tactics that are employed either to conceal information or to intentionally create a false impression. The true topic of this chapter is deception. The concern here is less with deliberate lying and more with the creation of false or misleading impressions through concealment and obfuscation.

Every organization possesses facts that it may conceal. Corporations do not want to divulge trade secrets that could help competitors. Information about marketing strategies and new product introduction could be disastrous if revealed to competitors in advance. In business, as in sport, a certain level and type of secrecy is essential and the need for secrecy requires strategies for concealment. If communication of secret is needed, then it must be encoded to protect it from competitors. Databases must be secured. Access to sensitive information must be protected and efforts may be undertaken to detect and combat intelligence moves by competitors.

However, the type of secrets that I want to focus on are what we may call dirty secrets. These are not trade secrets nor details of business plans, marketing strategies nor ideas for product development. What I have in mind are secrets about real or potential wrong-doing, hence the adjective *dirty*. It is common knowledge that firms have trade secrets that they will protect; it is not common knowledge that firms have dirty secrets that they conceal. Dirty secrets must be concealed not just from competitors but also from governmental and regulatory agencies, from the press, and from the public. The act of concealment of dirty secrets must also be concealed because the fact of a cover-up implies the existence of a dirty secret that is being covered. In this regard, efforts to hide dirty secrets are different from steps taken to conceal business information. Everyone knows that firms have trade secrets; it is not common knowledge that firms have dirty secrets.

Kramer and Messick (1996) argued that decision makers in organizations often act as if they were intuitive lawyers. In contrast to intuitive scientists, whose goal is to discover truth and the causal structure of the world, intuitive lawyers are concerned with advancing their interests and those of their clients and shielding those interests from harm by others. Kramer and Messick were writing about individual decision makers coping with the complexities of organizational decisions that pit one set of interests against another, either in the short term versus the long term or the individual against the broader group. The metaphor of the intuitive lawyer is applicable to the issues to be discussed here, and indeed in many instances, decision making is not done by metaphorical intuitive lawyers, it is done by actual lawyers who are defending and promoting the interests of the organization. However, one distinction between the perspective taken here and that adopted by Kramer and Messick is that here I treat the organization as the unit of analysis. So biases and strategies that psychologists discuss at the level of the individual, I discuss at the level of organizations. Several new elements are introduced by this perspective shift and these are discussed presently. It is important only to keep in mind that the mechanisms that create self-serving processes in organizations are often different from those that create analogous processes in individuals (see for instance, Allison, Messick, & Goethals, 1989; Greenwald, 1980; Kunda, 1990; Taylor, 1989). Thus, I am writing about organizational level phenomena that resemble and are functionally related to individual processes.

One of the difficulties in writing about strategies that underlie organizational efforts to conceal dirty secrets is that successful efforts are never publicized. By definition, if an organization is successful in hiding a dirty secret, the secret is never discovered. Thus, the only cases that are available for analysis are those of failed or partly failed attempts at concealment. I do not pretend that my selection of cases to discuss in this chapter is in any way scientific. In fact the cases that I use to illustrate the strategy and tactics of concealment are, generally speaking, those that have been described recently by the investigative press. In particular, there have been many recent reports of strategies used by the tobacco industry over the past several decades. Of particular interest are the confidential documents that were obtained from Brown and Williamson Tobacco Corporation, an American cigarette manufacturer. These documents were made available on the World Wide Web by Professor Stanton Glantz and his staff at the University of California, San Francisco and were later described in a series of articles in the *Journal of the American Medical Association* (*JAMA*) and in a book called *The Cigarette Papers* (*TCP*; Glantz, Slade, Bero, Hanauer, & Barnes, 1996). I rely on this book for many of my illustrations. This case is particularly interesting in that the strategy for concealment by the tobacco industry was successful for many years. These recent revelations disclose some of the elements of a successful strategy. However, the negotiations with the tobacco industry are ongoing as I write this in the summer of 1997 and doubt remains whether this industry's dirty secrets and the details of its efforts to conceal them will be revealed (France, DeGeorge, & Carey, 1997).

TYPES OF DIRTY SECRETS

Dirty secrets may be of many different types. Some may be criminal acts, as was the case in the New York Police Department when Frank Serpico and David Durk reported becoming celebrated whistle-blowers (Lardner, 1993). These secrets can also be related to false and deceitful business practices, like the false sales records alleged in the case of Bausch & Lomb (Maremont, 1995). In this case, it was alleged that nonexistent sales were recorded in order for some business units to meet sales targets. Dirty secrets may also have to do with practices that are either illegal or deceptive, as in the allegations against Prudential Securities in the sale and marketing depiction of risky investments as being as safe as certificates of deposit (Eichenwald, 1995).

One class of dirty secrets that has a special relevance to this chapter is the knowledge that a consumer product is harmful in ways that the consumer does not suspect or appreciate. Asbestos was such a product whose history has been told in part (Sharplin, 1993). The Ford Pinto is another celebrated product of this type (Birsch & Fielder, 1994; Kunen, 1994). Of course cigarettes qualify as products with dangerous qualities, as are risky investment products (Eichenwald, 1995). Other potentially hazardous products include drugs, pesticides and herbicides, alcoholic beverages, food additives, automobiles, airplanes, clothing, toys, household cleaners, and plastic bags. In short, nearly every product made is potentially hazardous to some consumers under some circumstances.

Part of the interest in allegedly dangerous products derives from the complexities surrounding the judgment of dangerousness. For instance, the scientific data regarding the health effects of silicone breast implants are anything but clear in their implications. Whereas some persons are absolutely certain that these devices can produce a variety of diseases (Byrne, 1996), others claim that the epidemiological evidence does not justify such a conclusion (Angell, 1996). Thus, the judgment of harm itself may be debatable.

Moreover, if a manufacturer produces a product that is potentially dangerous and fails to either take steps to mitigate the danger or to warn consumers of the danger, the manufacturer may be held morally responsible for the harm caused and may be found legally liable for compensatory and punitive damages. Punitive damages may be warranted if the producer is found to have acted in reckless disregard of the well-being of the consumers. The judgment of reckless disregard may be justified, for instance, if the manufacturer knew of the dangers; had the capacity to either correct the problem or to warn consumers; and intentionally decided not to do so, possibly for sound business reasons. To protect against such allegations, a firm needs to be careful about revealing what it knew when about hazards and what it did with this knowledge. And it is precisely this need that creates the incentive to conceal and possibly misrepresent what was known when.

Who Knows What

One important difference between individual-level biases and organizational processes hinges on the questions of who knows what. What does it mean to say that an organization, a firm, or a corporation knows, for instance, that a product is harmful? Does this mean that the medical staff believes this? Does it mean that the legal group knows it? Does it mean that it is common knowledge among the members of the board of directors? Transposing the language of individual cognition to organizations raises the questions about how knowledge is distributed and how the responsibility for distributing knowledge is allocated within the organization. There may be a small group of individuals within a company who know of product flaws or illegal acts, and it may be in their interest to keep that knowledge from their superiors. The distribution of information creates *de facto* ingroups and outgroups, with the ingroups sharing the information among themselves while concealing it from the outgroups. Because of this possibility, not all individuals within an organization can be held responsible for dirty secrets. This possibility can be exploited to shield individuals, generally high-ranking individuals, from blame and responsibility. The concept of *plausible deniability*, so-named in the Iran-Contra hearings, is a sophisticated expression of precisely this notion. The idea is that information should be shared with the senior decision maker, in the original case, President Ronald Reagan, in such a way as to allow this person to claim ignorance of the actions and knowledge of the subordinates. The concept of plausible deniability is thus a structural concept in that the defense against blame derives from the structure of the organization, not from a psychological process. Many of the processes that I describe in this chapter are organizational in this same way.

There are at least two general strategies for concealing dirty secrets. The first of these I call *knowledge shields*. Knowledge shields are procedures, processes, or structures that prevent information about organizational secrets from being possessed by persons outside of the organization (or unauthorized persons within the organization). Many of these shields are legal or legalistic in nature. Some are perfectly acceptable when used to protect trade secrets and proprietary information. They become corrupt when the same procedures are used to protect dirty secrets or to cover up illegal and immoral strategies.

The second general strategy is the creation of *smoke machines*. Smoke machines are designed to obscure, blur, confuse, distract, or otherwise direct attention away from some features of an issue and, possibly, toward other, less unfavorable aspects of it. Smoke machines are of many types. Their importance in the concealment of dirty secrets is that they attempt to alter the nature of information to make the information more favorable to the organization. Smoke machines can either manipulate the valence of the information, how favorable or unfavorable it seems, or the certainty of the information.

Knowledge Shields

A perfectly legitimate type of knowledge shield is the *confidentiality agreement* that many firms require employees to sign on leaving the firm. Confidentiality agreements generally prohibit an employee from divulging information about business practices after employment is terminated. Similar types of agreements are noncompetition agreements in which ex-employees promise not to work for a competitor or on a product that competes with the firm's products for some period of time following separation. These types of agreements are perfect reasonable devices for firms to use to discourage ex-employees from divulging information that could be useful to a competitor and harmful to the firm.

The status of confidentiality agreements is somewhat different if these contracts are used to enforce concealment of illegal or immoral activities. If an ex-employee knew of crimes being committed within the organization, a confidentiality agreement might compromise the person's obligation to report the crime to appropriate authorities. Confidentiality agreements might be used to enforce silence among ex-employees about continuing crimes.

A recent case in point is that of Dr. Jeffrey Wigand, who was the head of research for Brown and Williamson Tobacco Corporation (BW) until 1993. When Dr. Wigand left BW, he signed a confidentiality agreement. However, in 1994, during congressional hearings about the safety of cigarettes, Dr. Wigand heard Thomas E. Sandefur, then CEO of BW, testify, under oath, that he did not believe that cigarettes were addictive. According to Wigand, Sandefur perjured himself with this testimony because Wigand had heard Sandefur say on many occasions that cigarettes were addictive. If Wigand were to honor his confidentiality agreement with BW, he could not reveal the conversations that he had or had heard on this point. But to conceal this information would be to fail to report a felony in the perjured testimony.

Confidentiality agreements might lose their effectiveness if organizations and employers were unwilling to enforce them. Lawsuits are used for this purpose. If confidentiality agreements were routinely broken with no consequences to the ex-employee, they might have little value. Hence organizations use lawsuits and the threat thereof to enforce silence. A suit against an ex-employee may not only result in damages against the person, it also sends a signal to other employees that it is costly to violate the agreement. In this case referred, Dr. Wigand was sued by BW for violating his agreement (this despite the fact that his testimony was initially subpoenaed as part of a lawsuit brought by the state of Mississippi's suit against the tobacco industry). But the use and threat of lawsuits to conceal dirty secrets is not limited to ex-employees.

Dr. Wigand was interviewed by reporter Mike Wallace in an exposé of the dirty secrets held by BW. The interview was intended to be broadcast in November, 1995, on CBS' Sunday news program, *60 Minutes* (Kaplan, 1995). Shortly before the scheduled broadcast, however, the interview was cancelled. The legal staff at CBS determined that by broadcasting the interview, CBS might be legally liable for having induced Dr. Wigand to violate his agreement with BW. Killing the broadcast was controversial, both within CBS and nationally. The legal fear was not based on the possibility that the information in the interview was libelous. There was no reason to doubt the veracity of Wigand's claims. The broadcast was killed because of the confidentiality agreement and the prospect that BW would sue CBS for having caused Wigand to breach the agreement. So the agreement was used not only to silence Wigand but also to silence those who might reveal his knowledge.

60 Minutes eventually did broadcast the interview with Wigand. He was also deposed in the suit brought by the state of Mississippi against the tobacco industry, including BW. The 135-page deposition of Wigand found its way to the *Wall Street Journal*, which posted the document on its Internet Site. The *Journal* published a summary of the document in its January 26, 1996 edition (Freedman, 1996). BW sued Wigand for breach of contract. However, their efforts to silence him and to minimize the impact of his testimony did not stop with the suit. According to an article in the *Wall Street Journal* on February 1, 1996 (Hwang & Geyelin, 1996), BW complied a 500-page file about Wigand, attempting to discredit him and portraying him as a habitual liar. This document had little to do with the allegations that BW's CEO, Mr. Sandefur, had lied under oath, that the corporation knew that smoking was harmful, that Wigand had been told to stop work on a safe cigarette because of the legal suggestion that their current products might be unsafe, or that additives that were known to be toxic were intentionally added to pipe tobacco to improve taste. This personal attack on Wigand was based on a detailed examination of his personal history by a private investigation firm hired to accumulate as much damaging evidence as possible about all aspect of Wigand's life. According the *Journal*, investigators examined Wigand's dissertation for evidence of plagiarism, they examined his resumes for erroneous statements, they examined his driver license applications, and they got a videotape of a mock employment interview and examined his assertions there for accuracy. The *Journal*'s assessment of the validity of the allegations contained in this document is that they "are backed by scant or contradictory evidence. Some of the charges—including that he pleaded guilty to shoplifting—are demonstrably untrue" (Hwang & Geyelin, 1996, p. A1).

An employee or ex-employee can only be sued for divulging secrets if the employee can be identified as the whistle-blower. If documents are leaked anonymously, no one can be punished. Anonymity can puncture the knowledge shield. Scism and Paltrow (1997) described a tactic used by Prudential Insurance Co. to guarantee the identifiability of a leak. Prudential was being sued for failing to prevent its agents from fraudulently misrepresenting the sales of new insurance policies to its customers. The company strenuously fought to keep documents that displayed how much was known of this practice from being made public. One such document was a report prepared in 1994 by Coopers and Lybrand, an external auditor. In an effort to deter employees from leaking this report, Prudential had each copy numbered and had a different error inserted into each copy. If a copy were leaked or copied, Prudential could identify which copy it was and identify the person who had responsibility for its safekeeping.

Efforts to destroy a critic's credibility are attempts to minimize the damage done by information once it is released. This function of a personal attack, as I show in the case of the attack on Dr. Stanton Glantz, is part of the smoke machine. However, another consequence of personal attacks against critics is to discourage criticism and to increase the perceived costs of whistle-blowing. From this perspective, these attacks are knowledge shields.

It appears that the tobacco industry created a complex legal strategy to shield its information from outsiders. Wigand testified, for instance, that BW's legal department routinely stamped sensitive scientific documents "confidential" or "attorney/client" even though the documents were not part of litigation activities. One purpose for the classification was to allow BW to resist producing such documents during the discovery part of litigation, preventing the individuals suing BW from discovering what the company knew. Wigand also testified that the legal department of BW edited minutes of scientific meetings to delete references that could, if discovered in litigation, support the inference that BW knew that its products were harmful or addictive. Liability concerns came to determine the research agenda. Research on making a safer cigarette was terminated, according to Wigand, because of the legal liability such an effort entailed. It seems ironic that efforts to find a safer product were, according to Wigand, derailed because such efforts, if revealed, could be construed as evidence that the company knew its current products were not safe. Thus did BW's efforts to shield its knowledge that cigarettes might be made safer paralyze its efforts to actually make them safer.

A final tactic to prevent the leakage of dirty secrets might be called *patterned amnesia*. Patterned amnesia refers to an organizational inability to recall crucial items of information that might reveal either the dirty secrets or the process of concealment.

Memory retrieval processes in organizations consist of the aggregated human memory of decision makers and of the physical evidence. The physical evidence consists both of archival evidence in the form of reports, memos, research documents, and recordings, for instance, and other forms of physical evidence that could indicate what an organization did or did not do, knew or did not know. When I use the phrase *patterned amnesia*, I intend to connote that the amnesia in not merely a generalized inability to recall facts, retrieve documents, or produce evidence, but rather a strategic retrieval failure that conceals dirty secrets. The most celebrated instance of patterned amnesia in pubic life was the mysteriously erased 18-minute gap on the White House tapes during the Watergate scandal. (At least the appearance of unpatterned amnesia could have been created if multiple mysterious gaps had been discovered on the tapes.)

The locus of much organizational amnesia is often difficult to pinpoint. When people cannot recall precisely what occurred and documents cannot be found, it is hard to determine who should have known and what documents should have been available. Kunen (1994) provided an excellent illustration of this state.

On May 14, 1988, a school bus from Carrollton, Kentucky was involved in a head-on collision with a pickup truck driven by a drunk young man. Twenty seven of the passengers on the bus were killed and of them, 24 were children between the ages of 10 and 19. All of the victims were killed by fire or smoke. Both the front and rear doors of the bus had been blocked. There were no fractured skulls or broken bones. Fire, not the collision, had killed the victims. These facts were important in subsequent litigation because there was evidence that Ford Motor Company, who had manufactured the chassis for the bus, had been aware of the hazardous placement of the gas tank under the front steps of the bus and had failed to correct the hazard.

Specifically, a new federal standard (FMVSS 301–75) was to be enforced in 1976 that would effect, among other things, the placement and protection of fuel tanks in automobiles (like the infamous Ford Pinto) and school buses. This new standard would require that the fuel tanks on school buses, located beneath the front steps of the bus, be covered by a steel guard. The concern was that if the tank was ruptured during an accident, a fire could result that would prevent occupants from leaving through the front door. In order to come into compliance with this new standard, Ford engineered its production line, arranged to have the guards manufactured and sent to the production facility, and stood ready by May 20, 1976 to install fuel tank cages on all buses that went through the line. Documentation for all of the details of this alteration was produced, showing that Ford was prepared to be in compliance with new federal regulations.

But then something interesting happened. A memo was sent on June 23, 1976, directing the plant not to install the fuel tank shield because the implementation of the new standard was to be postponed until April 1, 1977. (The U.S. Senate passed the delaying legislation the day after the Ford memo was sent: June 24, 1976.) Despite Ford's readiness to make the safety improvement, the decision was made to postpone it until the law demanded the safer bus. The bus that was involved in the crash was made during this period and the fire would not have happened, in all likelihood, had Ford not rescinded the order to begin the installation of the fuel tank guards.

Who decided to delay implementation? In Kunen's (1994) own words,

> While a meticulous paper trail documented the instructions, approvals, and concurrences regarding putting the cage on, no documentation could be found fixing the responsibility for leaving it off (or more precisely, making it optional, which resulted in leaving it off). In fact an almost complete institutional amnesia seems to have afflicted the corporation and everyone in it on

this point. After the Carrollton crash, Ford engineer Keith Lewis helped conduct a genteel ("I didn't want to offend anybody") in-house investigation. "A lot of people asked around," he said, and "nobody could clearly identify who made the decision."

"[The decision] may have been as a result of meetings with any number of the components in the company," design engineer Kraemer would explain. "You can't define it exactly. If you work for a big company, there are many, many ways that things get done." (p. 174)

The one thing that most people were generally sure of was that the decision was not made by them or in their units. The decision was made somewhere in management, according to the engineers. The reluctance to accuse specific persons of wrong-doing creates an organizational network of uninformed finger-pointers, each of whose one piece of crucial knowledge is that responsibility does not reside in their unit.

Patterned amnesia is created by more detailed tactics than mere forgetting. The destruction of documents and other evidence is a common tactic to prevent information from being retrieved. In the dispute about reports of medical problems arising from the use of silicone breast implants, John Swanson, Dow Corning's ethics officer whose wife become ill after having breast enhancements implanted, resigned from his position at Dow Corning because he became aware that officials in the company were destroying reports they had received from the field, alerting them to a growing incidence of medical problems with the implants (Byrne, 1996). These documents, naturally, would belie the corporation's claim that it had no knowledge of medical problems associated with its breast implants. The destruction of documents or the erasure of tapes represents only the most blatant of tactics to create organizational amnesia for dirty secrets.

Dr. Wigand of BW described a far more sophisticated strategy that he alleged was used by the BW legal staff. Wigand testified that members of the legal department at BW controlled access to scientific research and had the power to prevent him from reading research documents produced by BW, despite his position as the head of the research unit. If the documents were potentially troublesome in liability suits, the documents could be stamped "Confidential" or "Attorney/Client Privilege" to shield the documents from discovery during lawsuits. In other words, the scientific research that could either have resulted in a safer cigarette or in the identification (and subsequent removal) of harmful additives was isolated and controlled by the legal department for the protection of the organization. Wigand testified that some documents were sent to company headquarters in London to prevent their disclosure to litigants. These documents were not destroyed, they were hidden in another country. Wigand seemed to have felt that he was part of the outgroup from whom the dirty secrets were to be concealed. The shrinking ingroup seemed to have discovered the principle that the fewer people who share a secret, the more secure the secret. Thus were research documents concealed from the research boss.

One final tactic that Dr. Wigand mentioned in his testimony was that the legal department of BW deleted about 12 pages from the minutes of a BW research meeting. The pages that were deleted dealt with the issues of finding a safer cigarette and nonaddictive nicotine substitutes (Freedman, 1996).

TCP suggests one additional tactic to create amnesia, at least in BW. BW is owned by British American Tobacco (BAT), a British firm with offices throughout Europe. *TCP* (Glantz et al., 1996, p. 439) suggests that lawyers kept research results isolated in Europe that may have been embarrassing in litigation in the United States. Research conducted in overseas laboratories that may have confirmed hypotheses that cigarettes were addictive and harmful may have been confined to Europe and concealed from American scientists. Thus could BAT's international structure have been used to foster patterned amnesia.

Dr. Wigand's testimony creates the impression of an organization whose legal strategy to defend against potential product liability suits included the aggressive construction of amnesia for facts, discussions, research, or activities that would have disclosed dirty secrets about the firm's knowledge that cigarettes were harmful and addictive. One detail from a different cigarette manufacturer, Philip Morris, confirms this impression.

Dr. Victor DeNoble claimed that he was hired by Philip Morris to conduct research with rats on the addictive properties of nicotine (Schorr & MacIntyre, 1996). DeNoble is a behavioral pharmacologist who used operant conditioning techniques to study the reinforcing properties of drugs. After having achieved some success in demonstrating that nicotine showed similar reinforcing properties to cocaine, DeNoble requested permission to publish his findings in the scientific literature. Philip Morris refused to grant permission. Furthermore, the request for permission brought his work to the attention of the legal department, who requested to visit his laboratory to understand the potentially important work he was doing. After having the project explained, the legal department shut the laboratory down. DeNoble stated that several days after he was told that his work was going to be discontinued, he came to the lab to find that the whole laboratory had disappeared. The animals were gone, the computers were gone, the wiring was pulled, and even the benches had disappeared. It is as if the lab had never existed.

Smoke Machines

The creation and maintenance of knowledge shields deserves more attention than I have allocated to it in this brief introduction. But I leave this topic in order to have some space to discuss the equally interesting phenomenon of organizational smoke machines. By smoke machines I refer to the procedures, strategies, and institutions whose goal is to create doubt, suspicion, and uncertainty, particularly about allegations that would reveal or imply the existence of dirty secrets. Even if knowledge shields are effective, opponents of an organization may develop evidence that contradicts an organization's assertions. This evidence, typically unfavorable to the organization, must be discredited. Although there are many tactics that organizations have developed to rebut criticism, it is poetic, perhaps, that the tobacco industry has perfected the strategy of blowing smoke at the claims. That is to say, rather than to directly rebut claims about the harmful effects of tobacco products, the industry has claimed that there is insufficient evidence to support such allegations.

Tobacco industry strategists understand that the public will tend to discount assertions, made by the industry, defending its products and attacking industry critics. The solution to this credibility deficit is to create sham objectivity via institutions that appear to be independent and objective but that are in fact outlets for the tobacco industry and its communications. Perhaps the best illustration of the creation of sham experts was the establishment of the Tobacco Industry Research Committee (TIRC) in 1954, an organization whose name was changed to The Council for Tobacco Research (CTR) in 1964. According to Glantz et al. (1996, p. 33), the tobacco industry announced the formation of this group in response to medical reports linking lung cancer and smoking. The TIRC was empowered to fund independent research to determine the validity of these reports. Glantz et al. (1996, p. 34) reproduce an advertisement that appeared in January, 1954, announcing the formation of the TIRC. The ad stressed TIRC's objectivity and independence. It was to be headed by a scientist with impeccable credentials and would have a scientific advisory board of disinterested medical and scientific scholars.

Documents discussed in *TCP* reveal, however, that the TIRC and later the CTR were actually intended all along to be public relations organs of the tobacco industry. Decisions about what projects to fund were often made by lawyers for the tobacco companies, and memos from the public relations firm of Hill & Knowlton (HK), which had been hired by the tobacco industry in 1953 to combat the negative impact of the growing evidence linking smoking to disease, indicate that HK considered TIRC to be a PR organization. TIRC and, later, CTR had one major objective to pursue, according to the tobacco industry, and that was, according the documents reviewed by *TCP*, to keep the smoking–health controversy alive by claiming that there was no definitive proof that smoking caused lung cancer or other diseases. One memo from BW's Vice-President and General Council Ernest Pepples to the CEO of BW in 1978 made it clear that, "Originally, CTR was organized as a public relations effort" (Glantz et al., 1996, p. 44).

The use of sham organizations has become something of a trademark of the tobacco industry. A recent article in the *Wall Street Journal* (Richards, 1997) described efforts by Californians for Scientific Integrity to discredit a study by Dr. Stanton Glantz, the industry critic who published the industry documents in *TCP*, that purported to show that a ban on smoking in restaurants in some communities in California did not produce an adverse economic impact on the restaurants. Californians for Scientific Integrity is funded by the tobacco industry, according to Richards (1997). The National Smokers Alliance, also funded by the tobacco industry, has also attempted to discredit Glantz' work.

(I do not want to leave the impression that sham organizations are used by the tobacco industry only to discredit or challenge health claims about smoking. Noah, 1996, reported that two organizations, Government Direct and Oregon Executive Committee, funded an effort to place a referendum on the Oregon ballot that would require the state to reimburse all health-care providers, including massage therapists, acupuncturists, and other naturopath therapists. These two organizations were both funded by the Tobacco Institute and the point of the referendum was to make the Oregon medical establishment dilute its support for a measure that would have raised the state tax on cigarettes by 30 cents. This measure made the Oregon Medical Association fight two fronts, rather than putting all of its support behind the tax increase. More recent, Boncompagni & Abramson, 1997, described an organization called the New York Society for International Affairs, which pays for junkets to foreign destinations for influential state legislators. Mr. Andrew Whist, the president of the Society, is also the senior vice-president for external affairs at Philip Morris, and the director of the Society also works for Philip Morris under Mr. Whist. The Society's office is a chair in Mr. Whist's home. Most of the funding for the Society comes from Philip Morris. Mr. Whist denies that the trips that are sponsored by the Society are tobacco junkets.)

In an advertisement run in the *New York Times* on May 26, 1994, R. J. Reynolds more or less acknowledges their own loss of credibility. This ad reprinted a column by a Mr. J. Sullum that criticized an EPA study of the dangers of second-hand smoke. In bold print under the reprinted piece were the words, "If we said it, you might not believe it." Of course, one might not believe it even if someone else said it.

What are the messages that the tobacco industry puts into the mouths of its sham experts?

The most persistent message that the industry has broadcast is that there is no definitive evidence that smoking causes cancer or other diseases. They wish to create the illusion of controversy where there is in fact none. This illusion relegates what most independent medical authorities have taken as a fact for decades, to the status of a claim, hypothesis, possibility, or accusation. If the public can be sold the illusion, then the industry can pretend to be seeking the truth, seeking evidence, seeking to find the answers. However, as we saw with the TIRC, these searches are little more than efforts to keep the issue smoky. Tactics that have been employed to keep the smoke machine pumping include the claim that experts disagree. In fact one of the goals suggested for TIRC was to seek scientists who would support the tobacco industry's position and to give them a pulpit from which to express their views. Because the struggle is a public relations struggle, the publication of industry views in the scientific literature is unnecessary. Thus, according to Richards (1997), the criticism of Glantz' work was not submitted to a peer-reviewed journal for publication. It was used as PR by National Smokers Alliance.

The illusion of controversy can be enhanced not only by alleging that experts disagree, but also by critical scrutiny of published work unfavorable to the industry. The tobacco smoke machine examines research reporting unfavorable findings with minute critical detail. The industry called the 1962 report of the Royal College of Physicians incomplete (Glantz et al., 1996, p. 40). It criticized the report for failing to discuss air pollution as a possible cause of lung cancer, thereby suggesting that cigarettes may have been wrongly identified as the sole cause. When the Surgeon General's report was released in 1964, the recommendation was made in a BW memo "to attack the Surgeon General's Report itself by pointing out its gaps and omissions, its reliance on statistics, its lack of clinical evidence, etc., etc." (Glantz et al., 1996, p. 53). It is essential to note that the critical scrutiny is not merely a reflection of a general skepticism or scientific conservatism. It is completely one-sided, directed against unfavorable reports and not against favorable ones or documents sympathetic to the industry. The standard of proof implicit in the tobacco industry's position is that tobacco is innocent until proven guilty, and the proof must be beyond any reasonable doubt. This standard is, of course, appropriate in criminal trials, not public health matters.

The smoke machine did not deal only with medical research. It was also used to create new issues, thereby deflecting attention away from health–addiction concerns, to redefine concepts, like addiction, to make the concepts more favorable to the industry, and it shifted responsibility from the makers of cigarettes and tobacco products to the consumer of the products. These tactics are interrelated, of course, because they are all part of effort to claim that smoking is a personal choice, that smokers chose to smoke voluntarily and, hence, accept whatever health risks might be associated with smoking (warnings are, after all, printed on every pack), and that the real issue is establishing the procedures and institutions to accommodate smokers and non-smokers in a tolerant society.

Medical definitions of addiction refer to several features including the development of tolerance to a drug, withdrawal problems, brain mechanisms, and the intoxicating qualities of the drug. The tobacco industry focuses only on the intoxication criterion to argue that cigarettes are not addictive. They also point to the sizable number of people who have stopped smoking as evidence that smoking is a choice. However, other data that the industry ignores indicate that most people who try to stop smoking cannot and that most people who smoke feel themselves to be addicted to cigarettes. Moreover, Glantz et al. (1996, p. 65) described evidence that BAT had contract research conducted for them by European research organizations into the physiological and behavioral effects of nicotine. Some of the results of this research were described in a 1963 report that detailed the effects of nicotine in the body. The report also discussed nicotine addiction.

If nicotine and cigarettes are addictive, then the concept that consumers freely choose to smoke is compromised. The addiction concept has to be discredited, therefore, in order for the industry to blow smoke at the health issue by saying that the real issue is people's right to choose to smoke. One advertising blitz stressed the need for accommodation to protect the rights of smokers. In a full-page advertisement that was run in the *New York Times* on March 24, 1994, R. J. Reynolds Tobacco Company had the following statement:

> We believe that the solution to most smoking issues can be found in *accommodation*, in finding ways in which smokers and non-smokers can co-exist peacefully. And we encourage dialogue and discussion that will help solve the issues without Government intervention.

Obviously this media strategy is an effort to shift the debate about cigarettes from health to civil rights. Moreover, the strategy has been at least partly successful at the level of state legislatures. By 1994, 28 states and the District of Columbia had passed laws that prohibited employers to deny employment to smokers (Janofsky, 1994). These laws appear to have resulted when firms declared that they would no longer hire smokers in order to cut health care costs. Suits were brought, often with the support of the American Civil Liberties Union, to declare such laws unconstitutional invasions of employees' privacy.

The final element of this feature of the smoke machine deals with the admittedly complex question of responsibility for the harm that arises from smoking. One the one hand, if smokers began smoking with full knowledge of the risks that smoking entailed, it would be wrong to blame the manufacturers of cigarettes for smoking-related illness. The fact that cigarette packs contain written warning labels also tends to shift the responsibility for harm from the producer to the smoker. One item that the industry generally ignores, however, is the fact that the warning labels do not warn of addiction and most adult smokers began smoking when they were children and psychologically incapable of making informed judgments about risks and rewards.

POSTSCRIPT

Until recently, the strategies of the tobacco industry, the use of knowledge shields and smoke machines, had been relatively successful. The industry has remained relatively unregulated by governmental agencies and it had lost precious few liability suits. That all seems to be changing. As I write this chapter in the summer of 1997, the legal environment has undergone a major change. One tobacco company, the Liggett Group, has reached a settlement with several states that are suing to recover health costs and also to impose punitive damages for deceptive and possibly fraudulent practices. Documents that were turned over by Liggett documented meeting with other firms in which defensive strategies were discussed. A tentative agreement has been reached between all of the American tobacco companies, on the one hand, and states that are suing for health-related costs, on the other. This agreement must be approved by the Republican Congress and the Democratic President. One of the sticking points of the agreement concerns the disclosure of documents that have not been previously publicized. A recent court ruling in Florida rejected the industry claims that some concealed documents were entitled to attorney–client privilege, arguing that the lawyers were working on "lobbying, public relations, and general business activities," not offering legal opinions (Geyelin, 1997). As these documents become available, we will learn more not only about what the tobacco industry knew when, but also about how the industry manipulated ignorance, uncertainty, and deception to its advantage and its customers' detriment.

The ideas I have described in this chapter are in their early stages. It seems a reasonable hypothesis that firms will be tempted to create ignorance by using knowledge shields and to create uncertainty through the use of smoke machines when people within the firm become aware of potentially embarrassing, immoral, or illegal actions the firm took or failed to take. The efforts may be reactive, as when critics are attacked, or proactive, as in the establishment of sham organizations. It seems reasonable to hypothesize that the more severe the perceived damage that would result from disclosure, the more intense the efforts at concealment. Furthermore, today's efforts must include concealment of yesterday's concealment, so the burden on a firm to maintain knowledge shields and smoke machines grows as time passes. The strategic decision for sharing or concealing knowledge would seem to reside in the answer to the question of whether, in the long run, it is better to be out with a dirty secret and accept the immediate blame and–or punishment, or to attempt concealment and risk far more serious consequences. We need to be reminded that Richard Nixon was forced to resign as President of the United States in 1974 because of the attempted cover-up of the Watergate break-in, not because of the break-in itself.

ACKNOWLEDGMENTS

This chapter was improved by comments from an anonymous reviewer, Terry Boles, Phil Tetlock, and Leigh Thompson. I am very grateful for their careful reading and thoughtful comments.

REFERENCES

Allison, S. T., Messick, D. M., & Goethals, G. R. (1989). On being better but not smarter than others: The Muhammad Ali effect. *Social Cognition, 7*, 275–295.

Angell, M. (1996). *Science on trial*. New York: Norton.

Birsch, D. & Fielder, J. H. (1994). *The Ford Pinto case*. Albany: State University of New York Press.

Bok, S. (1982). *Secrets: On the ethics of concealment and revelation*. New York: Pantheon.

Boncompagni, T. S., & Abramson, J. (1997, August 4). Tobacco-funded group gives legislators free trips. *Wall Street Journal*, pp. A20.

Byrne, J. A. (1996). *Informed consent*. New York: McGraw-Hill.

Collins, J. C., & Porras, J. I. (1994). *Built to last*. New York: HarperCollins.

Eichenwald, K. (1995). *Serpent of the rock*. New York: Harper.

France, M., DeGeorge, G., & Carey, J. (1997, July 14). So much for smoking out big tobacco's secrets. *Business Week*, No. 3525, 28.

Freedman, A. M. (1996, January 26). Cigarette defector says CEO lied to congress about view of nicotine. *Wall Street Journal*, pp. A1.

Geyelin, M. (1997, August 6). Official in Florida finds evidence on tobacco group teens program. *Wall Street Journal*, p. B10.

Glantz, S. A., Slade, J., Bero, L. A., Hanauer, P., & Barnes, D. E. (1996). *The cigarette papers*. Berkeley: University of California Press.

Greenwald, A. G. (1980). The Totalitarian ego: Fabrication and revision of personal history. *American Psychologist, 35*, 603–618.

Hwang, S. L., & Geyelin, M. (1996, February 1). Brown & Williamson has 500 page dossier attacking chief critic. *Wall Street Journal*, p. A1.

Janofsky, M. (1994, April 28). States challenge employment bans faced by smokers. *New York Times*, p. B1.

Kaplan, D. A. (1995, November 20). Smoke gets in CBS's eye. *Newsweek, 96*.

Kramer, R. M. & Messick, D. M. (1996). Ethical cognition and the framing of organizational dilemmas: Decision makers as intuitive lawyers. In D. M. Messick & A. Tenbrunsel (Eds.), *Codes of Conduct* (pp. 59–85). New York: Russell Sage Foundation.

Kunda, Z. (1990). The Case for motivated reasoning. *Psychological Bulletin, 108*, 480–498.

Kunen, J. S. (1994). *Reckless Disregard*. New York: Simon & Schuster.

Lardner, J. (1993, July 5). The Whistle-blower-Part 1. *New Yorker*, Vol. *LXIX*, No. 20, 52–70.

Maremont, M. (1995, October 23). Blind ambition. *Business Week*, No. 3447, 78–92.

Noah, T. (1996, October 29). Election unites acupuncturists, tobacco lobby. *Wall Street Journal,* p. B2.

Richards, B. (1997, July 23). Pro-tobacco groups step up attacks on longtime foe. *Wall Street Journal,* p. B1.

Scism, L., & Paltrow, S. J. (1997, August 7). Prudential's auditors gave early warnings about sales abuses. *Wall Street Journal,* p. A1.

Schorr, D., & MacIntyre, L. (1996). Smoke in the eye (N. Docherty and J. Gilmore, Producers). In D. Fanning (Executive Producer), *Frontline.* Boston, MA: WGBH/Frontline.

Sharplin, A. (1993). Johns-Manville and Riverwood-Schuller. *Case Research Journal, 13,* 15–40.

Taylor, S. E. (1989). *Positive illusions.* New York: Basic Books.

EMOTIONAL AND
MOTIVATIONAL SYSTEMS

5

Effects of Epistemic Motivation on Conservatism, Intolerance, and Other System-Justifying Attitudes

John T. Jost
Stanford University

Arie W. Kruglanski
Linda Simon
University of Maryland at College Park

> *There is a basic antinomy between openness to change and the desire to preserve a pre-existing view or conviction.*
> —Jones and Gerard (1967, p. 227)

Social and political institutions are maintained in part by the attitudes and beliefs that are held by individuals belonging to those institutions. The community of social scientists agrees on precious few things, but it is widely accepted as an axiom of social science that cognitive support for prevailing social arrangements is essential to the survival of those arrangements (e.g., Eyerman & Jamison, 1991; Giddens, 1979; Jones & Gerard, 1967; Kelman, 1969; Kluegel & Smith, 1986; Lane, 1962; Muller, Jukam, & Seligson, 1982; Piven & Cloward, 1977; Tyler & Smith, 1998; Weatherford, 1992). The assumption that social systems require and gain stability through legitimation is common to theoretical perspectives founded by such diverse figures as Marx, Weber, and Durkheim and it is accepted by contemporary structuralists, functionalists, status-expectation states theorists, feminists, symbolic interactionists, social constructionists, and even postmodern social theorists (e.g., Abercrombie, 1980; Berger & Luckmann, 1967; Berger, Ridgeway, Fisek, & Norman, 1998; DiMaggio & Powell, 1983; Elster, 1989; Giddens, 1979; Habermas, 1975; House, 1990; MacKinnon, 1989; Sampson, 1983; Scheff, 1990).

Elites, leaders, and other authorities who benefit from the status quo seem well aware of the power of socially shared cognitions to forgive or forsake the social order (Tyler, 1990), and so vast amounts of material and cultural resources are devoted to the production and dissemination of ideology (Carragee, 1993), the purpose of which is to bolster the subjective sense that present arrangements are fair and just (Habermas, 1975). Dissidents and revolutionaries, on the other hand, cultivate the perception that the status quo is rotten, unfair, and devoid of reason and justification (Martin, Scully, & Levitt, 1990). Struggles over the adoption or rejection of social forms as complex and wide-ranging as capitalism or socialism are won or lost in the cognitive domain.

It seems likely that certain kinds of attitudes are especially conducive to the preservation of existing social systems, to the extent that they justify social inequality that might otherwise sow the seeds of discontent (e.g., Moore, 1978). This cognitive bolstering is the result, at least, if not the function, of ideologies that are avowedly traditional or conservative in content, anti-democratic in style or procedure, intolerant or discriminatory in application, and final or irreversible in consequence (e.g., Milburn & Conrad, 1996). Although it is, of course, possible to distinguish among different types of conservative and right-wing ideologies in terms of their motives and values (e.g., Tetlock & Mitchell, 1993), attitudes fitting the above descriptions may be referred to as "system justifying," insofar as they possess the property of providing social and cognitive support for the present state of social relations (Jost, 1995, 1996; Jost & Banaji, 1994; Stangor & Jost, 1997). More specifically, system justifying attitudes serve to rationalize outcomes, so that inequalities of status, power, wealth, or prestige are provided with ideological justifications. For example, the stereotype that African Americans are less intelligent or less hard-working than European Americans serves to justify socio-economic differences between these groups and to increase the sense that the socio-economic system that produces such differences is fair and legitimate (Jost & Banaji, 1994).

It is also plausible that one of the functions of society is to provide organization and clarity for the individual and to reduce his or her epistemological uncertainty. In other words, social organizations facilitate the meeting of cognitive needs as well as material needs. This point is made by Berger and Luckmann (1967) in their famous treatise on *The Social Construction of Reality*. They noted that: "Institutions also, by the very fact of their existence, control human conduct by setting up predefined patterns of conduct, which channel it in one direction as against the many other directions that would theoretically be possible" (p. 55). In a world that is unpredictable and enormously complex, social systems and organizations help to reduce the number of potential solutions to problems of human knowledge and action. To paraphrase Walker Percy in the novel *The Moviegoer*, a person is truly lost when he or she has difficulty ruling out the merely possible. A starting theoretical assumption, then, is that a dialectical or reciprocal relationship exists between the social and cognitive needs of the individual to manage his or her environment and the organization of large-scale social systems that serve to simplify and structure human experience (Berger & Luckmann, 1967; DiMaggio & Powell, 1983; Pfeffer, 1998).

In this chapter, we investigate the cognitive and motivational underpinnings of attitudes toward social and organizational systems. Specifically, we draw on the theory of lay epistemics to address individual and situational variations in the manner and extent to which people are motivated to possess knowledge that is secure, stable, and permanent (Kruglanski, 1989). One independent variable in particular, the need for cognitive closure, has been found to predict reliance on social stereotypes, biases in person perception, resistance to persuasive influence, and rejection of opinion deviates (Kruglanski & Webster, 1996). In other words, this cognitive style, which is responsive to environmental demands and situational variations, seems to be associated with the preservation of existing social arrangements. Building on past research on the need for cognitive closure, we present new correlational and experimental evidence that connects epistemic motivational tendencies to "seize" and "freeze" upon information that is readily accessible to the formation of system-justifying attitudes.

THE INDEPENDENT VARIABLE: EPISTEMIC MOTIVATION

According to Kruglanski's (1989) theory of lay epistemics, people differ in the extent to which they are motivated to seek out and possess knowledge that is secure, stable, and unlikely to change. In other words, a general cognitive-motivational orientation toward the social world is proposed that is either open and exploratory, on the one hand, or closed and immutable, on the other hand (Kruglanski & Webster, 1996). This tension is what Jones and Gerard (1967) described as a "basic antinomy" (p. 227) and they argued that although "there is an undeniable tendency toward conservatism reflected in the economizing principle of applying past solutions to present problems, there must also be countermeasures that make for openness and flexibility" (p. 228). According to Kruglanski and Webster (1996), individuals differ from one another, and they differ from situation to situation, in the extent to which they are open to novel information and are willing to consider cognitive alternatives to the status quo.

One empirical approach to the study of epistemic motivation is to understand it in terms of chronically accessible individual differences. Part of this chapter is devoted to reviewing evidence of this type. Specifically, we consider correlational results linking "uncertainty motivation" (Sorrentino & Hancock, 1986), "personal need for structure" (Thompson, Naccarato, & Parker, 1989), and the "need for cognitive closure" (Webster & Kruglanski, 1994) to system-justifying attitudes and behaviors. The evidence suggests that people who are relatively tolerant of ambiguity and uncertainty are less likely to use stereotypes and other attitudes as a way of rationalizing inequality and preserving the status quo.

Because dispositional accounts provide an incomplete picture of the causes of human behavior by identifying traits and characteristics that appear to be stable properties of individual actors but in fact show considerable variance when the situational context is altered (e.g., Mischel & Peake, 1982; Pfeffer, 1985, 1998), a second way of approaching epistemic motivation is to examine the impact of situational variables. Factors such as time pressure, environmental noise, task attractiveness, and dispositional characteristics have been found to influence the extent and nature of information processing (e.g., Dijker & Koomen, 1996; Kruglanski & Freund, 1983; Kruglanski & Webster, 1991; Kruglanski, Webster, & Klem, 1993; Ordonez & Benson, 1997; Schaller, Boyd, Yohannes, & O'Brien, 1995; Stapel, 1997; Webster & Kruglanski, 1994). For example, the presence of environmental noise tends to curtail extensive informational searches and leads people to "seize" on a quick answer or solution and to "freeze" on this particular solution without considering alternatives. It seems that specific features of the person and the organizational environment, both independently and in interaction (Pfeffer, 1998), tend to affect the processes through which knowledge is developed and shared as well as the particular contents of that knowledge.

The need for cognitive closure, whether varied situationally or measured dispositionally, has been associated with tendencies to: engage in social stereotyping (Kruglanski & Freund, 1983), succumb to primacy effects in impression formation (Kruglanski & Freund, 1983; Webster & Kruglanski, 1994), commit the correspondence bias (Webster & Kruglanski, 1994), resist persuasive influence (Kruglanski et al., 1993), and to reject opinion deviates (Kruglanski & Webster, 1991). Although these and related dependent variables may not ordinarily be classified as examples of conservative or system justifying attitudes or behaviors, it is certainly the case that the function of each is to preserve existing social forms of the organization and to inhibit innovation and change, suggesting that an integrative conception of attitudes related to the status quo may be warranted. This is one major goal of the theory of system justification (e.g., Jost, 1996; Jost & Banaji, 1994; Stangor & Jost, 1997). Thus, the demands of the immediate situation on one's attentional and cognitive capacities may well affect social and political tendencies to embrace or eschew organizational change.

DEPENDENT VARIABLES: POLITICAL CONSERVATISM AND OTHER SYSTEM-JUSTIFYING ATTITUDES

According to the theory of system justification, people tend to accept exist-ing institutions and procedures as fair, legitimate, natural, and inevitable (Jost, 1996; Jost & Banaji, 1994; Stangor & Jost, 1997), in part because they are taught from childhood on to engage in such ideological work (e.g., Tyler & McGraw, 1986), in part because they are motivated to conserve cognitive and behavioral resources (e.g., Kluegel & Smith, 1986), and in part because they are motivated to preserve the sense that the world is a fair place in which people get what they deserve and deserve what they get (e.g., Lerner, 1980). One major (and overdetermined) function of attitudes, stereotypes, and social judgments, then, is to justify existing social arrangements. Sys-tem justification refers to a set of social, cognitive, and motivational tenden-cies to rationalize inequality and to preserve the status quo through ideo-logical means (Jost, 1996). To engage in system justification is to put forth attitudes that are inherently right-wing and conservative; that is, to develop and communicate what Pratto, Sidanius, Stallworth, and Malle (1994) re-ferred to as "hierarchy enhancing legitimizing myths."

Wilson (1973) proposed a general psychological definition of conserva-tism as "resistance to change and the tendency to prefer safe, traditional and conventional forms of institutions and behaviour" (p. 4), and this defi-nition is sufficiently broad to fit with our emphasis on system justification. According to Wilson's "dynamic" theory, conservatism is the product of (partially unconscious) motives and needs having to do with fear and anxiety. The central tenet of the theory is that "the common basis for all the various components of the conservative attitude syndrome is a *gener-alized susceptibility to experiencing threat or anxiety in the face of uncertainty*" (Wilson, 1973, p. 259, emphasis in original). This account lends itself very well to an analysis in terms of the need for cognitive closure, insofar as the construct refers to a motivated tendency to reduce uncertainty and achieve knowledge that is secure and stable (e.g., Kruglanski & Webster, 1996). The adoption of conservative and system justifying beliefs, then, should be enhanced by the chronic and temporary activation of cognitive-motivational needs associated with the preservation of the familiar and the rejection of the unfamiliar.

The hypothesized connection between epistemic motivation and various manifestations of political conservatism is explored in correlational and experimental research studies that are described in the remainder of this chapter. First, we present evidence linking individual differences in epistemic motivation to authoritarianism, dogmatism, political conservatism, and social stereotyping. Next, correlational evidence is presented that connects the need for cognitive closure to one politically conservative attitude—namely, support for the death penalty—that reflects an unambiguous desire for swift and punitive action. Finally, we report on experimental studies that demonstrate that increasing the need for cognitive closure has the effects of decreasing political tolerance and weakening commitment to democratic social norms, unless values for tolerance are chronically or temporarily accessible. Taken as a whole, this evidence suggests that the epistemic needs of individuals do play a substantial role in the preservation of unequal social systems and the formation of normative decisions that may be expedient but are restrictive and difficult to change.

INDIVIDUAL DIFFERENCES
IN EPISTEMIC MOTIVATION

It is a familiar notion in social science since the height of research on the "Authoritarian Personality" (Adorno, Frenkel-Brunswik, Levinson, & Sanford, 1950) that individual difference variables would predict social intolerance, scapegoating of deviates, and generalized support for the social system. As Gordon Allport (1954) put it, "the cognitive processes of prejudiced people are in general different from the cognitive processes of tolerant people" (p. 175). Contemporary researchers have documented the extent to which cognitive complexity decreases as one moves from left to right across the ideological spectrum (Tetlock, 1983), the extent to which racism increases with political conservatism, even among highly educated people (Sidanius, Pratto, & Bobo, 1996), and the extent to which individual difference measures of "right-wing authoritarianism" (Altemeyer, 1988; Peterson, Doty, & Winter, 1993) and "social dominance orientation" (Pratto et al., 1994) are capable of predicting a wide range of anti-social attitudes and behaviors.

Work on epistemic motivation has stressed individual differences in the less value-laden propensity to consider a wide range of cognitive alternatives before engaging in decision making but these, too, are linked to social and political attitudes. Sorrentino and Hancock (1986, p. 249), for example, argued that some people are more "certainty-oriented" than others and that they "are in fact persons who would like to keep things the way they are" and that such "persons are not interested in finding out new information about themselves or the world." Studies show that people who are identified as "certainty-oriented" on the basis of a diagnostic instrument tend to rely more on cognitive heuristics, categorical thinking, and social stereotyping than do "uncertainty-oriented" people and they also display less evidence of creativity and innovation (Huber & Sorrentino, 1996).

A "personal need for structure" (PNS) scale was developed by Thompson, Naccarato, and Parker (1989) to measure the extent to which individuals seek out situations that are organized, predictable, and structured and the extent to which they avoid situations that are ambiguous, uncertain, and unpredictable. This scale has been found to correlate moderately with measures of authoritarianism, dogmatism, and mental rigidity (Neuberg & Newsom, 1993). People who score high on the PNS scale are more likely to ascribe traditional gender stereotypes (such as emotionality, irrationality, childishness, and gullibility) to female targets than to male targets under conditions of ambiguity, whereas people who score low on the scale do not differentiate between male and female target persons who are otherwise described in similar terms.

Research by Schaller et al. (1995) suggests that the personal need for structure is associated with the formation of erroneous group stereotypes. High PNS individuals tend to draw straightforward conclusions about group characteristics (such as intelligence) on the basis of simple performance outcomes (number of anagrams solved) without taking into account task difficulty and other situational constraints, which are used by the more attributionally complex individuals who score low on the PNS. All of these findings indicate that epistemic motives exacerbate the system-justifying tendency to use stereotypes as a way of rationalizing outcomes and justifying inequality (see Jost & Banaji, 1994).

Webster and Kruglanski (1994) also developed and validated an individual difference measure that taps this type of epistemic motivation. The 42-item "need for cognitive closure" scale possesses five factors or subscales, which are described as: (a) preference for order and structure; (b) emotional discomfort associated with ambiguity; (c) impatience with regard to decision-making; (d) desire for security and predictability; (e) closed-mindedness. Items include: "I think that having clear rules and order at work is essential for success," "I'd rather know bad news than stay in a state of uncertainty," and, "I don't like to go into a situation without knowing what I can expect from it." There is evidence, some of which is already in the published literature and some of which is new to this chapter, that links the individual difference variable of need for closure to system justifying dependent variables. We turn now to a consideration of that evidence.

Need for Cognitive Closure
and General Political Conservatism

The "need for closure" (NFC) scale has been widely validated and compared with a variety of other dispositional measures, some of which are related to system justification and political conservatism (Webster & Kruglanski, 1994). Correlations between the need for cognitive closure and the authoritarianism F scale, for example, have been found to be positive and significant at $r = +.27$ (Webster & Kruglanski, 1994). The scale correlates also with dogmatism ($r = +.29$) and intolerance of ambiguity ($r = +.29$) at $p < .01$ (Webster & Kruglanski, 1994), providing indirect evidence that the relationship between need for closure and conservatism is reasonably close. The point is not to suggest that NFC is redundant with political conservatism but that there may be a relatively unexplored connection between individual motives to acquire epistemological certainty and the contents of particular political ideologies.

To tighten the theoretical and empirical connection between epistemic motivation and political conservatism, we administered batteries of measures that included the need for cognitive closure scale and a single-item measure of self-reported liberalism–conservatism to two large samples of undergraduate students at the University of Maryland in the Fall of 1995 and the Spring of 1996. In the first sample, comprised of 613 respondents, the correlation between need for closure and conservatism was +.21, which is statistically significant at the $p < .001$ level. In the second sample of 733 students, the correlation was slightly higher at $r = +.26$ ($p < .001$). Thus, there is some direct evidence available that the need for cognitive closure is associated (albeit modestly) with attitudes that are favorable toward political conservatism.

A study conducted in Germany demonstrates that NFC scores increase steadily as one moves across the political spectrum from left to right. Democratic socialists score lower on NFC than members of the Green Party, who score lower than members of the Social-Democratic Party, who score lower than members of the Free-Democratic Party, who score lower than members of the right-wing Christian-Democratic Party (Kemmelmeier, 1997). Because this research examines five political parties, it is possible to compare both linear and non-linear models of the relation between cognitive style and political orientation (e.g., Sidanius, 1985; Tetlock, 1983). Kemmelmeier's (1997) results yield no evidence for the notion that extreme individuals at both ends of the political spectrum exhibit greater cognitive rigidity (e.g., Shils, 1954) nor evidence for Sidanius' (1985) suggestion that politically extreme individuals tend to exhibit greater flexibility and sophistication in their thinking, insofar as the need for closure relates to these variables. Instead, there appears to be a linear relationship between cognitive style and political ideology (e.g., Adorno et al., 1950; Tetlock, 1983) such that NFC is related positively to conservative and right-wing ideological thinking.

The methodological weakness of correlational studies, of course, is that determinations of causality are not possible. From these findings, interesting as they are in terms of linking general cognitive orientations to the specific contents of political ideologies, it is impossible to determine whether a need for epistemological certainty leads one to embrace right-wing ideologies or whether conservative political parties increase the desire (or even the tendency) to acquire secure and permanent knowledge. In any case, there does appear to be a connection between the epistemic needs of the individual and the ideologies shared by members of political parties and other organizations.

Need for Cognitive Closure and Attitudes Toward Capital Punishment

Support for the death penalty reflects the holding of attitudes that are politically conservative in the sense that they are associated more with right-wing than left-wing ideologies. Punitiveness in general has long been associated with the syndrome of right-wing authoritarianism (Adorno et al., 1950; Altemeyer, 1988; Peterson et al., 1993). In addition, pro-capital punishment attitudes may be expected to satisfy hypothesized needs of conservatives to make decisions that are unambiguous, certain, and final. To examine the possibility that individual needs for cognitive closure in general would be associated with the endorsement of specific ideological opinions, a small-scale study was carried out at the University of California at Santa Barbara.

Nineteen undergraduate students at U.C.S.B. completed the need for cognitive closure scale and an attitude questionnaire designed by Ellsworth and Ross (1983) to gauge opinions about capital punishment. The latter questionnaire presents nine crimes (e.g., "intentional killing of a policeman or prison guard," "kidnapping during which no death occurs") and asks respondents which of three scaled positions they would advocate for each crime: (a) no death penalty, (b) discretionary death penalty (the jury would have the choice to recommend or not recommend the death penalty), and (c) mandatory death penalty (the jury would have to recommend the death penalty if they were to reach a guilty verdict). By assigning scores of 0, 1, and 2 to these respective choices and then averaging across the nine items, it is possible to calculate an overall attitude score with regard to capital punishment and to compare this score with the need for cognitive closure.

As expected, the need for cognitive closure was associated with attitudes that are favorable toward the death penalty. The correlation between the overall need for closure score and endorsement of capital punishment was +.47, which was found to be significant at the $p < .05$ level. It has been argued that the NFC scale is more useful as a multidimensional scale than as a unidimensional instrument (Neuberg, Judice, & West, 1997). Two of the sub-scales of the NFC scale were found to be especially strongly related to attitudes toward the death penalty. They were the discomfort with ambiguity ($r = +.66$, $p < .01$) and the preference for order ($r = +.55$, $p < .02$) sub-scales. Although this evidence is correlational (and so causal conclusions are difficult to draw), these findings suggest that Wilson (1973) may be right. Conservative opinions, such as favoring capital punishment, may satisfy cognitive–motivational needs to reduce uncertainty, ambiguity, and chaos.

From this perspective, it makes sense that the need for cognitive closure should predict attitudes toward capital punishment for at least two related reasons. The first reason is that the endorsement of capital punishment is related in terms of content to conservative and right-wing ideologies, with their demands for law and order (e.g., Milburn & Conrad, 1996). The second reason is that recommending the death penalty is to make a decision that is final, unambiguous, and permanent; such decisions almost surely gratify those who are especially high on the need for cognitive closure (Kruglanski & Webster, 1996). Few decisions in the social world are as final and long-lasting as the decision to sentence someone to death, although it is true that political conservatives frequently bemoan the due process appeals that serve to prolong "closure".

SITUATIONAL FACTORS AFFECTING EPISTEMIC MOTIVATION AND SYSTEM JUSTIFICATION

In addition to developing an individual difference measure of the need for cognitive closure, researchers have developed experimental paradigms for inducing the need for cognitive closure (e.g., Kruglanski & Webster, 1996; Webster & Kruglanski, 1994). One such paradigm involves exposing research participants to environmental noise while they are performing cognitive tasks. The noise, which is bothersome but not unbearable, makes the completion of other tasks more difficult and uncertain and lowers people's motivation to engage in effortful cognitive searches, thereby heightening the need to "seize" and "freeze" on an accessible and satisfying solution. In other words, these circumstances increase one's need to achieve cognitive closure, which, in turn, exacerbates system-justifying behaviors such as rejecting opinion deviates, promulgating stereotypes of the outgroup, and making use of the linguistic intergroup bias (Kruglanski & Webster, 1996).

In experimental research described later this chapter, we conducted new studies to investigate the effects of enhancing the need for cognitive closure on political intolerance and preference for autocratic (as opposed to democratic) decision-making schemes. Both of these tendencies are theoretically related to system justification, which refers to cognitive and behavioral orientations that are supportive of right-wing ideologies and other attempts to reinforce hierarchical social relations and to inhibit progressive social or organizational change (Jost, 1996). Based on the foregoing theoretical analysis and correlational data, it was hypothesized that increasing the need for cognitive closure would increase political intolerance and adherence to autocratic norms.

A second theoretical possibility was also considered: that increasing the need for cognitive closure would increase reliance on ideological values that are either chronically accessible or situationally primed. This possibility was supported by prior research in which non-ideological types of beliefs were found to impact judgment most strongly under the joint conditions of high knowledge activation and high need for closure (e.g., Ford & Kruglanski, 1995; Thompson, Roman, Moskowitz, Chaiken, & Bargh, 1994). Roch and Samuelson (1997), too, found that chronically accessible individual differences in social value orientation were more likely to affect resource allocations under conditions of high uncertainty compared to conditions of low uncertainty. The research described here makes use of variations in terms of cognitive accessibility and epistemic motivation in more explicitly ideological domains.

In one study, political liberals and political conservatives were exposed to manipulations of epistemic motivation and their reactions to an anti-American target person were monitored. In a follow-up study, values of political tolerance were made cognitively accessible to participants just before they were required to evaluate the anti-American target under conditions of high versus low need for cognitive closure. Thus, it was possible to explore the independent and combined effects of epistemic motivation and accessibility of ideological beliefs on political intolerance.

Need for Cognitive Closure and Political Intolerance Among Liberals and Conservatives

Thus far, we have considered differences in epistemic motivation between people subscribing to left-wing and right-wing ideologies. In another line of research, we have taken liberals and conservatives and exposed both groups to conditions that are expected to heighten the need for cognitive closure. One empirical possibility is that both groups tend to behave more like system-justifying conservatives under such circumstances. Another possibility is that increasing the need for closure leads people to rely on chronically accessible attitudes; that is, to defend their enduring ideological beliefs in an even stronger fashion than before. Although some evidence suggests that epistemic needs for closure and for certainty are better served by ideologies that are traditional, conservative, or right-wing in content (e.g., Kemmelmeier, 1997; Neuberg & Newsom, 1993; Schaller et al., 1995; Webster & Kruglanski, 1994), our experimental research also demonstrates that situational manipulations of epistemic motivation can lead people to adhere more strongly to their initial ideological positions, whether these are more associated with the political left or the political right.

On the basis of pre-screening sessions involving a five-item measure of liberal versus conservative attitudes, research participants were selected from the top and bottom quartiles so that two groups emerged—one that was relatively high in liberalism and one that was relatively high in conservatism. The five items that were used to differentiate these groups had to do with the favorability of attitudes directed toward Bill Clinton, Newt Gingrich, legalized abortion, prayer in school, and increases in military spending. Liberals were defined as people holding favorable attitudes toward the first and third of these objects and unfavorable attitudes toward the rest. Conservatives were defined as people having unfavorable attitudes toward the first and third of these and favorable attitudes toward the others. Thus, we started with two groups that were presumed to differ in terms of chronically accessible ideological values.

The goal of the study was to investigate how these chronic ideologies would be affected by an increase in the need for cognitive closure, as caused by the presence of ambient noise. In particular, we were interested in effects on political intolerance, which was operationalized in terms of evaluations of foreigners who express anti-American attitudes. It was theorized that such evaluations would reflect a commitment to the status quo and a reluctance to entertain criticisms of the social and political system. An experimental procedure for studying political intolerance was borrowed from Greenberg, Simon, Pyszczynski, Solomon, and Chatel (1992), who investigated the effects of death anxiety on political intolerance.

According to this procedure, participants are instructed that the purpose of the research is to assess foreign views of the United States and American reactions to those views. Participants are presented with two brief essays that are ascribed to foreign exchange students. One of these essays adopts a strong pro-American stance (e.g., "In this country, people can go to school and train for the job they want. Here anyone who works hard can make their own success . . .") and the other adopts a strong anti-American stance (e.g., "The system here is set up for rich against the poor. All people care about here is money and trying to have more than other people"). After reading each of these essays, participants are asked to evaluate the foreign target by indicating how much they like and agree with the target person, how intelligent and how knowledgeable he is, and how valid his arguments are. An overall political (in)tolerance score is calculated by averaging across the five ratings.

Before presenting the effects of chronic ideology and environmental noise on political intolerance, let us consider the effects of environmental noise on the need for cognitive closure, as measured by four items that serve as manipulation checks. The wordings of these items and mean responses to each under noise versus control conditions are presented in Table 5.1. An overall need for closure index is calculated by averaging across these four items. Scores on the index are significantly higher under conditions of noise than no noise, suggesting that the noise manipulation

TABLE 5.1
Means (and SDs) on the Need for Cognitive Closure
as a Function of Environmental Noise

Item	No Noise	Noise
How much thought did the task require?	5.31	5.68
	(1.74)	(1.83)
To what extent were you in a hurry to complete the task?	3.67	5.17
	(1.27)	(1.66)
To what extent did you wish the experiment to be over?	4.67	5.88
	(2.08)	(2.05)
How much confidence did you have in your judgment?	6.59	7.46
	(2.22)	(1.22)
Overall index of need for cognitive closure	5.21	6.04
	(1.34)	(1.18)

does induce a need for cognitive closure (see also Webster & Kruglanski, 1994).

As expected, there were effects of liberal versus conservative ideology and high versus low need for cognitive closure on political intolerance. Mean evaluations of the pro-American and anti-American foreign students by experimental condition are presented in Table 5.2. As can be seen, effects of ideology and epistemic motivation emerge only for evaluations of the anti-American target; there are no differences for the pro-American target. Liberals are significantly more tolerant of the anti-American foreigner in

TABLE 5.2
Means (and SDs) on Evaluation of Pro-American and Anti-American
Targets as a Function of Political Ideology and Environmental Noise

Pro-American Target		
Political Ideology	No Noise	Noise
Liberal	6.14	6.49
	(1.12)	(1.09)
Conservative	6.19	6.63
	(1.53)	(1.10)
Anti-American Target		
Political Ideology	No Noise	Noise
Liberal	4.01	5.29
	(1.29)	(1.20)
Conservative	3.33	2.88
	(0.96)	(1.01)

Note. Higher numbers reflect more favorable evaluations.

general than are conservatives. This validates our measure of political intolerance as well as the assumption that liberal political ideologies are more open to criticisms of the social system than are conservative political ideologies.

Of greater interest, however, is the fact that political ideology interacts with the need for cognitive closure to predict political intolerance. Environmental noise slightly increases political intolerance among conservatives, but it significantly decreases political intolerance (or increases tolerance) among liberals. Thus, increasing the need for cognitive closure appears to increase reliance on chronically accessible ideological attitudes; it leads conservatives to further engage in system justification, but it leads liberals to further tolerate criticism of the system. A follow-up study offered the opportunity to replicate these effects under conditions in which political values are made situationally accessible through priming techniques.

Need for Cognitive Closure and Political Intolerance Following Priming of Tolerant Values

The experimental procedures for inducing the need for cognitive closure and for measuring political intolerance were repeated in a follow-up study. Instead of pre-selecting liberals and conservatives, a priming technique was used in this study to make the value of political tolerance high or low in salience. This was accomplished by having participants respond to an alleged attitude survey that consisted of either innocuous statements such as, "It is important to have goals in life" (in the control condition) or statements that primed tolerant attitudes such as, "It is important to be tolerant of those with different opinions" (in the experimental condition). It appears that this priming procedure affected political intolerance under conditions of noise and no noise.

Once again, there were no effects on evaluations of the pro-American target. For evaluations of the anti-American target, however, an interaction effect between type of prime and need for closure was observed. For people exposed to the tolerance prime, noise increased political tolerance of an anti-American target. For people exposed to the neutral prime, there was no significant effect of noise on tolerance (see means in Table 5.3). Thus, it seems that a heightened need for cognitive closure can result in increased political tolerance but only when tolerant values are highly accessible, either because of enduring political convictions or because of contextual priming.

Taken together, these studies demonstrate that situational manipulations of the need for cognitive closure do affect political intolerance. Specifically, environmental noise increases the likelihood that political conservatives will derogate a foreign student who is expressing an opinion that is critical of the United States. However, political liberals and people who are primed

TABLE 5.3
Means (and SDs) on Evaluation of Pro-American and Anti-American
Targets as a Function of Prime Type and Environmental Noise

	Pro-American Target	
Prime Type	No Noise	Noise
Tolerant	6.19	6.38
	(1.09)	(1.02)
Neutral	6.08	6.06
	(1.04)	(0.82)

	Anti-American Target	
Prime Type	No Noise	Noise
Tolerant	3.98	5.65
	(1.17)	(0.97)
Neutral	3.86	4.04
	(0.96)	(1.22)

Note. Higher numbers reflect more favorable evaluations.

explicitly with tolerant attitudes are less likely to derogate the anti-American target under conditions of noise, indicating that epistemic motivation and knowledge accessibility jointly determine social attitudes. Other studies, to which we now turn, investigate the effects of need for closure and knowledge activation on a different type of system justifying dependent variable; namely, the preference for an autocratic decision-making scheme over a democratic one.

Need for Cognitive Closure and Preferences for Autocratic Versus Democratic Systems Among Men and Women

According to a meta-analytic review conducted by Eagly, Makhijani, and Klonsky (1992), men and women differ in terms of their preferences for democratic versus autocratic systems of leadership. More specifically, the bulk of research indicates that women tend to espouse more democratic values than do men and that men espouse more autocratic arrangements than do women. The study described here makes use of this gender-related individual difference variable (Major & Deaux, 1982) in much the same way that our earlier study made use of individual differences between political liberals and conservatives. A theoretical assumption was made, then, that there would be differences between men and women in terms of chronically accessible preferences for democratic versus autocratic preferences (cf. Pratto et al., 1994).

Following traditional and contemporary research on authoritarian attitudes (e.g., Adorno et al., 1950; Altemeyer, 1988; Peterson et al., 1993), it was further assumed that a connection exists between preferences for autocratic rule and system-justifying tendencies to preserve existing inequalities and to oppose progressive social change. The idea is that autocratic preferences reflect a desire for structure, hierarchy, and inequality (especially the way in which it is operationalized here), whereas democratic preferences reflect a desire for tolerance, pluralism, and equality. Thus, even in the context of a democratic society, ideologies of system justification should be associated more with autocratic than democratic preferences, insofar as the former attitudes help to conserve and concentrate power and to restrict opportunities for full and equal participation. Still, future research is needed to determine the extent to which the variety of system-justifying attitudes discussed here are linked empirically.

In an experiment on the effects of need for closure and ideological accessibility on preferences for autocratic versus democratic systems, 72 male undergraduate students and 72 female undergraduate students from the University of Maryland participated in same-sex triads. In the first part of the experiment, participants completed a "Symbolic Meaning Insight Task" in which they were asked to look at 10 modified Chinese language characters and to determine the meaning of each of character. It was alleged that this task could be used to measure a person's "insight into the symbolic nature of the character." All participants were given false feedback indicating that they had scored "in the 70th percentile, which is actually really good."

Participants were then assigned to same-sex discussion groups with two other people, one of whom was said to have also scored in the 70th percentile, and the other of whom was said to have scored in the 85th percentile, which the experimenter commented was "one of the highest scores I have ever seen." After receiving instructions not to discuss their individual scores on the Symbolic Meaning Insight Task, participants joined the two other group members to engage in a collective decision-making task in which all three people were required to discuss and come to a consensual decision about the meaning of five new modified Chinese characters. Half of the groups were exposed to ambient noise during their group discussions and the other half were not. Our interest was in whether democratic or autocratic styles of leadership predominated in these different groups of men and women under conditions of high and low need for closure.

Perceptions of and preferences for democratic versus autocratic arrangements were measured in three different ways, immediately following actual group discussions. First, participants were asked to evaluate the leadership potential of their two fellow group members on four items (e.g., "To what extent do you think this person is likely to be an efficient leader?"; "To what extent did this person appear to be capable of exerting a leadership role?"). Combining across these evaluation items, it was possible to determine the extent to which participants differentiated between the leadership potentials of their two fellow group members (one of whom had allegedly scored in the 70th percentile, and the other of whom had allegedly scored in the 85th percentile). It was theorized that preferences for autocratic styles of leadership would result in greater differentiation between the two fellow group members, whereas preferences for democratic leadership would result in lesser differentiation between the other group members. Secondly, participants were asked to estimate the extent to which democratic versus autocratic norms had predominated in their group discussions. This was achieved by asking participants how much they agreed or disagreed (on nine-point scales) with each of the following statements: "In this group, decisions were made by the group leader," and "In this group, decisions were made by discussing until consensus was reached." These items tapped perceptions of whether democracy or autocracy had prevailed during the group sessions. Thirdly, participants were asked to indicate their general preferences by agreeing or disagreeing with the following items: "When I am a member of a group, I prefer that decisions be made by the group leader," and "When I am the leader of a group, I prefer that decisions be made by the group leader." We investigated the effects of gender and epistemic motivation on each of these three dependent variables, all of which were designed to tap preferences for autocratic versus democratic social arrangements.[1]

Analysis of variance was performed on mean group judgments of differentiation between the leadership potentials of one's co-workers. This analysis revealed a statistically reliable two-way interaction between gender and the need for cognitive closure, as manipulated through environmental noise. As can be seen by inspecting means reported in Table 5.4, men showed greater differentiation (and hence greater tendencies to exhibit autocratic attitudes) than did women, but only under conditions of noise. For this dependent variable, then, both chronic accessibility of autocratic values and high need for closure seem to be required.

With regard to perceptions and preferences for autocratic versus democratic procedures, however, the situational manipulation of need for closure seemed to increase reliance on autocracy and decrease the use of democracy among men and women alike. Mean responses for two perception items and two preference items are presented in Table 5.5, broken down by gender and noise condition. Although men in general appear to hold more

---

[1]The data were analyzed using the three-person discussion group as a unit of analysis, so that a single data point represents the mean ratings of three individual participants. One group of men was dropped from the analysis because they admitted that they had never discussed the symbolic meaning task and therefore failed to reach any decisions whatsoever.

TABLE 5.4
Mean Leadership Differentiation Between Coworkers
as a Function of Gender and Environmental Noise

Gender	No Noise	Noise
Male	0.13	1.00
(SD)	(1.49)	(1.66)
n	12	12
Female	0.33	0.29
(SD)	(0.77)	(1.78)
n	12	12

Note. Higher numbers reflect greater differentiation between coworkers.

TABLE 5.5
Means (and SDs) on Perceptions of and Preferences for Democratic Versus
Autocratic Leadership as a Function of Gender and Environmental Noise

Item	Gender	No Noise	Noise
In this group, decisions were made by the group leader.	Male	6.67	7.33
		(1.15)	(1.37)
	Female	4.00	6.58
		(2.44)	(1.16)
In this group, decisions were made by discussing until consensus was reached.	Male	4.75	3.58
		(0.75)	(1.51)
	Female	6.92	4.50
		(2.06)	(1.45)
When I am a member of a group, I prefer that decisions be made by the group leader.	Male	5.83	7.58
		(2.44)	(0.90)
	Female	3.42	6.00
		(2.81)	(1.76)
When I am the leader of the group, I prefer that decisions be made by the group leader.	Male	8.25	8.75
		(0.75)	(0.45)
	Female	4.10	7.33
		(2.87)	(1.23)

Note. Higher numbers indicate greater agreement with the statement.

favorable attitudes toward autocratic arrangements than do women, enhancing the need for cognitive closure did increase the favorability of autocratic options among women as well as men. Thus, it seems that both chronically accessible ideological preferences and contextual variations in epistemic motivation play important roles in determining whether autocratic or democratic procedures are followed.

Although our experiment does provide some support for the notion that men and women exhibit different preferences with regard to procedural arrangements and leadership styles (Eagly et al., 1992; Major & Deaux, 1982), the use of gender as a proxy variable for the chronic accessibility of autocratic versus democratic values is not ideal. For that reason, an additional experiment was conducted to examine the effects of priming certain value orientations so that the relations among knowledge accessibility, epistemic motivation, and autocratic preferences might be further explored. Once again, we were interested in whether an increase in the need for cognitive closure would result in a general preference for procedures and solutions that are closed, expedient, and autocratic, or whether it would result in the increased use of whatever preference is made cognitively accessible.

Need for Cognitive Closure and Preferences for Autocratic Versus Democratic Systems Following Priming of Autocratic Versus Democratic Values

For another experiment on the effects of epistemic motivation on political values, 72 female introductory psychology students at the University of Maryland were recruited. Early in the experimental session, participants completed an Attitude Assessment scale that was surreptitiously designed to prime a particular value orientation, following a procedure used by Katz and Hass (1988). There were three different versions of the seven-item Attitude Assessment scale: (a) an autocratic version, which contained five items that were intended to make autocratic values salient (e.g., "In general, I prefer a President who makes decisions for himself rather than one who consults with advisors"); (b) a democratic version, which contained five items that were intended to make democratic values salient (e.g., "In general, I prefer a President who consults with advisors rather than one who makes decisions for himself"); and (c) a neutral version, in which all seven items were innocuous and unrelated to political values (e.g., "It's better to have tried and lost than never to have tried at all"). Participants in each of these three conditions were asked simply to indicate their levels of agreement or disagreement with each of the survey statements on nine-point scales.

Following this priming procedure, participants received two hand-written statements that were ascribed to other undergraduate students. One of these statements espoused a democratic leadership style and the other one espoused an autocratic leadership style; the order of the two statements was counter-balanced. The democratic statement emphasized the person's desire to let everyone have a say in the decision but that ultimately a vote should be taken and the majority should rule, whereas the autocratic statement emphasized the person's desire to be viewed as a leader and in control and that because he or she was a fair person, it made sense for him or her to make the decisions for the group. Participants were asked to evaluate the author of each statement by estimating how much she would like that person, how much she agreed with the leadership style expressed, whether she would like to have that person as a group leader, and so on.

All evaluations were completed under conditions of noise or relative silence. A composite measure of evaluation was computed, and this served as the dependent variable of interest here.

The experimental design was a 3 (Democratic vs. Autocratic vs. Neutral Prime Type) × 2 (Noise vs. No Noise Condition) × 2 (Democratic vs. Autocratic Target Person). Analysis of variance yielded a pair of main effects (prime type and target person), a pair of two-way interactions (prime type × target person and noise condition × prime type), and a three-way interaction involving prime type, target person, and noise condition. Cell means and standard deviations are presented in Table 5.6.

First, a main effect of prime type indicates that evaluations of all targets were less favorable in the autocratic prime condition ($M = 5.09$) than in the neutral ($M = 5.50$) or democratic ($M = 5.75$) prime conditions. A main effect of the target person establishes that the democratic target was evaluated more favorably ($M = 6.02$) than the autocratic target ($M = 4.87$). An interaction between prime type and target person supports a matching hypothesis: The democratic target was evaluated more favorably following the democratic prime than the autocratic prime, whereas the autocratic target was evaluated more favorably following the autocratic prime than the democratic prime (see Table 5.6).

TABLE 5.6
Means (and SDs) on Evaluation of Democratic and Autocratic
Targets as a Function of Prime Type and Environmental Noise

	Noise Condition		
	Prime Type		
Target Person	Democratic	Neutral	Autocratic
	(n = 12)	(n = 11)	(n = 12)
Democratic	7.33	6.26	3.89
	(1.05)	(1.74)	(1.08)
Autocratic	4.79	5.29	6.08
	(1.66)	(1.78)	(1.55)
	No Noise Condition		
	Prime Type		
Target Person	Democratic	Neutral	Autocratic
	(n = 11)	(n = 10)	(n = 11)
Democratic	6.41	6.13	6.18
	(1.13)	(0.97)	(1.76)
Autocratic	4.43	4.26	4.19
	(0.99)	(1.04)	(1.31)

Note. Higher numbers reflect more favorable evaluations.

The effects of prime type were also moderated by the presence versus absence of ambient noise, as reflected in a two-way interaction between prime type and noise condition. This finding indicates that the effects of the prime were more pronounced under conditions of noise than under conditions of no noise, suggesting once again that increasing the need for cognitive closure magnifies the impact of accessible information on social judgment in general.

Probably the most important finding of this study, however, is the three-way interaction involving prime type, target person, and the noise manipulation of the need for closure. It appears that under conditions of noise, when people are likely to seize readily accessible notions, the democratic primes improved evaluations of democratic targets and autocratic primes improved evaluations of autocratic targets. Under conditions of no noise, the effects of the prime on evaluations of the target were considerably weaker (see Table 5.6). Thus, the results of this study suggest further that increasing the need for cognitive closure through the presentation of environmental noise leads people to rely on whatever ideological values are salient. In this case, the noise made democratically primed people more favorable toward a democratic leader (and less favorable toward an autocratic leader), and it made autocratically primed people more favorable toward an autocratic leader (and less favorable toward a democratic leader). The punch line of these studies, then, is that knowledge accessibility and epistemic motivation play a joint role in determining preferences for autocratic versus democratic leaders and procedures.

THE ROLE OF EPISTEMIC PROCESSES IN THE MAINTENANCE OF SOCIAL AND POLITICAL ORGANIZATIONS

We have argued that social cognition plays a major role in the perpetuation of social and organizational systems (e.g., Eyerman & Jamison, 1991; Jost, 1995; Kluegel & Smith, 1986; Scheff, 1990; Tyler & Smith, 1998). More specifically, we have identified a connection between the tendency to "seize" and "freeze" upon existing knowledge structures—referred to as the need for cognitive closure (Kruglanski & Webster, 1996; Webster & Kruglanski, 1994)—and the tendency to preserve the status quo by adopting attitudes that are authoritarian, politically conservative, intolerant of dissent, and discouraging of full democratic participation. These myriad judgments and evaluations may be viewed as contributing to the stability of existing social arrangements insofar as they serve the system-justifying functions of providing cognitive support for traditional forms of social organization, rationalizing inequality among social groups, and resisting opportunities for change or revision (Jost, 1995, 1996; Jost & Banaji, 1994; Stangor & Jost, 1997). In other words, factors that increase cognitive and motivational needs to make up one's mind quickly and to shorten informational searches tend also to strengthen normative and ideological adherence to the status quo, unless contrasting values of tolerance and liberalism happen to be readily accessible.

If people are committed to tolerating criticism or dissent, either because of enduring ideological values or because they are reminded temporarily of the moral value attached to political tolerance, then enhancing the need for closure is capable of producing an increase in tolerance for dissent. Thus, the need for cognitive closure might result in an erosion of support for the system under some circumstances, as when the call for social change and revolutionary action is made salient in the environment, or among certain people who are ideologically predisposed to favor social change and reject the social system. One implication of this analysis, then, is that circumstances that increase the need for closure might produce a polarization of ideological values. Under heightened need for closure, our evidence suggests that conservatives will probably become more extreme in their protection of conservative stability, progressives will probably become more extreme in their demand for progressive change, democrats will probably become more extreme in their commitment to democracy, and autocrats will probably become more extreme in their preferences for autocracy.

What are the social and organizational conditions that might be expected to increase the need for cognitive closure among people? A good deal of research, including that presented here, indicates that factors such as noise, distraction, and time pressure are especially likely to increase the need for closure (e.g., Dijker & Koomen, 1996; Kruglanski & Webster, 1996; Webster & Kruglanski, 1994). Noise, distraction, and time pressure are nearly ubiquitous features of the urban environment (Milgram, 1977) the technological age (Gergen, 1991), and the mass media (McGuire, 1986). What this means is that modern society itself produces the very conditions that lead people to "seize" and "freeze" upon existing notions without considering cognitive alternatives, even in consequential ideological domains.

Threatening economic conditions such as unemployment, inflation, recession, resource scarcity, and market uncertainty would probably also have manifestations in terms of the cognitive and motivational needs of individual citizens and corporate agents (e.g., Haunschild, 1994; Podolny, 1994; Roch & Samuelson, 1997). If Wilson (1973) is correct, anxiety and uncertainty about the future should lead one to adopt attitudes that are conservative, traditional, and resistant to change. There is a deep irony here, given that periods of harsh economic conditions are probably those that are most in need of progressive social change. When movements of change do grow out of such frustrating material circumstances, it has been observed that they often take the form of right-wing mobilizations that tend to emphasize law and order and other promises to reduce ambiguity and uncertainty (e.g., Milburn & Conrad, 1996).

Our evidence suggests that there is indeed a content-based asymmetry such that the need for cognitive closure appears to be satisfied more effectively by the emergence and maintenance of shared knowledge that is politically conservative, socially intolerant, anti-democratic, and system jus-tifying in general than by knowledge that poses a challenge to the status quo. Some evidence indicated that increasing the epistemic needs of indi-viduals to reach conclusions that are secure and stable may spark a re-newed commitment to values that are tolerant, democratic, and progres-sive, but only if these values are highly salient to the individual, either because of his or her enduring value system or because of the immediate social context. Ultimately, whether innovation and change are likely to take place in society and in institutional organizations depends on both the ideological milieu and, as our research emphasizes, the relative propensity of the individual to approach the world in an open, searching, and explora-tory fashion.

ACKNOWLEDGMENTS

All of the research reported herein was funded by NIMH Grant R01-MH52578 and NSF Grant SBR-9417422, both administered to Arie W. Kruglanski. We thank Pamela Haunschild, John M. Levine, Jeffrey Pfeffer, and Keith Rozen-dal for their helpful comments on previous drafts of this chapter. Prepara-tion of the manuscript was facilitated by Juliana A. Mott and Maureen L. Taylor.

REFERENCES

Abercrombie, N. (1980). *Class, structure, and knowledge*. New York: New York University Press.

Adorno, T. W., Frenkel-Brunswik, E., Levinson, D. J., & Sanford, R. N. (1950). *The authoritarian personality*. New York: Harper.

Allport, G. W. (1954). *The nature of prejudice*. Reading, MA: Addison-Wesley.

Altemeyer, B. (1988). *Enemies of freedom: Understanding right-wing authoritarianism*. San Francisco: Jossey-Bass.

Berger, J., Ridgeway, C., Fisek, M. H., & Norman, R. Z. (1998). The legitimation and delegitimation of power and prestige orders. *American Sociological Review, 63*, 379–405.

Berger, P., & Luckmann, T. (1967). *The social construction of reality*. New York: Doubleday/Anchor.

Carragee, K. M. (1993). A critical evaluation of debates examining the media hegemony thesis. *Western Journal of Communication, 57*, 330–348.

Dijker, A. J., & Koomen, W. (1996). Stereotyping and attitudinal effects under time pressure. *European Journal of Social Psychology, 26*, 62–74.

DiMaggio, P. J., & Powell, W. W. (1983). The iron cage revisited: Institutional isomorphism and collective rationality in organizational fields. *American Sociological Review, 48*, 147–160.

Eagly, A. H., Makhijani, M. G., & Klonsky, G. B. (1992). Gender and the evaluation of leaders: A meta-analysis. *Psychological Bulletin, 111*, 3–22.

Ellsworth, P. C., & Ross, L. (1983). Public opinion and capital punishment: A close examination of the views of abolitionists and retentionists. *Crime and Delinquency, 29*, 116–169.

Elster, J. (1989). *Nuts and bolts for the social sciences.* Cambridge, England: Cambridge University Press.

Eyerman, R., & Jamison, A. (1991). *Social movements: A cognitive approach.* University Park: Pennsylvania State University Press.

Ford, T. E., & Kruglanski, A. W. (1995). Effects of epistemic motivations on the use of accessible constructs in social judgement. *Personality and Social Psychology Bulletin, 21*, 950–962.

Gergen, K. J. (1991). *The saturated self.* New York: Basic Books.

Giddens, A. (1979). *Central problems in social theory: Action, structure and contradiction in social analysis.* Berkeley: University of California Press.

Greenberg, J., Simon, L., Pyszczynski, T., Solomon, S., & Chatel, D. (1992). Terror management and tolerance: Does mortality salience always intensify negative reactions to others who threaten one's worldview? *Journal of Personality and Social Psychology, 63*, 212–220.

Habermas, J. (1975). *Legitimation crisis.* Boston: Beacon Press.

Haunschild, P. (1994). How much is that company worth? Interorganizational relationships, uncertainty, and acquisition premiums. *Administrative Science Quarterly, 39*, 391–411.

House, J. S. (1990). Social structure and personality. In M. Rosenberg & R. H. Turner (Eds.), *Social psychology: Sociological perspectives* (pp. 525–561). New Brunswick, NJ: Transaction Publishers.

Huber, G. L., & Sorrentino, R. M. (1996). Uncertainty in interpersonal and intergroup relations: An individual-differences perspective. In R. M. Sorrentino & E. T. Higgins (Eds.), *Handbook of motivation and cognition: Foundation of social behavior* (pp. 591–619). New York: Guilford.

Jones, E. E., & Gerard, H. B. (1967). *Foundations of social psychology.* New York: Wiley.

Jost, J. T. (1995). Negative illusions: Conceptual clarification and psychological evidence concerning false consciousness. *Political Psychology, 16*, 397–424.

Jost, J. T. (1996). *Ingroup and outgroup favoritism among groups differing in socioeconomic success: Effects of perceived legitimacy and justification processes.* Unpublished doctoral dissertation, Yale University.

Jost, J. T., & Banaji, M. R. (1994). The role of stereotyping in system-justification and the production of false consciousness. *British Journal of Social Psychology, 33*, 1–27.

Katz, I., & Hass, R. G. (1988). Racial ambivalence and American value conflict: Correctional and priming studies of dual cognitive structures. *Journal of Personality and Social Psychology, 55*, 893–905.

Kelman, H. C. (1969). Patterns of personal involvement in the national system: A social-psychological analysis of political legitimacy. In J. Rosenau (Ed.), *International politics and foreign policy* (pp. 276–288). New York: The Free Press.

Kemmelmeier, M. (1997). Need for closure and political orientation among German university students. *Journal of Social Psychology, 137*, 787–789.

Kluegel, J. R., & Smith, E. R. (1986). *Beliefs about inequality: Americans' views of what is and what ought to be.* New York: deGruyter.

Kruglanski, A. W. (1989). *Lay epistemics and human knowledge: Cognitive and motivational bases.* New York: Plenum.

Kruglanski, A. W., & Freund, T. (1983). The freezing and unfreezing of lay inferences: The effects of impressional primacy, ethnic stereotyping, and numerical anchoring. *Journal of Experimental Social Psychology, 19*, 448–468.

Kruglanski, A. W., & Webster, D. W. (1991). Group members reactions to opinion deviates and conformists at varying degrees of proximity to decision deadline and of environmental noise. *Journal of Personality and Social Psychology, 61*, 215–225.

Kruglanski, A. W., & Webster, D. W. (1996). Motivated closing of the mind: "Seizing" and "freezing". *Psychological Review, 103*, 263–283.

Kruglanski, A. W., Webster, D. M., & Klem, A. (1993). Motivated resistance and openness to persuasion in the presence or absence of prior information. *Journal of Personality and Social Psychology, 65*, 861–876.

Lane, R. E. (1962). *Political ideology: Why the American common man believes what he does.* New York: The Free Press.

Lerner, M. J. (1980). *The belief in a just world: A fundamental delusion.* New York: Plenum.

MacKinnon, C. A. (1989). *Toward a feminist theory of the state.* Cambridge, MA: Harvard University Press.

Major, B., & Deaux, K. (1982). Individual differences in justice behavior. In J. Greenberg & R. Cohen (Eds.), *Equity and justice in social behavior* (pp. 43–76). London: Academic Press.

Martin, J., Scully, M., & Levitt, B. (1990). Injustice and the legitimation of revolution: Damning the past, excusing the present, and neglecting the future. *Journal of Personality and Social Psychology, 59*, 281–290.

McGuire, W. J. (1986). The myth of massive media impact: Savagings and salvagings. In G. Comstock (Ed.), *Public communication and behavior* (Vol. 1, pp. 173–257). Orlando, FL: Academic Press.

Milburn, A. M., & Conrad, D. S. (1996). *The politics of denial.* Cambridge, MA: MIT Press.

Milgram, S. (1977). *The individual in a social world: Essays and experiments.* New York: McGraw-Hill.

Mischel, W., & Peake, P. (1982). Beyond déjà vu in the search for cross-situational consistency. *Psychological Review, 89*, 730–755.

Moore, B., Jr. (1978). *Injustice: The social bases of obedience and revolt.* White Plains, NY: M. E. Sharpe.

Muller, E. N., Jukam, T. O., & Seligson, M. A. (1982). Diffuse political support and antisystem political behavior: A comparative analysis. *American Journal of Political Science, 26*, 242–261.

Neuberg, S. L., Judice, N., & West, S. G. (1997). What the need for closure scale measures and what it does not: Toward differentiating among related epistemic motives. *Journal of Personality and Social Psychology, 72*, 1396–1412.

Neuberg, S. L., & Newsom, J. T. (1993). Personal need for structure: Individual differences in the desire for simple structure. *Journal of Personality and Social Psychology, 65*, 113–131.

Ordonez, L., & Benson, L., III. (1997). Decisions under time pressure: How time constraint affects risky decision making. *Organizational Behavior and Human Decision Processes, 71*, 121–140.

Peterson, B. E., Doty, R. M., & Winter, D. G. (1993). Authoritarianism and attitudes toward contemporary social issues. *Personality and Social Psychology Bulletin, 19*, 174–184.

Pfeffer, J. (1985). Organizations and organizational theory. In G. Lindzey & E. Aronson (Eds.), *Handbook of social psychology* (3rd ed., Vol. 1, pp. 379–440). Reading, MA: Addison-Wesley.

Pfeffer, J. (1998). Understanding organizations: Concepts and controversies. In D. Gilbert, S. T. Fiske, & G. Lindzey (Eds.), *Handbook of social psychology* (4th ed., Vol. 2, pp. 733–777). New York: McGraw-Hill.

Piven, F. F., & Cloward, R. A. (1977). *Poor people's movement: Why they succeed, how they fail.* New York: Vintage Books.

Podolny, J. (1994). Market uncertainty and the social character of economic exchange. *Administrative Science Quarterly, 39*, 458–483.

Pratto, F., Sidanius, J., Stallworth, L. M., & Malle, B. F. (1994). Social dominance orientation: A personality variable predicting social and political attitudes. *Journal of Personality and Social Psychology, 67*, 741–763.

Roch, S. G., & Samuelson, C. D. (1997). Effects of environmental uncertainty and social value orientation in resource dilemmas. *Organizational Behavior and Human Decision Processes, 70*, 221–235.

Sampson, E. E. (1983). *Justice and the critique of pure psychology*. New York: Plenum.

Schaller, M., Boyd, C., Yohannes, J., & O'Brien, N. (1995). The prejudiced personality revisited: Personal need for structure and formation of erroneous group stereotypes. *Journal of Personality and Social Psychology, 68*, 544–555.

Scheff, T. J. (1990). *Microsociology: Discourse, emotion, and social structure*. Chicago: The University of Chicago Press.

Shils, E. A. (1954). Authoritarianism: "Right" and "left". In R. Christie & M. Jahoda (Eds.), *Studies in the scope and method of "The authoritarian personality"* (pp. 24–49). Glencoe, IL: The Free Press.

Sidanius, J. (1985). Cognitive functioning and sociopolitical ideology revisited. *Political Psychology, 6*, 637–662.

Sidanius, J., Pratto, F., & Bobo, L. (1996). Racism, conservatism, affirmative action, and intellectual sophistication: A matter of principled conservatism or group dominance? *Journal of Personality and Social Psychology, 70*, 476–490.

Sorrentino, R. M., & Hancock, R. D. (1986). The role of information and affective value: A case for the study of individual differences and social influence. In M. P. Zanna, J. M. Olson, & C. P. Herman (Eds.), *Social influence: The Ontario Symposium* (Vol. 5, pp. 244–268). Hillsdale, NJ: Lawrence Erlbaum Associates.

Stangor, C., & Jost, J. T. (1997). Individual, group, and system levels of analysis and their relevance for stereotyping and intergroup relations. In R. Spears, P. J. Oakes, N. Ellemers, & S. A. Haslam (Eds.), *The social psychology of stereotyping and group life* (pp. 336–358). Oxford, England: Blackwell.

Stapel, D. A. (1997). *What we talk about when we talk about knowledge accessibility effects*. Doctoral dissertation, University of Amsterdam. Amsterdam: Heap Publishers.

Tetlock, P. E. (1983). Cognitive style and political ideology. *Journal of Personality and Social Psychology, 45*, 118–126.

Tetlock, P. E., & Mitchell, G. (1993). Liberal and conservative approaches to justice: Conflicting psychological portraits. In B. A. Mellers & J. Baron (Eds.), *Psychological perspectives on justice* (pp. 235–255). Cambridge, England: Cambridge University Press.

Thompson, E. P., Roman, R. J., Moskowitz, G. B., Chaiken, S., & Bargh, J. A. (1994). Accuracy motivation attenuates covert priming: The systematic reprocessing of social information. *Journal of Personality and Social Psychology, 66*, 474–489.

Thompson, M. M., Naccarato, M. E., & Parker, K. E. (1989, June). *Assessing cognitive need: The development of the Personal Need for Structure and Personal Fear of Invalidity scales*. Paper presented at the annual meeting of the Canadian Psychological Association, Halifax, Nova Scotia.

Tyler, T. R. (1990). *Why people obey the law*. New Haven, CT: Yale University Press.

Tyler, T. R., & McGraw, K. M. (1986). Ideology and the interpretation of personal experience: Procedural justice and political quiescence. *Journal of Social Issues, 42*, 115–128.

Tyler, T. R., & Smith, H. J. (1998). Social justice and social movements. In D. Gilbert, S. T. Fiske, & G. Lindzey (Eds.), *Handbook of social psychology* (4th ed., Vol. 2, pp. 595–629). New York: McGraw-Hill.

Weatherford, M. S. (1992). Measuring political legitimacy. *American Political Science Review, 86*, 149–165.

Webster, D. M., & Kruglanski, A. W. (1994). Individual differences in need for cognitive closure. *Journal of Personality and Social Psychology, 67*, 1047–1062.

Wilson, G. D. (Ed.). (1973). *The psychology of conservatism*. London: Academic Press.

6

Accountability Theory: Mixing Properties of Human Agents With Properties of Social Systems

Philip E. Tetlock
The Ohio State University

This chapter links two levels of analysis that are only occasionally brought together: experimental work on judgment and choice and institutional analyses of accountability and power relationships. Bringing the two together does not initially look promising. Experimental work on judgment and choice typically unfolds in a political vacuum in which researchers do their best to make subjects feel as unaccountable for their opinions as possible. The goal is to reproduce the spectacular successes of the physical sciences by studying the workings of the human mind in pure form in settings that minimize the distortions of social context. Analysts of accountability and power relationships in organizations—from Weber (1922/1978) to Meyer (1983) to Williamson (1993)—have largely reciprocated the indifference, showing little curiosity about the psychology of the human agents who populate complex collectivities. The overriding questions are "who depends on whom for what?"; "what are the ground rules for evaluating both performance and accounts for nonperformance?" and "what are the consequences of acting inexcusably?" Once we understand these resource-dependency and normative constraints within which people work, we can do a fine job predicting how people will respond, with the assistance of only the crudest caricatures of human nature—certainly no need for anything fancier than variants of *homo sociologicus* (approval-seeking creatures who are highly sensitive to the appropriateness of their conduct vis-à-vis prevailing cultural rules—Meyer, 1983; Zetterberg, 1957) or variants of *homo economicus* (utility-maximizing or boundedly rational creatures who pursue their self-interest with varying degrees of ruthlessness and skill—Becker, 1996; Williamson, 1993).

This chapter takes up the challenge of convincing each camp that it has something to learn from the other. To microcognitivists, the argument in a nutshell is this: The social–political context within which people make the vast majority of decisions affects how people think, not just what people are willing to say they think (mere strategic manipulation of response thresholds). The functionalist metaphors that dominate laboratory work on judgment and choice—the intuitive scientist in the social cognition tradition (Fiske & Taylor, 1991) and the intuitive economist in the behavioral decision theory tradition (Kahneman & Tversky, 1979)—are too restrictive. Thought serves multiple, interrelated functions and one key function—communicating and justifying one's opinions to others—has been given short shrift. To macroinstitutionalists (whether they subscribe to one of the old-fashioned, role-theoretic schools of thought or to one of the new-fangled, microeconomic schools that stress problems of principal–agent coordination or transaction–cost minimization), the argument will be strikingly similar: You, too, could expand the explanatory power of your models if you worked with less restrictive models of the human agent. People need not be either norm-following automatons or amoral calculators of personal or organizational advantage. There are plenty of more psychologically nuanced options.

Working from the premise that you cannot defeat a point of view unless you advance an alternative, the first part of this chapter lays out the core assumptions and testable predictions of accountability theory. Epistemologically, the theory is of the middle-range Mertonian type. Although it rests on some quite abstract assumptions about human beings and the social worlds they inhabit, it does not dally long at these nose-bleed heights. There are fairly straightforward rules for generating specific hypotheses about how people cope with the sorts of accountability demands that frequently arise in everyday life in complex pluralistic societies. Substantively, the theory is pitched at a meso or intermediate level of analysis: The focus is on neither the individual nor on social structures but rather on the individual's relationship to social structures. The theory represents a self-conscious effort to bridge micro and macro by integrating the most robust findings and perspicacious insights from each tradition.

The second half of the chapter shifts from theory to evidence. It summarizes findings that should shake the faith of cognitivists that they can safely ignore social context and the faith of institutionalists that they can safely ignore the cognitive and emotional complexities of human agency. Herein lies the acid test for accountability theory. Any meso-level theory worth its salt should stimulate discoveries that irritate both micro and macro reductionists.

CORE PROPOSITIONS
OF ACCOUNTABILITY THEORY

Over the last 15 years, I have been developing a model of social judgment and choice (originally known as the "social contingency model"—Tetlock, 1985b, 1992) that is premised on a view of people as intuitive politicians. The central function of judgment and choice is neither to make causal sense of the world (the defining motive for intuitive scientists in attribution theory) nor to maximize profit in competitive markets (the defining motive for intuitive economists), but rather to protect one's social identity in the eyes of key constituencies. The core function of thought becomes assessing the relative justifiability of response options. Consciously or unconsciously, people often find themselves engaged in internalized dialogues of the form: "If I did this, what would others say? What could I say in return? What conclusions should reasonable observers draw about my competence or character?"

Of course, metaphors are not explanations. It does not clarify much to say that people are intuitive politicians. Some politicians have been notoriously pragmatic and flexible, capable of conjuring up compelling personas for each and every audience they care to charm or intimidate; others have earned reputations for extraordinary rigidity, an unwillingness to change their minds (or to abandon principle, defenders might say) to save their careers or even lives. Whereas there is a voluminous body of research that unpacks what it means to characterize people as intuitive scientists or economists, there is but a handful of studies that shed light on the various possible senses in which people might be said to be intuitive politicians. Accountability theory is an initial effort to fill this conceptual niche. The four foundational assumptions of the model can be summarized simply:

Accountability as a Universal Feature of Decision Environments. Accountability is a ubiquitous feature of judgment and choice outside the psychological laboratory. It links individual decision makers to the institutions within which they live and work by reminding them of the need to: (a) act in accord with prevailing norms and (b) advance compelling justifications or excuses for conduct that deviates from those norms. No social system can function for a sustained period without accountability checks on group members (Axelrod, 1984; Edgerton, 1985). Of course, social systems cannot rely exclusively on external modes of social control for maintaining order (Kramer & Tyler, 1996). The transaction costs of monitoring everybody all the time would be staggering. The theory therefore stipulates that trust and norm internalization are necessary but hardly sufficient for the smooth functioning of institutions.

Audience-Approval Motive. People seek approval for both intrinsic and extrinsic reasons. Evidence for an intrinsic motivation comes from studies that point to a propensity—that appears early in human development—to respond automatically and viscerally to frowns, angry looks, and other signs of censure. We can interpret this robust finding (Baumeister & Leary, 1995) in either a social–learning framework (over a lifetime, other people become incredibly potent secondary reinforcers via their association with primary drive reduction) or in an evolutionary framework (people have been naturally and sexually selected to be sensitive to disapproval because the survival of our ancestors hinged on maintaining the goodwill of their fellow hominids). Evidence for extrinsic motivation comes from the exchange theory tradition (Rusbult, Farrell, Rogers, & Mainous, 1988) in which people seek approval primarily in response to *asymmetric resource dependency* (other people control resources we value to a greater degree than we control resources they value).

Motive Competition. Social approval is a critical, but by no means the only operative, motive. The model identifies four additional motives that may conflict with or transform the expression of the approval motive. These include the goals of achieving cognitive mastery of causal structure (emphasized by classic attribution theory; Kelley, 1967), minimizing mental effort and achieving simple forms of closure (emphasized by theories of social cognition—Fiske & Taylor, 1991), maximizing benefits and minimizing the costs of relationships (emphasized by exchange theories—Blau, 1964), and holding true to internalized principles and convictions (emphasized by theories of ego development as well as cognitive consistency—Festinger, 1957; Loevinger, 1976). The model also posits that the five core motives vary lawfully in strength as a function of both individual differences and situational context. For example, individual difference scales such as social anxiety, public self-consciousness, self-monitoring, and need for affiliation moderate the approval motive; and scales such as need for cognition, need for closure, and tolerance for ambiguity moderate willingness to invest cognitive effort in solving accountability predicaments. Situational manipulations—like failure–success or the size of the material incentive to act opportunistically—might be thought of as altering the perceived importance of social approval or the temptation to defect, respectively; manipulations like the ability of the audience to detect sloppy or self-serving thinking should motivate complex self-critical thought; manipulations like cognitive load (distractions or time pressure) should affect decision makers' ability to engage in complex, self-critical thought.

Linking Motives to Coping Strategies. The final component of the model links broad motivational orientations to specific coping strategies by identifying how each motive can be amplified or attenuated by the interpersonal and institutional context. The conceptual formula for generating predictions from the model is to identify situational or dispositional variables that either increase or decrease the perceived importance of a motive or the perceived feasibility of achieving that motive in a given context.

From the standpoint of accountability theory, every request for justification raises the question of how one will define oneself in the eyes of either external constituencies or internalized ones. There is potential to enhance or damage one's reputation on a wide range of social identity dimensions: cooperative or confrontational, duplicitous or candid, flexible or rigid, opportunistic or principled, decisive or vacillating, a can-do implementer or chronic complainer. I now consider five identity-defining choices that frequently arise in accountability predicaments.

To Accommodate the Audience or to Be True to One's Self. One basic identity-defining question is whether one will accommodate one's attitudes to others or be true to one's inner convictions (Cialdini, Levy, Herman, Kozlowski, & Petty, 1976; Jones & Wortman, 1973; Tetlock, 1983a). Attitude shifting is likely to the degree the approval motive is strong: The audience should be powerful (it should control resources that the decision maker values but the decision maker should control little that the audience values) and the audience should be firmly committed to its position and intolerant of other positions (a further incentive for accommodation). Attitude shifting is, however, a feasible strategy only to the degree that one knows the views of the anticipated audience and attitude shifting becomes a psychologically costly strategy to the degree that it requires compromising basic convictions (triggering dissonance) and it becomes socially costly to the degree that it requires backtracking on past commitments (making one look duplicitous or sycophantic to others). But when these preconditions have been satisfied, attitude shifting represents a cognitively efficient, politically expedient strategy that undermines neither one's self-concept as a principled being nor one's reputation for integrity in the wider social arena.

Self-Criticism Versus Self-Justification. Another identity-defining choice requires positioning oneself on the flexibility–rigidity (opportunism–principled) dimension. One can respond to accountability by trying to anticipate reasonable objections of critics and factoring them into one's own position (hence pre-emptive self-criticism) or one can direct mental effort toward generating plausible reasons that bolster one's own position (hence self-justifying). In each case, accountability motivates thought but in the former coping strategy, the thoughts take a dialectically complex form (on the one hand, ... on the other ...) and in the latter, the thoughts tend to be evaluatively simple (all run in support or opposition to one theme).

Accountability theory predicts pre-emptive self-criticism when: (a) decision makers are accountable either to an audience with unknown views (there is thus reason to anticipate objections from both ends of the political spectrum) or to two audiences with conflicting views who recognize the legitimacy of the other point of view (there is thus reason to search for complex compromise solutions); (b) decision makers perceive the audience or audiences to be powerful (and equally powerful if more than one audience); (c) decision makers perceive the audience or audiences to be cognitively sophisticated (and equally sophisticated if more than one audience); (d) decision makers do not hold strong private views and are unconstrained by public commitments.

Defensive bolstering, the cognitive mirror image of pre-emptive self-criticism, is most likely to be activated when decision makers: (a) are accountable to powerful audiences that are not believed to be knowledgeable about the topic; (b) are accountable for past statements as acts that cast some doubt on their competitiveness or morality and that cannot be retracted or reversed; (c) recognize that it is impossible to deny responsibility for the conduct in question.

To Duck, to Mediate or to Plunge Into Controversy. People are often accountable not just to a single audience but to two or more audiences who may disagree deeply over what should be done. Accountability theory posits that people cope with contradictory constituency demands in one of three distinct ways. First, people may engage in decision avoidance which, in turn, can take three forms: buck-passing (transferring responsibility to others), procrastination (delaying the decision), and obfuscation (shrouding one's position in opaque bureaucratic language). These decision-avoidance tactics are especially likely when the conflicting constituencies are powerful and roughly equally so, the constituencies deny the legitimacy of the other point of view (an apparently irreconcilable conflict), there are no institutional precedents for evading taking a stand, and decision makers' own views are relatively weak. A second strategy—align oneself with one or another constituency—becomes tempting when the conflicting constituencies deny each other's legitimacy, there are no institutional precedents for decision avoidance, one audience is more powerful than the other and favors a position similar to one's own preference, and the decision makers themselves hold strong views to which they are publicly committed. A third strategy—try to mediate the conflict—is likely to be activated when the disputants are both powerful and equally powerful, they acknowledge the legitimacy of the other point of view (so the conflict appears, in principle, to be resolvable) and there are no precedents for decision evasion.

To Implement or Resist the Collective Mission? Thus far, the focus has been on contexts in which people feel accountable for verbal opinions or preferences but not for actual work performance (be it assembling more widgets, upping billable hours for the firm, or generating more publications for tenure). In work settings, the identity-defining choice is often particularly painful: between good organizational citizenship (which may require enormous commitments of time and energy) and resisting the performance standards (which may jeopardize one's livelihood).

Accountability theory identifies a set of optimal preconditions for promoting internalization of new performance-appraisal standards, including the perception that the standards are high but reasonably so, the perception that everyone must work hard, that the standards were set through fair procedures, the belief that the standards are indeed necessary for the survival of the organization, and the prior existence of strong normative commitments to good citizenship within the organization. Accountability theory also identifies conditions for promoting covert or overt forms of resistance. Resistance is especially likely when people perceive that the standards were: (a) unreasonably high (employees see no method of achieving them that does not involve either unethical conduct or superhuman effort); (b) set in a procedurally unjust manner (employees feel their point of view was ignored); (c) not essential for organizational survival (but rather work to the advantage of some small group—such as top management—within the organization). The preferred first line of resistance is some variant of the voice option. Drawing on the arguments of Hirschman (1970) and the evidence of Tyler (1990), accountability theory predicts that people (especially those high in self-esteem and whose sense of fair play has been violated) will take advantage of opportunities to protest burdensome standards, to offer accounts for performance shortfalls, and to appeal to higher authorities. Accountability theory also predicts that the availability of opportunities to exercise the voice option will both enhance the legitimacy of the accountability regime and reduce the sense of anger triggered by the imposition of unfair performance standards (cf. Tyler 1990).

The mere existence of the voice option can reinforce loyalty to the system. Eliminating the voice option triggers more destructive forms of resistance that undermine both organizational loyalty and efficiency. People may express their resentment either by remaining within the organization (and engaging in corner-cutting or disengaging from their role responsibilities) or by exiting the organization. Corner-cutting is the preferred coping response when people are alienated from the accountability regime and perceive large loopholes in performance appraisal standards, regard dismissal as highly unlikely and exit as highly unattractive. Exit is the preferred coping response when people are alienated from the accountability regime, see no loopholes to be exploited, and regard dismissal for nonperformance as likely and exit as more attractive than the status quo (cf. Rusbult et al., 1988; Withey & Cooper, 1989).

When all six forms of resistance to illegitimate accountability regimes have been blocked, the theory predicts grudging compliance—a prediction consistent with Withey and Cooper's (1989) portrait of some loyalists as "entrapped persons" who have abandoned hope of successfully exercising either the voice or exit options. Grudging compliance is typically a less satisfactory outcome (from an organizational perspective) than internalization of the accountability mandate. Grudging compliance carries a high price tag in terms of demoralization of work force (the feeling of being treated with contempt and intrusively monitored) as well as in terms of transaction and implementation costs (the agents of social control need to be continually on guard that subordinates have not come up with new ingenious strategies for identifying loopholes, disengaging from their roles, or appealing to external authorities). In the spirit of a long line of social theorists—from Weber to Parsons to Hirschmann—accountability theory affirms that effectively functioning social systems are populated by people who are motivated to do the right thing even when no one is watching.

Diffusing Sacrifice Versus Concentrating Pain. A burdensome requirement of managerial roles in both the private and public sectors is the task of implementing budget cuts. One strategy is to spread the required sacrifice across many constituencies, thereby avoiding severe impact on any one constituency. Another is to target the budget cuts on a small subset of constituencies that might be chosen on efficiency grounds (the least productive) or on political grounds (the least connected). The theory predicts that decision makers who have internalized egalitarian values should be especially likely to spread the sacrifice widely when the budget cut is relatively small (few will notice the pain if it is spread across the board), when it is difficult to identify distinctive pockets of inefficiency (making it hard to justify singling anyone out), and when the groups that have been singled out for deep budget cuts in the past have demonstrated a formidable ability to mobilize political protest when roused to wrath. By contrast, decision makers who have internalized the neoclassical economic value of efficiency (and fear "demosclerosis"—Rauch, 1994) should concentrate cuts on specific constituencies to the degree they confront large budget cuts, can easily distinguish more from less efficient work units, and know that groups singled out for deep budget cuts have little capacity to resist.

IMPLICATIONS OF ACCOUNTABILITY THEORY FOR THE MICRO AND MACRO LEVELS OF ANALYSIS

Meso-level theories are subject to attack from two contradictory directions: from micro theorists who doubt that fundamental psychological principles are transformed in any noteworthy fashion in organizational or political settings and by macro theorists who doubt that well documented regularities of social systems will be appreciably altered by delving into lower-level phenomena. Advocates of meso-level theories (such as myself) have a difficult job in convincing these skeptics that the "epistemic value-added" offsets the loss of parsimony that both micro and macro variants of reductionism have to offer.

Lessons for Cognitivists

Some cognitive theorists—let us call them cognitive fundamentalists as a shorthand—suspect that accountability theory has little to contribute to our understanding of human thought. These scholars invoke an implicit disciplinary division of labor originally proposed by Miller and Dollard (1946), in which experimental psychologists dedicate themselves to discovering basic laws of thought and action, whereas social scientists tackle the task of documenting the cultural and political content (expectancies, norms, beliefs, and values) on which the basic laws operate. From this standpoint, accountability theory may shed light on what people think or at least on what people say they think but it sheds no light on how people think. These basic—it is tempting to call them "presocial"—laws such as psychophysical principles of perception or associationist principles of connectionist networks are poor prospects to be affected by social pressures to justify one's views to others (cf. Arkes, 1991).

The extent to which the cognitive fundamentalists are right is, in one sense, a definitional issue. It surely is possible to identify some features of information processing—perceptual contrast effects, for example—that are unaffected by social context. But it is extremely implausible to dismiss all accountability effects as mere public posturing (for a comprehensive review, see Lerner & Tetlock, 1999). Five methodologically distinct lines of evidence now converge on the conclusion that accountability affects not only what people think, but also how they think:

Pre- Versus Post-Exposure-to-Evidence Accountability. If accountability simply influences response thresholds (turning people, for example, into cautious fence sitters reluctant to stray from the safe midpoints of attitude scales), it should not matter when people learn of being accountable. But if accountability influences how people initially encode and draw inferences from evidence, its effects should be much more pronounced when people learn of being accountable before exposure to the evidence on which they are basing their judgments. Studies of overattribution (Tetlock, 1985a), primacy effects (Tetlock, 1983b), and overconfidence (Kassin, Castillo, & Rigby, 1991; Tetlock & Kim, 1987) all suggest that: (a) preexposure accountability is a substantially more potent de-biasing manipulation than is postexposure accountability, and (b) its debiasing effectiveness is at least partly mediated by its power to motivate effort-demanding self-critical thought.

Canceling the Anticipated Accountability Session. If accountability merely affects response thresholds, such effects should disappear as soon as people learn that the anticipated interview session will be canceled. But audience-induced shifts in beliefs and attitudes often persist even after the anticipated interview with the evaluative audience has been canceled (Cialdini et al., 1976; Lerner, Goldberg, & Tetlock, 1998; Pennington & Schlenker, 1996).

Structural Complexity of Confidential Thought Protocols. Relative to unaccountable subjects, accountable subjects often report more complex patterns of argumentation (thoughts that have a dialectical "on the one hand" vs. "on the other" quality to them) in response to thought-protocol measures, notwithstanding strong assurances of confidentiality that minimize concerns for impression management (Tetlock, Skitka, & Boettger, 1989).

Accountability × Cognitive Load Effects. Cognitive-load manipulations such as distraction and time pressure often disrupt accountability effects in exactly the ways one would expect if the ways that suggest that the underlying processes require active attention and effort (Kruglanski & Freund, 1983). If people coped with accountability by engaging solely in low effort or mindless adjustments of response thresholds, cognitive load should not interfere with these effects.

Complex Patterns of Effects. Accountability often has rather differentiated effects on dependent variables that are difficult to dismiss as simple response-threshold adjustments: improving calibration of confidence without degrading resolution in confidence-setting tasks (Siegal-Jacobs & Yates, 1996; Tetlock & Kim, 1987), reducing dispositional attributions in low-choice conditions of essay attribution paradigms but not in high-choice conditions (Tetlock, 1985a), and enhancing differential-accuracy scores in person perception (Tetlock & Kim, 1987).

Accountability theory should interest cognitivists in part because it clarifies empirical boundary conditions on the cognitive-miser portrait of human nature: It specifies when people can be motivated to be thoughtful and resistant to various cognitive biases. But accountability theory should also be of interest because it suggests normative boundary conditions on the cognitive-miser portrait. It does so by raising troublesome questions concerning when cognitive theorists are justified in labeling response tendencies—such as overattribution, overconfidence, and dilution—as errors or biases (cf. Tetlock, Lerner, & Boettger, 1996). The intuitive politician metaphor warns us that observers of varying ideological or intellectual persuasion will often disagree over what constitutes both cognitive bias and appropriate accountability correctives. What counts as rational will often be tightly coupled to one's view of human nature and of the good society. Consider the potential for attaching opposing value spins on each of the coping strategies reviewed earlier:

1. Strategic attitude shifting might be applauded by collectivists as tactful and diplomatic or deplored by individualists as duplicitous; conversely, self-expression might be denounced as insensitive or commended as honest and candid;

2. Pre-emptive self-criticism could be praised as a thoughtful and balanced approach to problems that protects people from cognitive biases such as overattribution, overconfidence, and belief perseverance (Tetlock, 1992) or it could be viewed with suspicion, as a sign of mental confusion (increased susceptibility to the dilution effect—Tetlock & Boettger, 1989) or timidity (increased loss aversion—Tetlock & Boettger, 1994—and unwillingness to punish aggressors in mixed-motive games—Tetlock, McGuire, & Mitchell, 1991);

3. Defensive bolstering could be praised as principled or decisive (Suedfeld, 1992) or condemned as a rigid, self-righteous style of thinking that promotes escalating commitment to projects with large sunk costs (Staw, 1980);

4. Decision evasion strategies could be viewed as manifestations of (appropriate) modesty about one's competence to make certain judgment calls or as moral cowardice (Tetlock & Boettger, 1994);

5. Exercising the voice option could be seen as legitimate protest and justified assertiveness or as whiny and self-serving;

6. Loophole exploitation might be derided as fraudulent or depicted more dispassionately as an understandable—if not laudable—effort by employees to assert some meager measure of control in their bleak Dickensian lives;

7. The exit option might be viewed as desertion and organizational treason or as a rational response to signals from the labor market.

In short, the law of perverse consequences seems to hold. For every cognitive bias or behavioral pathology that accountability attenuates, there seems to be a mirror-image bias or pathology that accountability exacerbates. The intuitive-politician metaphor reminds us of the inherent contestability of claims of cognitive bias and irrationality.

Lessons for Institutionalists

Institutional theorists—from Weber (1922/1978) to Jensen and Meckling (1976) to Williamson (1993)—have often exhibited every bit as cavalier an attitude toward psychological assumptions as cognitive fundamentalists have toward social context. In this view, once we know the economic inter-dependencies and normative ground rules that bind actors to each other, we have no need for differentiated psychological models of the human agent (see March & Olsen, 1998, for a synoptic overview of such formulations). It is sufficient for advocates of *homo sociologicus* to posit that people are socially sensitive creatures who are attuned prevailing norms and rhetorical conventions for legitimating action and for advocates of *homo economicus* to posit that people are relentless opportunists who create and comply with prevailing norms only insofar as compliance facilitates the pursuit of tangible material outcomes.

Institutional theorists make a mistake, however, if they think they can indefinitely get by with such sketchy and stereotyped assumptions about the human agents who populate collectivities. They will run into difficulties, arguably insuperable ones, when circumstances require making assumptions about how these agents will cope with cross-pressures—situations in which external normative principles conflict with each other or with material incentives or with internalized beliefs about fairness and ideological convictions. Here we discover the usefulness of a more nuanced view of humanity: To predict which of these competing influences is likely to prevail, under what conditions, and for which subgroups of respondents, we need to draw on theories of ambivalence and decision conflict (Festinger, 1957; Janis & Mann, 1977), theories of distributive and procedural justice (Tyler & Smith, 1998), dual-process theories of social cognition (Fiske & Neuberg, 1990; Kruglanski & Webster, 1996), and theories of emotion (Frijda, 1988) and taxonomies of individual differences (John, 1990)—all from which accountability theory borrows quite liberally.

Accountability theory posits that as long as people believe that the social contract linking them to the organization is being honored (leaders are respecting internal norms of distributive and procedural justice as well as the rules of the broader society), most people will approximate the ideal type of *homo sociologicus*, responding to routine problems on normative autopilot (analogous to Langer, Blank, & Chanowitz, 1978, mindless scripted processing). When the psychological bond between the individual and the collective is, however, challenged—as occurs when decision makers are caught in cross-pressures in which constituencies make demands that either contradict each other or decision makers' internalized values—accountability theory predicts that people will shift into cognitive high gear—into vigilant modes of information processing that produce heightened awareness of complex cues, willingness to change one's mind in response to probative evidence, and tolerance for dissonance and trade-offs. But vigilance need not lead to counternormative conduct. Inasmuch as people conclude that the organization is still treating them in a fundamentally fair fashion, cross-pressures may energize cognitive and social efforts to contribute to collective goals—trying hard, for example, to craft integratively complex compromises between constituencies who disagree deeply or are looking for creative means of achieving burdensome new performance requirements. Vigilance induced by cross-pressures leads to deviance only when it is coupled with cognitive assessments that one has been treated contemptuously and that, in turn, trigger emotional reactions of anger and indignation. Here, accountability theory warns that cross-pressures will encourage coping strategies among individuals that may be detrimental to organizational survival. Subordinates who feel subject to unfair accountability regimes will direct less cognitive effort toward solving serious collective problems and more effort toward designing stratagems of decision avoidance (buck-passing, procrastination, and obfuscation), of protest and excuse making (the voice options), of loophole exploitation, and of exiting the organization altogether. In short, people will devote less thought to their jobs and more thought to how to paralyze, sabotage or leave the organization—hardly a good omen for the efficiency or stability of the unit.

This chapter focuses on three specific cases of cross-pressures:

1. How people cope with accountability to conflicting constituencies who may be of equal or unequal power and who may or may not respect each other. Accountability theory tells us when to expect strategic entry into interpersonal alliances, decision evasion tactics (buck-passing, procrastination, and obfuscation), when to expect coalition building, and when to expect integrative problem solving;

2. How people cope with accountability to demanding performance standards that they do or do not perceive as legitimate and that can or cannot be appealed. Accountability theory tells us when to expect internalization of the standard and good faith efforts to achieve it and when to expect overt or covert forms of resistance to authority that include exercising variants of the voice option (such as protest, offering justifications and excuses, and appealing to higher authorities), exploiting loopholes in the performance appraisal system, and exercising the exit option;

3. How people cope with accountability in resource allocation tasks in which specific and general interests collide (creating the threat of demo-sclerotic policy choices—Olson, 1982) or in which equality versus efficiency collide (thus activating what Okun, 1975, called the big trade-off).

Testing the full array of predictions derivable from accountability theory will obviously be a long-term, multimethod undertaking that will require lab simulations, interviews and surveys, content analysis, and ethnographic case studies. I focus here on one particular method for testing the expanded version of accountability theory presented here: a questionnaire study of private and public sector managers (n = 259) that probes how they would respond in hypothetical situations in which the antecedent conditions for various coping strategies have been systematically activated or de-activated (for more empirical details, see Tetlock, 1998).

Accountability to Conflicting Managers

This scenario asked respondents to role play a purchasing agent accountable to two senior managers, one intent on minimizing cost even at the risk of slighting quality and the other intent on maximizing quality even if that proves expensive. The 2^3 factorial design manipulated: (a) relative power—the managers were either equally powerful or one was more powerful than the other; (b) political polarization—the feuding managers either did or did not recognize the legitimacy of the other's point of view; (c) the legitimacy of decision evasion—respondents learned that the previous incumbent in their job had always taken direct responsibility for these types of purchasing decisions or had developed an elaborate system for diffusing responsibility onto outside consultants.

We then asked managers how they thought they would respond and how they thought most other managers would respond in this situation (the two types of rating-scale judgments correlated .44). The results revealed that: (a) decision makers who were accountable to two equally powerful managers with irreconcilable perspectives were most likely to adopt the decision-evasion options of buck-passing, procrastination, and obfuscation. This finding is consistent with the mental-manager postulate of accountability theory—why go to all the cognitive work, and assume all the political risk, of developing an integrative solution when the prospects of acceptance are so dim; (b) decision makers who were accountable to conflicting audiences of unequal power who do not recognize each other's legitimacy often aligned themselves with the audience they considered more powerful (in essence, a variant of strategic attitude shifting); (c) decision makers who were accountable to two equally powerful managers with contradictory but potentially reconcilable perspectives tried to mediate the conflicts via integrative problem solving. Only when there are reasonable prospects for viable compromise and when neither party can be safely ignored should we expect intuitive politicians to invest the cognitive and political effort into developing integratively complex solutions. Here, again, we find evidence that people are reasonably prudent cognitive managers who deploy scarce mental resources in accountability predicaments only when they think it will make a difference.

At this juncture, critics might raise a familiar objection: We are merely measuring socially desirable posturing in our questionnaires. To be sure, it is true that subjects are more likely to attribute the more attractive coping response of integrative problem solving to themselves than to other managers and are more willing to assign to other managers the less attractive coping responses of buck-passing, procrastination, and coalition building than to themselves. But putting aside this not-too-surprising effect, respondents do sometimes endorse socially undesirable coping strategies. There is a surge of anger and of willingness to endorse these deviant responses for oneself and even more so for other managers when people feel that they have fallen into a fundamentally unfair accountability regime (cf. Rousseau, 1995) that, for example, places its employees in the middle of an irreconcilable conflict between two senior supervisors. The organization has broken faith with them and they now feel justified in resorting to coping strategies that in other contexts they would have deemed less than honorable. Structural equation modeling bears this claim out: Accountability to irreconcilable constituencies increases decision evasion disproportionately among respondents who perceive the situation to be deeply unfair and who report anger at the organization for allowing such a situation to emerge. The unfairness of the accountability regime justified, in the eyes of about 40% of respondents, resorting to the coping tactics that pretest subjects from the same population judged to be unprofessional and even cowardly: passing the buck, procrastinating, and creating ambiguity about where they really stand (smoke-and-mirrors obfuscatory tactics).

Accountability to Rising Performance Standards

Three vignettes explored responses to accountability for achieving rising performance standards. The first vignette asked managers to imagine a scenario in which their immediate supervisor had indicated that their work unit would now be accountable for achieving dramatically higher minimal performance standards. The 2^3 design manipulated: (a) the severity of the threat to organizational survival—Managers were told that these new performance standards were widely believed to be essential for the long-term viability of the organization. Other times, respondents believed that the guidelines were not a response to any imminent threat but were simply part of a precautionary strategy to pre-empt threats that may emerge in the future; (b) the perceived legitimacy of the standard-setting process—Some managers thought that there had been careful consultation with employees to ensure that the standards were judged as fair. Other times, the managers thought the standards had been imposed by administrative fiat; (c) the perceived feasibility of attaining the new standard within managers' own work units—Sometimes managers were told that the standard could be achieved by fairly straightforward restructuring of work roles and other times they were told that the standard would be extremely difficult to achieve even if sweeping layoffs were implemented and already productive employees were placed under even more pressure.

Two accountability theory predictions were supported: (a) the strongest internalization of the performance standard ("make the organization's goals my goals") occurred among decision makers who saw the standard as dictated by economic necessity, as reached in a procedurally fair fashion that treated them with respect, and as attainable with available resources; (b) the strongest resistance to the standard—endorsement of the protest option—occurred when people perceive the standard to have been economically unnecessary, procedurally unjust, and unattainable with available resources. Mediational analysis suggested that willingness to protest was almost entirely driven by both perceptions of the illegitimacy of the new standard and emotional reactions of anger at being treated in so cavalier and capricious a fashion by senior management.

The next scenario further explored responses to unjust accountability. Here, all subjects were led to believe that the procedures for setting standards had not been fair; that the threats to organizational survival had not been compelling; and that the prognosis for achieving the new standards, even with wrenching reforms, had been poor (the least conducive conditions for internalization). Accountability theory now predicts smoldering resentment of the new accountability regime that should take either active or passive forms. The vignette explored three preconditions in a 2^3 factorial design for activating resistance tactics: whether decision makers believe that their immediate superiors will listen to protests against the arbitrariness of the standards or to excuses and justifications for performance shortfalls and whether decision makers believe it is feasible to appeal to higher authorities. The results revealed that decision makers appealed to higher authorities only when they perceived all voice options with respect to immediate supervisors—protests, excuses, and justifications—to be futile. Of special interest here, however, is how respondents coped when all variants of the voice option had been experimentally foreclosed. Here we observed a surge of interest in locating and exploiting loopholes in the performance appraisal system. This was true, moreover, even though pretest subjects rated loophole exploitation—in plain language, cheating—as the least acceptable of all the coping strategies. Accordingly, it is especially instructive that approximately 30% of respondents were prepared to endorse this option to an appreciable degree when they felt that the organization viewed their point of view as utterly inconsequential. Once again, mediational analysis showed that: (a) people who endorsed the socially undesirable option reported greater anger and more intense perceptions of unfairness; (b) the impact of eliminating voice options on loophole exploitation was largely mediated by these emotional and perceptual reactions.

The third scenario in this sequence drove managers to further points of hypothetical desperation. Here we depicted the rising performance standards as illegitimate and also foreclosed all variants of the voice option by informing subjects that there was no willingness among upper management to heed protests or to consider justifications or excuses for performance shortfalls and there was no opportunity to appeal to a higher authority (no voice as a constant background condition). We then manipulated the feasibility of three resistance tactics in a 2^3 design: (a) loophole exploitation (by telling managers that the performance standards did or did not contain loopholes that permitted low-effort solutions); (b) role disengagement (by telling managers that they could or could not be easily fired for failing to achieve the new performance standards); (c) exit (by telling managers to assume that they could or could not easily find just as good a job as their current one in the external labor market). The results revealed that when managers believed that the exit option had been foreclosed and that they could be easily dismissed for failing to achieve the demanding new standards, they were most willing to endorse the least socially desirable of all the coping strategies (loophole exploitation; about 35% endorsement of 5 or greater on a 9-point scale). Curiously, however, when managers believed that all three additional resistance strategies had been foreclosed—loophole exploitation, role disengagement, and exit—there was a significant increase in internalization of the accountability mandate. We call this coping strategy "bitter compliance" because managers remain as convinced as their counterparts who are cheating, resigning, or sinking into tenured apathy that the regime is unfair and remain as angry about the situation as do the others. But when the illegitimate accountability regime becomes efficiently oppressive and there is no viable exit option, we observe a dissociation of the intrapsychic correlates of overt or covert rebellion in other contexts and behavioral intentions (cf. Withey & Cooper, 1989). People with their hypothetical backs up against the wall will do what they perceive as necessary for their social and financial survival.

Accountability for Resource Allocation Decisions

The final scenario also takes the form of a 2^3 factorial, this time manipulating the size of the budget cut that managers must implement (the pain of a small cut can be more easily distributed across many constituencies than the pain of a large cut), the difficulty of distinguishing more efficient from less efficient production units (the easier it is to single out pockets of inefficiency, the easier it is to justify targeting budget cuts in that sector), and the capacity of potential targets of budget cuts to mount embarrassing protests if they feel they have been hit too hard.

Here both the political orientations of managers and their work experience in the private versus public sectors moderated the attractiveness of the "equality heuristic" (Messick, 1993) as a strategy of coping with budget cuts. Relative to conservatives, liberal public-sector managers diffused budget cuts across many constituencies, especially when they could invoke the double-barreled justification, "it is hard to single out the inefficient and if we try, there will be a big political stink." Relative to liberals, conservative private-sector managers concentrated budget cuts on the inefficient, especially when they were easy to identify and were politically impotent. Whereas conservatives found the decision process relatively easy and straightforward, liberals reported more ambivalence-related distress and generated more complex trade-off cognitions. Further evidence that liberals found the budget-cutting role more inherently conflicted was their greater interest in transferring responsibility for making decisions to "a committee that includes a representative cross-section of managers within the organization." Conservatives were quite content to let this particular buck stop with them.

CONCLUDING REMARKS

Skeptics can raise a host of obvious objections to the scenario methodology employed here. Moreover, they are right: The findings cry out for conceptual replication in both lab and field research designs that rely less heavily on self-report responses to hypothetical scenarios. The current project is best viewed as but a preliminary effort to extend the largely laboratory-based literature into more macro settings where accountability demands often take more subtle and complex forms. But these obligatory disclaimers to the side, the data are consistent with the general logic of accountability theory, which depicts people as intuitive politicians who are possessed by contradictory motives (the quest for constituency approval frequently conflicts with such goals as minimizing mental effort and preserving one's self-image as an autonomous being worthy of respect). The data are also consistent with a cognitive portrait of the intuitive politician as a creature with a capacity to deploy its limited cognitive resources in flexible and strategic ways (people as mental managers rather than cognitive misers). The accountability relationships within which we are embedded can direct thought down a variety of psychological paths: toward attitude shifting or candid self-revelation; toward self-justification or self-criticism; toward internalization of organizational goals or exploring the options of protest, subversion, and exiting the relationship; and toward seeking out viable integrative solutions or developing rationalizations for evading responsibility and for engaging in office politics and coalition building. If our goal is to link micro theories of social cognition with macro theories of institutions—to develop meso-level theories of sociocognitive functioning—accountability theory is a reasonable step toward that end.

A closing comment: A good meso-level theory of judgment and choice should be a nuisance. It should circumscribe and occasionally overturn generalizations on which micro and macro theorists stake their reputations. Accountability theory passes the nuisance test in several interrelated ways. It should vex cognitivists by highlighting: (a) when social pressures to justify one's views motivate complex, self-critical thought that confers immunity to well-replicated cognitive biases; (b) the degree to which judgments of cognitive bias hinge on one's ideological or theoretical outlook (what looks cognitively dysfunctional may be politically functional—at least from certain points of view). It should vex institutionalists by highlighting when both *homo sociologicus* and *homo economicus* prove inadequate (at least underspecified) guides for predicting how people cope with complex political and organizational dilemmas of accountability. People often eschew efficiency goals that violate internalized norms of distributive or procedural justice and they often violate organizational norms when they feel the organization has shown a cavalier disregard for their point of view. Cognitive, emotional, and behavioral responses to accountability regimes depend, in no small measure, on how people feel about how they have been treated.

ACKNOWLEDGMENTS

Preparation of this chapter was assisted by National Science Foundation grant SBR #732396, by the Mershon Center of The Ohio State University and by the Institute of Personality and Social Research of the University of California, Berkeley.

REFERENCES

Arkes, H. R. (1991). Costs and benefits of judgment errors: Implications for debiasing. *Psychological Bulletin, 110*, 486–498.

Axelrod, R. M. (1984). *The evolution of cooperation*. New York: Basic Books.

Baumeister, R. F., & Leary, M. F. (1995). The need to belong: Desire for interpersonal attachments as a fundamental human motive. *Psychological Bulletin, 117*, 497–529.

Becker, G. (1996). *The economic way of looking at behavior: The Nobel lecture*. Stanford, CA: Hoover Institution on War, Revolution, and Peace, Stanford University.

Blau, P. M. (1964). *Exchange and power in social life*. New York: Wiley.

Cialdini, R. B., Levy, A., Herman, C. P., Kozlowski, I. T., & Petty, R. E. (1976). Elastic shifts of opinion: Determinants of direction and durability. *Journal of Personality and Social Psychology, 34*, 663–672.

Edgerton, R. B. (1985). *Rules, exceptions, and social order*. Berkeley: University of California Press.

Festinger, L. (1957). *A theory of cognitive dissonance*. Stanford, CA: Stanford University Press.

Fiske, S. T., & Neuberg, S. L. (1990). A continuum of impression formation, from category-based to individuating processes: Influence of information and motivation on attention and interpretations. In M. P. Zanna (Ed.), *Advances in experimental social psychology*, (Vol. 23, pp. 1–74). New York: Academic Press.

Fiske, S. T., & Taylor, S. (1991). *Social cognition*. New York: McGraw-Hill.

Frijda, N. H. (1988). The laws of emotion. *American Psychologist, 43*, 349–358.

Hirschman, A. O. (1970). *Exit, voice, and loyalty: Responses to decline in firms, organizations, and states.* Cambridge, MA: Harvard University Press.

Janis, I. L., & Mann, L. (1977). *Decision making: A psychological analysis of conflict, choice, and commitment.* New York: The Free Press.

Jensen, M., & Meckling, W. (1976). Theory of the firm: Managerial behavior, agency costs, and ownership structure. *Journal of Financial Economics, 3*, 305–360.

John, O. P. (1990). The "Big Five" factor taxonomy: Dimensions of personality in the natural language and in questionnaires. In L. A. Pervin (Ed.), *Handbook of personality: Theory and research* (pp. 66–100). New York: Guilford.

Jones, E. E., & Wortman, C. (1973). *Ingratiation: An attributional approach.* Morristown, NJ: General Learning Press.

Kahneman, D., & Tversky, A. (1979). Prospect theory: An analysis of decision under risk. *Econometrica, 47*, 263–291.

Kassin, S. M., Castillo, S. R., & Rigby, S. (1991). The accuracy-confidence correlation in eyewitness testimony: Limits and extensions of the retrospective self-awareness effect. *Journal of Personality and Social Psychology, 5*, 698–707.

Kelley, H. H. (1967). Attribution theory in social psychology. In D. Levine (Ed.), *Nebraska Symposium on Motivation* (Vol. 15, pp. 192–240). Lincoln: University of Nebraska Press.

Kramer, R. M., & Tyler, T. R. (Eds.). (1996). *Trust in organizations: Frontiers of theory and research.* Thousand Oaks, CA: Sage.

Kruglanski, A. W., & Webster, D. (1996). Motivated closing of the mind: Seizing and freezing. *Psychological Review, 103*, 263–268.

Kruglanski, A. W., & Freund, T. (1983). The freezing and unfreezing of lay-inferences: Effects on impressional primacy, ethnic stereotyping, and numerical anchoring. *Journal of Experimental Social Psychology, 19*, 448–468.

Langer, E. J., Blank, A., & Chanowitz, B. (1978). The mindlessness of ostensibly thoughtful action: The role of 'placebic' information in interpersonal interaction. *Journal of Personality and Social Psychology, 36*, 635–642.

Lerner, J., Goldberg, J., & Tetlock, P. E. (in press). Sober second thought: The effects of accountability, anger, and authoritarianism on attributions of responsibility. *Personality and Social Psychology Bulletin.*

Lerner, J., & Tetlock, P. E. (in press). Accounting for the effects of accountability. *Psychological Bulletin.*

Loevinger, J. (1976). *Ego development—conceptions and theories.* San Francisco: Jossey-Bass.

March, J. G., & Olsen, J. (in press). The institutional dynamics of international political orders. *International Organization.*

Messick, D. M. (1993). Equality as a decision heuristic. In B. Mellers & J. Baron (Eds.), *Psychological perspectives on justice* (pp. 11–31). New York: Cambridge University Press.

Meyer, J. W. (1983). Conclusion: Institutionalization and the rationality of formal organizational structure. In J. W. Meyer & W. R. Scott (Eds.), *Organizational environments: Ritual and rationality* (pp. 261–282). Beverly Hills, CA.: Sage.

Miller, N. E. & Dollard, J. (1946). *Social learning and imitation.* New Haven, CT: Yale University Press

Okun, A. M. (1975). *Equality and efficiency, the big trade-off.* Washington, DC: Brookings Institution.

Olson, M. (1982). *The rise and decline of nations: Economic growth, stagflation, and social rigidities.* New Haven, CT: Yale University Press.

Pennington, J., & Schlenker, B. R. (1996). *Accountability for consequential decisions: Justifying ethical judgments to audiences.* Unpublished manuscript.

Rauch, J. (1994). *Demosclerosis: The silent killer of American government.* New York: Times Books.

Rousseau, D. M. (1995). *Psychological contracts in organizations: Understanding written and unwritten agreements.* Thousand Oaks, CA: Sage.

Rusbult, C. E., Farrell, D., Rogers, G., & Mainous, A. G. (1988). Impact of exchange variables on exit, voice, loyalty, and neglect: An integrative model of responses to declining job satisfaction. *Academy of Management Journal, 31,* 599–627.

Siegel-Jacobs, K., & Yates, J. F. (1996). Effects of procedural and outcome accountability on judgment quality. *Organizational Behavior and Human Decision Processes, 65*(1), 1–17.

Staw, B. M. (1980). Rationality and justification in organizational life. In B. Staw & L. Cummings (Eds.), *Research in organizational behavior* (Vol. 2, pp. 45–80). Greenwich, CT: JAI.

Suedfeld, P. (1992). Cognitive managers and their critics. *Political Psychology, 13*(3), 435–453.

Tetlock, P. E. (1983a). Accountability and complexity of thought. *Journal of Personality & Social Psychology, 45,* 74–83.

Tetlock, P. E. (1983b). Accountability and the perseverance of first impressions. *Social Psychology Quarterly, 46,* 285–292.

Tetlock, P. E. (1985a). Accountability: A social check on the fundamental attribution error. *Social Psychology Quarterly, 48,* 227–236.

Tetlock, P. E. (1985b). Accountability: The neglected social context of judgment and choice. In B. Staw & L. Cummings (Eds.), *Research in organizational behavior* (Vol. 7, pp. 297–332). Greenwich, CT: JAI.

Tetlock, P. E. (1992). The impact of accountability on judgment and choice: Toward a social contingency model. *Advances in Experimental Social Psychology, 25,* 331–376.

Tetlock, P. E. (1998). *Cognition biases and organizational correctives: Do both disease and cure reside in the eye of the ideological beholder?* Unpublished manuscript, Ohio State University.

Tetlock, P. E., & Boettger, R. (1989). Accountability: A social magnifier of the dilution effect. *Journal of Personality & Social Psychology, 57,* 388–398.

Tetlock, P. E., & Boettger, R. (1994). Accountability amplifies the status quo effect when change creates victims. *Journal of Behavioral Decision Making, 7,* 1–23

Tetlock, P. E., & Kim, J. I. (1987). Accountability and judgment processes in a personality prediction task. *Journal of Personality and Social Psychology, 52,* 700–709.

Tetlock, P. E., & Lerner, J. S. (in press). The social contingency model of judgment and choice: Multi-functional but still dual-process? In S. Chaiken & Y. Trope (Eds.), *Dual process theories in social psychology.* New York: Guilford.

Tetlock, P. E., Lerner, J. S., & Boettger, R. (1996). The dilution effect: Judgmental bias, conversational convention, or a bit of both? *European Journal of Social Psychology, 26,* 915–935.

Tetlock, P. E., McGuire, C. & Mitchell, G. (1991). Psychological perspectives on nuclear war. *Annual Review of Psychology, 42,* 239–276.

Tetlock, P. E., Skitka, L., & Boettger, R. (1989). Social and cognitive strategies for coping with accountability: Conformity, complexity, and bolstering. *Journal of Personality & Social Psychology, 57,* 632–640.

Tyler, T. R. (1990). *Why people obey the law.* New Haven, CT: Yale University Press.

Tyler, T. R., & Smith, H. J. (1998). Social justice. In S. Fiske, D. Gilbert, & G. Lindzey (Eds.), *Handbook of social psychology* (4th ed., pp. 595–629). Boston, MA: McGraw-Hill.

Weber, M. (1978). *Economy and society* (G. Roth & K. Wittich, Eds. and Trans.). Berkeley: University of California Press.

Williamson, O. E. (1993). Opportunism and its critics. *Managerial and Decision Economics, 14,* 97–107.

Withey, M., & Cooper, W. (1989). Predicting exit, voice, loyalty, and neglect. *Administrative Science Quarterly, 34,* 521–539.

Zetterberg, H. L. (1957). Compliant actions. *Acta Sociologica, 2,* 188–192.

Zucker, L. G. (1977). The role of institutionalization in cultural persistence. *American Sociological Review, 42,* 726–743.

Zucker, L. G. (1991). Postscript: Microfoundations of institutional thought. In W. W. Powell & P. J. DiMaggio (Eds.), *The new institutionalism in organizational analysis* (pp. 103–106). Chicago: University of Chicago Press.

7

Some Like It Hot: The Case for the Emotional Negotiator

Leigh L. Thompson
Northwestern University

Janice Nadler
University of Illinois, Urbana–Champaign

Peter H. Kim
University of Southern California

The classic analysis of the organization is based on the information-processing agent whose decisions result from rational analysis (March, 1988). Similar analyses have been applied to virtually all micro-organizational activity, including individual decision making and interpersonal decision making, or negotiation. It is not too surprising that the study of negotiation has been mentalized, given the cognitive revolution that preceded its development. With cognition as the dominant model of negotiation, the descriptive and prescriptive analysis of negotiation is largely divorced from considerations of affect and emotion. The negotiator is commonly depicted as a faulty information processor who uses judgmental heuristics that often lead to inefficient bargaining outcomes (cf. Neale & Bazerman, 1991; Thompson & Hastie, 1990). When the negotiator falls short, it is attributed to the fallibility of his or her information processing system. Affect, when it is examined, is viewed as a nuisance, obstacle, ploy, or byproduct of negotiation. Prescriptive analyses of negotiation behavior uniformly argue that negotiators should take the high road and focus on cognitive, decision-making principles as a way out of the information-processing quagmire. In contrast, we argue that the negotiator who behaves in a purely cognitive fashion will not be as effective in achieving his or her goals as the emotional negotiator. In this chapter, we challenge the view that emotion is a nuisance or hindrance in negotiation and argue that the effective negotiator is an emotional negotiator.

Our assertion that emotion is important at the negotiation table is not new. There is a growing sense that the affective life of negotiation has been ignored to the detriment of theoretical development and application (Barry & Oliver, 1996; Carnevale & Isen, 1986; Keltner, 1994; Kramer, Newton, & Pommerenke, 1993; Neale & Bazerman, 1991). In this chapter, we advance the following propositions:

1. Affect and emotion play a large role at the bargaining table;
2. Affect and emotion are not always reducible to the individual; they are meaningful at the group and organizational level;
3. An emotionally skilled negotiator manages emotional experience and emotional expression at the bargaining table.

We examine two different roles of affect in negotiation: emotion as experienced by negotiators, and emotion as expressed by negotiators.[1] These two roles are interrelated and can occur simultaneously within one person. But experienced and expressed emotions have different consequences in negotiation and we examine them in turn.

THE EMOTIONAL NEGOTIATOR: EXPERIENCED EMOTION

The emotions that negotiators feel can become a factor in the negotiation in two ways. First, negotiators might experience emotion prior to the start of the negotiation and bring that experience with them to the negotiation table. For example, the morning before a big meeting with a new supplier, Tim is overjoyed when he learns that he has been selected for the promotion for which he has been hoping. When Tim walks into the meeting, he is still thinking about the promotion and all of the wonderful new opportunities it will bring. The meeting with the supplier goes much better than anticipated and Tim thinks his supervisor will be quite pleased with the deal he reached.

---

[1]*Affect* is a generic term for a range of preferences, evaluations, moods, and emotions (Fiske & Taylor, 1991). *Mood* is a low-intensity, diffuse, and relatively enduring affective state (Forgas, 1995). Emotions typically have a more definite cause than moods (Forgas, 1995), and have a more specific focus (e.g., being "in" a good mood vs. being happy "about" something in particular; Clore, Schwarz, & Conway, 1994). Although we use all three terms (emotion, mood, and affect) in this chapter, we use affect in a very broad sense to refer to the entire constellation of emotion and feeling states that are experienced by negotiators and characterize the negotiation process.

In this example, a negotiator brought emotion to the bargaining table from an earlier, unrelated experience. As we will see, exogenous emotion can affect both negotiation outcomes as well as negotiator attitudes toward those outcomes.

The second kind of experienced emotion that plays a role in negotiation is endogenous emotion—that is, emotion that develops during the negotiation itself. For example, when Marcia received her phone bill, she did not recognize some of the charges, so she called the phone company for clarification. Within the first few minutes of the conversation, the phone company representative became argumentative and defensive, which made Marcia so angry that she hung up and immediately switched to another long distance carrier. In this way, emotion that develops during the negotiation affects negotiation outcomes and attitudes. We examine these two types of experienced emotions in turn.

EXOGENOUS EMOTION

In the earlier example involving Tim's negotiation with the new supplier, Tim's positive emotions surrounding his promotion spilled over into his negotiation later in the day. Negotiators might desire to stop experiencing their earlier emotions once they enter the negotiation room. In general, people try to control sad moods, anxiety, worry, anger, and on occasion, people try to control positive moods when they are unwanted (Wegner & Bargh, 1998). But such attempts at suppressing emotion often fail, especially when people simply try to suppress the thoughts that accompany the unwanted emotions. In these cases, the thoughts themselves often subside temporarily but the emotions are often intensified in the attempt to suppress thoughts about them (Wegner & Bargh, 1998). In sum, although negotiators might try to avoid bringing their earlier emotions with them to the negotiating table, this is not always possible.

THE CONSEQUENCES OF EXOGENOUS EMOTION FOR NEGOTIATORS

When negotiators experience exogenous emotion during the negotiation, those emotions can affect the negotiation in several different ways. Affect influences the way people make judgments, solve problems, remember, and process social information (Forgas & Bower, 1987; Isen, Means, Patrick, & Nowicki, 1982). When asked to make a judgment about some target, people often use a heuristic strategy of assessing their feelings to simplify the judgmental task, especially when the judgment requires integration of large amounts of information (Schwarz & Clore, 1996). These processes are all implicated during the course of a typical negotiation. We discuss in the next section some of the specific ways in which exogenous emotion (both positive and negative) impact negotiation outcomes and negotiator attitudes.

Positive Mood Enhances Postnegotiation Attitudes and Outcomes

Negotiators who come to the bargaining table already in a positive mood look at the world through rose-colored glasses. Compared to negotiators in neutral moods, those in positive moods:

- believe they perform as well or better than their opponent;
- believe that they compare favorably to other negotiators in their own position;
- are more satisfied with their outcomes;
- perceive their teams to be more cohesive than other teams; and
- prefer using less competitive strategies to resolve future conflicts.

In short, regardless of actual outcome, negotiators in positive moods display a rosy glow after the negotiation experience. But does positive affect result in better objective outcomes for negotiators?

Positive Affect Improves Negotiation Effectiveness

Negotiators induced to adopt a positive mood prior to negotiating are generally more effective in both integrative and distributive negotiation tasks than are negotiators in a neutral or negative mood. For example, on bargaining tasks with integrative potential, positive-mood negotiators achieve better individual outcomes (Kramer et al., 1993), and better joint outcomes (Carnevale & Isen, 1986) than do neutral-mood negotiators. If both parties are in a positive mood during the negotiation, they increase the total available resources as well as their own share of that total more than negotiators who are both in a neutral mood.

In addition to outperforming neutral-mood negotiators, positive-affect negotiators are also more successful than negative-affect negotiators in claiming a larger share of resources. On fixed-sum bargaining tasks, for example, negotiators in a positive mood who negotiate with negative-mood negotiators achieve a larger share of the resources than do negative-mood negotiators who negotiate with positive-mood opponents (Forgas & Moylan, 1996).

There are a number of factors that contribute to the greater success of negotiators induced to adopt a positive mood prior to negotiating. When planning their negotiation strategy, positive-affect negotiators anticipate using more cooperative strategies (e.g., "support the opponent's choices so they will support mine") than do negative-affect negotiators, whereas negative-affect negotiators plan to be more competitive (e.g., "do not support the opponent's choices so that mine have a better chance") than positive affect negotiators (Forgas & Moylan, 1996). Positive-affect negotiators may overestimate the likelihood that their opponents will be cooperative, leading positive-affect negotiators to expect that cooperation is a good strategy. Negotiators in a good mood rate themselves as more trusting of the opponent than do negotiators in a neutral mood, suggesting that positive mood leads to a more cooperative orientation (Kramer et al., 1993). Negative-affect negotiators, on the other hand, expect their opponent to be uncooperative. Negotiators in a good mood use fewer contentious tactics (such as threats, positional commitments, contrived arguments designed to pressure the opponent to concede, and efforts to raise one's status in the eyes of the opponent) compared to negotiators who are in a neutral mood (Carnevale & Isen, 1986).

Of course, cooperation in and of itself cannot ensure an increase in the total available resources, nor can it guarantee that a negotiator will increase her own share of the total resources. For example, in a negotiation with integrative potential, adopting a cooperative attitude might lead each negotiator to compromise on all issues, as opposed to maximize joint gains. Superior negotiated outcomes require insight and information exchange. Positive-affect negotiators do just that: They propose more alternatives, make more requests for their opponent's reaction to offers, and propose more trade-offs (concessions on certain items to gain on others) than their neutral-mood counterparts in face-to-face negotiations (Carnevale & Isen, 1986). Furthermore, negotiators in a good mood engage in more information exchange and show better recognition of integrative solutions than those in negative moods.

The success of positive-affect negotiators in experimental tasks is not surprising given that positive mood has been linked to creative thinking (Isen, Daubman, & Nowicki, 1987), flexible thinking (Murray, Sujan, Hirt, & Sujan, 1990), and more motivated thinking (Pretty & Seligman, 1984). For example, on the Remote Associates Test, which is based on the associative memory structure thought to be related to creative thinking (e.g., what do the words blue, cottage, and Swiss have in common?), positive-affect participants perform better than neutral or negative-affect participants (the answer: cheese; Isen, Daubman, & Nowicki, 1987). In addition, when asked to generate a list of unique features of different television programs, positive-affect participants performed better than neutral-mood participants (Murray et al., 1990).

Positive-affect negotiators are more confident about achieving their goals prior to the negotiation than are negotiators in a neutral mood (Kramer et al., 1993). Negotiators in a good mood make more concessions than negotiators in a neutral mood (Baron, 1990). This result has mixed implications for the positive-affect negotiator. In a bargaining task with integrative potential, more concessions could lead to better outcomes if negotiators recognize opportunities for trade-offs or if the bargaining zone is so small that concessions are needed to prevent impasse. A negotiator in a good mood could make concessions to induce concessions from the opponent. On fixed-sum tasks, however, making more concessions may lead to worse outcomes—each unmatched concession relinquishes more of the resource pie to the opponent.

In sum, negotiators who are experiencing a positive mood when they negotiate achieve better individual outcomes and better joint outcomes than their neutral- and negative-mood counterparts. Positive-affect negotiators are more cooperative and use fewer contentious tactics than negotiators in neutral or negative moods. Negotiators in a good mood propose more alternatives, make more requests for information, and are more confident about achieving their goals than do neutral or negative mood negotiators. Positive mood has been linked to creative thinking: Happy negotiators are more imaginative about proposing solutions that maximize joint payoffs.

Negative Affect Hinders Negotiation Effectiveness

Just as positive emotions enhance negotiation outcomes, negative emotion can have a detrimental effect on the quality of negotiated settlements. For example, when a negotiator is made to look foolish by the opponent in the presence of an audience and feels embarrassment or humiliation during the course of the negotiation, the negotiator is likely to retaliate despite the fact that this may worsen own outcomes (Brown, 1968). Negotiators who feel high anger and low compassion toward the other party are less accurate in judging each other's interests and achieve lower joint gains than negotiators with low anger and high compassion (Allred, Mallozzi, Matsui, & Raia, 1996).

Negative emotions arising from an acrimonious relationship hinder effective negotiation. Negotiators with an acrimonious history are more concerned with their own outcome than are negotiators who have a harmonious or neutral history (Loewenstein, Thompson, & Bazerman, 1989). Whereas negotiators with a harmonious or neutral history dislike advantageous unequal outcomes (i.e., where they come out ahead of the other party), negotiators with an acrimonious history prefer advantageous but unequal outcomes—equity concerns diminish with acrimony.

ENDOGENOUS EMOTION

The assertion that negotiation is an emotional interaction seems to contradict the very foundation of negotiation theory, which posits that negotiators are rational actors. Without the communication and experience of emotion in negotiation, people lack information pertinent to their understanding of their relationships with others. Emotions have primarily relational, rather than personal, meanings and thus hold the dyad or group together as a system (Gallois, 1994; Parkinson, 1995). In this sense, getting emotional is not a personal reaction, but rather involves making claims about one's identity or definition of the social situation. Because negotiation is a highly rule-governed interaction, negotiators may feel a tension between maintaining a relationship, expressing their feelings, and saving face.

Thus far, we have made the argument that emotion is an integral part of negotiation. However, we have not explained how endogenous emotion is indeed the part, parcel, and glue of negotiated interaction. Next, we discuss two key principles that illustrate the presence and power of endogenous emotion in negotiated interaction: social facilitation and emotional contagion.

SOCIAL FACILITATION OF EMOTION

Social facilitation refers to the principle that behaviors performed in the presence of others will be facilitated, augmented, or exaggerated to the extent that they are well-learned and debilitated to the extent that they are not well-learned (Zajonc, 1965). For example, joggers on paths speed up when an observer is facing them (Strube, Miles, & Finch, 1981); experienced pool players improve their game when others are watching, but inexperienced players get worse (Michaels, Blommel, Brocato, Linkous, & Rowe, 1982); and cyclists ride faster in races with others than when racing alone (Triplett, 1898).

The presence of others—whether they be coactors, partners, opponents, or mere onlookers—also affects the expression of emotions in interactions. For example, people laugh longer and think comedy shows are more humorous when an experimenter or others are present than when they are alone (Donoghue, McCarrey, & Clement, 1983). The social facilitation of emotion is largely nonconscious; people are generally not aware that their emotions are more intense when experienced in the presence of others. Negotiated interaction may be more emotionally exaggerated when people are in the presence of others than when they are alone. Consider a negotiation concerning a joint venture between two business firms, each represented by an agent. The agents might decide to come to the negotiation alone, or they each might decide to bring five of their most trusted advisors. The presence of others in the meeting should augment the emotions felt by the negotiators, whether they are positive or negative.

EMOTIONAL CONTAGION

Whereas the social facilitation of emotion refers to how emotions are intensified in the presence of others, emotional contagion is a process in which the emotions experienced by one person are transmitted to another person.

Thus, one person catches or is infected with the emotions of another (Hatfield, Cacioppo, & Rapson, 1993). The process of emotional contagion consists of three mechanisms. The first process is mimicry, wherein people copy the facial expressions, voice tone, posture, and movement of others. The second process is the feedback about our emotions that our facial, vocal, and postural behaviors provide to us. The third is the actual contagion process. We discuss each next.

Mimicry

People mimic the facial, vocal, and postural movements of others, but they are not aware that this occurs. Probably the most common experience of mimicry is yawning, which is infectious and largely out of our control. Laughter is equally contagious. Like yawning and laughter, emotional mimicry is not a controlled, deliberate process; it is automatic and often irrepressible. It is difficult or impossible for people to consciously and deliberately mimic others because the process of mimicry is too complex and too fast. When people deliberately attempt to mimic others, they are often perceived as phonies (Davis, 1985). Mimicry is so natural in social interactions that it is expected; people feel uncomfortable in the absence of behavioral synchrony.

We do not always mimic others; sometimes we countermimic. For example, people who are competing in fixed-sum games show counterempathic facial responses to the opponent's facial expression (e.g., smiling when the other is upset; Englis, Vaughan, & Lanzetta, 1981). However, when people share the same fate, such as when their outcomes are jointly shared, they show empathic facial responses (e.g., smiling when the other is pleased or is winning; Englis, Vaughan, & Lanzetta, 1981). Thus, people who fall prey to the fixed-pie perception should be less likely to mimic their opponent than people who see joint interests. Negotiators who perceive the possibility for joint gain may be more inclined to synchronize their behavior with that of the opponent.

Whereas vocal mimicry and synchrony are crucial for smooth interaction between individuals, there is an important exception. Mimicry of positive facial expressions and emotions is conducive for pleasant social interaction but in the case of negative expression and emotion, mimicking others is often not desirable. Indeed, when people are forced to interact with strangers or with people whose attitudes differ markedly from their own, they try to keep their voices and bodies from betraying their antipathy (Cappella & Palmer, 1990), presumably so as to salvage the interaction. For example, well-adjusted couples are better at resisting quid pro quo behavior in angry exchanges, whereas unhappy couples seem trapped in destructive tit-for-tat exchanges; anger is likely to spark an angry response (Gottman, 1979). The same principle is true in negotiated interactions.

Emotional Feedback Systems

Our emotional experience is a result of feedback from our own vocal, facial, and postural expressions (James, 1890/1981). Our emotional experience is affected moment to moment by the activation and feedback resulting from mimicry (Laird, 1984; Strack, Martin, & Stepper, 1988). Simply stated, if I smile at you during a social interaction, the activation of the smile on my face will increase my emotional feelings of happiness and joy. On the other hand, if I am clenching my fists and grinding my teeth, I am more likely to feel aggressive and hostile. Moreover, feedback about emotional states is not limited to facial expression. Vocal feedback can also influence emotional experience, such as vocal pitch and vocal tone. Basic emotions are linked with specific patterns of intonation, vocal quality, rhythm, and pausing (Clynes, 1980; Scherer, 1982). Further, postural position and movement mimicry also affect our emotional experience. Therefore, even if we attempt to use emotions in only a strategic manner in negotiations, emotional feedback may induce us to ultimately experience these emotions to some degree. Thus calculated or feigned emotion may instigate real emotion.

Catching the Emotion of Others

People tend to catch—that is, feel—the emotions of others. People not only tend to catch positive emotions but also negative emotions (Coyne, 1976). Unlike mimicry, where we copy the behavior of another person, catching another's emotion involves actually feeling what the other person is feeling. For example, when people talk to depressed people, they feel sad and anxious themselves (Howes, Hokanson, & Loewenstein, 1985). Probably the best-known illustration of emotional contagion by social psychologists is the Schachter and Singer (1962) studies of arousal, labeling, and emotion. In these studies, participants were made to feel aroused and then put in the presence of a confederate who adopted a particular mood (e.g., angry, delighted). Participants who experienced arousal and no obvious explanation for their arousal adopted the mood of the confederate (contagion). In contrast, participants who were not aroused did not show emotional contagion; nor did participants who were aroused but provided with a physiological reason for their arousal. According to Schachter and Singer (1962), the experience of emotion involves cognitive appraisal. When people become aroused, they look for an appropriate label for their feelings; if a label is absent or ambiguous, they look to the behavior of others to interpret their own arousal.

Conclusion

Despite the prominent role that experienced emotion plays in negotiation, cognitive models have been used almost exclusively for descriptive and prescriptive analyses of negotiation behavior. The emotion that negotiators experience influences the discovery and creation of resources, choice of cooperative or competitive strategies, the number of alternatives and requests for information, the accuracy with which negotiators judge one another's interests, and how negotiators feel about the negotiation outcome as well as about their own performance. Thus, rather than ignoring or suppressing the emotion implicit in the negotiation process, perhaps negotiators should acknowledge the emotional nature of the task and attempt to engender those emotions that facilitate the discovery and development of resources.

Therefore, to the extent possible, negotiators should adjust their own mood to try to capitalize on the advantages of both positive and negative affect. Negotiators who mimic emotions and experience emotional contagion are likely to be more accurate in judging the true emotions of the other person. Conversely, negotiators who fail to engage in behavioral synchrony of emotional expression with the other party probably will not be as effective as negotiators who are emotionally responsive. Additionally, because happy negotiators are better at expanding the resources available to both parties, negotiators can benefit from inducing positive affect in their opponents as well as in themselves. The role of emotion as a form of social communication in negotiation is discussed at greater length in the next section.

THE EMOTIONAL NEGOTIATOR: EXPRESSED EMOTION

Emotions are not only experienced (i.e., felt) but can also be expressed. The expression of emotion can serve a useful communicative purpose. For example, I might express anger at a prospective buyer of my house who makes me an offer that is 50% below my asking price. The prospective buyer understands my anger to signify my unwillingness to accept an offer far below my asking price. Alternatively, emotional expression can be detrimental if it serves only to interfere with the goals of the negotiation parties. For example, the prospective buyer in this example might react to my anger by deciding that he would prefer to make an offer on a different house, rather than dealing with an emotional seller.

In this section we examine the ways in which the expression of emotion in negotiation can be successfully managed. The management of emotion in negotiation is considered from two different points of view. We first examine how negotiators can use emotional expression and understanding to their advantage during the course of a negotiation. Second, we consider how negotiators can avoid emotional expression when such expression would interfere with conflict-management goals.

STRATEGIC USE OF EMOTION IN NEGOTIATION

It is often believed that to manage one's emotion is to reduce emotional feeling and response—that is, to become devoid of emotion. However, managing emotions does not mean removing the emotional aspect of negotiation. Rather, it means developing a set of strategies to effectively monitor, shape, and influence our own and others' emotional expressions so as to better achieve our goals in negotiations.

EMOTIONAL TUNING

An important element of emotion management is the negotiator's ability to adapt, regulate, and manage the emotions of others. Although certain conditions may facilitate or hinder emotional mimicry and contagion, it is often beyond a person's control. In this section, we consider controlled and deliberate mechanisms used by individuals in social interaction.

A large body of research suggests that communicators tailor messages to their audience (Higgins, 1992; Zajonc, 1960). The same is true for negotiators who attempt to communicate with bargaining opponents. When people formulate a message for an intended recipient, they take their recipient's background, knowledge, attitudes, and opinions into consideration (for a review, see Hardin & Higgins, 1995; Higgins, 1992). For example, when communicators perceive their audience dislikes a particular person or idea, they structure their message to present it more negatively. It is in this sense that people cognitively tune to their social interaction partners. Cognitive tuning represents a form of control or management in that to the extent that we tune with our audience, we can be more persuasive and achieve our social interaction goals (Higgins, 1992).

We suggest that in addition to cognitively tuning to one's audience by taking into account another's information, opinions, or knowledge, people emotionally tune to their audience by considering their current emotional state and emotional disposition. We propose a Maxim of Regulation whereby people tailor their messages to an audience so as to regulate the other person's emotional reactions. We further suggest that people in many situations, including negotiation, attempt to maintain what they perceive to be a happy mood in others and alleviate what they perceive to be a negative mood. Further, we propose that to the extent that people anticipate a negative reaction, they attempt to minimize the likelihood of its occurrence by tailoring the expression of their own emotions. Consider, for example, an employee who wants to talk to a supervisor about a raise. If the supervisor is known to be extremely temperamental and moody, the employee may express more positive emotion than if the supervisor is considered to be generally relaxed and calm.

Our discussion thus far has argued that communicators and, in particular, negotiators tune their messages to the perceived emotional state and reactions of the other party. We have labeled this process *emotional tuning* and we argue it is basic to social interaction. However, it is not always the case that communicators desire to tune to their opponent or teammate in negotiation situations. Communicators may employ at least four qualitatively different types of tuning: basic tuning, supertuning, antituning, and nontuning (Hardin & Higgins, 1995; Higgins, 1992). Thus far, we have discussed the principles of basic tuning.

Supertuning. Supertuning is used when people desire to achieve a high shared sense of reality with their audience, such as when the audience has high power or high status. In these situations, negotiators may be highly motivated to achieve shared reality with the other party. For example, a person attempting to negotiate a raise from his or her superior is likely to supertune, so as to achieve a shared emotional reality during the negotiation.

Antituning. Antituning occurs when people desire to block out the other person or dissociate themselves from interaction. Negotiators may correctly infer the other party's emotional state but might not be motivated to regulate the opponent's or partner's emotional reactions. Indeed, sometimes negotiators might be motivated to resist achieving a shared sense of emotional reality with the other party. When a salesperson telephones during the dinner hour, we may cut him or her off in midsentence, stating that we are not interested, and hang up.

Nontuning. Nontuning occurs when people simply are disinterested in achieving a shared sense of reality with the other person. For example, an employee who has already accepted an offer at another firm might have no interest in emotionally tuning to his supervisor during their discussion of the employee's performance evaluation.

Understanding which mode is employed by negotiators is not entirely straightforward. Although negotiation situations are commonly characterized by differences in perceptions and beliefs, this does not mean that negotiators will consistently antitune or nontune to an opponent; further, negotiators do not necessarily supertune with a partner or teammate at the negotiation table. For example, low-power persons may engage in more supertuning in interactions with high-power persons than vice versa. Consider a young couple negotiating the purchase of a new home with a seller. Whether the couple or the seller engage in supertuning is likely to be a function of which party is less interested in the deal going through. If the couple is also interested in a different house, they are less likely to super-tune. Similarly, if the seller is currently sitting on an offer, supertuning may not occur.

TRANSACTIVE EMOTION: THE DEVELOPMENT OF EMOTIONAL SYSTEMS IN GROUPS

Negotiators can also tune to the emotions of members of their own negoti-ating team. Negotiating dyads, teams, and groups have a group-level affec-tive tone (George, 1990; Sessa, 1996; Smith & Crandell, 1984). George (1990) distinguished negative affect groups whose members feel nervous, worried, anxious, upset, and distressed from positive affect groups, whose members feel enthusiastic, energetic, and assured. However, to characterize a group as having an affective tone, the affective reactions of the members of the group must be consistent. For example, consider two groups, each com-posed of four persons; in one group, all members are moderately positive in affective tone; in the other group, two members are high in positive affect and the other two are low in positive affect. The first group would be characterized as having its own affective tone; the second group would not. In a study of real work groups in organizations, George reported individual affect in groups tended to be consistent, suggesting that positive and nega-tive affect were real group-level constructs. Furthermore, group affect was related to behavior: For example, positive affect groups had fewer sick days than negative affect groups.

Transactive memory refers to a shared system within a group for the encoding, processing, storage, and retrieval of information (Wegner, 1986). According to the transactive memory model, individuals in dyads and groups develop implicit roles concerning the reception, storage, and re-trieval of group-relevant information. Roles are assigned on the basis of two primary criteria: expertise and circumstance. For example, a team of nego-tiators may expect their legal counsel to collect and retrieve the legal aspects of their negotiation deal; this relieves the rest of the team from encoding such information. In other cases, responsibility for information is more circumstantial and depends on a person's temporary location, and so forth.

We suggest similar systems develop within dyads and groups for perceiv-ing, signaling, feeling, and expressing emotion. We call such systems *trans-active emotion*. Consider for example, a negotiating team in which one partner consistently loses his temper at the negotiation table. Initially, this loss of control may upset the other member of the team and hinder their effectiveness as a team. Over time, however, as the team works together, the other partner may not only come to expect her partner to lose his temper but depend on her partner to fulfill this role as it becomes part of an overall bargaining strategy.

Emotional roles may be developed by teams for the purpose of strategic gain in negotiations. Consider, for example, the classic good cop–bad cop routine. In the classic routine, a suspect is held for questioning about a crime. However, the investigators do not have sufficient evidence to convict the suspect. They must rely on a confession. The method involves the bad cop working over the suspect, treating him or her badly, without respect or sympathy. Then, the bad cop disappears for a few minutes and the good cop enters. The good cop offers the suspect coffee and cigarettes and claims to be on the side of the suspect. The good cop suggests a plan of how the two of them can ward off getting more heat from the bad cop. The plan involves a confession on the part of the suspect. The badgered suspect, thankful for the kindness, confesses. In this example, the emotional system is created by one party (consisting of two investigators) and involves engendering emotions in the opponent (the suspect). However, this is not the only way that transactive emotion may develop. We propose that transactive emotional systems develop on the same side of the negotiation table, as well as across the bargaining table, as opponents develop expectations for one another's behaviors and roles.

PRESCRIBED EMOTIONS

We have discussed how group members come to agree, either implicitly or explictly, to take on certain emotional roles. There are times, however, when emotional roles are imposed, rather than agreed on. Groups and organizations can explicitly or implicitly prescribe the amount (one can feel too angry or not angry enough), the direction (one can feel sad when one should feel happy) and the duration of a feeling, and even the object of emotion (Hochschild, 1979). These prescriptions may take the form of display rules, which influence which emotions members of a social system ought to express (Ekman, 1973), or feeling rules, which define what we should feel in various circumstances (Hochschild, 1979). Bill collectors, for example, are required to display urgency (high arousal with a hint of irritation) to debtors but are not required to internalize the emotion (Hochschild, 1983); Mary Kay teaches her beauty consultants to offer fake enthusiasm to customers when they do not feel genuine enthusiasm (Ash, 1984). Flight attendants at Delta, however, are given explicit feeling rules, which require that they imagine being hosts in their own home and view the passengers as their guests (Hochschild, 1983).

The value of prescribing emotions lies in their potential for acting as "control moves" (Goffman, 1959) that influence the behavior of people who are the targets of displayed feelings (Rafaeli & Sutton, 1989). For example, the good cop–bad cop strategy mentioned previously represents a classic example of how differences in expressed emotions can be used to influence a suspect's behavior. These control moves, in turn, represent a valuable tool for encouraging desired behavior, avoiding competitiveness, and gaining concessions in the negotiation of disputes.

Consider a negotiation in which an organizational representative seeks to speed the delivery of parts from a supplier. This representative is more likely to succeed if he or she displays positive emotions to encourage the supplier's cooperativeness, for example, than if the representative appears neutral and less interested in their rapport. Both positive and negative emotions can influence reactions in targets that may improve the emotional party's position in a negotiation.

Strategic Avoidance of Emotion in Negotiation

Up to this point, we have discussed how negotiators can use their awareness of emotional experience and expression to negotiate more effectively. But the emotional nature of negotiation cannot always be tightly controlled by the participants. To the extent that certain negotiations become emotionally taxing to the point where they interfere with participants' goals, it can be beneficial for the parties to make use of certain emotion avoidance strategies. Specifically, negotiators can employ neutralizing, buffering, or normalizing strategies as a way of avoiding emotion (Ashforth & Humphrey, 1995).

NEUTRALIZING EMOTIONS

When emotion is undesirable, negotiators can take advantage of existing roles and standardized procedures to substitute for interpersonal relations and thereby inhibit the development and expression of emotions. For example, organizations often require dissatisfaction to be expressed in formalized grievance procedures that not only provide an impartial method for resolving conflict but also reduce its expression due to its time-consuming nature. As a result, the potential for strong emotions to exacerbate conflicts is reduced.

Consider a conflict in which an employee believes that he or she is being treated unfairly by a supervisor. By requiring complaints to be filed through a formal grievance procedure, the employee is cued to take the time to consider the issues, consider the evidence that supports his or her position, and provide well-reasoned justifications for this position. The supervisor, in turn, has an opportunity to fashion counterarguments and justifications and a neutral party is used to settle this conflict in the most appropriate way.

Thus, by relying on a formalized grievance procedure, the opportunity for the conflict to erupt in heated accusations, exacerbate harmful emotions, and increase the difficulty of reaching a negotiated settlement is reduced.

BUFFERING EMOTIONS

When the expression of emotions cannot be prevented, parties may use buffering to compartmentalize emotionality and rationality (Ashforth & Humphrey, 1995). The buffering of emotions is frequently accomplished through the differentiation of roles. Customer service representatives, receptionists, public relations experts, and other "frontage" personnel (Goffman, 1959) are given the task of managing the often emotional demands of the public. This enables the backstage personnel to perform the routine tasks necessary to fulfill the public's demands.

Consider a conflict situation in which a client believes that he or she has been mistreated by a company representative and travels to that representative's office to express his or her dissatisfaction. By using a secretary to block access to the representative and require the scheduling of an appointment for a later date, organizations require that the dissatisfied client wait until the most heated emotions have been dissipated. These actions are likely to reduce the intensity of conflict and improve the organization's position in the negotiation.

NORMALIZING EMOTION

Despite efforts to neutralize or buffer emotions, expression of disruptive and socially unaccepted emotions occasionally does occur. In these situations, negotiators may attempt to maintain or restore the status quo. This goal may be achieved by (a) diffusing or lessening unacceptable emotions or (b) reframing the meaning of the emotions. Negotiators may attempt to diffuse disruptive and socially unacceptable emotions by promoting the use of normalizing and face-saving rituals. Negotiators may also rely on norms that require apologies after emotional outbursts to acknowledge at least partial responsibility and express remorse (Ashforth & Lee, 1990).

Alternatively, the meaning of unacceptable emotions can be reframed through rationalization, to lessen one's responsibility for an event or to lessen the apparent severity of the consequences (Ashforth & Lee, 1990). Client escorts at abortion clinics, for example, collectively work to interpret their occasional emotional outbursts at antiabortion protesters as a humanistic and justified response to provocation (Dilorio & Nusbaumer, 1993). By attributing emotional outbursts to external causes, the potential for these workers to take a personal affront to the negative emotions of others is reduced.

FINAL THOUGHTS

Emotion and Rationality. We have argued that emotion is not only a natural part of a negotiated interaction but that it is essential for effective negotiation. Our assertion, however, appears to fly in the face of traditional views of negotiation which view effective negotiation as achieved through rational action, commonly devoid of emotion. Here, we wish to take up two issues related to this point. The first is whether rationality really precludes emotion and affect. The second is whether a negotiator who is truly devoid of emotion, but highly rational, is effective.

Rationality and emotion are not contradictory—indeed, it can be rational for a person to behave in an emotional fashion (Frank, 1988). Consider, for example, an exit negotiation between a employee of a firm and his supervisor. The supervisor has determined that the firm should let the employee go but realizes that it is wise to offer the employee attractive compensation and benefits so as to avoid possible recrimination by the revengeful employee. From a purely objective standpoint, it is not in the employee's interests to seek revenge or initiate a lawsuit. However, if the employee becomes enraged because he feels that he has been dealt with unjustly, he may decide to seek revenge even when, in purely material terms, it does not pay. To the extent the supervisor realizes this, she may alter her approach and perhaps offer the employee more benefits. In this situation, the employee, by acting emotionally, maximizes his interests. The supervisor, by believing the employee may seek revenge, has also acted rationally. It is in this sense that emotion and rationality are not contradictory. The key, of course, in this and other situations is that the negotiator's behavior and expression of emotion must be credible. This, of course, involves the skills of signaling. A pure rational analysis of this situation would suggest that the employee's threat to retaliate with a lawsuit is not credible because it is not economically worthwhile. However, if the supervisor believes that his emotions will get the better of him, she will treat his emotions credibly. One implication, therefore, of the use of emotion in negotiation is that expression of emotion is effective only to the extent to which negotiators are able to signal emotions that are credible. Obviously, if a negotiator can convince the opponent that he is crazy, this can be an effective strategy.

The second issue we would like to raise concerns the flip side of the previous question. That is, to the extent that a negotiator is devoid of emotion and behaves in a fully rational fashion, will he or she be as effective (or more effective) than the negotiator who is emotional, as we have described? Virtually every prescriptive treatment of negotiation cautions the negotiator to avoid letting emotions rule behavior. Our speculation is that the negotiator who is unable or unwilling to engage in basic behavioral synchrony of emotional expression, neither mimicking or conveying emotion, will not be as effective as the negotiator who is emotionally responsive. Further, we do not suggest that emotional negotiators are consistently effective; we think that there are many emotional negotiators who are extremely ineffective.

Our point is to make the case for the emotionally skilled negotiator. There are several reasons underlying our view that the emotional negotiator is an effective negotiator. First, the emotionally skilled negotiator is more likely to have an accurate perception of the other parties as derived from his or her ability to detect emotions in his or her opponent. People who mimic emotions and experience emotional contagion are more accurate in judging the true emotions of the other person than those who do not catch others' emotions. Second, the emotional negotiator is more likely to be able to infect his or her opponent with emotion in a way that serves his or her interests. Third, the emotional negotiator is more likely to be able to develop and effectively utilize emotional systems on the same side and across the negotiating table. Consider, for example, how a purely rational negotiator, devoid of emotional expression and experience, would deal with a teammate or partner who was highly emotional. Consider how this same negotiator would deal with an emotional opponent.

Our argument is that the emotionally skilled negotiator does not seek to suppress or control his or her emotions but, rather, to use his or her emotions and those of the other party in a manner that achieves his or her goals. Further, we believe that the consideration of emotion does not imperil nor contradict the role of rationality in negotiation.

Positive Versus Negative Emotion. The empirical literature reviewed here on the impact of emotion on negotiation outcomes suggests that to be effective, negotiators should create a positive mood prior to the negotiation. This recommendation does not seem to square with intuition. First, if positive mood consistently leads to more favorable negotiation outcomes, then why do negotiators get angry or upset so frequently in bargaining situations? Whether we are buying a car, trying to get a refund, allocating household chores, discussing which job candidate should be hired, or bidding on a house, it is not unusual to experience and-or display negative emotions.

A deeper examination of emotion in negotiation suggests that negative emotions may not always be detrimental. For example, negotiators may demonstrate resolve and firmness by appearing tough; acting angry, irritated, and upset. Indeed, the absence of expressed negative affect may be viewed by an opponent as an indication that the negotiator does not care much about the issue or is willing to acquiesce. For example, just prior to the Gulf War in 1991, U.S. Secretary of State James Baker met with the foreign minister of Iraq, Tariq Aziz, and Saddam Hussein's half brother, Barzan al-Tik-riti (Friedman, 1991). Baker stated his position very clearly to his opponents: If Iraq did not move out of Kuwait, the United States would attack. Barzan al-Tikriti telephoned Hussein and told him, "The Americans will not attack. They are weak. They are calm. They are not angry. They are only talking" (Triandis, 1994). Six days later, the United States went to war against Iraq, resulting in the death of about 175,000 Iraqi citizens and property damage in the amount of about $200 billion (Triandis, 1994).

This example suggests that negotiators should act tough to make their opponent understand their priorities. Acting tough sometimes requires expressing anger, irritation, and exasperation. Ironically, James Baker's failure to display anger and irritation during the negotiations with Iraq was probably a result of extensive diplomacy training in which diplomats are taught to suppress instinctive displays of anger and other negative emotions. The expression of negative emotions, which seems to occur quite automatically in some situations, may actually serve us well. The paradox, then, is: Effective negotiation outcomes are best achieved by maintaining positive affect during the negotiation but we must act tough, and get angry and upset to show we are serious.

In high-stakes negotiations, negotiators expect their opponents to display negative emotions such as anger to demonstrate the importance of those issues. Presumably this was the expectation of Hussein's half brother, Barzan al-Tikriti, during the negotiations with the United States prior to the Gulf War. The display of negative emotion in circumstances where stakes are high therefore might promote effective negotiation outcomes by allowing negotiators to effectively communicate their priorities while motivating them to avoid suboptimal outcomes on the issues that are most important.[2]

A New Look at Emotion. Emotion in the organizational literature is given a bad name. It is virtually synonymous with: (a) the loss of control, (b) negative mood, and (c) irrational behavior (i.e., behavior that is later regretted and flies in the face of short- and long-term interest). We suggest that this is an overly narrow and, often, erroneous view of emotion. We propose a new look at emotion in interpersonal decision making that views emotion as: (a) more positive than negative (positive moods are more pervasive than are negative moods), (b) expressions of interpersonal relation-

---

[2]It should be kept in mind that the term "high stakes" is relative to the participants and the situation. Whereas a negotiation over whether to go to war is considered high stakes to a diplomat, a negotiation over the price of a house or an annual raise in salary is high stakes to an average citizen.

ships (i.e., emotion is not so much an exogenously determined as an endogenous indicator of the relationship between individuals); and (c) emotions are not necessarily contradictory with cognition and in many cases are more consistent with cognition than are inconsistent. It is most likely that people notice incongruity between thought and emotion much more than they notice congruity.

In arguing that negotiators are by nature emotional beings and that negotiation is an emotional interaction, we do not argue that negotiators are necessarily emotionally competent. The standard prescriptive negotiation advice is to void oneself of emotion. This is where we part with traditional views. We argue that negotiators should not (and really cannot) effectively void themselves of emotion; rather, we argue that the emotionally competent negotiator must be aware of his or her own emotional reactions and those of the other party. We argue that a simple awareness of the processes we discussed will place the negotiator at an advantage at the bargaining table. The ability to manipulate these processes will even be a greater advantage.

ACKNOWLEDGMENT

The research in this chapter was supported by grants from the National Science Foundation (SBR9022192).

REFERENCES

Allred, K. G., Mallozzi, J. S., Matsui, F., & Raia, C. P. (1997). The influence of anger and compassion on negotiation performance. *Organizational Behavior and Human Decision Processes, 70*, 175–187.

Ash, M. K. (1984). *Mary Kay on people management.* New York: Warner Books.

Ashforth, B. E., & Humphrey, R. H. (1995). Emotion in the workplace: A reappraisal. *Human Relations, 48*(2), 97–125.

Ashforth, B. E., & Lee, R. T. (1990). Defensive behavior in organizations: A preliminary model. *Human Relations, 43*, 621–648.

Baron, R. A. (1990). Environmentally induced positive affect: Its impact on self-efficacy, task performance, negotiation, and conflict. *Journal of Applied Social Psychology, 20*(5), 368–384.

Barry, B., & Oliver, R. L. (1996). Affect in dyadic negotiation. *Organizational Behavior and Human Decision Processes, 67*(2), 127–143.

Brown, B. R. (1968). The effects of need to maintain face on interpersonal bargaining. *Journal of Experimental Social Psychology, 4*, 107–122.

Cappella, J. N., & Palmer, M. T. (1990). Attitude similarity, relational history, and attraction: The mediating effects of kinesic and vocal behaviors. *Communication Monographs, 57*, 161–183.

Carnevale, P. J. D., & Isen, A. M. (1986). The influence of positive affect and visual access on the discovery of integrative solutions in bilateral negotiation. *Organizational Behavior and Human Decision Processes, 37*, 1–13.

Clore, G. L., Schwarz, N., & Conway, M. (1994). Affective causes and consequences of social information processing. In R. S. Wyer & T. K. Srull (Eds.), *Handbook of Social Cognition* (Vol. 1, pp. 323–417). Hillsdale, NJ: Lawrence Erlbaum Associates.

Clynes, M. (1980). The communication of emotion: Theory of sentics. In R. Plutchik & H. Kellerman (Eds.), *Emotion: Theory, research, and experience: Theories of emotion* (Vol. 1, pp. 271–304). New York: Academic Press.

Coyne, J. C. (1976). Toward an interactional description of depression. *Psychiatry, 39,* 28–40.

Davis, M. R. (1985). Perceptual and affective reverberation components. In A. B. Goldstein & G. Y. Michaels (Eds.), *Empathy: Development, training, and consequences* (pp. 62–108). Hillsdale, NJ: Lawrence Erlbaum Associates.

Dilorio, J. A., & Nusbaumer, M. R. (1993). Securing our sanity: Anger management among abortion escorts. *Journal of Contemporary Ethnography, 21,* 411–438.

Donoghue, E. E., McCarrey, M. W., & Clement, R. (1983). Humour appreciation as a function of canned laughter, a mirthful companion, and field dependence: Facilitation and inhibitory effects. *Canadian Journal of Behavioural Science, 15,* 150–162.

Ekman, P. (1973). *Darwin and facial expression.* New York: Academic Press.

Englis, B. G., Vaughan, K. B., & Lanzetta, J. T. (1981). Conditioning of counter-empathic emotional responses. *Journal of Experimental Social Psychology, 18,* 375–391.

Fiske, S. T., & Taylor, S. E. (1991). *Social cognition.* New York: McGraw-Hill.

Forgas, J. P. (1995). Mood and judgment: The affect infusion model (AIM). *Psychological Bulletin, 117,* 39–66.

Forgas, J. P., & Bower, G. H. (1987). Mood effects on person perception judgements. *Journal of Personality and Social Psychology, 53,* 53–60.

Forgas, J. P., & Moylan, S. U. (1996). *On feeling good and getting your way: Mood effects on expected and actual negotiation strategies and outcomes.* Unpublished manuscript.

Frank, R. H. (1988). *Passions within reason.* New York: Norton.

Friedman, T. L. (1991, January 10). Confrontation in the gulf. *The New York Times,* p. A1, col. 6.

Gallois, C. (1994). Group membership, social rules, end power: A social-psychological perspective on emotional communication. *Journal of Pragmatics, 22,* 301–324.

George, J. M. (1990). Personality, affect, and behavior in groups. *Journal of Applied Psychology, 75*(2), 107–116.

Goffman, E. (1959). *The presentation of self in everyday life.* Garden City, NY: Doubleday.

Gottman, J. M. (1979). *Marital interaction: Experimental investigations.* New York: Academic Press.

Hardin, C., & Higgins, E. T. (1995). Shared reality: How social verification makes the subjective objective. In R. M. Sorrentino & E. T. Higgins (Eds.), *Handbook of motivation and cognition: Foundations of social behavior* (pp. 28–84). New York: Guilford.

Hatfield, E., Cacioppo, J. T., & Rapson, R. L. (1993). Emotional contagion. *Current Directions in Psychological Science, 2*(3), 96–99.

Higgins, E. T. (1992). Achieving "shared reality" in the communication game: A social action that creates meaning. *Journal of Language and Social Psychology, 11,* 107–131.

Hochschild, A. R. (1979). Emotion work, feeling rules, and social structure. *American Journal of Sociology, 85*(3), 551–575.

Hochschild, A. R. (1983). *The managed heart.* Berkeley: University of California Press.

Howes, M. J., Hokanson, J. E., & Loewenstein, D. A., (1985). Induction of depressive affect after prolonged exposure to a mildly depressed individual. *Journal of Personality and Social Psychology, 49,* 1110–1113.

Isen, A. M., Daubman, K. A., & Nowicki, G. P. (1987). Positive affect facilitates creative problem solving. *Journal of Personality and Social Psychology, 52,* 1122–1131.

Isen, A. M., Means, B., Patrick, R., & Nowicki, G. P. (1982). Some factors influencing decisionmaking strategy and risk taking. In M. S. Clark & S. T. Fiske (Eds.), *Affect and cognition* (pp. 243–261). Hillsdale, NJ: Lawrence Erlbaum Associates.

James, W. (1981). *The principles of psychology.* Cambridge, MA: Harvard University Press. (Original work published 1890)

Keltner, D. (1994, May). *Emotion, nonverbal behavior, and social conflict.* Paper presented to the Harvard Project on Negotiation, Cambridge, MA.

Kramer, R. M., Newton, E., & Pommerenke, P. L. (1993). Self-enhancement biases and negotiator judgment: Effects of self-esteem and mood. *Organizational Behavior and Human Decision Processes, 56,* 110–133.

Laird, J. D. (1984). The real role of facial response in the experience of emotion: A reply to Tourangeau and Ellsworth, and others. *Journal of Personality and Social Psychology, 47,* 909–917.

Loewenstein, G., Thompson, L., & Bazerman, M. H. (1989). Social utility and decision making in interpersonal contexts. *Journal of Personality and Social Psychology, 57,* 426–441.

March, J. G. (1988). *Decisions and organizations.* Oxford, England: Basil Blackwell.

Michaels, S. W., Blommel, J. M., Brocato, R. M., Linkous, R. A. & Rowe, J. S. (1982). Social facilitation in a natural setting. *Replications in Social Psychology, 2,* 21–24.

Murray, N., Sujan, H., Hirt, E. F., & Sujan, J. (1990). The influence of mood on categorization: A cognitive flexibility interpretation. *Journal of Personality and Social Psychology, 59,* 411–425.

Neale, M. A., & Bazerman, M. H. (1991). *Cognition and rationality in negotiation.* New York: The Free Press.

Parkinson, B. (1995). *Ideas and realities of emotion.* New York: Routledge.

Pretty, G. H., & Seligman, C. (1984). Affect and the overjustification effect. *Journal of Personality & Social Psychology, 46,* 1241–1253.

Rafaeli, A., & Sutton, R. I. (1989). The expression of emotion in organizational life. In L. L. Cummings & B. M. Staw (Eds.), *Research in organizational behavior* (pp. 1–42). Greenwich, CT: JAI.

Schachter, S., & Singer, J. E. (1962). Cognitive, social, and physiological determinants of emotional state. *Psychological Review, 69,* 379–399.

Scherer, K. (1982). Methods of research on vocal communication: Paradigms and parameters. In K. R. Scherer & P. Ekman (Eds.), *Handbook of methods in non-verbal behavior research* (pp. 136–198). New York: Cambridge University Press.

Schwarz, N., & Clore, G. L. (1996). Feelings and phenomenal experiences. In E. T. Higgins & A. W. Kruglanski (Eds.), *Social psychology: Handbook of basic principles* (pp. 433–465). New York: Guilford.

Sessa, V. I. (1996). Using perspective taking to manage conflict and affect in teams. *Journal of Applied Behavioral Science, 32,* 101–115.

Smith, K. K., & Crandell, S. D. (1984). Exploring collective emotion. *American Behavioral Scientist, 27*(6), 813–828.

Strack, F., Martin, L. L., & Stepper, S. (1988). Inhibiting and facilitating conditions of the human smile: A nonobtrusive test of the facial feedback hypothesis. *Journal of Personality and Social Psychology, 54,* 768–776.

Strube, M. J., Miles, M. E., & Finch, W. H. (1981). The social facilitation of a simple task: Field tests of alternative explanations. *Personality & Social Psychology Bulletin, 7,* 701–707.

Thompson, L., & Hastie, R. (1990). Judgment tasks and biases in negotiation. In B. H. Shepherd, M. H. Bazerman, & R. J. Lewicki (Eds.), *Research in Negotiation in Organizations* (pp. 31–54). Greenwich, CT: JAI.

Triandis, H. C. (1994). *Culture and social behavior.* New York: McGraw-Hill.

Triplett, N. (1898). The dynamogenic factors in pacemaking and competition. *American Journal of Psychology, 9,* 507–533.

Wegner, D. (1986). Transactive memory: A contemporary analysis of the group mind. In B. Mullen & G. Goethals (Eds.), *Theories of group behavior* (pp. 185–208). New York: Springer-Verlag.

Wegner, D. M., & Bargh, J. A. (1998). Control and automaticity in social life. In D. T. Gilbert & S. T. Fiske (Eds.), *The handbook of social psychology*. Boston, MA: McGraw-Hill.

Zajonc, R. B. (1960). The process of cognitive tuning in communications. *Journal of Abnormal and Social Psychology, 61*, 159–167.

Zajonc, R. B. (1965). Social facilitation. *Science, 149*, 269–274.

8

Social Uncertainty and Collective Paranoia in Knowledge Communities: Thinking and Acting in the Shadow of Doubt

Roderick M. Kramer
Stanford University

> *The greatest threat to innocence is the awareness that not everyone else is innocent.*
>
> —March and Olsen (1989, p. 31)

Knowledge communities can be conceptualized as groups or organizations whose primary purpose is the development and promulgation of collective knowledge. Knowledge communities are a prevalent and increasingly important form of contemporary organization. For example, all of the major social sciences are organized as knowledge communities consisting of numerous researchers whose common goal is the advancement of knowledge within their discipline (Porter, 1995). At a more microlevel, organizations within an industry, or even small groups within a single organization, often find it useful to participate in strategic collaborations (Zucker, Darby, Brewer, & Peng, 1996) or "learning alliances" (Khanna, Gulati, & Nohria, 1995) in order to mutually benefit from their unique knowledge and distinctive competencies.

Within such communities, knowledge is typically disseminated through a variety of mechanisms. These include formal routines and procedures, such as publication of original research in scholarly journals and presentation of work-in-progress at academic conferences. Knowledge is also disseminated through various informal mechanisms, such as circulation of unpublished manuscripts and–or the exchange of preliminary ideas and data through electronic mail. Whether formal or informal, such mechanisms are intended to facilitate the steady accumulation, integration, and rapid diffusion of emerging insights and innovations within the community.

As these mechanisms illustrate, the vitality of intellectual exchange within a knowledge community—and the cumulative progress such exchange engenders—hinges on myriad acts of more or less spontaneous cooperation. For example, the pace of progress within a scientific community depends, in no small measure, on the willingness of individual researchers to voluntarily share new ideas and data as they become available. The vibrancy of such a community also depends on individuals' willingness to contribute to, and actively participate in, the various institutions (e.g., professional associations and conventions) that support and sustain the community.

Although cooperation is crucial to the success of a knowledge community, individual acts of cooperation are not without risks. Individuals who unilaterally decide to share valuable information with others, for example, may find their intellectual capital co-opted. Given such risks, it is not surprising that concerns about trust often loom large within groups and organizations that are organized as knowledge communities. In talking about the dynamics of collaboration within the highly competitive biotech industry, Zucker, Darby, Brewer, and Peng (1996) noted that, "Trust is extraordinarily important in communicating discoveries in biotechnology because of their high scientific and commercial value. The resulting intense competition produces an information dilemma, *with contradictory incentives to communicate the new knowledge and withhold it*" (p. 90, emphasis added).

While recognizing its importance, social scientists have also noted that trust within such collectives is often difficult to create and sustain (Arrow, 1974; Barber, 1983). One of the barriers to trust is that individuals sometimes have doubts or suspicions about the trustworthiness of other members of the community. They sometimes worry that others are not contributing equally to the collective enterprise or that others might exploit their own cooperative efforts. These doubts and suspicions foster a reluctance to unilaterally initiate cooperative exchanges, as well as a wariness in responding to the seemingly cooperative gestures of other individuals. The history of research on the AIDS epidemic provides a nice example of the deleterious impact of distrust and suspicion on the accumulation and diffusion of knowledge within the scientific community. Because of their mutual distrust and suspicion of each other, researchers at various labs were initially reluctant to share emerging insights and empirical findings. This significantly impeded progress in understanding both the severity of the disease and attempts to trace its origins (Shilts, 1987).

Unfortunately, our understanding of the processes that contribute to distrust and suspicion within knowledge communities remains far from complete. Although recent theory and research provides many useful insights into how trust develops and thickens over time within various communities (e.g., Putnam, 1993), the mechanisms that contribute to the development and spread of distrust and suspicion are less perfectly understood. A primary aim of this chapter, accordingly, is to examine this important problem.

Contemporary trust theory and empirical research on trust suggests a number of useful perspectives that might be brought to bear on understanding why trust is sometimes problematic in such situations. For example, structural accounts (Burt & Knez, 1996; Granovetter, 1985; Zucker, 1986)—as well as recent work linking trust, social capital, and cooperation (Putnam, 1993)—indicate how different social configurations or ties among interdependent actors can influence the production of trust or distrust among them. Other research has examined how social psychological processes such as in-group bias influence perceptions of trust and distrust across group boundaries (e.g., Brewer, 1981).

While drawing on these previous contributions, the present chapter takes a different approach to conceptualizing the antecedents and consequences of collective distrust and suspicion in knowledge communities. Specifically, it attempts to elucidate the role social cognitive processes play in the development of distrust and suspicion among interdependent decision makers in collective contexts. Specifically, I examine how basic cognitive processes such as decision makers' self-consciousness and tendency to ruminate about others' motives and intentions affect trust-related judgments. I argue that such cognitive processes can contribute to the emergence of irrational or exaggerated forms of distrust and suspicion within a knowledge community.

The chapter is organized as follows. First, I conceptualize knowledge communities as posing a trust dilemma for individual decision makers.[1] I then argue that one of the factors that exacerbates judgment and choice in trust dilemmas is uncertainty about others' motives, intentions, and behavior. Next, I present a framework for thinking about how individuals cope with such uncertainty. I then describe a laboratory paradigm that was developed to test some hypotheses derived from this framework. Some findings from a representative study using this paradigm are presented next, followed by a discussion of some of the implications of these findings for understanding the problem of trust in knowledge communities.

KNOWLEDGE COMMUNITIES AS TRUST DILEMMAS

As just noted, a knowledge community consists of a group of interdependent decision makers who are engaged in an ostensibly collaborative enterprise, but one in which individualistic (i.e., self-interested and competitive) motives are also present. When individuals decide to engage in trusting behavior in mixed-motive situations of this sort, they create for themselves both opportunity and vulnerability. The opportunity arises from the perceived gains that accrue to individuals if and when their acts of trust are reciprocated by others. The vulnerabilities derive from the potential costs associated with misplaced trust in such situations: When individuals engage in trusting behavior, and others fail to reciprocate or decide to actively exploit that trust, they place themselves in harm's way.

From a judgment and decision-making perspective, trusting behavior is interesting, therefore, because it entails a more or less conscious decision by individuals to expose themselves to the risk of a potential loss in the hope of reaping some benefit from their behavior. As Luhmann (1979) noted, this fundamental tension or choice conflict is at the heart of the problem of trust. A central question in trust research, accordingly, has been the basis on which individuals' willingness to bear such risks is predicated.

Brewer (1981) provided a very useful analysis of this question. The basic structure of a trust dilemma, she noted, can be represented using a simple 2×2 choice matrix. Each decision maker has to decide whether or not to engage in some trusting behavior. For example, in a learning alliance, individuals have to decide how much of their scarce time and attention to invest in the collaborative venture. The trade-offs associated with this decision can be formulated in terms of the perceived consequences (costs and benefits) of trust versus distrust. As is well known to social scientists who study such dilemmas, this matrix has the familiar structure of a one-trial Prisoner's Dilemma game, such that the protection of self-interests always dictates the nontrusting choice. No matter which decision others in the alliance make, each individual's own outcomes are better if she or he elects not to trust, even though the outcomes associated with mutual nontrusting choices result in less than optimal outcomes for everyone involved.

This simple representation of a trust dilemma draws attention to the two types of decision error individuals can make in such situations: *misplaced trust* (e.g., continuing to invest resources in the joint venture when others are not reciprocating) and *misplaced distrust* (failing to invest such resources when others either have done so or would have done so).

Each of these errors entails potential costs. In the case of misplaced trust, individuals, who engage in trusting behavior when others do not endure all of the costs—both short-term and long-term—associated with their cooperative behavior. For example, as noted earlier, those who cooperate may find their intellectual capital exploited by opportunistic others. Individuals who engage in trusting behavior also bear the less obvious, but often quite substantial, opportunity costs associated with cooperation: Individuals who engage in trust-based behavior may squander scarce attentional resources on a joint venture, whereas others devote their time and effort toward furthering their own more individualistic goals.

The longer-term and sometimes delayed costs of misplaced trust may also be rather substantial. First, the erosion of confidence in others that attends the experience of misplaced trust may have pervasive and long-lasting effects. For example, the psychological residues of misplaced trust may inhibit individuals' willingness to initiate cooperative actions in future encounters. Additionally, there may be serious reputational costs associated with misplaced trust: Within many knowledge communities—especially those that are highly competitive—being labeled by others as gullible may increase the likelihood an individual will be exploited again. Thus, individuals who trust indiscriminately may acquire a reputation for exploitability that may make them vulnerable to future predation. Recognition of this problem prompted Axelrod (1984) to emphasize that not only is the willingness to initially cooperate critical to getting a cooperative regime going but establishing one's provokability was critical to sustaining it.

On the other hand, the costs of misplaced distrust are far from trivial and hardly any more attractive. For example, individuals who routinely engage in a strategy of presumptive distrust—in an attempt to minimize the risks associated with misplaced trust—necessarily forego all of the opportunities for joint gain that mutual trust makes possible. In the parlance of negotiation theory, mutual distrust leaves all of the gains to trade through collaboration on the table. Moreover, when aggregated over members of a community, the collective costs of misplaced distrust may be quite substantial, as Shilts' (1987) tragic chronicle of retarded progress toward understanding the extent of the AIDS epidemic documented.

How do individuals resolve these tensions and trade-offs inherent in collective trust dilemmas? Research on social uncertainty and choice behavior in trust dilemmas provides one perspective to this question.

SOCIAL UNCERTAINTY AND JUDGMENT IN TRUST DILEMMAS: THE INTUITIVE SOCIAL AUDITOR IN ACTION

Much of the analysis articulated in the previous section simply reiterates the familiar observation that the decision to trust others is largely about decision makers' anticipations of the benefits and risks associated with their decisions. In situations where mutualistic trust is high, the benefits of cooperation are likely to loom large in such anticipations, enhancing individuals' willingness to engage in trusting behavior. In situations where suspicion casts its shadow over the expectational landscape, the prospect of both immediate losses and future vulnerabilities may loom large, inhibiting risk taking.

From a social judgment perspective, such anticipations can be viewed from the standpoint of how individuals calibrate their expectations about other people's behavior in such situations. The calibration of expectations, in turn, hinges on the social inferences individuals draw from their observations of others' behavior, including the attributions they make about others' motives and intentions (Kelley & Stahelski, 1970). Unfortunately, in most knowledge communities, such inferences are complicated by the fact that significant *social uncertainty*—uncertainty about others' motives and intentions—may exist.

Theoretical models of trust development provide several clues as to how individuals respond to such uncertainty. Several theorists (e.g., Deutsch, 1958; Lindskold, 1978; Rotter, 1980) have noted that judgments about others' trustworthiness (or lack of it) are largely history-dependent processes. According to such models, trust thickens or thins as a function of the cumulative history of interactions among interdependent parties. Evidence that interactional histories play a critical role in the formation of judgments about others' trustworthiness comes from several sources. First, there is a substantial body of experimental research that links specific patterns of behavioral interaction with changes in perceived trustworthiness. For example, studies by Lindskold (1978) and Axelrod (1984) demonstrate that reciprocity in exchange relations enhances perceptions of others' trustworthiness and cooperativeness, whereas the absence of reciprocity erodes such perceptions.

In noting the formative role that interactional histories play in the emergence of trust, these models draw attention to the fact that individuals' judgments about others' trustworthiness are anchored, at least in part, on their a priori expectations about others' behavior and the extent to which subsequent experience supports or discredits those expectations. In support of such assertions, empirical studies show that interactions that reinforce individuals' expectations about others' trustworthiness increase trust, whereas interactions that violate those expectancies tend to undermine trust (Deutsch, 1958; Messick et al., 1983; Rotter, 1980).

Other research in this vein demonstrates that the attributions individuals make about others' observed behavior also play an important role in judgments about their trustworthiness (see, e.g., Deutsch, 1973; Hilton, Fein, & Miller, 1993; Vorauer & Ross, 1993). These causal attributions have been shown to be centrally involved in the process of drawing inferences about others' motives, intentions, and dispositions. Often, these inferences have been portrayed as reasonably systematic or orderly forms of social judgment, consistent with the idea that people resemble intuitive scientists trying to make sense of the social worlds they inhabit (Kelley, 1973).

In their purest form, such models seem to imply a rather straightforward arithmetic to the calculus of trust within a collaborative alliance, with some actions adding to the steady accumulation of trust and others subtracting from it. Stated somewhat differently, the reservoir of trust fills or empties as a direct function of experiential history. Boyle and Bonacich's (1970) analysis of trust development is representative of such perspectives. Individuals' expectations about trustworthy behavior, they posit, tend to change, "in the direction of experience and to a degree proportional to the difference between this experience and the initial expectations applied to it" (p. 130).

The portrait of the decision maker that emerges from this research then, is that of a relatively vigilant and fastidious intuitive bookkeeper or social auditor who maintains a rather strict accounting of the various exchanges and transactions that constitute the history of their relationship with the other parties with whom they are interdependent. Of course, social psychologists have long been appreciative of the myriad ways that various cognitive biases undo people's attempts to make sense of their social worlds. In the spirit of that theme, I consider next how the well-intentioned attempts by the intuitive social auditor to calibrate or judge others' trustworthiness might be led astray by several ordinary, and seemingly rather benign, cognitive processes.

COLLECTIVE PARANOIA IN TRUST DILEMMAS: THE INTUITIVE SOCIAL AUDITOR GONE ASTRAY

As noted previously, trust theorists have often viewed people's judgments regarding others' trustworthiness from the standpoint of the specific social inferences they draw from scrutinizing their interactional histories. Recent research suggests there are a variety of social cognitive processes that can influence how such interactional histories are construed, contributing to the development of exaggerated forms of distrust and suspicion (Fenigstein & Vanable, 1992; Zimbardo, Andersen, & Kabat, 1981). This research proceeds from the intuition that paranoid-like social cognitions appear to be quite prevalent and are often observed, even among normal individuals who find themselves in social situations that they construe as potentially threatening. As Fenigstein and Vanable (1992) noted in this regard, people in such situations:

> often manifest characteristics—such as self-centered thought, suspiciousness, assumptions of ill will or hostility, and even notions of conspiratorial intent— that are reminiscent of paranoia . . . on various occasions, one may think one is being talked about or feel as if everything is going against one, resulting in suspicion and mistrust of others, as though they were taking advantage of one or were to blame for one's difficulties. (pp. 130–133)

Drawing on this work, I have been interested in understanding how collective paranoia gets started in social systems such as knowledge communities. In particular, I have been interested in identifying social cognitive processes that contribute to the emergence of reciprocal paranoia among groups of interdependent decision makers. An intuitive feel for what I mean by collective paranoia in a social system, and the role that social cognitive processes might play in its development, is provided by Burt's (1992) provocative thought experiment, which he characterized as the "atavistic driver experiment." He asked us to imagine the following situation:

> You're on the freeway. There is a car ahead of you going 65. Pull up so your front wheels are parallel to his. Stay there. This won't take long. If he speeds up, speed up. If he slows down, slow down. You feel the tension, which you know is also building in the near car. He looks over. Is this a threat? . . . For the moment when you stood in common time and place, you were competitors. Break the parallelism and the competition is gone. (p. 4)

"Competition," Burt went on to argue, "is an intense, intimate, transitory, invisible relationship created between players by their invisible relations with others. It is being cheek and jowl with respect to the passing environment that makes the drivers competitors" (p. 4).

If we revise Burt's thought experiment slightly and imagine instead that we are the innocent driver, speeding along on a lonely stretch of freeway late at night, when suddenly it is the other car that pulls up to us. After a few abortive attempts to break the perceived parallelism in behavior, few of us, I suspect, would not experience some paranoia and perhaps even not a little fear: Are we being followed? If so, why? What have we done? Did we cut the driver of the other car off at some point earlier on the freeway? Does he have us mixed up with someone else?

In all-too-brief a moment, the presumption that our world is a safe and innocent place has been shattered and we find ourselves locked in a tense psychological standoff. Yet, in many respects, all of the tension and drama resides within our own heads, fueled by a cascading chain of cognitions—all of which are aimed at trying to make sense of a profoundly disturbing and threatening occurrence.[2]

There are many facets of psychological life within knowledge communities that share the subtle and ephemeral features Burt described. An anecdote related by a young screenwriter at a workshop for writers held at UCLA several years ago provides a nice example:

> I had just thought of a new idea for a screenplay. I immediately started working on writing it up. About three weeks later, I was talking to one of my film professors about my idea. When I finished telling him what I was thinking of doing, he mentioned someone at [another film school] who was working on almost the same idea. He was very excited about the fact that others were working on this idea because he said it showed it was a "hot" concept. But I became really depressed. Suddenly, I started to worry about what they [sic] were working on. Was their idea exactly the same as mine? How far along were they? Was I behind? From that point on, I stopped feeling relaxed about my screenplay—especially when about four months later the other person contacted me by e-mail. They must have heard I was working on a similar

idea as well. They wanted to know how my script was going and asked me to send them my draft when it was ready. Their message was very friendly—even cheery—and they seemed like a nice enough person. But I found it hard not to get a little paranoid about the whole thing. A lot of the fun went out of writing the script from that point on.

I suspect few of us in the social sciences have not had a similar kind of experience—we have discovered what we regard as a new problem or have an original insight about some existing problem. We set about happily proceeding to work on developing our hypothesis, only to discover shortly thereafter that someone else is working on it or has had a similar idea. Suddenly, the leisurely pursuit of inquiry is transformed into a competitive race of some sort. Much like the startled driver on Burt's imaginary freeway, we are suddenly in an uncomfortable and potentially threatening competition with someone whose motives and intentions are not fully transparent. We would like to assume the best (that there is no threat here), but we fear the worst.

Burt's thought experiment and the experience of the hapless screen-writer nicely capture some of the complex interpersonal phenomenology underlying judgment and choice in trust dilemma situations. They are also richly evocative of the kinds of cognitive responses individuals have to such dilemmas. In particular, I would like to argue next that they implicate two rather common cognitive responses: (a) rumination about the other party and (b) heightened self-consciousness about one's own predicament.

Other-Focused Rumination and Social Judgment in Trust Dilemmas

One adaptive heuristic that individuals use when trying to reduce the sort of social uncertainty inherent in such situations is to think about the features of the situation and the nature of the party (or parties) with whom one is interdependent. For example, we might try to make sense of what the other party is thinking about, what their motives and intentions might be, and try to predict their behavior.

People's commonsense beliefs and intuitions about effortful or mindful thinking lead them to associate tangible benefits with thinking about their problems. Indeed, there is a long tradition in Western philosophy and culture that places a premium on the merits of introspection and constructive rumination.

Unfortunately, psychological research on rumination does not support many of these intuitions (see Wyer, 1996, for a comprehensive overview of this research). Instead, it suggests that thinking about one's problems or situations often does not help very much, either with respect to producing greater clarity regarding one's difficulties or with respect to generating superior insights about how to cope with them. This is particularly the case when rumination has a depressive or fatalistic cast to it (Lyubomirsky & Nolen-Hoeksema, 1993; Tesser, 1978). For example, research on *dysphoric rumination*—the tendency for individuals to think about, imagine, or rehearse unpleasant or anticipated negative events—suggests a number of reasons why rumination about others' motives and intentions might contribute to enhanced suspicion and distrust of them. First, rumination following negative events has been found to increase negative thinking about them and contributes to a pessimistic explanatory style when trying to make sense of them (Lyubomirsky & Nolen-Hoeksema, 1993). Second, research has shown that dysphoric rumination can lead individuals to overestimate the likelihood of worst case scenarios when imagining the outcomes associated with various courses of action (Kramer, Meyerson, & Davis, 1990). Third, and somewhat ironically, rumination has been found to increase individuals' confidence in the interpretations and explanations they have generated to explain events (Wilson & Kraft, 1993).

Extrapolating from this previous work, several hypotheses regarding the effects of rumination on trust-related judgment suggest themselves. First, it seems reasonable to hypothesize that rumination about others' motives and intentions in situations where concerns about trust already loom large will increase individuals' distrust and suspicion of others' behavior. In particular, one might argue that the more individuals ruminate about the intentions and motives underlying the behavior of other actors with whom they are interdependent in a trust dilemma situation, the greater their tendency to make more sinister attributions regarding that behavior. On the basis of previous research, it can also be hypothesized that rumination about others' motives and intentions will increase the ruminator's confidence in their judgments.

Heightened Self-Consciousness and Social Judgment in Trust Dilemmas

A second social cognitive process that is implicated in the dynamics of Burt's atavistic driver scenario, I would argue, is a form of heightened and dysfunctional self-consciousness: Our sudden awareness of the other car alongside ours prompts an intense scrutiny not only of the other driver's motives and intentions but of our own actions as well: "Have I done anything to contribute to this situation? What can I do to influence what the other person is thinking about me? Can I communicate peaceful or cooperative intent by my actions? What is my relationship to the other party? What do I do now?" Thus, paying close attention to others with whom one is interdependent, perhaps paradoxically, can enhance feelings of being under intense scrutiny by them in return.

Research on the effects of situationally-induced self-consciousness on social judgment bear out some of these intuitions regarding the relationship between heightened self-consciousness and onset of paranoid-like ideation. First, a number of studies have shown that heightened self-consciousness increases individuals' tendency to make overly personalistic attributions about others' intentions and motives (Buss & Scheier, 1976; Fenigstein, 1979; Fenigstein & Vanable, 1992; Pyszczynski & Greenberg, 1987). Fenigstein (1979) characterized this as the "overperception of self-as-target bias." In response, he argued, self-conscious individuals tend to feel suspicious, looking for reasons why they are being observed.

Such concerns, in turn, prompt them to contemplate the motives or intentions that might be behind others' imagined or perceived scrutiny of them. This contemplation of others' motives and intentions lies at the core of suspicion. As Fein and Hilton (1994) noted, suspicion can be defined as:

> a psychological state in which perceivers actively entertain multiple, possibly rival, hypotheses about the motives or genuineness of another person's behavior. Moreover, *suspicion involves the belief that the actor's behavior may reflect a motive that the actor wants hidden from the target of his or her behavior.* (pp. 168–169, emphasis added)

As this definition suggests, it is the inherent aversiveness of uncertainty about others' motives and intentions and thoughts that contribute to the development of paranoid-like self-consciousness. This dynamic is nicely suggested by a clever piece of research by Zimbardo, Andersen, and Kabat (1981). Their research took as a point of departure an interesting, although at the time poorly understood, clinical observation. Clinicians working within institutional settings had often informally noted an apparent correlation between gradual hearing loss and the onset of paranoid-like ideation. Specifically, paranoid delusions appeared to be more prevalent among individuals who had experienced deafness later in life and whose deafness had a gradual and therefore undiagnosed onset and course. For example, it was noted that elderly hospitalized patients diagnosed as paranoid had significantly elevated levels of deafness compared to patients with other affective disorders.

Zimbardo et al. suggested that when hearing loss is gradual and unexpected, the patients suffering from that loss, as well as those around them, tended to remain unaware of the loss. As a consequence, for both the person experiencing the loss and those experiencing the behavior engendered by that loss, a set of complex attributional dynamics was set into play. In particular, they argued, paranoid thinking emerges as a:

> cognitive attempt to explain the perceptual anomaly of not being able to hear what people in one's presence are apparently saying. Judging them to be whispering, [the patient] may ask, "about what" or "why me?" Denial by others

that they are whispering may be interpreted by the hard of hearing person as a lie since it is so clearly discrepant with observed evidence. Frustration and anger over such injustices may gradually result in a more profound expression of hostility. (p. 1529)

The initial responses of the hard-of-hearing person can be construed as quite rational attempts to make sense of their experience ("Did I commit some faux pas without realizing it?"; "What have I done to make others reject me?"). As they find their attempts at sensemaking frustrated by others, their efforts become more vigorous and pressing.

However, the aggressive behavior driven by such concerns creates a cognitive dilemma for observers of the behavior as well. As Zimbardo et al. noted:

Observers, without access to the perceptual data base of the person experiencing the hearing disorder, judge these responses to be bizarre instances of thought pathology. As a consequence, others may exclude the hard-of-hearing person, whose suspiciousness and delusions about their alleged plots become upsetting. (p. 1529)

Zimbardo et al. went on to describe the interactional dynamics that cement the spiraling pattern of distrust and suspicion between both the hard-of-hearing person and those who surround him or her: "Over time, social relationships deteriorate, and the individual experiences both isolation and loss of the corrective social feedback essential for modifying false beliefs. *Within a self-validating, autistic system, delusions of persecution go unchecked*" (p. 1529, emphasis added). In a compelling demonstration of this argument, Zimbardo et al. experimentally replicated these dynamics by hypnotically inducing gradual hearing loss among students and then observing what happened to them during their social encounters.

Zimbardo et al.'s findings suggest how self-consciousness about one's predicament leads to a form of heightened vigilance and scrutiny of others.

Extrapolating from this work, one can hypothesize that when individuals experience a state of heightened self-consciousness, they tend to overconstrue others' behavior in self-relevant terms. In the context of a trust dilemma, this can lead to heightened suspicion and distrust of others with whom one is interdependent, especially when the meaning of their behavior is highly uncertain or ambiguous.

Summary

On the basis of previous theory and research, I have argued that certain basic social cognitive processes—such as rumination about others' intentions and motives and situationally induced self-consciousness—can contribute to the development of exaggerated judgments of distrust and suspicion in trust dilemma situations. In the next section, I describe a laboratory paradigm that was designed to explore some of these social cognitive dynamics within the context of a simulated learning alliance.

A LABORATORY METHODOLOGY FOR STUDYING COLLECTIVE SUSPICION IN TRUST DILEMMAS

To create a laboratory analogue of a learning alliance, it was essential to find a task that (a) possessed the structural properties of a multiactor trust dilemma, and (b) that would allow the creation of high levels of social uncertainty within the dilemma. A task that integrates and exploits critical features of two well-known laboratory tasks in social psychology seems to meet these criteria. The first task is a multiactor, common resource pool management task that has been widely used in previous research to study social dilemma behavior (see, e.g., Brann & Foddy, 1988; Messick et al., 1983; Parker et al., 1983). In this analogue, small groups of interdependent decision makers ostensibly share access to a pool of scarce but replenishable resources. Across a series of choice trials, individuals have an opportunity to withdraw or contribute resources to the common pool. In between decision trials, the pool size is replenished according to some variable replenishment rate function. Thus, the state of the common resource (i.e., whether it is relatively full or empty) depends primarily on the collective decisions of the interdependent decision makers (how wisely or foolishly their consumption behavior is vis-à-vis the replenishment factor).

Although the laboratory analogue in this instance is socially and computationally simpler than many real-world social dilemma situations, it nonetheless preserves many of the psychological tensions associated with such situations—including the choice conflict between pursuit of individual, short-term interests and collective, longer-term interests. For example, as individuals in these experiments discover that the common resource pool they are sharing with others is being depleted due to collective overconsumption of resources, participants often experience the kind of acute decision dilemma associated with real-world social dilemmas ("I'd like to cooperate by taking less in order to preserve the common pool, but I'm reluctant to do so if others won't reciprocate").

The second task incorporated in this analogue has been used by previous researchers primarily to study social judgment and interaction processes. It is based on the well-known autokinetic effect (Sherif, 1935). In this task, individuals are typically asked to make judgments about the apparent motion of a small dot of light in a darkened room. Although in actuality this dot is completely stationary, it appears to move in a random pattern because of uncontrolled movements of the human eye. Because of this compelling perception of apparent motion, the task has been shown to be ideally suited to study a variety of social psychological processes—such as peer pressure and social norms—that influence the subjective construal of motion (see, e.g., Jacobs & Campbell, 1961; Sherif, 1935; Zucker, 1977). Combining features of these two tasks yields a novel task that captures many of the psychological facets and social dynamics of collective distrust and suspicion (see Kramer, 1994, for a fuller exposition of the history and rationale for this methodology).

Overview of the Task and Procedures

Participants are recruited six at a time, ostensibly for a study of interdependent decision making. The studies are conducted at night, in a room equipped with blackout shades, so that the setting can be rendered completely dark. Upon their arrival at the laboratory, participants are seated at a long table containing a Macintosh II computer with color monitor. Six joysticks are connected by individual cables to a cable box and ostensibly connected to the computer. Each student is seated next to one of these joysticks. The joysticks are separated by large partitions, so that visual access to other participants is eliminated. In addition, as soon as they are seated, participants wear large headphones for the duration of the session. These precautions minimize the possibility of both verbal and nonverbal communication between participants during decision making.

Individuals are told they will be participating in a decision-making task with five other individuals. They are told the task involves the use of shared resources (points). Their attention is then directed toward a small point of light that is displayed on an otherwise black computer screen. Each person is assigned a specific segment of the monitor's screen space equal to 60 degrees of arc ($\frac{1}{6}$ of 360 degrees) that radiates from the dot located at the center of the screen to the borders of the screen (e.g., the person with Joystick #1 is assigned the upper right segment, the person with Joystick #2 the middle right, etc.).

Participants are told that the point of light (dot) is controlled by their joysticks, such that moving the joystick in any direction moves the dot in that direction. If the joysticks are not moved, they are told, the dot will remain more or less stationary, except for small, random fluctuations produced by the computer.

Participants are informed they will have an opportunity to earn money during the study, based on how many resources (points) they accumulate during the time allotted for the study. The location of the dot determines how many resources each person accumulates. They are told that as long as the dot is stationary, each individual can accumulate the same amount of money (one cent per second). Thus, there is the possibility that each person in the group can earn up to $0.60 per minute, as long as no one attempts to move the dot from its center position. Whenever the dot is off-center and in one person's assigned segment, however, that person earns 1.5 cents per second, whereas the other five individuals receive only 0.5 cents per second. Thus, if that individual manages to keep the dot in his or her segment for a full minute, he or she will earn $0.90, while the other individuals receive only $0.30. Participants are told the computer will keep a tally of the accumulating points. This information will remain confidential (i.e., only the experimenter will know how many points they have accumulated, and they will be individually and privately paid at the end of the task).

The task is described as difficult because of several features. First, participants are told that, for any given second, the computer is programmed to respond only to one person's joystick inputs; thus, if one person has control of the dot, the others are locked out for that instant by the computer. Thus, there is a maximum of 60 decision opportunities per minute. Second, they are told the computer is programmed to introduce a slight delay between joystick movements and movements of the dot. Third, they are told the computer has been programmed according to a "stochastic, fluctuation algorithm," so that the dot will sometimes move slowly and randomly even when no one is intentionally moving a joystick. These instructions are intended to increase an individual's vigilance and involvement with the task while increasing attributional ambiguity regarding perceived movements of the dot.

Although participants are led to believe that movement of the dot is controlled by their joysticks, in actuality the joysticks have no effect on the dot's location on the screen. The dot is stationary. However, the dot appears to drift off-center in response to participants' uncontrolled eye movements. Thus, although perceived movement of the dot is vivid and compelling, it is purely subjective. Any differences in the perceived magnitude of movement across the four conditions of the study can be attributed entirely to the manipulations of the independent variables described later this chapter.

To summarize, the task structure, payoff schedule, and operational features of the computer system are designed to create a collective trust dilemma in which a group of interdependent decision makers must choose between self-restraint (not moving the dot, a decision that maximizes collective long-term payoffs) and self-interest (i.e., increasing one's own gain at others' expense).

It is important to note that, in this kind of trust dilemma, individuals may move the joystick for reasons other than self-interests or pure greed. For example, even if some individuals are not motivated by a desire to increase their own payoffs, they may decide to move their joysticks in a defensive or retaliatory fashion to thwart someone else's perceived attempt to do so. Thus, social inferences about others' motives or intentions based on their observed behavior (joystick behavior) are shrouded in ambiguity: It is hard to know whether others are acting out of selfishness, self-protection, or an attempt to retaliate against other transgressors in the group.

The Phenomenology of Study Participants

Data collected during intensive pilot testing and debriefing suggest how well this laboratory paradigm induces states of collective distrust and suspicion. For example, one participant stated, "I can't believe what I am seeing. Everyone seems to be trying to cheat!" Another participant muttered, "You can't trust anyone."

Interestingly, by the end of these sessions, some individuals had even developed fairly elaborate images of the dispositions or personalities of the other participants, based entirely on what they perceived as systematic patterns of dot movement.[3] "This group really s--ks. That purple guy is the worst p---k. He keeps trying to pull it [the dot] into his own zone. Yellow seems to be fighting with him a lot ... Blue seems to be about the only unselfish person in this game besides me."

Manipulation of Independent Variables

To manipulate self-consciousness, the study employed procedures similar to those used in previous research (Carver & Scheier, 1981; Fenigstein, 1979). Participants were told one purpose of the experiment was to see how individuals coped with complex interdependent decision-making environments in abstract task environments. Such behavior, it was explained, was predictive of real-world ability. In the High Self-Consciousness Condition, participants were told their decision behavior would be videotaped using a nightcam lens so that the experimenter could monitor how well they were coping with the task. A video camcorder was conspicuously mounted in a corner of the room facing toward the group, with its red light blinking, indicating the camera was on.

Individuals in the Low Self-Consciousness Condition were provided with the same information about the purpose of the experiment but were told that they would be orally debriefed at the end of the session. In this condition, the mounted camera was in the room but the lens cap was on and the camera lens was pointed toward the floor.

To manipulate rumination, participants were told the task would last approximately 700 seconds (12 minutes) and would be divided into two periods of roughly equal duration. They were told the breaks were to provide them with an opportunity to rest and relax their eyes. In actuality, they provided an opportunity to interject a rumination manipulation.

Halfway through the task, the researcher asked the participants to stop and take a break. To fill the time, they were asked to write a brief assessment. Participants in the High Rumination Condition were asked to "try and imagine what the motives, intentions, and strategies of the other five people with whom you are interacting are and then write them down." Those assigned to the Low Rumination Condition were told the researchers were interested in learning more about the experience level of MBAs with personal computers. Accordingly, they were asked to write about their general level of previous experience using PCs. This condition was designed to parallel the distraction–control conditions used in previous rumination research (cf. Lyubomirsky & Nolen-Hoeksema, 1993).

Results of the Study

The primary aim of this research was to explicate some of the cognitive antecedents and consequences of collective distrust and suspicion. A number of measures were used to assess how self-consciousness and rumination affected individuals' distrust and suspicion regarding others' motives, intentions, and behavior during the task (Table 8.1 provides a summary of these major findings).

Perceived Suspicion. On completion of the task, individuals were asked to indicate how suspicious they were that others in their group were trying to take resources from the common pool. An analysis of variance of these data revealed several effects. First, there was a main effect for self-con-

TABLE 8.1
Effects of Self-Consciousness and Rumination
on Collective Attributions and Judgments

	Self-Consciousness			
	Low		High	
	Rumination			
	Low	High	Low	High
Dependent Variables				
Suspicions regarding others' motives and intentions	3.71	4.85	5.07	5.35
Estimated total time the dot was off center position	384.64	519.64	506.78	537.14
Estimated occurrences of cheating	34.85	63.85	53.42	57.64
Trustworthiness of group	4.57	2.78	3.00	2.71
Attraction toward group	4.92	2.71	3.14	3.21
Willingness to interact again	4.64	2.64	3.07	3.00
Confidence in future interaction	4.85	2.85	3.07	3.07
Confidence in judgment	4.21	5.28	4.71	4.92

sciousness and a main effect for rumination. As is evident in Table 8.1, individuals in the High Self-Consciousness Condition were more suspicious of others' intentions and motives ($M = 5.21$) compared to those in the Low Self-Consciousness Condition ($M = 4.28$). There was also a main effect for rumination, such that those in the High Rumination Condition were more suspicious ($M = 5.10$) compared to those in the Low Rumination Condition ($M = 4.39$). The interaction between self-consciousness and rumination was not significant, however.

Perceived Untrustworthiness. To assess individuals' perceptions of the extent to which others in their group had actually engaged in untrustworthy behavior, individuals were asked to estimate how much time they thought the dot was off-center because of another group member's attempts to increase his or her earnings. Individuals in the High Self-Consciousness Condition estimated that the dot was off-center for a significantly longer period of time ($M = 521.96$ seconds) compared to those in the Low Self-Consciousness Condition ($M = 452.14$ seconds). A similar pattern was observed for rumination (Ms of 528.39 and 445.71 seconds for the High and Low Rumination Conditions, respectively). There was also an interaction between self-consciousness and rumination. As can be seen in Table 8.1, individuals' estimates of cheating behavior were substantially lower in the Low Self-Consciousness–Low Rumination Condition compared to the other three conditions.

Perceptions of Collective Cheating. Perceptions of collective cheating were viewed as another proxy for distrust. Individuals were asked to estimate the number of specific instances of cheating they thought they had detected, operationalized as having perceived movement of the dot into one or more group members' segments during the task. There was a main effect for rumination, such that individuals in the High Rumination Condition thought they had detected more instances of cheating ($M = 60.74$ episodes) compared to those in the Low Rumination Condition ($M = 44.13$ episodes). Although the main effect for self-consciousness was not significant, there was an interaction between rumination and self-consciousness. As can be seen in Table 8.1, the lowest levels of perceived cheating occurred in the Low Self-Consciousness–Low Rumination Condition.

Perceptions of Collective Trustworthiness. To assess how self-consciousness and rumination affected attributions regarding collective trustworthiness, participants were asked to indicate how trustworthy ($1 =$ Not at all; $7 =$ Very) they felt their group as a whole had been during the task. A 2×2 analysis of variance revealed main effects for both self-consciousness and rumination, as well as a significant interaction between self-consciousness and rumination. As can be seen in Table 8.1, as self-consciousness increased, individuals' perceptions of others' trustworthiness decreased (*M*s of 2.85 and 3.67 for the High and Low Self-Consciousness Conditions, respectively). Similarly, rumination contributed to a decline in perceived trustworthiness (*M*s of 2.74 and 3.78 for the High and Low Ruminations Conditions, respectively). However, these effects were least pronounced in the Low Self-Consciousness–Low Rumination Condition.

Perceptions of Future Trustworthiness. To assess how rumination and self-consciousness affected perceptions of future trustworthiness, individuals were asked to indicate how interested they would be in interacting with these same people again on another task. There was a marginally significant main effect for self-consciousness, a significant main effect for rumination, and a significant interaction between self-consciousness and rumination.

They were also asked to indicate how confident they were that, given another opportunity, their groups would behave in a more trustworthy fashion the next time. There was a significant main effect for self-consciousness, a significant main effect for rumination, and a significant interaction between self-consciousness and rumination,. As is readily apparent from inspection of the means in Table 8.1, the pattern of results for each of these variables closely parallel their previous perceptions and judgments; that is, in each case, rumination and self-consciousness impaired collective trust and confidence, with the least evidence of this pattern emerging in the Low Self-Consciousness–Low Rumination Condition.

Attributional and Perceptual Confidence. An interesting question is how confident people in this situation were that their distrust and suspicion were warranted. To assess the effects of self-consciousness and rumination on individuals' confidence in their social perceptions and judgments, participants were asked to indicate on a 7-point scale how confident they were (1 = Not at all, 7 = Very) that their judgments were accurate. Analyses of variance revealed that rumination increased individuals' confidence in their judgments about others' motives and intentions, such that those in the High Rumination Condition reported significantly more confidence ($M = 5.10$) compared to those in the Low Rumination Condition ($M = 4.46$).

Implications and Conclusions

A primary goal of the present research was to contribute to our understanding of some of the psychological barriers to trust that may reside within knowledge communities and other forms of collaborative learning. Specifically, I have attempted to demonstrate how some rather ordinary social cognitive processes might adversely and unintentionally influence trust-related judgments, thus undermining the stability of a cooperative venture. In putting these findings in perspective, several points merit attention. First, the results of the present study demonstrate how merely ruminating about others' intentions and motives can influence subsequent judgments regarding those intentions and motives. While adding to an impressive and accumulating body of evidence regarding the effects of rumination on social judgment, they also extend those results in an important direction. Previous research on rumination has focused almost exclusively on the effects of self-focused rumination on individuals' perceptions of their own psychological states (e.g., their level of depression). In contrast, little attention has been afforded in these studies to the question of how rumination about others' psychological states affect social perception and judgment of their states. The results of the present study begin to shed some light on this problem.

These results also show that ruminating about others' motives and intentions, somewhat ironically, can increase individuals' confidence in the veridicality of their judgments and attributions about others' motives and intentions. It might seem surprising that effortful rumination would increase individuals' confidence in their judgments in this fashion. After all, on prima facie grounds, one might argue just the opposite. For example, using a discounting logic, one might argue that the more individuals ruminate about the cause of an external event, the more likely they would be to generate larger numbers of alternative interpretations for it, resulting in decreased confidence in any one interpretation. However, the findings from the present study suggest just the opposite. Other research suggests such a pattern is not surprising, however. For example, Wilson and Kraft (1993) have produced similar results and have proposed a reasonable explanation for them. "Because it is often difficult to get at the exact roots of [many] feelings," they suggested "repeated introspections may not result in better access to the actual causes. Instead, people may *repeatedly focus on reasons that are plausible* and easy to verbalize" (p. 410; emphasis added). The results of the present study seem consistent with this argument.

Framed more broadly, such results suggest the operation of an interesting effort heuristic (i.e., "Since I've thought so much about this problem, my inferences regarding it must be pretty sound"). Such a heuristic implies individuals believe there exists a rough proportion or equivalence between attempts at retrospective sensemaking (expenditure of cognitive effort) and the quality of sensemaking that flows from them (the outcome of such effort). (Psychoanalysis, with its standard presumption that decades of intense introspective rumination by patient and therapist are prerequisite to therapeutic insight, seems to be predicated on precisely such a heuristic.) Viewed from this perspective, these findings have implications for understanding not only the origins of irrational distrust and suspicion but also why such distrust and suspicion might be relatively resistant to disconfirmation or extinction.

In assessing the generality of the observed relationship between rumination and suspicious cognitions, it is important to emphasize that I am not arguing here that rumination necessarily contributes to social suspicion in all situations. For example, in the context of positive social relationships—such as those that might be found within a more cooperative alliance (e.g., a knowledge community in which collective trust in others' intentions and motives is high)—rumination might actually accentuate perceptions of collective trustworthiness. As previous research has shown, rumination leads to attitude change in the direction of individuals' pre-existing attitudes and beliefs. For example, Wilson and Kraft (1993) found that rumination about a positively regarded loved one resulted in an increase in positive evaluations of the relationship with that person!

The findings regarding self-consciousness also merit some comment. The present research employed a common, but admittedly somewhat artificial, method used by social psychologists to induce heightened self-consciousness in a laboratory setting. This was expedient from the standpoint of rigorously and reliably assessing the effects of self-consciousness on social judgment in an experimental context. However, questions about the external validity of the manipulation should be raised. What does self-consciousness have to do with judgment and choice in real-world trust dilemmas? I would like to suggest that self-consciousness in many social situations serves as a cue or signal that something is amiss in the social situation—something that is potentially threatening and worthy of one's attention. In naturalistic settings, such concerns prompt individuals to search for the cause of their anxiety or discomfort. In other words, when individuals feel self-conscious, they are motivated to look outward for a cause for their self-consciousness, prompting a series of cognitions centered around attempts to make sense of the feeling. Much like Zimbardo et al.'s patients, people are motivated to ask what or who is making them self-conscious, and why. Thus, in real-world settings, self-consciousness may be a rather natural response to situations in which threat or danger is perceived to be present, even though the nature and magnitude of the threat remains uncertain. In such settings, paying attention to such cues is often quite adaptive.

This heightened self-consciousness, of course, is one of the hallmarks of the paranoid style of cognition. As Colby (1981) noted:

> Around the central core of persecutory delusions [that preoccupy the paranoid person] there exists a number of attendant properties such as suspiciousness, hypersensitivity, hostility, fearfulness, and self-reference that lead the paranoid individual to interpret events that have nothing to do with him [sic] as bearing on him personally. (p. 518)

As the popular saying goes, "Just because you're paranoid doesn't mean they aren't out to get you."

Although a primary aim of the present research was to explore how and why exaggerated forms of distrust and suspicion develop among potential collaborators within knowledge communities, the results of the present research have some implications for thinking about the conditions that might help create and sustain collective trust in such situations.

A first approach to creating collective trust is to implement what Messick and Brewer (1983) termed "structural solutions" that help mutual trust and cooperation get a toehold. Miller (1992) offered an excellent example of this kind of socially constructed and self-reinforcing dynamic within a knowledge-based organization. In recounting the philosophy of HP founder William Hewlett, he noted that the HP way, "consists of the policies and actions that flow from the belief that men and women want to do a good job, a creative job, and that if they are provided with the proper environment they will do so.

"The reality of cooperation," Miller went on to note:

> is suggested by the open lab stock policy, which not only allows engineers access to all equipment, but encourages them to take it home for personal use ... the open door symbolizes and demonstrates management's trust in the cooperativeness of the employees ... The elimination of time clocks and locks on equipment room doors is *a way of building a shared expectation among all the players that cooperation will most likely be reciprocated*, creating *a shared "common knowledge" in the ability of the players to reach cooperative outcomes*. (p. 197, emphases added)

Because such acts are so manifestly predicated on confidence in the other members of a group, they tend to breed confidence in the group as a whole in turn. As a consequence, collective trust over time becomes institutionalized (at the collective level) and internalized (at the individual level).

Hedges are another cognitive process that may play an important role in the development and maintenance of collective trust within knowledge communities (Meyerson, Weick, & Kramer, 1996). The purpose of a hedge is to lessen the perceived risks of trust by reducing dependence on specific others and thereby reducing perceived vulnerability to moderate, tolerable levels. Hedges guard against or minimize the dangers of misplaced trust. Hedges imply an attitude that is somewhat equivocal: Trust the other, but not completely.

An established screenwriter at the same workshop attended by the writer described earlier provided a nice illustration of a hedge she uses strategically to solve the trust dilemma the first writer alluded to:

When I finish a script, I send lots of copies of it out to all of my contacts. I also register it at the Screenwriter's Guild. By sending it out simultaneously to lots of people in the industry, I never worry about sharing my ideas with someone I don't know because the idea is out there and credited to me. So I can feel good, and at the same time, pretty well protected against being ripped off.

By disseminating her script widely to many strangers and friends within the industry, this person feels she creates a base of common knowledge that attenuates the trust dilemma by reducing the costs of misplaced trust.

As this example suggests, hedges function much like BATNAs (best alternatives to a negotiated agreement) in negotiations. BATNAs free negotiators to press their case because they reduce the perceived downside should bargaining fail. The existence of a hedge allows one to enter into a risky activity because the worst case outcomes associated with misplaced trust are at least somewhat anticipated and preemptively defended against. The posture of hedging is reflected in Weick and Roberts' (1993) observation, based on their research on accidents in flight operations off nuclear carriers, that people who avoid accidents in such situations live by the credo, "Never get into anything without making sure you have a way out" (p. 640). Having a way out allows individuals to act in a trusting manner precisely because they have a way out. As a cognitive process, hedging thus entails the creation of psychological failsafe mechanisms; they provide the needed reassurance that precedes risky ventures.

Hedges imply an orientation that resembles the attitude of wisdom described by Meacham (1983) as a stance of simultaneously believing and doubting, understanding and questioning. The initial trusting behavior that is liberated by the existence of a hedge can set off a cycle of reciprocal engagements in which trust becomes mutual and reinforcing: Trust allows one to engage in certain behaviors and these behaviors, in turn, reinforce and strengthen members' trust in each other. As Putnam (1993) noted in his study of the evolution of cooperation in Italian civic communities, trust within such communities not only "lubricates cooperation [but] *cooperation itself breeds trust*" (p. 171, emphasis added). And it is this "steady accumulation of social capital," he suggested, that plays a fundamental role in the development of collective trust and cooperation. It may seem rather ironic that hedges—which represent acts of partial distrust—allow cycles of mutualistic trust to get jump-started even among wary individuals, but this, of course, is precisely their utility.

Although hedges may contribute to the emergence and resilience of collective trust, the process of hedging is not without its own risks and disadvantages. First, if others in an alliance discover that what they initially construed as an act of trust by another individual was, in actuality, predicated on a hedge (i.e., that person's presumption of partial distrust), the self-reinforcing cycle described previously may be undermined. Also, people who acquire a reputation for playing it too safe by hedging all of their bets may not inspire much trust at all and may even contribute to a collective diminution of trust.

Second, and perhaps ironically, having a hedge may unintendedly reduce or diminish individuals' commitment to a collaborative venture or alliance. When the going gets a little problematic or rough within such a collaboration, those with attractive alternatives readily available may simply decide to act on them and go elsewhere. Hedged trust may be abandoned too readily, therefore, precisely because it can be abandoned. Of course, this is precisely the intuition behind self-management strategies predicated on behavioral precommitment: Such strategies recognize that, if decision makers want to maximize their commitment to a course of action, they should burn their bridges so that retreat from commitment is rendered more difficult.

There is another potential danger associated with hedging, one that is perhaps less obvious. The process of creating hedges necessarily presupposes or requires anticipatory ruminations about things that might go wrong in a relationship. Although intended as an adaptive form of preemptive pessimism (cf. Norem & Cantor, 1986), there is evidence that the cognitive strategy of engaging in such worst case thinking can lead to unintended effects: As the results of the present study imply, such pessimistic rumination can lead to diminished expectations and exaggerated distrust and suspicion.

Another promising approach for avoiding some of the problems surrounding trust in knowledge communities is enhanced communication among members (see Messick & Brewer, 1983, for a recent overview of evidence regarding the beneficial effect of communication on cooperation). To the extent that individuals in a knowledge community recognize the difficulties that attend inferring motives and intentions from others' behavior, they may also realize that similar ambiguities attend their own actions (i.e., that their behavior creates interpretive predicaments for others). In response, individuals may proactively undertake constructive attempts to clarify their motives and intentions. In other words, just as people understand the need to obtain reassurance from others regarding their intentions and motives, they also may recognize the need to provide others with reassuring information as well. Economists and game theorists have frequently argued, of course, that cheap talk of this sort is meaningless and should be discounted. Certainly there are contexts where talk is cheap and should be ignored. For example, in arms races, actions do speak louder than words. However, in more benign contexts, cheap talk serves a variety of useful social functions, including the reduction of ambiguity and the provision of partial, even if incomplete, reassurance. Cheap talk may also build positive feelings and rapport, contributing to the development of collective identities that can help override individualistic motives and parochial orientations. Thus, although such talk may be cheap, it is often far from worthless.

As a final comment, it is interesting to think about the potentially powerful impact of collective talk on cooperation and trust within knowledge communities—the kinds of language we use when talking about the character of relationships within a knowledge community and the sort of mutual expectations about norms of conduct and obligations that tie us together. Within contemporary science, for example, one can find very different, competing construals of the social character of knowledge communities. On the one hand are those views that portray knowledge communities as Hobbesian jungles in which relentless Darwinian forces play out. Lewontin (1980), for example, advanced the view that:

> What every scientist knows, but few will admit, is that the requirement for great success [in science] is great ambition. Moreover, the ambition is for personal triumph over other men, not merely over nature. Science is a form of competitive and aggressive activity, a contest of man against man that provides knowledge as a side product. That side product is the only advantage over football. (p. 186)

For other scientists, the same landscape is suffused with very different personal values and collective orientations. For example, the German physicist Heinz Maier-Leibnitz—who trained two students who went on to win Nobel Prizes—affirmed an alternative vision of science as a knowledge community in which collective trust was a valuable asset, to be cultivated and guarded:

> I don't know whether the word *honesty* is the best word. It's the search for truth in your work. You must criticize yourself, you must consider everything that may contradict what you think, and you must never hide an error. *And the whole atmosphere should be so that everybody is like that. And later, when you are head of a lab or an institute, you must make a great deal of effort to help those who are honest, those who don't work only for their careers and try to diminish the work of others*. This is the most important task that a professor has. It's absolutely fundamental. (cited in Csikszentmihalyi, 1996, p. 166, emphasis added)

Whether the social landscape of a knowledge community is sinister or benign is often in the eye of the beholder. We should be mindful of the collective costs of these different construals in terms of realizing the benefits of collective trust or bearing the costs of collective distrust. As Frank (1988) noted,

Our views about human nature are not merely a subject of debate among behavioral scientists. They also have important practical consequences. . . . Our beliefs about human nature help shape human nature itself. What we think about ourselves and our possibilities determines what we aspire to become. (p. xi)

Thus, collective talk is not cheap either.

NOTES

1. Within the social psychological and organizational literatures, a variety of different terms have been used to describe such dilemmas, including *communication dilemma* (Bonacich & Schneider, 1992), *information dilemma* (Zucker, Darby, Brewer, & Peng, 1996), and *concealment* or *revelation dilemma* (Kramer & Messick, 1996).
2. This experience actually happened to me. I was driving alone one night on a major California freeway when a car raced up behind me and pulled alongside at the last minute. I saw the driver roll his window down and begin shouting at me. Having grown up on the Los Angeles Freeways, I knew this often means you have cut someone off, they are armed, and your life expectancy has suddenly been considerably truncated. I was prepared for the worst. I decided to roll down my window, however, and make at least an attempt at what I hoped would be a deft (and life-saving) Rogerian-style empathic intervention aimed at reconciliation. It was then that the driver shouted, "Your right rear tire is loose!" and sped off with a friendly wave. I immediately stopped my car and discovered he was right. I had just bought new tires at Sears and the person who installed them had put the hubcaps on without securely fastening the lugnuts—my tires were literally hanging onto the axles.
3. It is interesting, in this regard, that when the autokinetic effect (which is a truly random movement) is linked to a situation in which collective perceived control over movement of the dot is high, individuals do not experience the dot's movement as random at all but rather perceive highly patterned movements based on slowly developing beliefs about what others in the group are doing.

ACKNOWLEDGMENTS

Earlier versions of these ideas were presented at the Society of Experimental Social Psychology, Academy of Management Meetings, Michigan University Graduate School of Business, and Stanford University Psychology Department. Comments from participants at those conferences and colloquia are gratefully acknowledged. I am also thankful for comments provided by Ron Burt, Bill Barnett, Jane Dutton, Chip Heath, John Levine, Jim March, David Messick, Karl Weick, Phil Zimbardo, and two anonymous reviewers.

REFERENCES

Arrow, K. (1974). *The limits of organization*. New York: Norton.
Axelrod, R. M. (1984). *The evolution of cooperation*. New York: Basic Books.
Barber, B. (1983). *The logic and limits of trust*. New Brunswick, NJ: Rutgers University Press.

Bonacich, P., & Schneider, S. (1992). Communication networks and collective action. In W. G. Liebrand, D. M. Messick, & H. A. M. Wilke (Eds.), *A social psychological approach to social dilemmas* (pp. 113–140). Oxford, England: Pergamon.

Boyle, R., & Bonacich, P. (1970). The development of trust and mistrust in mixed-motives games. *Sociometry, 33,* 123–139.

Brann, P., & Foddy, M. (1988). Trust and the consumption of a deteriorating resource. *Journal of Conflict Resolution, 31,* 615–630.

Brewer, M. B. (1981). Ethnocentrism and its role in interpersonal trust. In M. B. Brewer & B. E. Collins (Eds.), *Scientific inquiry and the social sciences* (pp. 151–165). San Francisco: Jossey-Bass.

Burt, R. (1992). *Structural holes.* Cambridge, England: Cambridge University Press.

Burt, R., & Knez, M. (1996). Third-party gossip and trust. In R. M. Kramer & T. R. Tyler (Eds.), *Trust in organizations* (pp. 68–89). Thousand Oaks, CA: Sage.

Buss, D. M., & Scheier, M. F. (1976). Self-consciousness, self-awareness, and self-attribution. *Journal of Research in Personality, 10,* 463–468.

Carver, C. S., & Scheier, M. F. (1981). *Attention and self-regulation: A control theory approach to human behavior.* New York: Springer-Verlag.

Colby, K. M. (1981). Modeling a paranoid mind. *The Behavioral and Brain Sciences, 4,* 515–560.

Csikszentmihalyi, M. (1996). *Creativity.* New York: HarperCollins.

Deutsch, M. (1958). Trust and suspicion. *Journal of Conflict Resolution, 2,* 265–279.

Deutsch, M. (1973). *The resolution of conflict.* New Haven, CT: Yale University Press.

Fein, S., & Hilton, J. L. (1994). Judging others in the shadow of suspicion. *Motivation and Emotion, 18,* 167–198.

Fenigstein, A. (1979). Self-consciousness, self-attention, and social interaction. *Journal of Personality and Social Psychology, 37,* 75–86.

Fenigstein, A., & Vanable, P. A. (1992). Paranoia and self-consciousness. *Journal of Personality and Social Psychology, 62,* 129–138.

Frank, R. H. (1988). *Passions within reason: The strategic role of the emotions.* New York: Norton.

Granovetter, M. (1985). Economic action and social structure: The problem of embeddedness. *American Journal of Sociology, 91,* 481–510.

Hilton, J. L., Fein, S., & Miller, D. T. (1993). Suspicion and dispositional inference. *Personality and Social Psychology Bulletin, 19,* 501–512.

Jacobs, R. C., & Campbell, D. T. (1961). The perpetuation of an arbitrary tradition through successive generations of a laboratory microculture. *Journal of Abnormal and Social Psychology, 62,* 649–658.

Kelley, H. H. (1973). Causal schemata and the attribution process. *American Psychologist, 28,* 107–123.

Kelley, H. H., & Stahelski, A. J. (1970). The inference of intentions from moves in the prisoner's dilemma game. *Journal of Experimental Social Psychology, 6,* 401–419.

Khanna, T., Gulati, R., & Nohria, N. (1995). The dynamics of learning alliances: Competition, cooperation, and relative scope. *Harvard Business School Weekly Paper* No. 95-055. Cambridge, MA: Harvard Business School.

Kramer, R. M. (1994). The sinister attribution error. *Motivation and Emotion, 18,* 199–231.

Kramer, R. M., & Messick, D. M. (1996). Ethical cognition and the framing of organizational dilemmas: Decision makers as intuitive lawyers. In D. M. Messick & A. E. Tenbrunsel (Eds.), *Codes of conduct: Behavioral research into business ethics* (pp. 162–185). New York: Russell Sage Foundation.

Kramer, R. M., Meyerson, D., & Davis, G. (1990). How much is enough? Psychological components of "guns versus butter" decisions in a security dilemma. *Journal of Personality and Social Psychology, 58,* 984–993.

Lewontin, R. (1980). Honest Jim Watson's big thriller about DNA. In P. Stent (Ed.), *The Double helix: Text, commentary, reviews, original papers* (pp. 73–90). New York: Norton.

Lindskold, S. (1978). Trust development, the GRIT proposal, and the effects of conciliatory acts on conflict and cooperation. *Psychological Bulletin, 85,* 772–793.

Luhmann, N. (1979). *Trust and power.* New York: Wiley.

Lyubomirsky, S., & Nolen-Hoeksema, S. (1993). Self-perpetuating properties of dysphoric rumination. *Journal of Personality and Social Psychology, 65,* 339–349.

March, J. G., & Olsen, J. (1989). *Institutions.* New York: The Free Press.

Meacham, J. A. (1983). Wisdom and the context of knowledge: Knowing that one doesn't know. *Contributions in Human Development, 8,* 111–134.

Messick, D. M., & Brewer, M. B. (1983). Solving social dilemmas: A review. *Personality and Social Psychology, 4,* 11–44.

Messick, D. M., Wilke, H., Brewer, M. B., Kramer, R. M., Zemke, P., & Lui, L. (1983). Individual adaptations and structural changes as solutions to social dilemmas. *Journal of Personality and Social Psychology, 44,* 294–309.

Meyerson, D., Weick, K. E., & Kramer, R. M. (1996). Swift trust and temporary groups. In R. M. Kramer & T. R. Tyler (Eds.), *Trust in organizations: Frontiers of theory and research* (pp. 166–195). Thousand Oaks, CA: Sage.

Miller, G. J. (1992). *Managerial dilemmas: The political economy of hierarchies.* New York: Cambridge University Press.

Norem, J. K., & Cantor, N. (1986). Defensive pessimism: Harnessing anxiety as motivation. *Journal of Personality and Social Psychology, 51,* 1208–1217.

Parker, R., Lui, L., Messick, D., Brewer, M., Kramer, R., Samuelson, C., & Wilke, H. (1983). A computer laboratory for studying resource dilemmas. *Behavioral Science, 28,* 298–304.

Porter, T. M. (1995). *Trust in numbers: The pursuit of objectivity in science and public life.* Princeton, NJ: Princeton University Press.

Putnam, R. (1993). *Making democracy work.* Princeton, NJ: Princeton University Press.

Pyszczynski, T., & Greenberg, J. (1987). Self-regulatory perseveration and the depressive self-focusing style: A self-awareness theory of reactive depression. *Psychological Bulletin, 102,* 122–138.

Rotter, J. B. (1980). Interpersonal trust, trustworthiness, and gullibility. *American Psychologist, 35,* 1–7.

Sherif, M. (1935). A study of some factors in social perception. *Archives of Psychology, 31,* No. 187, 107–119.

Shilts, R. (1987). *And the band played on: Politics, people and the AIDS epidemic.* New York: St. Martin's Press.

Tesser, A. (1978). Self-generated attitude change. In L. Berkowitz (Ed.), *Advances in experimental social psychology* (Vol. 21, pp. 181–227). New York: Academic Press.

Vorauer, J. D., & Ross, M. (1993). Making mountains out of molehills: An informational goals analysis of self- and social perception. *Personality and Social Psychology Bulletin, 19,* 620–632.

Weick, K. E., & Roberts, K. H. (1993). Collective mind in organizations: Heedful interrelating on flight decks. *Administrative Science Quarterly, 38,* 357–381.

Wilson, T. D., & Kraft, D. (1993). Why do I love thee? Effects of repeated introspections about a dating relationship on attitudes towards the relationship. *Personality and Social Psychology Bulletin, 19,* 409–418.

Wyer, R. S. (1996). *Ruminative thoughts (Advances in social cognition, Vol. IX).* Mahwah, NJ: Lawrence Erlbaum Associates.

Zimbardo, P. G., Andersen, S. M., & Kabat, L. G. (1981). Induced hearing deficit generates experimental paranoia. *Science, 212,* 1529–1531.

Zucker, L. G. (1977). The role institutionalization in cultural persistence. *American Sociological Review, 42,* 726–743.

Zucker, L. G. (1986). Production of trust: Institutional sources of economic structure, 1840–1920. In B. M. Staw & L. L. Cummings (Eds.), *Research in organizational behavior* (Vol. 8, pp. 53–111). Greenwich, CT: JAI.

Zucker, L. G., Darby, M. R., Brewer, M. B., & Peng, Y. (1996). Collaboration structure and information dilemmas in biotechnology: Organizational boundaries as trust production. In R. M. Kramer & T. R. Tyler (Eds.), *Trust in organizations: Frontiers of theory and research* (pp. 90–113). Thousand Oaks, CA: Sage.

COMMUNICATION AND
BEHAVIORAL SYSTEMS

9

Normative Influences in Organizations

Robert B. Cialdini
Arizona State University

Renee J. Bator
State University of New York at Plattsburgh

Rosanna E. Guadagno
Arizona State University

In a case study on leadership in a computer consulting firm, one consultant had this to say about the corporate environment:

> You had a management which knew what people [employees] could do, which took an interest in them and made demands. There were very strict guidelines during that time. If you had a "conference" that went on half the night, there were no excuses for not arriving at the right time the following morning. If you did not arrive on time you got a public reprimand. You had to be there at 8 o'clock in the morning, in fresh shape. You were allowed to do whatever you wanted until then.... (Alvesson, 1992, p. 189)

This example illustrates that in organizations, as in any group, there are rules for behavior that are understood by all group members. These rules may or may not be formal, written rules. There also may be unwritten exceptions to the written rules that govern organizational behavior. When these rules are unwritten, they must be transmitted or taught to new group members. These rules for behavior are called *norms*. Although they do serve as guidelines for socially appropriate behavior, some norms are explicit rules and some are implied or unspoken. Both kinds of norms are equally important. Members of a group who behave in ways consistent with the normative rules for behavior receive greater acceptance and approval from the group than the members who deviate from the group norms (Turner, 1991).

How do people learn which attitudes and behaviors are important in their group? What types of normative rules do people learn? How are norms transmitted to new group members? And, how do these norms change over time? There are a number of means by which group members form, transmit, and learn the rules for appropriate behavior.

Hardin and Higgins (1996) conceived of normative influence in terms of what they called shared reality. They argued that shared reality is formed and sustained for individuals when their experience and sense of reality is shared with others. This formation and transmission of reality occurs through a social verification process, which occurs when individuals receive feedback from other group members on the appropriateness of their view of reality. From this perspective, social interaction is necessary for the establishment of reality for group members. In addition, a perceiver's notion of shared reality helps regulate the self; one's social environment alters one's concept of self. Conversely, one's social environment and the individuals in that environment are affected by one's perception of self. Thus, shared reality and the social verification process provide a mechanism by which individuals define themselves and their social environment and therefore form social norms.

The purpose of this chapter is to review the literature on social norms in an attempt to understand more about normative processes that occur in organizations. We start with an overview of the social psychological research on norms. Next, we review the organizational psychology literature on norms and attempt to integrate the two bodies of research. Then, we review certain applications of different types of normative behavior and analyze them in terms of our integrated view of norms. Finally, we conclude with a series of suggestions on ways to modify or establish norms within organizations.

A REVIEW OF THE LITERATURE ON *NORMS*

Many of the topics of interest to persuasion researchers are based on social *norms*—understood rules for accepted and expected behavior (Myers, 1993). Adherence to these rules typically allows one to avoid rejection and gain social approval. In a number of classic experiments, social psychologists have manipulated the presence of a norm and repeatedly found adherence to it when it was salient.

Sherif's (1937) work on conformity is one of the earliest investigations to demonstrate the powerful influence of norms. In this study, participants were seated in a dark room with only a pinpoint of light directed at a wall.

Without a reference point, the light appeared to move slightly and participants were asked how far it moved from its original position. For half of the participants, the first set of trials occurred on an individual basis and a second set of trials was conducted in a group format. The other half of the participants underwent the group conditions first and then the individual conditions. The participants who first experienced the group condition responded with highly consistent estimates within each group; these measurements were stable over the series of group trials. When these participants moved on to the individual trials, the pattern of their responses from the group condition remained in force. Those participants who underwent the individual condition first established more divergent estimates of movement, varying by as much as 7 inches from person to person. But when these participants were then placed in the group context, their responses converged in the first trial and their compromised responses continued over the series of group trials. This research demonstrated that under conditions of uncertainty, people incorporate the judgments of others into their own judgments.

Aronson and O'Leary (1982–1983) took advantage of the power of norms in their research to investigate means to reduce water consumption on a university campus. When a large sign reading:

(1) Wet down
(2) Turn water off
(3) Soap up
(4) Rinse off

was hung in the men's shower room, only 6% complied with the request. However, when the sign was removed and an undergraduate confederate modeled the posted routine, 49% followed his lead. When two confederates were employed to model, compliance rose to 67%. This experiment provides further evidence that humans look to the actions of others to learn how to respond in an uncertain situation and the more people demonstrating the same behavior, the more powerful the influence.

Looking to one's social network for information regarding the proper behavior has definite adaptive qualities because the actions of others provide a good indication of what is likely to be approved and effective conduct in the situation (Cialdini, 1993). Festinger (1954) suggested that when what constitutes appropriate behavior is uncertain, people come to rely increasingly more on the social reality. In an ambiguous situation, the actions of surrounding others provide guidelines for behavior. An individual is especially likely to attend to and follow the lead of others when the environment is uncertain, the number of others from whom to gauge what is appropriate is large, and those being observed are similar or successful (Cialdini & Trost, 1998).

Two kinds of social norms have been distinguished: *Descriptive norms*, which describe what most others do in a situation, and *injunctive norms*, which describe what most others approve or disapprove there. It is important to distinguish between descriptive and injunctive norms because they differ in their power and strength across situations. We first describe the research on descriptive norms, which are found to influence individuals when it is the only normative information available. Next we examine the research on injunctive norms, which tend to be more powerful motivators of behavior as their influence carries across environments.

DESCRIPTIVE NORMS

Cialdini, Kallgren, and Reno (1991) executed a research program to examine the impact of descriptive and injunctive norms. In their first three experiments, they examined the effect of descriptive norms on participants' decisions to litter. In Experiment 1, the researchers manipulated the environment to be either heavily littered (representing a prolittering descriptive norm) or free of litter. In addition, the researchers manipulated the salience of this descriptive information. In the high-norm salience condition, a confederate littered the environment and in the low-norm salience condition, the confederate just walked through the area. The researchers found that participants littered more in the littered environment compared to the clean environment. This supported the hypothesis that individuals will follow the behavior of others in order to determine how to behave. In the high-norm salience conditions, this effect was even stronger: A confederate who littered produced the most littering in the study when the environment was already littered but produced the least littering when the environment started out clean. Thus, bringing attention to the existing norms of the situation spurred participants to follow the norms.

In the second experiment, the researchers found that a single piece of litter in a clean environment could also serve as a norm salience manipulation by prompting the participants to notice the state of the environment. In this case, when the state of the environment was clean except for that single piece of litter, the participants noted the descriptive norm (that most people do not litter) and were especially likely to follow it by failing to litter themselves. Indeed, a single piece of litter lying in an otherwise clean environment generated less littering than did a litter-free environment. This finding attests to the importance of establishing cues that heighten the salience of a desirable norm if organizations wish that norm to be maximally effective.

Experiment 3 was a conceptual replication of Experiment 2 with a few minor changes. Once again, the researchers found an environment that made the antilittering descriptive norm salient (that with a single piece of litter) produced the least amount of littering. These three experiments demonstrated the power of descriptive norms as the participants noted and followed the behavior of others, especially when the norm was made prominent in participants' consciousness.

INJUNCTIVE NORMS

Cialdini et al. (1991) continued their program of research with a comparison of the power of descriptive versus injunctive norms (i.e., what is done versus what is approved). In Experiment 4, the researchers used a fully littered environment in which the litter was either scattered throughout the area (representing a prolittering descriptive norm) or swept into piles (representing an antilittering injunctive norm). They predicted that making the prolittering descriptive norm more salient, by having a confederate litter into an environment of scattered litter, would increase littering there. The more important prediction was that making the antilittering injunctive norm salient, by having a confederate litter into an environment of swept litter, would reduce littering there. These predictions were confirmed, suggesting the power of injunctive norm salience. Cialdini et al. concluded that, "shifting subjects' focus from descriptive (unswept litter) to injunctive (swept litter) normative cues resulted in differing behavioral tendencies that were nonetheless consistent with the type of normative information on which the participant had been focused" (p. 214).

Experiment 5 examined whether focusing participants on the antilittering injunctive norm through a priming process could reduce littering behavior. According to the notion of spreading activation (Anderson, 1976, 1983; Collins & Loftus, 1975; McClelland & Rumelhart, 1981), if norms are stored in memory in a network system as some evidence suggests (Harvey & Enzle, 1981), then priming norms that are differentially related to a target antilittering injunctive norm should differentially activate the target norm and lead to commensurate levels of littering. Flyers with various messages were tucked under the windshield wipers of cars in a library parking lot. The statements on the flyers were of varying conceptual proximity to the antilittering norm—from a specific "do not litter" appeal to messages of increasing distance from the antilittering norm (encouraging recycling, conserving energy, voting, and a visit to the local art museum). These messages were designed to prime (or activate) the antilittering norm more strongly the more conceptually proximate they were to the norm. The researchers expected the least littering when the antilittering norm was primed directly, with gradual increases in litter as the priming message was progressively distant from the issue of littering. The results supported the hypothesis;

there was a significant decrease in littering as participants became focused on issues that were more similar to the antilittering injunctive norm.

The program of research by Cialdini, Kallgren, and Reno (1991) provides instructive data regarding the power of normative information. Their first three experiments demonstrated that the least littering occurred when participants came on a single piece of litter in an otherwise clean environment. Focusing individuals in this way on the descriptive antilittering norm led to behavior consistent with that norm. Experiments 4 and 5 introduced injunctive information into participants' behavioral decisions and the results indicated that focusing individuals on the injunctive norm against littering led to reduced littering rates, even when the descriptive norm favored littering. This tells us that if an individual is confronted with a descriptive norm favoring undesirable behavior, it may be possible nonetheless to reduce such behavior by making a contradicting, injunctive norm salient.

In a later study, Cialdini, Kallgren, and Reno (1991) compared the power of injunctive versus descriptive information across situations. They found that injunctive information motivated participants' behavior even when it was transmitted in one situation and the participants' responses occurred in a different situation. Descriptive norms were much less powerful in their ability to motivate behavior across situations. The researchers concluded that injunctive social norms are the most widely applicable in their ability to encourage specific behaviors across a variety of situations and target populations.

More recently, research has applied the findings of Cialdini, Kallgren, and Reno (1991) to the development of antilittering public service announcements (Bator, 1997). In this research, antilittering injunctive information that was presented in a televised message successfully motivated antilittering behavior hours later in a different, heavily littered (where the descriptive norm was prolittering) environment. This finding supports the power of injunctive norms in their ability to direct behavior across situations.

How might normative behavior within organizations be interpreted from this perspective? What are the implications and conclusions for organizations? Although there are normative theories of behavior within organizational psychology, we can also interpret normative behavior in terms of the descriptive and injunctive norms. Before we discuss normative behavior within organizations and the transmission of group norms to new members, let us first review the way organizational researchers view normative behavior in organizations. Then, we look at specific organizational norms and discuss each from an integrated organizational and social psychological perspective.

A REVIEW OF ORGANIZATIONAL LITERATURE ON NORMS

Although any group will have a set of established behavioral norms, the content and transmission of these norms will vary greatly from group to group or from organization to organization. As an example of the content and transmission of norms varying across organizations, consider the following two new employee accounts of group dynamics. The first example illustrates fighting between groups:

> I was part of a technical team that was supposed to offer product support on a new product. When the roles of everyone were defined, the project group was very adamant about keeping control of their product in their jurisdiction, although they weren't the ones who developed the concept and proved it workable. We were! They refused to compromise and what was stupid was the director of engineering had to intervene. It was it like a bunch of kids fighting.

From this experience, the new employee got evidence that cooperation between groups was not the norm in this organization. A second example illustrates cooperation between groups: "We were meeting in a group to test circuitry. Everyone's idea was shared in the discussion, including mine. Even though I was new, they wanted to know what I thought" (Gundry & Rousseau, 1994, p. 1076). Unlike the first account, this employee got evidence that working together towards a common goal was normative in this organization.

Normative behavior also varies within any one organization (Cooke & Rousseau, 1988). Within one organization, norms may differ depending on the department. For example, a company might have an overall strong norm for high productivity but the content of the norm may differ within the organization (e.g., what an employee needs to do to be extremely productive may vary by his or her position in the company, as well as the specific norms in his or her department). Thus, norms differ across organizations in both their mode of transmission and in their content; norms also differ within organizations, with any one department holding norms that vary from those of another department.

Organizational researchers typically discuss normative behavior within organizations in terms of the *climate* and *culture* of the organization. *Climate* is defined as individuals' perceptions of their organizational group that are influenced by the characteristics of both the organization and the individual (Schneider & Hall, 1972). Climate can also be defined as the perceptions of organizational policies shared by most group members or, simply, "the way things are around here" (Cooke & Szumal, 1993). As we saw in the statement made by the consultant in the beginning of this chapter, employees in the consulting firm understood that everyone was expected to (and did) work as many hours as needed to get the job done. Thus, organizational climate encompasses the descriptive norms of an organization (Cooke & Szumal, 1993) because climate typifies what people actually do.

Culture is defined as "a set of cognitions shared by members of a social unit" (O'Reilly, Chatman, & Caldwell, 1991, p. 491). Additionally, culture is a reflection of the common ways of thinking and believing within an organizational group, as well as norms that are common behavioral expectations relevant to all group members (Cooke & Rousseau, 1988). One example of how culture affects behavior is that although employees of the computer consulting firm worked as many hours as needed to complete their projects, they also understood that, to avoid disapproval, they had to arrive promptly at 8 a.m. every morning regardless of how late they had worked the night before. Thus, whereas organizational climate provides more descriptive norm information, organizational culture provides more injunctive norm information (Cooke & Szumal, 1993).

There are two important characteristics of organizations with strong cultures or a strong set of injunctive norms: intensity and presence of crystallization. In an intense culture, group members elicit strong approval and disapproval responses to certain behaviors of individual group members that are central to its set of values. Employees in an intense culture, for example, may be disapproved of by both their supervisor as well as other group members if they arrive to work after 8 a.m. Crystallization refers to an almost unanimous agreement on the content of important values among group members (e.g., everyone in the consulting firm agreed that working long hours was important; Hackman, 1992; O'Reilly et al., 1991).

Factors that influence compliance to group norms include the content of the group norm, individual adherence to or rejection of the norm, and an individual's role in the group (Hackman, 1992). For example, norms that are highly crystallized and intense are more strictly adhered to by group members than norms that are not. So if there was little agreement regarding the importance of coming in early after working especially late, one would expect lower rates of compliance. Additionally, the greater the overall group cohesiveness, the stronger the compliance to the organizational behavioral norms by group members. In this case, members of a cohesive group would probably inquire with one another regarding the appropriate time to arrive at work after a late night on the job and this group affinity would provide encouragement to follow through with this act and disapproval if the individual did not arrive for work at 8 a.m. Additionally, it is permissible for high-status group members to deviate from a group norm without sanction, whereas the same behavior would be met with strong disapproval if a low-status member committed the same act (Hackman, 1992). For example, it is unlikely that the president of the consultancy firm would receive a reprimand for failing to arrive for work by 8 a.m.

Because the content of organizational norms differs across organizational groups, researchers have developed quantitative measures of norms within organizations. These include the Organizational Culture Profile (OCP; O'Reilly et al., 1991), which measures person–organization fit, and the Organizational Culture Inventory (OCI; Cooke & Rousseau, 1988), which evaluates the content of organizational norms and categorizes the organizational culture on the basis of the composition of its norms. Organizations in the same industry that are of similar sizes, hierarchical structures, age, and technological sophistication tend to have similar cultures (O'Reilly et al., 1991) as well as similar normative beliefs and values.

The concept of norms is readily applied to organizational contexts. An examination of norms from this perspective reveals that norms differ between organizations in terms of their mode of transmission and their content. Within organizations, norms may differ by department. The climate of an organization primarily describes what most people do (the descriptive norms). The culture of an organization refers more to what is expected or approved (the injunctive norms). One should expect stronger adherence to a norm depending on the intensity and presence of crystallization (unanimous agreement with the norm). Finally, measures have been developed to examine the person–organization fit (OCP) and a means to categorize the culture of an organization depending on the norms of that organization (OCI).

APPLICATION I: ORGANIZATIONAL DISHONESTY

What happens when organizations condone or support the use of dishonest business practices; when dishonesty becomes a part of the organizational culture and climate? According Cialdini's (1996) Triple Tumor of Dishonesty model, organizations that establish dishonest business practices as a socially acceptable behavioral norm stand to lose far more than they stand to gain. Although dishonest business practices usually lead to a short-term increase in profits, the long-term consequences are more costly (Stark, 1993). The three tumors refer to the major long-term detrimental consequences for an organization that engages in dishonest business practices.

The first tumor deals with the decrease in long-term profits due to an organization's bad reputation and loss of business or clients. For example, a company's climate might foster approval of its sales team promising to deliver goods to customers sooner than the goods are actually available, provided that this practice increases sales. Although sales will increase for a while, once customers learn that the company cannot keep its end of the bargain, the customers will not do business with the company again.

A good reputation is extremely important in business and deception, such as that previously described, can do much to undermine a company's reputation for honesty in business deals (Aaker, 1991; Labich, 1992; Steckmest, 1982; Weitz, Castleberry, & Tanner, 1992). Not only will the company lose business with the customers that were deceived but word of their dishonest business practices could tarnish their reputation. This may cause the company to lose business with potential new customers as well. Thus, as the model suggests, dishonest business practices may lead to a short-term increase in profit. However, the probable long-term losses make the acceptance of this norm questionable.

The second tumor of the Triple Tumor of Dishonesty model refers to the way an organizational norm of dishonesty will affect individuals within the organization. If the dishonesty norm does not fit with an employee's personal values, one of two things may happen: (a) An employee will not change his or her self-concept to be in line with the group norm and will not become accustomed to the organizational dishonesty or (b) an employee will change his or her self-concept to match the group norm and therefore become comfortable with the dishonest policy.

According to the Triple Tumor model, if no self-concept change occurs, the employee will become conflicted. Stress (Dewe, 1993), illness (Cohen, Tyrell, & Smith, 1991), and absenteeism will increase while job satisfaction and productivity decrease (Barnett, Marshall, Raudenbach, & Brennan, 1993). These problems may be exacerbated by an employee's behavioral compliance with the dishonest policies without a subsequent change in his or her belief system. The conflict experienced by an employee behaving in a way inconsistent with his or her personal beliefs enhances the likelihood that the employee will leave the company. In fact, research suggests that lower job satisfaction increases the probability that an individual will leave a company (Carsten & Spector, 1987). Thus, companies that engage in unethical business practices may have a higher employee turnover rate than companies that support honest business practices.

Conversely, if employees adjust their self-concepts to match the group norm, even stronger negative repercussions are likely. Although these employees are more likely to stay with the company, they may now see themselves as the type of person who engages in dishonest business practices and, as a result, they may see the organization as a place where it is normative to act this way. This suggests that the remaining employees may be more likely to cheat the organization as well as its business partners and clients. Attitudes and behavior such as this lead to increased employee theft and fraud (Brown, 1986; Jones & Terris, 1983; Terris & Jones, 1982).

Employee theft and fraud cost U.S. businesses about $120 billion per year (Buss, 1993) and this figure is expected to rise to $200 billion per year by the turn of the century (Govoni, 1992; Snyder, Blair, & Arndt, 1990). As the numbers illustrate, employee theft has become a serious and costly problem for organizations. Additional research suggests that once theft has become an accepted organizational group norm, the behavior is unlikely to stop (Payne, 1989). However, the norms regulating what and how much an employee can steal will vary by organization (Greenberg & Scott, 1996). Thus, in keeping with the model, once a norm of dishonesty is established in organizations, employees uncomfortable with this norm will leave the company, whereas the remaining employees will accept the norm and start to view themselves as less honest. This self-concept change may then lead to greater employee dishonesty, evidenced by increased employee theft and fraud within the organization as well as increased dishonesty in business deals.

If left untreated, employee theft should continue to be the pervasive social norm, repeatedly transmitted to new employees. So even with a high employee turnover rate, the dishonesty norm can persist (Jacobs & Campbell, 1961; Nielsen & Miller, 1997). Unfortunately, the current methods for dealing with this problem may also have negative repercussions. In fact, the means by which organizations deal with employee dishonesty may actually exacerbate the problem. Organizations often attempt to confront this problem not by changing the dishonesty norm but instead by spending increasing amounts of money on high-tech security and surveillance systems. These high tech systems facilitate the growth of tumor three—the cost of the surveillance of an organization's employees.

Although costly in monetary terms (Bylinski, 1991; Halpern, 1991), these security measures also may prove costly by giving employees the message that the organization does not trust its employees (Deci, Connell, & Ryan, 1989), decreasing the sense of organizational community. Employees see the organizational management as distrustful of them, which can facilitate a belief that management is the adversary. These beliefs may lead to employee hostility and retaliation (e.g., lack of cooperation among employees, attempts to bypass the security system, etc.), which in turn can generate increased costs in more advanced security and surveillance equipment. In fact, Greenberg and Scott (1996) reported that retaliation against management is one of two possible motives for employee theft. The other motive postulated by Greenberg and Scott is a desire to "even the score" for unfair treatment. This perceived unfair treatment is often an activity that employees view as insulting their sense of identity (Bies & Tripp, 1996).

The organizational management's expectation that employees will be dishonest and cannot be trusted may actually lead to greater dishonest behavior on the part of the employees (Tenbrunsel & Messick, 1998). The transmission of this expectation of dishonesty may lead to a self-fulfilling prophecy, with the employees acting in a more dishonest manner than usual because they are confirming or living up to management's expectations (Harris, Milich, Corbitt, & Hoover, 1992). In fact, research suggests that being instructed to observe a subordinate may actually lead supervisors to report that subordinate as less trustworthy even if the worker did nothing dishonest while under surveillance (Strickland, Barefoot, & Hockenstein, 1976). Additionally, the use of surveillance equipment may cause employees to attribute their honest behavior to the presence of the security systems rather than to an internal sense of honesty. So, in keeping with the Triple Tumor of Dishonesty model, this type of monitoring is likely to support the dishonest self-concept rather than encourage employees to view themselves as honest.

According to Coleman (1985), white-collar crime falls into one of two categories: organizational crime and occupational crime. Organizational crime is defined as crime committed with the approval and encouragement of the organization in order to advance the company. Occupational crime refers to employee theft within the organization for the personal gain of an individual employee. The Triple Tumor of Dishonesty Model suggests that companies that engage in organizational crime foster high levels of occupational crime. Acceptance of one type of crime leads to the growth of the other. Regardless of the type of tumor or the type of crime, once a norm of dishonesty is established, much like a real tumor, the problem grows as employees transmit the norm to one another. If not held accountable for their actions, a few dishonest employees, especially those in positions of leadership, may corrupt a company.

This issue of organizational dishonesty can be interpreted in terms of descriptive and injunctive norms. When organizations condone unethical business practices, it is not usually in the form of written company policy. Instead, the transmission of this injunctive information is more likely to occur by observation of what the supervisor does himself or herself, as well as the supervisor's approval of the unethical behavior of other employees. In these cases, the supervisor's behavior provides injunctive information that the organization's culture condones dishonesty.

In fact, research suggests that a supervisor may encourage employee theft by modeling the behavior or by tacitly approving the behavior on the part of his or her subordinates (Greenberg & Scott, 1996). The descriptive norm or climate favoring unethical behavior is probably transmitted through an examination of what one's coworkers are doing. If the organization has a strong culture or a strong set of injunctive norms, then one could say there is intensity and presence of crystallization. This means that there is strong approval for the profits associated with cheating one's clients and unanimous agreement with this goal. However, according to the model, this unethical behavior often leads to cheating within the organization, costly surveillance, a decreased sense of organizational community, and hostility toward the organization. The short-term profits associated with an injunctive and descriptive norm favoring dishonesty can result in serious, long-term loss.

APPLICATION 2: COMMUNICATING
GROUP NORMS TO NEWCOMERS

How do newcomers to an organization learn group norms? There are a number of possible ways. A new employee may learn injunctive norms by attending a new employee orientation, by noting the behavior of the supervisor, or by watching how the supervisor responds to the behavior of others. Descriptive norms may be gauged through observation of the behavior of other group members or by a description of behavioral norms as explained by established group members.

According to Gundry and Rousseau (1994), newcomers learn organizational norms through the experience of critical incidents. They defined a critical incident as an event that occurs early in a newcomer's tenure on the job, where the purpose of the incident and the consequences of the action can be easily understood by the newcomer. Newcomers use these critical events to shape their normative beliefs and their behavior. For example, a new employee learned that reference for authority was important norm within his organizational group:

> I was in a meeting held in the Executive conference room when a fellow engineer came in late. Reaching for the nearest chair, he sat down only to be informed that it was the Vice President's chair (its back was higher than all the others in the room), by the manager of a sister group in our department. This fellow was surprised at the ludicrousness of this comment since the VP wasn't even at the meeting, until the director of the department told him to find another seat. How absurd. (Gundry & Rousseau, 1994, p. 1075)

From this event, the engineer inferred that sitting in the vice president's chair is considered inappropriate by his group. If he wants to be accepted by the group, he will make sure that he never sits in the VP's chair. Thus, there are two components of a critical incident—the description of the event and the message inferred from it (Gundry & Rousseau, 1994).

The transmission of group norms to organizational newcomers usually focuses on two general issues or topics (Hackman, 1992). The first issue deals with information regarding the rewards and punishments available within the organizational environment as well as information on who controls the allocation of these rewards and punishments. The second issue focuses on normative information that provides details regarding the behaviors that lead to rewards as well as the behaviors that lead to avoidance of punishment. The following statement from a new employee exemplifies this:

> The company held two parties recently for this project. They were catered events at nearby restaurants. They were attended by many employees of this project at all different levels. Their purpose was to promote the application of hard work being performed by employees. (Gundry & Rousseau, 1994, p. 1075)

From this, a new employee should learn that hard work will lead to parties and other rewards for the workgroup and that he or she should attempt to increase productivity to earn future rewards.

If a newcomer wants to be successful and fit in, he or she will pay close attention to any information on the group norms within the particular organization leading to rewards and avoiding punishment. Thus, the effort a newcomer puts into learning group norms has a tremendous impact on his or her future in the organization. For example, the amount of effort an individual puts into learning the organizational norms, as measured by participation in optional organizational social events, is a significant predictor of job satisfaction (Chatman, 1991). Other factors affecting adherence to and understanding of organizational norms have to do with the crystallization of the normative structure. For example, the greater the cohesiveness of an organizational group, the more likely group members will conform to the group norms. Stronger group cohesion also leads to stronger belief systems that are resistant to modification even when they are outdated or inaccurate (Hackman, 1992). A strong belief system and a cohesive group make it easier for a newcomer to learn the normative rules for behavior.

As we saw in the previous application, if organizational dishonesty is one of the more valued group norms, adoption of this norm will help the newcomer fit in but it will also lead to negative long-term repercussions for both the employee and the organization. This is a crucial piece of information to consider, especially given that research shows that group norms persist even after original group members are no longer part of the group (Nielsen & Miller, 1997).

SUGGESTIONS FOR HARNESSING NORMATIVE INFORMATION IN ORGANIZATIONS

How can supervisors take advantage of descriptive and injunctive norms to create a work environment that fosters honest, productive employees? This chapter provides some guidelines in this domain. Whereas most organizations probably do suggest or imply a goal of honesty, our interpretation of the research indicates that organizations would be wise to make such descriptive and injunctive norms consistently salient. These norms have been found to be highly influential in motivating employee honesty and organizations should take advantage of this fairly simple yet powerful tactic. Because injunctive norms have been found to be more powerful than descriptive norms across situations and because injunctive norms are more dependent on supervisors' actions, these supervisors are the individuals who should emphasize the importance of honesty and productivity.

It is important that from the first interview with a prospective employee, supervisors should stress both injunctive and descriptive norms for honesty and productivity. In terms of injunctive norms for honesty, the interviewer should emphasize that the organization is based on honest business practices and a strong work ethic. He or she should explain that this philosophy is apparent not only from official corporate policy but also in the managers' behavior and (to include descriptive information) also in the behavior of the staff at every level of the organization. It is important to note that such an immediate emphasis of injunctive and descriptive norms for honesty and productivity should also help screen against employees who would be a poor fit.

It is especially important that these descriptive and injunctive norms be evident on the job. Supervisors should provide a strong example of their goals and messages and memos should attest to this common objective. If there is ever a problem, such that employees are found to be dishonest or unproductive, supervisors should refrain from describing the problem as a regrettably frequent one. Doing so would characterize dishonesty or low productivity as the descriptive norm. Instead supervisors should express strong disapproval for this uncommon behavior and employees should be reminded that most of the staff is honest and hardworking. Supervisors are urged to intervene in all instances of dishonesty (e.g., even theft of office supplies). Doing otherwise could lead to the spread of a protheft descriptive norm among employees, as well as an implied weak antitheft injunctive norm from the supervisors' lack of concern for this dishonest behavior. Again, supervisors are encouraged to express strong disapproval and emphasize that this behavior is unusual and unacceptable. Because humans tend to decide how to behave by looking to those around them, and often to those in positions of authority, organizations could benefit (in terms of honesty and productivity, or any other quality deemed desirable) by taking advantage of the power of descriptive and injunctive norms.

REFERENCES

Aaker, D. A. (1991). *Managing brand equity.* New York: The Free Press.

Alvesson, M. (1992). Leadership as social integrative action. A study of a computer consultancy company. *Organization Studies, 13*(2), 185–209.

Anderson, J. R. (1976). *Language, memory, and thought*. Hillsdale, NJ: Lawrence Erlbaum Associates.

Anderson, J. R. (1983). *The architecture of cognition*. Cambridge, MA: Harvard University Press.

Aronson, E., & O'Leary, M. (1982–1983). The relative effects of models and prompts on energy conservation. *Journal of Environmental Systems, 12*, 219–224.

Barnett, R. C., Marshall, N. L., Raudenbach, S. W., & Brennan, R. T. (1993). Gender and the relationship between job experiences and psychological distress. *Journal of Personality and Social Psychology, 64*, 794–806.

Bator, R. J. (1997). *Effective public service announcements: Linking social norms to visual memory cues*. Unpublished doctoral dissertation, Arizona State University, Tempe.

Bies, R. J., & Tripp, T. M. (1996). Beyond distrust: Getting even and the need for revenge. In R. M. Kramer & T. Tyler (Eds.), *Trust in organizations* (pp. 246–260). Thousand Oaks, CA: Sage.

Brown, T. S. (1986). Convenience store losses and employees' attitudes. *Psychological Reports, 58*, 35–42.

Buss, D. (1993, April). Ways to curtail employee theft. *Nation's Business* (Vol. 81), 36, 38.

Bylinski, G. (1991). How companies spy on employees. *Fortune* (Vol. 124), 131–140.

Carsten, J. M., & Spector, P. E. (1987). Unemployment, job satisfaction, and employee turnover. *Journal of Applied Psychology, 72*, 374–381.

Chatman, J. A. (1991). Matching people and organizations: Selection and socialization in public accounting firms. *Administrative Science Quarterly, 36*, 459–484.

Cialdini, R. B. (1993). *Influence: Science and practice* (3rd ed.). New York: Harper Collins.

Cialdini, R. B. (1996). Social influence and the triple tumor structure of organizational dishonesty. In D. M. Messick & A. Tenbrunsel (Eds.), *Behavioral research and business ethics* (pp. 44–58). New York: Russell Sage Foundation.

Cialdini, R. B., Kallgren, C. A., & Reno, R. R. (1991). A focus theory of normative conduct: A theoretical refinement and reevaluation of the role of norms in human behavior. *Advances in Experimental Social Psychology, 24*, 201–234.

Cialdini, R. B., & Trost, M. R. (1998). Social influence: Social norms, conformity, and compliance. In D. Gilbert, S. Fiske, & G. Lindzey (Eds.), *The handbook of social psychology* (4th ed., pp. 151–192). New York: McGraw-Hill.

Cohen, S., Tyrell, D. A., & Smith, A. P. (1991). Psychological stress and susceptibility to the common cold. *New England Journal of Medicine, 325*, 606–612.

Coleman, J. W. (1985). *The criminal elite: The sociology of white collar crime*. New York: St. Martin's Press.

Collins, A. M., & Loftus, E. F. (1975). A spreading-activation theory of semantic memory. *Psychological Review, 81*, 348–374.

Cooke, R. A., & Rousseau, D. M. (1988). Behavioral norms and expectations: A quantitative approach to the assessment of organizational culture. *Group and Organization Studies, 13*(3), 245–273.

Cooke, R. A., & Szumal, J. L. (1993). Measuring normative beliefs and shared behavioral expectations in organizations: The reliability and validity of the Organizational Culture Inventory. *Psychological Reports, 72*(3), 1299–1330.

Deci, E. L., Connell, J. P., & Ryan, R. M. (1989). Self determination in a work organization. *Journal of Applied Psychology, 74*, 580–593.

Dewe, P. (1993). Measuring primary appraisal. *Journal of Social Behavior and Personality, 8*, 673–685.

Festinger, L. (1954). A theory of social comparison processes. *Human Relations, 7*, 117–140.

Govoni, S. J. (1992). To catch a thief. *CFO*, 24–32.

Greenberg, J., & Scott, K. S. (1996). Why do workers bite the hands that feed them? Employee theft as a social exchange process. *Research in Organizational Behavior, 18*, 111–156.

Gundry, L. K., & Rousseau, D. M. (1994). Critical incidents in communicating culture to newcomers: The meaning is the message. *Human Relations, 47*, 1063–1087.

Hackman, J. R., (1992). Group influences on individuals in organizations. In M. D. Dunette & L. M. Hough (Eds.), *Handbook of industrial and organizational psychology* (Vol. 3, 2nd ed., pp. 199–267). Palo Alto, CA: Consulting Psychologists Press.

Halpern, S. (1991). Big boss is watching you. *Details*, 18–23.

Hardin, C. D., & Higgins, E. T. (1996). Shared reality: How social verification makes the subjective objective. In R. M. Sorrentino & E. T. Higgins (Eds.), *Handbook of motivation and cognition, Vol. 3: The interpersonal context* (pp. 28–84). New York: Guilford Press.

Harris, M. J., Milich, R., Corbitt, E. M., & Hoover, D. W. (1992). Self-fulfilling effects of stigmatizing information on children's social interactions. *Journal of Personality and Social Psychology, 63*, 41–50.

Harvey, M. D., & Enzle, M. E. (1981). A cognitive model of social norms for understanding the transgression-helping effect. *Journal of Personality and Social Psychology, 41*, 866–875.

Jacobs, R. C., & Campbell, D. T. (1961). The perpetuation of an arbitrary norm through several generations of a laboratory micro-culture. *Journal of Abnormal and Social Psychology, 62*, 649–658.

Jones, J. W., & Terris, W. (1983). Predicting employees' theft in home improvement centers. *Psychological Reports, 52*, 187–201.

Labich, K. (1992, April 20). The new crisis in business ethics. *Fortune* (Vol. 125), 167–176.

McClelland, J. L., & Rumelhart, D. E. (1981). An interactive activation model of context effects in letter perception. *Psychological Review, 8*, 375–407.

Nielsen, M. E., & Miller, C. E. (1997). The transmission of norms regarding group decision rules, *Personality and Social Psychology Bulletin, 23*(5), 516–525.

Myers, D. G. (1993). *Social psychology*. New York: McGraw-Hill.

O'Reilly, C. A., III, Chatman, J., & Caldwell, D. F. (1991). People and organizational culture: A profile comparison approach to assessing person-organization fit. *Academy of Management Journal, 34*(3), 487–516.

Payne, S. L. (1989). Self-presentational tactics and employee theft. In R. A. Giacalone & P. Rosenfeld (Eds.), *Impression management in the organization* (pp. 397–410). Hillsdale, NJ: Lawrence Erlbaum Associates.

Schneider, B., & Hall, D. T. (1972). Toward specifying the concept of work climate: A study of Roman Catholic diocesan priests. *Journal of Applied Psychology, 56*, 447–455.

Sherif, M. (1937). An experimental approach to the study of attitudes. *Sociometry, 1*, 90–98.

Snyder, N. H., Blair, K. E., & Arndt, T. (1990). Breaking the bad habits behind theft. *Business* (Vol. 40), 31–33.

Stark, A. (1993, May–June). What's the matter with business ethics? *Harvard Business Review* (Vol. 71), 38–48.

Steckmest, F. W. (1982). *Corporate performance: The key to public trust*. New York: McGraw-Hill.

Strickland, L. H., Barefoot, J. C., & Hockenstein, P. (1976). Monitoring behavior in the surveillance and trust paradigm. *Representative Research in Social Psychology, 7*, 51–57.

Tenbrunsel, A. E., & Messick, D. M. (1998). *Sanctioning systems, decision frames, and cooperation*. Unpublished Manuscript.

Terris, W., & Jones, J. (1982). Psychological factors related to employees' theft in the convenience store industry. *Psychological Reports, 51*, 1219–1238.

Turner, J. C. (1991). *Social influence*. Bristol, PA: Open University Press.

Weitz, B. A., Castleberry, S. B., & Tanner, J. F. (1992). *Selling: Building relationships*. Homewood, IL: Irwin.

10

Entrepreneurs, Distrust, and Third Parties: A Strategic Look at the Dark Side of Dense Networks

Ronald S. Burt
University of Chicago

This chapter is about the tension between two understandings of the role played by social networks in the distribution of information and control, and so resources, within markets and hierarchies. Structural hole theory focuses on the benefits of entrepreneurial opportunity. Network theories of cohesion focus on the benefits of security. They contradict one another on the issue of trust, a contradiction resolved by a network theory of trust and distrust induced by gossip. Distrust is a strategic research site for distinguishing the theories. I present illustrative evidence from words and phrases that senior managers use to explain why they have had so much trouble working with their most difficult colleague. As predicted by the gossip argument, the explanations are prone to hostility and character assassination when embedded in strong third-party ties. My summary conclusion from the review and evidence is that the cohesion argument is true but incomplete; incomplete in a way that eliminates the social capital contradiction between brokerage and cohesion.

TRUST IN PRIVATE GAMES

Let me begin with the part of the story on which everyone seems to agree: dyads. This is the most rudimentary social context for trust—two people in isolation. Their interaction games are private in the sense that their behavior is only displayed to one another, and trust is a function of the history of their exchanges with one another.

Private games are the setting for much of exchange theory in American sociology. Two prominent examples are Homans' (1961) analysis of social behavior, and Blau's (1964) analysis of social exchange (see Ekeh, 1974, for historical exegesis of the individualistic British–American version of exchange theory contrasted with the French collectivist variant from Durkheim and Levi-Strauss, and Blau, 1994, for Blau's contemporary view, esp. pp. 156–158, explaining his continued focus on dyadic exchange). Blau (1964) argued that trust develops because social exchange involves unspecified obligations for which no binding contract can be written. When you exchange sensitive information with someone, for example, trust is implicit in the risk you now face that the other person might leak the information. Putting aside Blau's moral obligation aspect of exchange to focus on parameters of cost-benefit calculation (cf. Ekeh, 1974), Coleman (1990) captured trust more concretely for his systems of two-party exchange: Trust is committing to an exchange before you know how the other person will behave. You anticipate cooperation from the other person but you commit to the exchange before you know how the other person will behave.

This is trust, pure and simple. Anticipated cooperation is a narrow segment in the spectrum of concepts spanned by richer images such as Barber's (1983) distinctions between trust as moral order, competence, and obligation. However, anticipated cooperation is much of the trust essential to people in organizations. The issue is not moral. It is flexible cooperation. This point is nicely illustrated in fieldwork by Macauley (1963) and Uzzi (1996). Macauley (1963) quoted one of his local Wisconsin purchasing agents:

> If something comes up, you get the other man on the telephone and deal with the problem. You don't read legalistic contract clauses at each other if you ever want to do business again. One doesn't run to lawyers if he wants to stay in business because one must behave decently. (p. 61)

Uzzi (1996) offered a similar quote from one of his New York garment district managers:

> With people you trust, you know that if they have a problem with a fabric they're just not going to say, "I won't pay" or "take it back." If they did then we would have to pay for the loss. This way maybe the manufacturer will say, "Hey, OK so I'll make a dress out of it. Or I can cut it and make a short jacket instead of a long jacket." (p. 12)

Macauley (1963) offered a nice summary quote from another of his local businessman: "You can settle any dispute if you keep the lawyers and accountants out of it. They just do not understand the give-and-take needed in business" (p. 61).

Viewed as anticipated cooperation, trust is twice created by repeated interaction; from the past and from the future. From the past, repeated experience with a person is improved knowledge of the person. Cooperation in today's game is a signal of future cooperation. Across repeated games with cooperative outcomes, you build confidence in the other person's tendency to cooperate. At minimum, the cumulative process can be cast as a statistical decision problem in which you become more certain of the other person across repeated samples of the other person's behavior. The repetition of cooperative exchange promotes trust. More generally, the cumulative process involves escalation. From tentative initial exchanges, you move to familiarity, and from there to more significant exchanges. The gradual expansion of exchanges promotes the trust necessary for them. Whatever the cumulative process, past cooperation is a basis for future cooperation (cf. Zucker, 1986, on process-based trust; Staw & Ross, 1987, on commitment escalation; Larson, 1992, on the importance of the long term for trust between firms; Lawler & Yoon, 1996, for laboratory evidence; Stinchcombe, 1990, on the information advantages of current suppliers for building trust; Gulati, 1995, for empirical evidence). Further, the history of cooperation is an investment that would be lost if either party behaved so as to erode the relationship—another factor making it easier for each party to trust the other to cooperate. Blau (1968) summarized the process as follows:

> Social exchange relations evolve in a slow process, starting with minor transactions in which little trust is required because little risk is involved and in which both partners can prove their trustworthiness, enabling them to expand their relation and engage in major transactions. Thus, the process of social exchange leads to the trust required for it in a self-governing fashion. (p. 454)

Where sociologists explain trust emerging from past exchanges (e.g., Coleman, 1990; Granovetter, 1992), economists look to the incentives of future exchanges (e.g., Gibbons, 1992; Kreps, 1990). The expectation that violations of trust will be punished in the future leads players to cooperate even if defection would be more profitable in a single play of the game. The information contained in past experience and the potential for future interactions are inextricably linked. A player's willingness to forego short-term gains is based on the expectation that current behavior will be used to predict future behavior.

The summary conclusion is that trust is correlated with relation strength. Repeated cooperation strengthens the relationship between two people, increasing the probability that they trust one another.

TRUST IN PUBLIC GAMES, COHESION ARGUMENT:
THIRD PARTIES FACILITATE TRUST

Relationships play out in a social setting of other people. The other people are third parties to the relationship and transform what was private into public. The dyadic story extends in a natural way to public games. If trust is likely within a strong relationship, it must be even more likely between people embedded in a network of friends and acquaintances. This extrapolation of the dyadic story is consistent with the idea of group cohesion, so I'll refer to the extrapolation as a cohesion argument. Applied to social networks, cohesion is a story about balance. Building on Heider's (1958) image of balance in relationships, key works on network balance and transitivity are Davis (1970), Davis and Leinhardt (1972), and Holland and Leinhardt (1970). Subsequent work was primarily methodological (for review, see Burt, 1982, pp. 71–73; Wasserman & Faust, 1994) but the central tenet of balance theory remained an equilibrium assumption that adjacent elements in social structure evolve toward consistency; that is, toward balance. *Ceteris paribus*, ego's relation to alter, should be consistent with ego's indirect relations to alter through third parties. If ego has a strong positive relation to someone, who feels the same way about alter, then ego should have a strong positive relation to alter. The stronger the aggregate connection between ego and alter through third parties, the more likely that ego and alter trust one another.[1]

Examples of the cohesion argument are numerous (e.g., see Bradach & Eccles, 1989; Nohria & Eccles, 1992; Swedberg, 1993; and several chapters in Smelser & Swedberg, 1994, esp. Powell & Smith-Doerr, 1994). Two prominent examples are Coleman's (1990) analysis of trust and social capital, and Granovetter's (1985, 1992) discussion of trust emerging from "structural embeddedness" (trust is more likely between people with mutual friends):

> My mortification at cheating a friend of long standing may be substantial even when undiscovered. It may increase when the friend becomes aware of it. But it may become even more unbearable when our mutual friends uncover the deceit and tell one another. (Granovetter, 1992, p. 44)

There is an analogous reputation effect in economic theory (e.g., Kreps, 1990): Indirect connections through mutual acquaintances (a) make game behavior more public, which (b) increases the salience of reputation, (c) making ego and alter more careful about the cooperative image they display, which (d) increases the probability of cooperation and trust between ego and alter.

ENTREPRENEURS AND STRUCTURAL HOLES

The strategic issue is deciding who to trust. It is on this issue that contradictions emerge. Under the brokerage principle in network theory, there is a competitive advantage to building certain relations: Resources flow disproportionately to people who provide indirect connections between otherwise disconnected groups. This is the principle underlying the structural hole theory of social capital and the competitive advantage the theory predicts for entrepreneurial managers (Burt, 1992). Brief introduction is sufficient for the purposes of this chapter (see Burt, 1997, for more detailed exegesis). The theory draws on network arguments that emerged in sociology during the 1970s (most notably Granovetter, 1973, on the strength of weak ties; Freeman, 1977, on betweenness centrality; Cook & Emerson, 1978, on the benefits of having exclusive exchange partners; and Burt, 1980, on the structural autonomy created by network complexity). More generally, sociological ideas elaborated by Simmel (1922/1955) and Merton (1957/1968), on the autonomy generated by conflicting affiliations, are mixed in hole theory with traditional economic ideas of monopoly power and oligopoly, to produce network models of competitive advantage.

Figure 10.1 illustrates the gist of the argument. In an imperfect market, there can be multiple rates of return because disconnections between individuals—holes in the structure of the market—leave some people unaware of the benefits they could offer one another. Structural holes are the gaps between nonredundant contacts. The hole is a buffer, like an insulator in an electric circuit. As a result of the hole between them, two contacts provide network benefits that are in some degree additive rather than redundant. In Fig. 10.1, James has a network that spans one structural hole (the relatively weak connection between a cluster reached through contacts 1, 2, and 3 versus the other cluster reached through contacts 4 and 5). The structural hole between the two clusters does not mean that people in the two clusters are unaware of one another. It means that the people are so focused on their own activities that they have little time to attend to the activities of people in the other cluster. A structural hole indicates that the people on either side of the hole circulate in different flows of information. The structural hole is an opportunity to broker the flow of information between people and control the form of projects that bring together people from opposite sides of the hole.

Robert took over James' job and expanded the social capital associated with the job. He preserves connection with both clusters in James' network, but expands the network to a more diverse set of contacts. Robert's network, adding three new clusters of people, spans 10 structural holes.

Information benefits are enhanced in several ways. The volume is higher simply because Robert reaches more people indirectly. The diversity of his

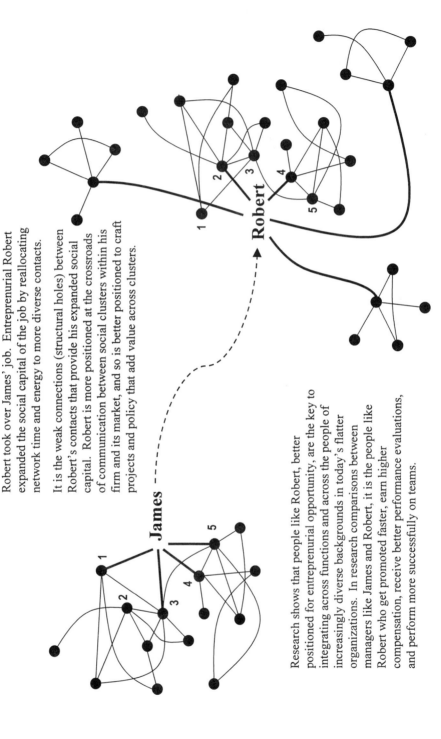

Robert took over James' job. Entreprenurial Robert expanded the social capital of the job by reallocating network time and energy to more diverse contacts.

It is the weak connections (structural holes) between Robert's contacts that provide his expanded social capital. Robert is more positioned at the crossroads of communication between social clusters within his firm and its market, and so is better positioned to craft projects and policy that add value across clusters.

Research shows that people like Robert, better positioned for entreprenurial opportunity, are the key to integrating across functions and across the people of increasingly diverse backgrounds in today's flatter organizations. In research comparisons between managers like James and Robert, it is the people like Robert who get promoted faster, earn higher compensation, receive better performance evaluations, and perform more successfully on teams.

contacts means that the quality of his information is also higher. One cluster is considered a single source of information because people connected to one another tend to know the same things at about the same time. Nonredundant clusters provide a broader information screen, providing better assurance of being informed of opportunities and impending disasters (access benefits). Furthermore, because Robert's contacts are only linked through him at the center of the network, Robert is the first to see new opportunities created by needs in one group that could be served by skills in other groups (timing benefits). Robert lies at the crossroads of social organization. He has the option of bringing together otherwise disconnected individuals where it would be rewarding. Further still, Robert's more diverse contacts means that he is more likely to be a candidate discussed for inclusion in new opportunities (referral benefits). These benefits are compounded by the fact that having a network that yields such benefits makes Robert more attractive to other people as a contact in their own networks.

The manager who creates a bridge between otherwise disconnected contacts has a say in whose interests are served by the bridge. The disconnected contacts communicate through the manager, giving the manager an opportunity to adjust the manager's image with each contact. As the broker between otherwise disconnected contacts, a manager is an entrepreneur in the literal sense of the word—a person who adds value by standing between others. Accurate, ambiguous, or distorted information is strategically moved between contacts by the broker. The information and control benefits reinforce one another at any moment in time and cumulate together over time.

Networks rich in structural holes present opportunities for entrepreneurial behavior. The network contains opportunities to build bridges between otherwise disconnected contacts. The behaviors by which managers develop these opportunities are many and varied but the opportunity itself is at all times defined by a hole in the social structure around the manager. In this framework, networks rich in the entrepreneurial opportunities of structural holes are entrepreneurial networks and entrepreneurs are people skilled in building the interpersonal bridges that span structural holes.

Managers with contact networks rich in structural holes are the individuals who know about, have a hand in, and exercise control over more rewarding opportunities. They monitor information more effectively than bureaucratic control. They move information faster, and to more people, than memos. Entrepreneurial managers know the parameters of organization problems early. They are highly mobile relative to bureaucracy, easily shifting network time and energy from one solution to another. More in control of their immediate surroundings, entrepreneurial managers tailor solutions to the specific individuals being coordinated, replacing the boilerplate solutions of formal bureaucracy. To these benefits of faster, better solutions, add cost reductions; entrepreneurial managers offer inexpensive coordination relative to the bureaucratic alternative.

In sum, managers with networks rich in structural holes operate somewhere between the force of corporate authority and the dexterity of markets, building bridges between disconnected parts of the firm where it is valuable to do so. In comparisons between otherwise similar people like James and Robert in Fig. 10.1, it is the people like Robert who are predicted by the hole argument to be more successful. They are. Managers with networks rich in structural holes receive more positive evaluations (Burt, Jannotta, & Mahoney, 1997; Rosenthal, 1996; cf., Fernandez & Gould, 1994; Krackhardt & Stern, 1988), earlier promotions (Burt, 1992; Gabbay, 1997; Podolny & Baron, 1997; Sparrowe & Popielarz, 1995), and higher compensation (Burt, 1997; Burt, Hogarth, & Michaud, 1997).

TENSION

Trust is critical to the value added by entrepreneurs but it is not developed as an issue in structural hole theory or the earlier network arguments about brokerage. Relations are taken for granted (Burt, 1980; Cook & Emerson, 1978; Freeman, 1977) or trust is put aside as person-specific and presumed resolved by the able entrepreneur (Burt, 1992).

There is reason to expect entrepreneurs to have special problems with trust. In the imaginary markets where competition is perfect, you can trust the system to provide a fair return on your investments. However, entrepreneurs thrive in imperfectly competitive markets; markets perforated by structural holes. In the reality of imperfect markets, you have to rely on personal contacts. Reconsider Robert and James in Fig. 10.1. The cohesion view is that James can have more trust in his contacts, and they in him, because of dense third-party connections reinforcing the individual relationships. Robert is at a disadvantage in this view because his relationships have no third-party support.

The awkward issue is that research on network structure and achievement shows that it is people like Robert, with networks rich in structural holes, who have the competitive advantage. Mizruchi (1992) provided a thorough review toward the conclusion that cohesion needs to be distinguished from business unity but it is more usual to see cohesion invoked by organization analysts as an antecedent to trust and cooperation. Thus the tension: Either trust is not critical to network entrepreneurs—a proposal that flies in the face of common sense—or the cohesion story is in some way flawed about how trust is associated with third parties.

TRUST IN PUBLIC GAMES, GOSSIP ARGUMENT: THIRD PARTIES AFFECT INTENSITY, NOT DIRECTION

The tension between brokerage and cohesion can be resolved with an alternative view of the connection between trust and social context. There is at least one significant difference between private and public that is ignored in the cohesion argument. The quality of information in public games is more complex. The two people in a private game have direct experience of one another. Third parties bring a qualitatively different kind of experience to the relationship. Third parties can enter the dyadic game in any of three roles: observer, intruder, or gossip. The minimum role is to observe; watching or listening but saying and doing nothing. The most intrusive role is to exercise some control over the game, guiding ego and alter toward a target relationship. Between these extremes is the rich diversity of ways in which third parties affect relationships by telling stories; not stories in the sense of deception, just stories in the sense of personal accounts, gossip, about the exchanges between people. These stories are the focus of a network argument in which trust and distrust emerge from gossip (Burt, 1998; Burt & Knez, 1995). The argument is about the bias created by gossip in ego's evaluation of alter's trustworthiness. For the purposes here, I present the intuition behind the argument and connect it with related arguments in other fields.

The gossip argument is anchored on ego deciding whether to trust alter, with ego and alter surrounded to some (measured) extent by third parties. Ego's decision is based on two kinds of information: personal experience with alter (which could be nothing or could be substantial) and vicarious experience in third-party stories about alter. To the extent that vicarious play invokes the emotions of actual play, stories about alter's behavior lead ego to feel as though he knows alter better than he does. The central point in the gossip argument is that ego's vicarious interaction with alter is a predictably biased sample of information on alter.[2] Predictions are based on social bias in ego's selection of third parties and the conversational etiquette of gossip that biases what ego hears from third parties.

The first social mechanism is a selection bias in ego's choice of third parties, call it a balance mechanism as discussed earlier in the cohesion argument. Faced with a decision about whether to trust alter, ego turns to trusted contacts for information about alter before asking less close contacts. People especially close to one another are likely to have similar views, so ego's trusted third parties are likely to report accounts of alter consistent with ego's own view of alter. In other words, a preference for trusted third parties before more distant contacts means that ego draws a sample of information on alter likely to reinforce ego's predisposition toward alter.

The second mechanism is a selection bias in the information that third parties share with ego; call it an etiquette mechanism. It is polite in casual conversation to go along with the flow of sentiment being shared. We tend to share in conversations those of our facts consistent with the perceived predispositions of the people with whom we speak, and facts shared with other people are facts more likely to be remembered. Thus, the biased sample of facts shared in conversations becomes the population of information on, and so the reality of, the people discussed.[3] Returning to ego's trust in alter, when ego expresses a predisposition toward alter (implicitly or explicitly), third parties with positive and negative information on alter can be expected to select, from their repertoire of stories about alter, a story consistent with the flow of the conversation. If ego seems to trust alter, the third party relays stories of games in which alter cooperated. If ego seems to distrust alter, the third party relays stories in which alter defected. Ego's predisposition toward alter is apparent from a variety of cues ranging from the subtle nuance of a raised eyebrow or a skeptical tone of voice when describing alter to the blatant signal of expressing a positive or negative opinion.[4] Having shared a story featuring certain alter behaviors, ego and the third party are thereafter more likely to think of alter in terms of the behaviors discussed. Thus, the etiquette mechanism encourages third parties to selectively disclose information on alter that is consistent with ego's predisposition toward alter, with the result of reinforcing ego's predisposition toward alter.[5]

The etiquette mechanism serves mutual interests: Etiquette is the foundation for civility. It allows people of diverse backgrounds and interests to ignore social differences that would otherwise interrupt the flow of conversation. Etiquette can be efficient. In the press of other demands, corroborating ego's predisposition ends the discussion without seeming rude. Corroboration brings closure with minimum effort. Etiquette strengthens relationships. Relaying a story about alter consistent with ego's predisposition highlights the social similarity between ego and third party with respect to other people—a concrete indicator that the third party's values are consistent with ego's. Moreover, there is the history of exchanges to consider. As third parties strengthen their relations with ego by offering information about alter consistent with ego's predisposition toward alter, ego strengthens his or her relation with the third party by asking for the information and responding to third-party opinion. When you and I discuss our views of John, we reinforce our relationship with one another and narrow the confidence interval around our joint opinion of John. Conversations about social structure are an integral part of building and maintaining relationships, with the primary effect of reinforcing the current structure (a familiar idea in sociology, illustrated in the extreme case by Durkheim's views on the social value of criminals is explained in note 10). Ego's search for information on whether to trust alter is less often a search *de novo* than it is a search for a quick update on stories vaguely recalled: "Didn't you once have some trouble working with John?"[6]

The two mechanisms need not be equally relevant to a situation. Balance could be dominant in small groups. Etiquette could be dominant in large groups differentiated in time or space. Whatever their relative impact on a specific pair of people, either mechanism is sufficient to bias vicarious play to be consistent with ego's predisposition toward alter.

That is the gist of the argument: (a) Ego has vicarious play with alter in third-party gossip; (b) the alter behavior to which ego is exposed is biased by balance or etiquette to be consistent with ego's predisposition toward alter; (c) the higher volume and greater homogeneity of information associated with third-party gossip make ego more certain about alter. Ego more certain means ego more likely to trust or distrust alter (as opposed to remaining undecided between the two extremes). Favorable opinion is amplified into trust. Doubt is amplified into distrust.[7]

Primary Prediction: Local Third-Party Effect

The predicted third-party effect is illustrated in Fig. 10.2. Strength of direct connection varies on the horizontal axis from a weak relationship at the left to a strong relationship at the right. Thin lines describe relations free of third parties. Bold lines describe relations embedded in strong third-party ties. Tracing the solid lines to the right of the graph, the probability of trust increases with the strength of a relationship. Third parties increase the probability of trust above and beyond the level expected from the strength of the relationship. Tracing the dashed lines to the left of the graph, the probability of distrust increases in weaker relationships. Third parties increase the probability of distrust above and beyond the level expected from the strength of the relationship. Third-party gossip amplifies relationships to positive and negative extremes, and anchors relations at the extremes, by making ego more certain of alter. At a given strength of relationship, ego's opinion of alter is more certain when embedded in a strong third-party connection. Ego more certain of alter is more likely to trust (or distrust) alter.[8]

Secondary Prediction: Broader Third-Party Effect

Trust and brokerage are now aligned. Rather than trust being a phenomenon in opposition to the value added by entrepreneurs, it is a natural correlate. Recall the tension between cohesion and brokerage illustrated by Robert and James in Fig. 10.1. The cohesion argument predicts that James can have more trust in his contacts, and they in him, because of the dense third-party connections reinforcing each individual relationship. Robert is

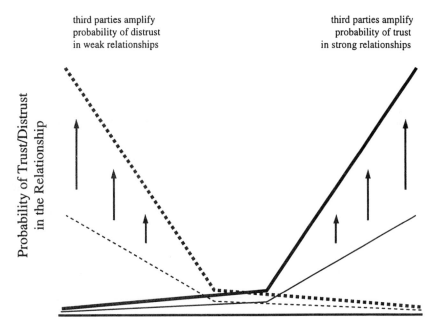

Third-party gossip amplifies relations to extremes, and anchors them at the extremes, by making ego more certain about alter. At a given strength of relationship, ego's opinion of alter is more certain when embedded in strong third-party ties. Ego more certain of alter is more likely to trust (or distrust) alter.

FIG. 10.2.   Amplified trust and distrust associated with third parties.

at a disadvantage in this view because his relationships have no third-party support. The awkward issue is that evidence on network structure and achievement shows that it is people like Robert, with networks rich in structural holes, who have the competitive advantage. Within the gossip argument, however, the advantage remains with Robert because he is less subject than James to the distortions of third-party gossip.

Information and control explain why Robert is less affected, in the same way that they define the competitive advantage of access to structural holes. With respect to information, Robert's advantage is not that he is less exposed than James to third-party gossip. The advantage is that he is exposed to more contradictory gossip. The structural holes among Robert's contacts mean that they circulate in separate flows of information. *Ceteris paribus*, Robert's contacts are more likely than James' to know different things about alter. More variance in the third-party gossip to which Robert is exposed has two implications: (a) Robert is more likely to be skilled in expecting and making sense of conflicting opinions; (b) Robert has an incentive to search for information from more distant third parties because his initial third-party accounts are less likely to corroborate one another.

With respect to control, the holes between Robert's contacts free him to negotiate third-party interpretations (as previously discussed under the control benefits of structural holes). James, working within a clique of interconnected contacts, will have more trouble breaking away from third-party interpretations of relations. The person in a clique who resists the shared opinion of other people in the clique is suspect and can expect peer pressure to conform to the shared opinion. Further resistance risks being ostracized from the clique. The danger of group-solidarity policies for building cooperation (e.g., cohesive teams) is that the conditions of strong relations and dense indirect connections that can make it easier to trust within the group intensify distrust of people who do not conform to group views and make it more difficult to trust beyond the group. The following results on character assassination are vivid illustration and the implications for rigid management are clear (cf. Janis', 1972, intuition about groupthink; Zucker, 1977/1991, on opinion rigidity in an ersatz office under very simple clique conditions of in-group communication).

In sum, managers like James in clique networks are exposed to more consistent third-party gossip about relationships and more peer pressure to conform to the gossip. Managers in clique networks can be expected to have less experience with making sense of inconsistent interpretations of events, be more accustomed to relying on third-party interpretations of events, and so show more evidence of the amplified trust and distrust associated with third-party gossip. To coin a colloquial phrase, cohesion is structural arthritis, an information inflammation of the organizational joints. On the other hand, managers like Robert, the network entrepreneur, are more likely to make accurate judgments about who to trust and who to distrust. Robert is forced and freed by the inconsistency of the third-party gossip around him to synthesize his own interpretation of new relationships.[9] Relative to James, Robert is more likely to make an accurate evaluation of whether he can trust alter and to make his accurate evaluation quickly. To the extent that accurate judgments about who to trust and who not to trust matter, as they surely do in organizations, Robert has a competitive advantage. It makes sense to see the accumulating research results in which managers like Robert are promoted faster, earn higher compensation, receive better performance evaluations, and serve on teams more recognized for superior performance.

STRATEGIC SIGNIFICANCE OF DISTRUST

The cohesion and gossip arguments are not everywhere equally contradictory. They make the same prediction about trust in strong relationships. Both arguments predict that the trust likely in a strong relationship is more likely when the relationship is embedded in a network of third parties (right of the graph in Fig. 10.2). Further, both arguments predict that distrust is more likely in weak relationships.

They differ in their predictions about the effects of third parties on distrust within weak relations. Cohesion predicts a direct effect in which strong third-party ties facilitate trust. The gossip argument predicts a contingent effect in which strong third-party ties amplify the emotional intensity, not direction, of ego's evaluation. The social process that makes ego more certainly positive can in the same way make for negative certainty. The direction of the third-party effect depends on ego's predisposition toward alter. The effect of third-party gossip is to amplify ego's predisposition into a certainty about alter. The doubt reasonable within a weak relationship festers into distrust.

DISTRUST

Thus, distrust is a strategic research site for resolving the tension between the structural hole emphasis on entrepreneurial opportunity and the cohesion emphasis on security. The research design is simple: Gather data on a sample of weak relationships, some embedded in strong third-party ties, others embedded in little or no indirect connection through third parties. If trust is more likely with the strong third-party ties, the gossip argument is rejected in favor of cohesion and we are forced back to the tension between manager success associated with structural holes, whereas trust is associated with the lack of structural holes. If, on the other hand, distrust is more likely with the strong third-party ties, then the gossip argument is supported over cohesion, which means that the tension between cohesion and structural holes is resolved with trust, a natural correlate of brokerage.

DERISION

The empirical test can be made in finer detail by analyzing the narratives associated with distrust. For simple reference, I refer to these narratives as derision. As third-party gossip amplifies the emotional intensity of distrust, it should make more severe and personal the rhetoric of derision.

Consider how one progresses to derision. Repeated interaction gives you reason to believe that a person cannot be trusted. Your initial meetings with a colleague, call him John, are difficult. You have little experience with John, so the difficulty of the initial meeting has alternative explanations—the problem could have been peculiar to those meetings (you caught John at a bad time or you were a little more difficult that usual) or a function of the situation in which you had to deal with John (the issue under discussion was complex and ambiguous, the interests of your respective constituencies are difficult to align, etc.). However, with repeated contact, all of it difficult, you realize that the problem is neither you nor the situation. The problem is John—and your advice to friends and colleagues is to avoid him. With each advisory discussion, you punish John for the trouble he caused you and do a service to friends better off avoiding John.

In fact, trust depends on derision. The sociology of the situation is that if we did not have an occasional unscrupulous colleague, we would have to make him up.[10] By sharing stories about people who behaved unscrupulously, we implicitly define scrupulous behavior and communicate the threat of what happens to unscrupulous people. Character assassination is a useful imagery here. It is not enough that the disreputable person behaved poorly in a difficult situation in which anyone might behave poorly. Character assassination requires more personal content and moral indignation (cf. Adams, 1977, chaps. 1–2, on "bad mouthing" or, more pertinently, Van Maanen, 1978, on "assholes").

Third-party gossip encourages an escalation in the rhetoric of derision. The gossip argument predicts that managers more exposed to third-party gossip have a vicarious feeling of repeated interaction such that they are more certain in their trust or distrust of a colleague. Extrapolating to the situation-to-person progression in attributing blame, managers more exposed to third-party gossip are more likely to interpret difficult relations in terms of the other person's personality—because they have heard corroborating stories about the other person. They are more certain that alter is the problem. A more certain manager is more likely to use strong words that express the certainty. Thus, difficult relations embedded in strong third-party ties are more likely to be described with severe and personal language attributing the difficulty to flaws in the other person's character.

There is a corollary network effect. The reality of negative relations is that they are more often than not a function of the two people involved than either person individually. A person with whom you have a difficult relationship enjoys positive relations with someone else.[11] Given the more diverse sources of information to which entrepreneurial managers are exposed, such managers are more likely to realize that difficult relations are not entirely the other person's fault. They should more often blame difficult relations on difficult situations and use neutral language in public explanations of the difficulty: "John and I just couldn't get together on that one." The reverse side to this prediction is that managers in clique networks are more likely to blame difficult relations on the other person and be more certain in public exclamations about the other's faults: "John and I didn't get together on that one, but of course everyone has trouble with John."

We each believe that the people whose reputations we erode with derision deserve it, but the truth is that few of us were eyewitnesses to the behavior deemed unscrupulous. Most of us were somewhere else, witnessing the behavior only vicariously through stories told by trusted colleagues. Moreover, we have little incentive to speak directly with the suspect person. You and I are brought together by sharing the story about unscrupulous behavior whether or not the story is true. Even if we were to speak directly with the suspect person, his or her version of the story would be deemed biased by self-interest. Only gossip seems to have the shimmer of unvarnished truth.

ILLUSTRATIVE EVIDENCE

Figures 10.3 and 10.4 contain illustrative evidence of the amplification in Fig. 10.2 predicted by the gossip argument. The evidence is discussed in detail elsewhere, so I am brief to the purpose of this chapter (see Burt & Knez, 1995, for further discussion of Fig. 10.3; Burt, 1998, for Fig. 10.4). The figures describe relationships with 3,015 colleagues cited as core contacts by a probability sample of 284 senior managers in a large electronic components and computing equipment manufacturer.

EXPECTED THIRD-PARTY EFFECTS ON TRUST AND DISTRUST

Contacts are sorted on two dimensions in Fig. 10.3; the strength of the manager's relationship with the cited contact (especially close, close, less close) and the strength of the manager's indirect connection through third parties to the contact (weak, strong). The third-party tie between manager and contact is strong if the manager's aggregate connection via third parties to the contact is stronger than the average for all 3,015 cited relationships. Bars in Fig. 10.3 indicate the probability of trust and distrust in each of the six network conditions distinguished by the strength of the direct and indirect connection between manager and contact.

The graph at the top of Fig. 10.3 shows the third-party effect on trust predicted by both cohesion and the gossip argument. These results are a quick construct-validity check to reassure you that the data conform to

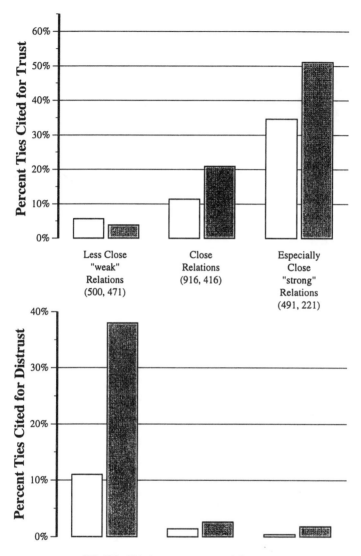

FIG. 10.3. Third parties, trust, and distrust.

predictions on which cohesion and gossip agree. A contact is trusted if he or she is someone with whom the manager would discuss leaving the firm for a new job elsewhere. The bars are higher to the right of the graph, showing that managers are more likely to trust people with whom they have an especially close relationship. The gray bars to the right are higher than the white bars, showing that the managers are still more likely to trust someone with whom they are strongly connected through third parties (29.8 chi-square, 3 d.f., $P < .001$). For example, 170 of the 491 especially close

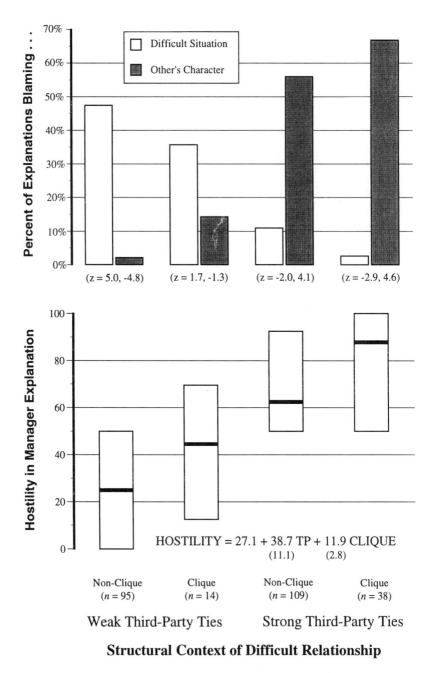

FIG. 10.4. Third parties, character assassination, and hostility in difficult relationships.

relations embedded in a weak third-party tie are cited as trusted contacts. That 35% (white bar) increases to 51% (gray bar) if the third-party tie is strong.

The graph at the bottom of Fig. 10.3 supports the gossip prediction over cohesion. Managers were asked, "Who has made it the most difficult for you to carry out your job responsibilities?" The question does not mention distrust explicitly but I take this citation to be an indicator of distrust for two reasons: It is associated with other kinds of relations as I would expect distrust to be and manager explanations for their citations indicate distrust of the uncooperative, repeated game kind (Burt & Knez, 1995). The point supporting the gossip argument is that distrust is associated with third parties (104.5 chi-square, 3 d.f., $P < .001$). Distrust is concentrated in weak relationships (as predicted by the cohesion and gossip arguments) but it is more likely in the weak relationships embedded in strong third-party ties (rejecting cohesion in favor of the gossip argument). The probability of a weak relationship being cited for distrust is .11 in the absence of third parties. That probability is more than three times higher if the weak relationship is embedded in a strong third-party tie (.38). In fact, third parties are more associated with amplified distrust than they are associated with amplified trust (evident in Fig. 10.3 from the larger ratio of gray to white bar for distrust in weak relations versus trust in strong relations, see Burt & Knez, 1995, pp. 269–270, for statistical analysis).[12] Not only is there a dark side to network density, it equals or exceeds the potency of the familiar positive side of third parties facilitating trust.

Anger and Blame

After naming their most difficult colleague, managers were asked to explain why the relationship was so difficult. The 256 explanations are tabulated in Fig. 10.4 and a selection of illustrative explanations are listed in Table 10.1 (number in parentheses to the left of each explanation is a hostility score based on repeated semantic differential evaluations, 0 for no hostility to 100 for clear hostility).[13] My hypothesis from the gossip argument is to expect more severe and personal language in the descriptions of difficult relations embedded in strong third-party ties. Blame is the principal theme to the manager explanations. The examples in Table 10.1 illustrate how managers clarified in their explanations who or what is to blame for their most difficult relationship. Some explanations blame the other person in the difficult relationship, others blame the situation (see Rodin, 1985; and Ross & Fletcher, 1985, for reviews of work on Heider's, 1958, personal versus situational attribution; Blount, 1995, for more recent review). Situational attributions include complex or ambiguous work assignments (blame the work), generic difficulties with supervisors or subordinates or matrix organization

TABLE 10.1
Illustrative Explanations of Most Difficult Relationship

Situational Attributions (n = 63)

---

(0) conflict of goals; what was good for him was bad for my group
(25) different management style and motivation
(0) I do not know; most likely a misunderstanding of my work rather than him personally
(0) language barrier was very difficult
(0) managed a parallel sales organization with a different philosophy
(13) personally we got along wonderfully, but people in her organization have a difficult style
(0) representative of an organization that has goals and objectives in opposition to mine
(0) she is under a lot of pressure and it spills over to the people around her

---

Competence Attributions (n = 103)

---

(13) does not understand his functional area
(25) her planning requests do not take into account time difference between New York and Europe
(100) incompetent; cannot make a decision and stick with it
(75) inexperienced; too emotional and immature to manage his organization
(50) micromanagement; poor understanding of our client group's needs
(25) mixed messages; no road map of clear direction
(0) not able to effectively affect change in organizational direction
(88) promoted too high, too fast; beyond her level of experience

---

Character Attributions (n = 90)

---

(100) dishonest; self-serving; no integrity
(100) divide and conquer person; takes credit for my work; disempowers
(100) egotistical; self-oriented; liar; worst manager I have ever met
(88) loses her temper and has a very unprofessional attitude with myself and external clients
(100) manipulative—insensitive to people—dishonest
(100) most territorial, uncooperative person I know
(100) my boss and a charlatan
(100) nasty, ill-tempered bitch
(100) not trustworthy; a back-stabber
(88) person cannot accept females
(88) shared private information with manager & peers
(100) unethical; uncooperative; unpleasant

Note. These are examples selected from the 63, 103, and 90 explanations respectively blaming the situation, the other person's competence, or the other person's character. Numbers in parentheses to the left are hostility scores (bottom of Fig. 10.4).

(blame the role), or the problem could be your own fault as well as the other person (share the blame). Personal attributions are more numerous and more complex. In reading through the explanations, I had to distinguish two kinds of personal attributions significantly different with respect to the predicted third-party effect. Competence attributions are more neutral about the other person's character. Integrity and cooperation are not issues so much as the person's abilities (e.g., "promoted too high, too fast; beyond her level of experience"). Character attributions explicitly blame the difficult relationship on a flaw in the other person's character (e.g., "egotistical; self-oriented; liar; worst manager I have ever met"). The hostility scores are correlated with, but distinct from, the three attribution categories (the attribution distinctions predict 47% of the variance in hostility scores).

Third parties are clearly associated with character assassination. The graph at the top of Fig. 10.4 shows how the three kinds of explanations are distributed across combinations of third parties and network structure. For example, the 95 difficult relations embedded in weak third-party ties within nonclique networks are 47% blamed on the situation (light gray bar), 51% blamed on the other person's competence, and 2% blamed on the other person's character (dark gray bar). The graph shows that the situational attributions are associated with weak third-party ties and character attributions are associated with strong third-party ties (106.6 chi-square, 4 d.f., $P < .001$). Character attributions are most associated with strong third-party ties within cliques (4.6 loglinear z-score in Fig. 10.4).

The more extreme emotions associated with third parties are also evident in respondent hostility toward the difficult colleague. Box plots at the bottom of Fig. 10.4 describe the distribution of hostility within each of four structural contexts; weak versus strong third-party ties within clique versus nonclique networks (box spans 25th to 75th percentile, bar within the box indicates median hostility). Hostility is higher on average in difficult relations embedded in a strong third-party tie. The third-party effect is stronger within cliques. The bars for cliques at the bottom of Fig. 10.4 are higher than the adjacent bars for noncliques. Hostility is significantly higher with strong third-party ties (11.1 t-test) and clique networks (3.3 t-test).

CONCLUSIONS

This has been a story in several parts that together trace a path to resolving a fundamental contradiction in contemporary understandings of organizations. I began with the tension between the network theory of structural holes defining entrepreneurial opportunity versus network theories of cohesion defining security, and so trust, within relationships. I then discussed an alternative to cohesion that resolves the tension; a network theory of trust emergent from third-party gossip. Distrust has a strategic significance for comparing the cohesion and gossip arguments. Cohesion and gossip both predict that trust is more likely within strong relations embedded in strong third-party ties and that distrust is more likely within weak relations. The two arguments differ in their predictions about the effects of third parties on weak relations: Cohesion predicts that third parties facilitate trust. The gossip argument predicts that third parties amplify feelings of distrust. With network data on several hundred people in electronic equipment and financial services, mostly middle and senior managers, I show an association between third parties and distrust within weak relationships. Probing further, the amplified feelings of distrust predicted by the gossip argument should be visible in the language used to explain why it was so difficult to work with the cited colleague. I used a content analysis of the explanations to show the hostility and character assassination associated with relations embedded in strong third-party ties. In sum, the evidence supports the gossip argument and so its explanation of trust and distrust is consistent with the predicted success of entrepreneurial managers in structural hole theory.

The implication is that third parties are dangerous around difficult relationships. It is not only that they are associated with amplified negative feelings, escalating to character assassination; there are also consequences beyond the immediate relationship. First, the relationship becomes less flexible because it is associated with more extreme emotions. Having reached the conclusion that alter is to blame for the prior difficulty, ego is less likely to trust him in the future (Blount, 1995). Having blamed alter for the difficulty, things will never be the same between the two people as they were before ego took to assassinating alter's character. Further, dense third-party connections between ego and alter mean that there are multiple people engaged in assassinating alter's character. Not only will alter have difficulty working with these people in future, she or he will have difficulty building new relations with employees exposed to their third-party gossip. The hardening wall between alter and the people around ego can be expected to elicit similar emotions from alter (e.g., Kramer, 1994, on paranoia and distrust, Sitkin & Stickel, 1996, on distrust spawned by TQM zealots). For behavior amplified and unforgiven in third-party gossip, alter is under pressure to leave the firm to escape third-party tormentors.

My theoretical conclusion is that the cohesion argument is true but incomplete, and incomplete in a way that eliminates the social capital contradiction between brokerage and cohesion. Cohesion's primary effect is rigidity, a kind of structural arthritis. It enhances trust between people already close at the same time that it amplifies distrust between people not close (see Portes & Landolt, 1996, for diverse examples). This rigidity can be a virtue in certain environments but in most contemporary markets and organizations, it is not. The brokerage story is the more general understanding of networks as social capital. Moreover, evidence of trust and distrust shows that managers with networks rich in structural holes are more likely to make accurate judgments about who they can trust, which means that they are less likely to make consequential errors in judgment about the character of individual colleagues. Cohesion remains a consideration on the issue of network dynamics. How does the network entrepreneur bring third parties into the deal to induce the cohesion benefits of trust and reliability without falling victim to the cohesion costs of distrust and character assassination?

NOTES

1. Social identity theory makes a similar prediction. One of the theory's predictions is that trust is more likely between people who perceive themselves members of the same group; that is, between people who have the same social identity (see Ashforth & Mael, 1989; Messick & Mackie, 1989, for reviews from business and psychology perspectives respectively; Kramer, Brewer, & Hanna, 1995, for more recent review and research results). There are two network components in ego's attachment to a group; cohesive ties to individual members of the group and a social boundary around the group. The relative and aggregate importance of these components for trust are the central empirical questions for social identity explanations of trust. The cohesive ties component is the cohesion argument discussed in the text and subject to the same problem resolved by the gossip argument that follows. The social identity prediction is broader because it includes the social boundary component in group identity. My critique of the cohesion argument that follows addresses only the more narrow prediction discussed in the text.

2. This is a scope condition to the gossip argument. Not included in the argument are third parties strategically inserted between ego and alter to strengthen or weaken their relationship. Beyond the exclusion of third-party facilitators and authority third parties in a corporate or legal hierarchy (e.g., Coleman, 1990, on complex relations; Black & Baumgartner, 1983; Black, 1993, on third parties in the legal process; and Morrill, 1995, for ethnographic illustration of the Black and Baumgartner view applied to managers), the gossip argument ignores third parties giving information to ego toward the goal of controlling or punishing alter (e.g., Black, 1995, "gossip is the handling of a grievance by an informal hearing in absentia—in the absence of the alleged offender" p. 855). Third parties in the gossip argument are responding to a friend's (ego) request for a story about alter. They are motivated by their relationship with ego and the rules of conversational etiquette. As Gambetta (1994) so nicely put it in his review, "Gossip does not work well if the receiver suspects ulterior motives behind the transmitter's story" (p. 11).

3. The etiquette mechanism is widely discussed (e.g., Grice, 1975, on the cooperative principle in conversation; Nyberg, 1993, on the need for deception in ordinary life; cf. Dunbar, 1996, on gossip as the human analogue to grooming between less linguistically social animals). Higgins (1992) reviewed evidence (cf. Klayman, 1995). For example, Higgins described an undergraduate subject given a written description of a hypothetical person (Donald). The subject is asked to describe Donald to a second student who walks into the lab. The second person is part of the experiment and primes the conversation by leaking his predisposition toward Donald ("kinda likes" or "kinda dislikes" Donald). The result is that subjects distort their descriptions of Donald toward the expressed predisposition. Positive predisposition elicits positive words about Donald's ambiguous characteristics and neglect of negative concrete characteristics. Negative predisposition elicits negative words about Donald's ambiguous characteristics and neglect of positive concrete characteristics.

4. The etiquette mechanism and its consequences are familiar to me from conversations with colleagues and senior managers but I know of no published field work that offers ethnomethodological analysis of sustained conversation between senior managers. Fortunately, the etiquette mechanism described in the text is a generic feature of gossip and so equally evident in conversation at lower levels and outside the corporation. Fine (1986) summarized his analysis of teenager gossip as follows:

> Teenagers must present actions which are susceptible to several possible interpretations in ways which are likely to be supported by other speakers, either through ratification utterances or by story-chaining. The audience members actively or tacitly ratify the speaker's remarks, even if they disagree with the talk in principle. Interactants have techniques by which they can express their disagreement—through later contrary examples (which, too, are usually not disagreed with) or by audience role distance through joking interjections. (p. 409)

This is precisely the etiquette mechanism of going along with the flow of the conversation and has the predicted consequence of amplifying certainty about others (e.g., Fine noted the exaggerated opinions in which some teenagers can "do no wrong," whereas others can "do no right.").

5. An alternative intuition is to say that ego is misled by a lower quality of information in gossip. For example, Gilovich (1987) showed undergraduates a video of a person describing "something you are not too proud of," then asked them to describe the person on audio tape and rate the person on 7-point scales from negative to positive. A second subject then hears the audio description and rates the person. Evaluations by the students with second-hand knowledge from audio tape are more extreme in blaming the person for the bad behavior. Gilovich argued that second-hand accounts elicit more extreme evaluations because the second-hand accounts tend to leave out mitigating circumstances and situational constraints. This intuition is an uncomfortable theoretical assumption because third-party accounts are reduced to "cheap talk," which should be discounted by ego (e.g., Gibbons, 1992, on cheap-talk games). Why should ego believe a third-party account stripped of situational details? The gossip argument asks for less naïveté on ego's part. The gossip argument is that third-party accounts are accurate but not representative. Other things being equal, each third party has positive and negative stories about alter. Ego receives complete stories, but not a representative set of stories. Ego cannot know she or he is getting a subset of information biased toward the positive (or toward the negative) because ego does not know the scope of each third party's information on alter.

6. This sentence on ego's search highlights the role that confirmation bias could play in the predicted effect of the etiquette mechanism. With respect to ego, alter, and third parties, the gist of the evidence is twofold: (a) Ego's search for information on alter is biased toward third-party stories consistent with ego's predisposition toward alter (see Klayman, 1995, for a review of evidence), and (b) ego is more likely to believe stories consistent with ego's predisposition toward alter (see Klayman, 1995). The first of these two points is the more unique to confirmation bias. Wason's (1960) "2-4-6 task" is an often-cited illustration. Klayman (1995) summarized the view from cognitive psychology:

> The experimenter has in mind a rule that generates sets of three numbers (triples). The subject must try to discover the generating rule by proposing triples, which the experimenter identifies as fitting or not fitting the rule. To begin, the experimenter tells the subject that the triple 2, 4, 6 fits the generating rule. From that point on, the subject proposes triples one at a time, with the experimenter responding yes or no. In the original version of this rule-discovery task, subjects were told to stop proposing triples when they were 'highly confident' they had the correct rule. Wason found that subjects often developed considerable confidence in a hypothesis on the basis of inconclusive data. When subjects formed a hypothesis about the rule that generated the triples (e.g., increasing by two), they most often tested instances that fit their hypothesis (e.g., 5, 7, 9; 10, 12, 14; 106, 108, 110). All these triples received 'yes' responses, and subjects became convinced that they had quickly found the rule. In most cases, they did not discover that Wason's rule was in fact more general, namely "numbers in ascending order.' Wason referred to this as confirmation bias,

because subjects performed tests that were aimed at confirming a current belief. To find the correct rule, subjects had to test triples that did not fit the rule they thought correct, such as 1, 2, 3. (pp. 388–389)

In short, ego tends not to look for evidence that could disconfirm his or her predisposition toward alter (see Klayman & Ha, 1987, on confirmation versus disconfirmation; cf., Burt's, 1998, contrast between a Groucho and a Gossip information search).

7. Notice how simply this eliminates the monitoring problem that Hechter (1987, 1990) used to drive his argument about dependence and formal control being necessary conditions for group solidarity. Hechter (1987) took issue with Axelrod's (1984) use of the live-and-let-live system of trench warfare to illustrate the idea that cooperation emerges in even the most difficult circumstances if players anticipate future interaction with one another. Hechter stressed the implicit monitoring necessary to the live-and-let-live system, the difficulty of monitoring even between the two armies that is analogous to a two-player game, and the implausibility of that monitoring (without formal controls) in games of more than two players (see Macy, 1991, for illustration with simulated prisoner's dilemma games; Knez & Camerer, 1994, for laboratory illustration with weakest-link coordination games). In other words, cooperation is more difficult in larger groups. Hechter's argument presumes that everyone monitors everyone else, whereupon monitoring is more difficult in larger groups. The gossip argument is less demanding. Everyone is relatively ignorant but increasingly informed by third parties with increasing indirect connection. All it takes is one third party to relay stories between a pair of people. Systemic properties of amplified trust and distrust emerge from the microsocial context around individual pairs of people. The monitoring problem reduces to realistic proportions. The whole population does not monitor your behavior, just your closest friends and coworkers (e.g., Janowitz & Shils, 1948/1991, on why the German *Wehrmacht* continued to function toward the end of World War II despite repeated defeats; monitoring was between buddies in the squad and the army was a system of interlocked squads; cf. Marshall, 1947/1978, on the corresponding effect of "tactical cohesion" in the American forces).

8. This prediction has an analogy in overconfidence research. Overconfidence refers to people who believe in something with a probability higher than is accurate (e.g., Kahneman, Slovic, & Tversky, 1982; see also Prendergast & Stole's, 1996, economic analysis of overconfidence in terms of information consistency as an indicator of accuracy). Here is typical evidence: For a sequence of predictions, plot each prediction on a vertical axis by the prediction's actual probability of being true and on a horizontal axis by the average subject's expressed probability of the prediction being true. To the extent that subjects are accurate, their expressed probabilities equal the actual probabilities so the data points define a 45-degree diagonal line between the axes. Subjects are overconfident to the extent that data points lie below the diagonal (indicating incorrectly high perceived probabilities). An analogous view of the third-party effect would have a horizontal axis measuring ego's evaluation of alter's trustworthiness (e.g., "On a scale of 0 to 100, indicate the probability that you trust alter to cooperate in the next game.") The vertical axis would be the actual probability (typically unobserved). Ego's perceived probability is expected to be amplified by third-party gossip. There is no measure of true probability but the strength of the direct connection between ego and alter is an indicator of the empirical evidence available to ego for his or her evaluation of alter trustworthiness. When the strength of direct connection between ego and alter is held constant and the probability of trust (or distrust) is inflated where ego is more exposed to third-party gossip, the result is evidence of an overconfidence effect induced by social context. The significant difference here is that there is no true probability of alter being trustworthy (see the "reality of negative relations" in note 11). The truth of alter is socially constructed between ego and selected third parties (e.g., Gambetta, 1994, "Plausibility is more relevant than truth. A convincing story gets

repeated because of its appeal not its truthfulness" p. 13.). The gossip argument is not about truth, it is about certainty.

9. With respect to synthesizing interpretations of events, the contrast between Robert and James is the contrast between Protestants and Catholics in Durkheim's (1897/1951) analysis of suicide:

> The only essential difference between Catholicism and Protestantism is that the second permits free inquiry to a far greater degree than the first ... the Catholic accepts his faith ready made, without scrutiny. ... A whole hierarchical system of authority is devised, with marvelous ingenuity, to render tradition invariable. All variation is abhorrent to Catholic thought. The Protestant is far more the author of his faith. The Bible is put in his hands and no interpretation is imposed upon him. The very structure of the reformed cult stresses this state of religious individualism. (p. 158)

I mention Durkheim's contrast first to better communicate my information-processing contrast between Robert and James by linking it to a more familiar information-processing contrast and second to highlight a disadvantage to being a manager like Robert, namely, the lack of social regulation. Durkheim contrasted Protestants and Catholics in service of explaining why the former are more prone to suicide. Religion serves its function in part by resolving unanswerable questions through social consensus but its social authority is less where individuals are in some significant way free to craft their own religion. Protestants are less protected from uncertainty by their religion and so are more prone to suicide when events go wrong. Similarly, the inconsistent third-party gossip that forces managers like Robert (relative to managers like James) to craft their own interpretations means that they are less certain about their interpretations. I show elsewhere (Burt, 1998, from which illustrative evidence is presented here in Fig. 10.4) that managers like Robert are less subject to the distortions of third-party gossip and past research has shown that they are more successful, but the research is yet to appear describing the consequences of the higher levels of uncertainty with which they live—presumably the usual stress correlates such as heart attack, although even with respect to emotional states, the social capital of complex networks can be argued to be positive (e.g., Coser, 1975; Marks, 1977; Sieber, 1974).

10. This point is illustrated in Durkheim's (1893/1933) classic analysis of the social value of criminals, productively developed in Erikson's (1966) analysis of crime waves. Durkheim offered text that enriches my few sentences (Durkheim, 1893/1933, the bulk of which is also quoted in Erikson's, 1966, argument):

> Of course, we always love the company of those who feel and think as we do, but it is with passion, and no longer solely with pleasure, that we seek it immediately after discussions where our common beliefs have been greatly combated. Crime brings together upright consciences and concentrates them. We have only to notice what happens, particularly in a small town, when some moral scandal has just been committed. They stop each other on the street, they visit each other, they seek to come together to talk of the event and to wax indignant in common. From all the similar impressions which are exchanged, from all the temper that gets itself expressed, there emerges a unique temper, more or less determinate according to the circumstances, which is everybody's without being anybody's in particular. That is the public temper. (p. 6)

11. The reality of negative relationships is clearly illustrated for me in peer evaluations among investment bankers. In one firm, for example, each officer is asked to name other officers in the firm with whom he or she had substantial and frequent business dealings during the preceding year, then asked to rate each cited colleague on a 5-point scale for the adequacy

of their job performance (1 for "unacceptable" to 5 for "outstanding"). Two features of the evaluations are illustrative: (a) Every officer is the object of negative and positive relations. Each officer has two or more people who say she or he is doing a poor job. The same officer has two or more people who say that he or she is doing a good job. In fact, the best predictor of the number of negative relations an officer receives is the total number of people citing the officer for any reason. More prominent officers have more admirers and more detractors. The total number of relations received has a .91 correlation with the number of positive relations and a .80 correlation with the number of negative relations. (b) Analysis of variance across the 31,394 interpersonal evaluations breaks down into 26% attributable to differences between respondents (some officers use lower ratings on average), 15% attributable to differences between subjects (some officers receive lower ratings on average), and the remaining 59% of the variance measures qualities specific to the respondent–subject pair of officers. In other words, the distinction between positive and negative relations is a function more of the two people involved than either person individually (see Kenny & Albright, 1987, for a similar result in relations between undergraduates).

12. It is tempting to conclude that third parties transmit negative gossip more readily than positive gossip, but I know only of anecdotal evidence on this point. Heath (1997) offered suggestive evidence. To find out whether people prefer to pass along good news or bad, Heath presented University of Chicago undergraduates with information about muggings in the university neighborhood. Some received more negative information (many muggings). The students were then asked how likely they would be to pass along the information in a conversation with an acquaintance if the topic of muggings came up. Students informed of an extremely high number of muggings were significantly more likely to claim that they would pass the information along. Heath had no behavioral data on whether students are actually more likely to pass along the more negative information and it is a long step from undergraduates to managers but the evidence is consistent, with results in Fig. 10.4 showing the stronger negative effect of third parties.

13. I had a computer display each explanation at random and elicit a three-category evaluation of how hostile the manager seemed toward the cited colleague; (0) not hostile, (50) maybe hostile, or (100) definitely hostile. The hostility score analyzed in the text for each explanation is the average of four evaluations spread over 4 days. Coding the explanations for hostility must remain a subjective measurement and therefore suspect, however, the repeated measures, strong correlation among the measures, and low autocorrelation between adjacent measures are reassuring (see Burt, 1998, for details).

ACKNOWLEDGMENTS

This chapter includes material from Burt (1997) on the structural hole argument and Burt (1998) on the gossip argument. For comments and new leads I am grateful to Sally Blount, Greg Janicik, Tory Higgins, Joshua Klayman, Richard Moreland, Joel Podolny, Holly Raider, James Schrager, and Adrian Tschoegl.

REFERENCES

Adams, R. M. (1977). *Bad mouth*. Berkeley: University of California Press.
Ashforth, B. E., & Mael, F. (1989). Social identity theory and the organization. *Academy of Management Review, 14*, 20–39.

Axelrod, R. (1984). *The evolution of cooperation.* New York: Basic Books.

Barber, B. (1983). *The logic and limits of trust.* New Brunswick, NJ: Rutgers University Press.

Black, D. (1993). *The social structure of right and wrong.* New York: Academic Press.

Black, D. (1995). The epistemology of pure sociology. *Law and Social Inquiry, 20,* 829–870.

Black, D., & Baumgartner, M. P. (1983). Toward a theory of the third party. In K. O. Boyum & L. Mather (Eds.), *Empirical theories about courts* (pp. 84–114). New York: Longman.

Blau, P. M. (1964). *Exchange and power in social life.* New York: Wiley.

Blau, P. M. (1968). Interaction: Social exchange. In D. L. Sills (Ed.), *The international encyclopedia of the social sciences* (Vol. 7, pp. 452–458). New York: The Free Press and Macmillan.

Blau, P. M. (1994). *Structural contexts of opportunities.* Chicago: University of Chicago Press.

Blount, S. (1995). When social outcomes aren't fair: The effect of causal attribution on preferences. *Organizational Behavior and Human Decision Processes, 63,* 131–144.

Bradach, J. L., & Eccles, R. G. (1989). Price, authority, and trust: From ideal types to plural forms. *Annual Review of Sociology, 15,* 97–118.

Burt, R. S. (1980). Autonomy in a social topology. *American Journal of Sociology, 85,* 892–925.

Burt, R. S. (1982). *Toward a structural theory of action.* New York: Academic Press.

Burt, R. S. (1992). *Structural holes.* Cambridge, MA: Harvard University Press.

Burt, R. S. (1997). The contingent value of social capital. *Administrative Science Quarterly, 42,* 339–365.

Burt, R. S. (1998). *Evidence of density, distrust, and character assassination.* Manuscript under review.

Burt, R. S., Hogarth, R. M., & Michaud, C. (1997). *The social capital of French and American managers.* Manuscript under review.

Burt, R. S., Jannotta, J., & Mahoney, T. (1998). Personality correlates of structural holes. *Social Networks, 20,* 63–87.

Burt, R. S., & Knez, M. (1995). Kinds of third-party effects on trust. *Rationality and Society, 7,* 255–292.

Coleman, J. S. (1990). *Foundations of social theory.* Cambridge, MA: Harvard University Press.

Cook, K. S., & Emerson, R. M. (1978). Power, equity and commitment in exchange networks. *American Sociological Review, 43,* 712–739.

Coser, R. L. (1975). The complexity of roles as a seedbed of individual autonomy. In L. A. Coser (Ed.), *The idea of social structure* (pp. 237–263). New York: Harcourt, Brace, Jovanovich.

Davis, J. A. (1970). Clustering and hierarchy in interpersonal relations: Testing two graph theoretical models on 742 sociograms. *American Sociological Review, 35,* 843–852.

Davis, J. A., & Leinhardt, S. (1972). The structure of positive interpersonal relations in small groups. In J. Berger, M. Zelditch, & B. Anderson (Eds.), *Sociological theories in progress* (pp. 218–251). New York: Houghton-Mifflin.

Dunbar, R. (1996). *Grooming, gossip, and the evolution of language.* Cambridge, MA: Harvard University Press.

Durkheim, E. (1933). *The division of labor in society* (G. Simpson, Trans.). New York: The Free Press. (Original work published 1893)

Durkheim, E. (1951). *Suicide.* (J. Spaulding & G. Simpson, Trans.). New York: The Free Press. (Original work published 1897)

Ekeh, P. P. (1974). *Social exchange theory.* Cambridge, MA: Harvard University Press.

Erikson, K. T. (1966). *Wayward puritans.* New York: Wiley.

Fernandez, R. M., & Gould, R. V. (1994). A dilemma of state power: Brokerage and influence in the national health policy domain. *American Journal of Sociology, 99,* 1455–1491.

Fine, G. (1986). The social organization of adolescent gossip: the rhetoric of moral education. In J. Cook-Gumperz, W. A. Corsaro, & J. Streeck (Eds.), *Children's worlds and children's language* (pp. 405–423). New York: deGruyter.

Freeman, L. C. (1977). A set of measures of centrality based on betweenness. *Sociometry, 40,* 35–40.

Gabbay, S. M. (1997). *Social capital in the creation of financial capital.* Champaign, IL: Stipes.

Gambetta, D. (1994). Godfather's gossip. *Archives Européen de Sociologie, 35,* 1–25.

Gibbons, R. (1992). *Game theory for applied economists.* Princeton, NJ: Princeton University Press.

Gilovich, T. (1987). Secondhand information and social judgment. *Journal of Experimental Social Psychology, 23,* 59–74.

Granovetter, M. S. (1973). The strength of weak ties. *American Journal of Sociology, 78,* 1360–1380.

Granovetter, M. S. (1985). Economic action, social structure, and embeddedness. *American Journal of Sociology, 91,* 481–510.

Granovetter, M. S. (1992). Problems of explanation in economic sociology. In N. Nohria & R. G. Eccles (Eds.), *Networks and organization* (pp. 29–56). Boston: Harvard Business School Press.

Grice, H. P. (1975). Logic and conversation. In P. Cole & J. Morgan (Eds.), *Syntax and semantics* (pp. 41–58). New York: Academic Press.

Gulati, R. (1995). Familiarity breeds trust? The implications of repeated ties for contractual choice in alliances. *Academy of Management Journal, 38,* 85–112.

Heath, C. (1997). Do people prefer to pass along good or bad news? Valence and relevance of news as a predictor of transmission propensity. *Organizational Behavior and Human Decision Processes, 68,* 79–94.

Hechter, M. (1987). *Principles of group solidarity.* Berkeley: University of California Press.

Hechter, M. (1990). On the inadequacy of game theory for the solution of real-world collective action problems. In K. S. Cook & M. Levi (Eds.), *The limits of rationality* (pp. 240–249). Chicago: University of Chicago Press.

Heider, F. (1958). *The psychology of interpersonal relations.* New York: Wiley.

Higgins, E. T. (1992). Achieving "shared reality" in the communication game: A social action that creates meaning. *Journal of Language and Social Psychology, 11,* 107–131.

Holland, P. W., & Leinhardt, S. (1970). A method for detecting structure in sociometric data. *American Journal of Sociology, 70,* 492–513.

Homans, G. C. (1961). *Social behavior.* New York: Harcourt Brace.

Janis, I. L. (1972). *Victims of groupthink.* Boston: Houghton Mifflin.

Janowitz, M., & Shils, E. A. (1991). Cohesion and disintegration in the Wehrmacht in World War II. In J. Burk (Ed.), *On social organization and social control* (pp. 160–175). Chicago: University of Chicago Press. (Original work published 1948)

Kahneman, D., Slovic, P., & Tversky, A. (Eds.). (1982). *Judgment under uncertainty: Heuristics and biases.* New York: Cambridge University Press.

Kenny, D. A., & Albright, L. (1987). Accuracy in interpersonal perception: A social relations analysis. *Psychological Bulletin, 102,* 390–402.

Klayman, J. (1995). Varieties of confirmation bias. *The Psychology of Learning and Motivation, 32,* 385–418.

Klayman, J., & Ha, Y. W. (1987). Confirmation, disconfirmation, and information in hypothesis testing. *Psychological Review, 94,* 211–228.

Knez, M., & Camerer, C. (1994). Creating expectational assets in the laboratory: Coordination in weakest-link games. *Strategic Management Journal, 15,* 101–119.

Krackhardt, D., & Stern, R. N. (1988). Informal networks and organizational crisis: An experimental simulation. *Social Psychology Quarterly, 51,* 123–140.

Kramer, R. M. (1994). The sinister attribution error: Paranoid cognition and collective distrust in organizations. *Motivation and Emotion, 18,* 199–230.

Kramer, R. M., Brewer, M. B., & Hanna, B. A. (1995). Presumptive trust and collective action in organizations: The role of identity-based trust. In R. M. Kramer & T. R. Tyler (Eds.), *Trust in organizations* (pp. 357–389). Newbury Park, CA: Sage.

Kreps, D. M. (1990). Corporate culture and economic theory. In J. E. Alt & K. A. Shepsle (Eds.), *Perspectives on positive political economy* (pp. 90–143). New York: Cambridge University Press.

Larson, A. (1992). Network dyads in entrepreneurial settings: A study of the governance of exchange relationships. *Administrative Science Quarterly, 37,* 76–104.

Lawler, E. J., & Yoon, J. (1996). Commitment in exchange relations: Test of a theory of relational cohesion. *American Sociological Review, 61*, 89–108.

Macaulay, S. (1963). Non-contractual relations in business: A preliminary study. *American Sociological Review, 28*, 55–67.

Macy, M. W. (1991). Learning to cooperate: Stochastic and tacit collusion in social exchange. *American Journal of Sociology, 97*, 808–843.

Marks, S. R. (1977). Multiple roles and role strain: Some notes on human energy, time, and commitment. *American Sociological Review, 42*, 921–936.

Marshall, S. L. A. (1978). *Men against fire.* Gloucester, MA: Peter Smith. (Original work published 1947)

Merton, R. K. (1968). Continuities in the theory of reference group behavior. In R. K. Merton (Ed.), *Social theory and social structure* (pp. 335–440). New York: The Free Press. (Original work published 1957)

Messick, D. M., & Mackie, D. M. (1989). Intergroup relations. *Annual Review of Psychology, 40*, 45–81.

Mizruchi, M. S. (1992). *The structure of corporate political action.* Cambridge, MA: Harvard University Press.

Morrill, C. (1995). *The executive way.* Chicago: University of Chicago Press.

Nohria, N., & Eccles, R. G. (Eds.). (1992). *Networks and organizations.* Boston: Harvard Business School Press.

Nyberg, D. (1993). *The varnished truth.* Chicago: University of Chicago Press.

Podolny, J. M., & Baron, J. N. (1997). Relationships and resources: Social networks and mobility in the workplace. *American Sociological Review, 62*, 673–693.

Portes, A., & Landolt, P. (1996, May–June). The downside of social capital. *American Prospect,* 18–21.

Powell, W. W., & Smith-Doerr, L. (1994). Networks and economic life. In N. J. Smelser & R. Swedberg (Eds.), *The handbook of economic sociology* (pp. 368–402). Princeton, NJ: Princeton University Press.

Prendergast, C., & Stole, L. (1996). Impetuous youngsters and jaded oldtimers: Acquiring a reputation for learning. *Journal of Political Economy, 104*, 1105–1134.

Rodin, J. (1985). The application of social psychology. In G. Lindzey & E. Aronson (Eds.), *The handbook of social psychology* (Vol. 2, pp. 805–881). New York: Random House.

Rosenthal, E. A. (1996). *Social networks and team performance.* Unpublished doctoral dissertation, University of Chicago.

Ross, M., & Fletcher, G. J. O. (1985). Attribution and social perception. In G. Lindzey & E. Aronson (Eds.), *The handbook of social psychology* (Vol. 2, pp. 73–122). New York: Random House.

Sieber, S. D. (1974). Toward a theory of role accumulation. *American Sociological Review, 39*, 567–578.

Simmel, G. (1955). *Conflict and the web of group affiliations.* (K. H. Wolff & R. Bendix, Trans.). New York: The Free Press. (Original work published 1922)

Sitkin, S. B., & Stickel, D. (1996). The road to hell: The dynamics of distrust in an era of quality. In R. M. Kramer & T. R. Tyler (Eds), *Trust in organizations* (pp. 196–215). Newbury Park, CA: Sage.

Smelser, N. J., & Swedberg, R. (Eds.). (1994). *Handbook of economic sociology.* Princeton, NJ: Princeton University Press.

Sparrowe, R. T., & Popielarz, P. A. (1995). *Weak ties and structural holes: The effects of network structure on careers.* Paper presented at the annual meetings of the Academy of Management, August, Vancouver, BC.

Staw, B. M., & Ross, J. (1987). Behavior in escalation situations: Antecedents, prototypes, and solutions. In L. Cummings & B. M. Staw (Eds.), *Research in organizational behavior* (Vol. 9, pp. 39–78). Greenwich, CT: JAI.

Stinchcombe, A. L. (1990). *Information and organizations.* Berkeley: University of California Press.

Swedberg, R. (Ed.). (1993). *Explorations in economic sociology.* New York: Russell Sage Foundation.

Uzzi, B. (1996). The sources and consequences of embeddedness for the economic performance of organizations: The network effect. *American Sociological Review, 61,* 674–698.

Van Maanen, J. (1978). The asshole. In P. K. Manning & J. Van Maanen (Eds.), *Policing* (pp. 121–138). New York: Random House.

Wason, P. C. (1960). On the failure to eliminate hypotheses in a conceptual task. *Quarterly Journal of Experimental Psychology, 12,* 129–140.

Wasserman, S., & Faust, K. (1994). *Social network analysis.* New York: Cambridge University Press.

Zucker, L. G. (1986). Production of trust: Institutional sources of economic structure, 1840–1920. In L. Cummings & B. M. Staw (Eds.), *Research in organizational behavior* (Vol. 8, pp. 53–111). Greenwich, CT: JAI.

Zucker, L. G. (1991). The role of institutionalization in cultural persistence. In W. W. Powell & P. J. DiMaggio (Eds.), *The new institutionalism in organizational analysis* (pp. 83–107). Chicago: University of Chicago Press. (Original work published 1977)

11

What Newcomers See and What Oldtimers Say: Discontinuities in Knowledge Exchange

Deborah H. Gruenfeld
Elliott T. Fan
Northwestern University

Many important aspects of knowledge about work are implicit in the cultures of workgroups (Trice & Beyer, 1993). Workgroup culture can be defined as the unspoken and often unrecognized beliefs and routines that guide members' actions (Levine & Moreland, 1991) and includes knowledge and expectations about group members, about group process, and about their relations to group performance (Gruenfeld & Hollingshead, 1993). The wisdom, insight, and expertise embedded in group culture are useful to organizations because they enable group members to behave automatically, without conscious thought, in ways that are consistent with the group's values and best practices. However, this lack of awareness also presents a problem for organizations. Because the unique knowledge embedded in distinct work groups is generally invisible to participants, the most critical lessons and insights are often tacit within their group of origin (Nonaka & Takeuchi, 1995). As a result, the presence of distinct group cultures can lead to a performance paradox in organizations, whereby knowledge gleaned by one group or team leads to improvements at the local group level that have no appreciable impact on organization-level performance (Rousseau, 1993).

The performance paradox illustrates a major challenge for organizational learning: to facilitate the transfer of tacit knowledge across group boundaries (Argote, Gruenfeld, & Naquin, in press; Olivera & Argote, chap. 13, this volume). Failure to overcome the paradox can result from two types of problems. One is the problem of consciousness (Argyris & Schon, 1978).

Group culture is enacted through habitual routines and is stored in habits of mind that operate at a subconscious level (Louis & Sutton, 1991). Hence, tacit knowledge about group work is typically unnoticed by those who possess it. Knowledge about group practices can be transmitted without explicit awareness (Berry & Broadbent, 1987); however, this is most likely to occur when insiders and outsiders are willingly engaged in their mutual socialization and adjust their values and behavior to increase their similarity (Moreland & Levine, 1989). In contrast, distinct organizational groups are often in competition for status and control, which motivates them to maximize their distinctiveness and maintain unique identities (Trice & Beyer, 1993).

Tacit knowledge can be made explicit when an unexpected challenge or obstacle to routine behavior stimulates active thinking about cultural practices (Kiesler & Sproull, 1982; Langer, 1986; Louis, 1980). However, communication of explicit knowledge between representatives of different groups poses additional obstacles. Representatives of knowledge donor groups must be motivated to make their insights available to others and representatives of knowledge recipient groups must be motivated to receive others' insights (Szulanski, 1994). Research on group problem solving shows that these motives are hard to come by. When members of such groups possess unique knowledge, they are less likely to share it with others than to discuss information they already have in common (Wittenbaum & Stasser, 1996). This is especially true when discussants are unfamiliar with one another because they represent different social groups (Gruenfeld, Mannix, Williams, & Neale, 1996; Williams, Mannix, Neale, & Gruenfeld, 1998). Moreover, the recipients of unique knowledge and opinion often process that information defensively and ultimately reject it because they wish to distance rather than align themselves with a social deviant (Levine, 1989; Nemeth, 1986; Wood, Lundgren, Ouellette, Busceme, & Blackstone, 1994; Wood, Pool, Leck, & Purvis, 1996).

In recent years, organizations have begun to experiment with various means of increasing group members' consciousness and communication of tacit knowledge, to facilitate intergroup learning (for reviews see Argote et al., in press; Mohrman, Cohen, & Mohrman, 1995). A common strategy has been to make group boundaries more permeable by moving members back and forth across them (Galbraith, 1990). In manufacturing, for example, many employees who used to work within a single functional area, such as engineering, are now full-time members of cross-functional teams, including representatives of engineering, marketing, and manufacturing departments. Participation on cross-functional task forces is another common organizational vehicle for intergroup knowledge transfer. Although participation on cross-functional teams is typically a full-time job assignment, whereas participation on task forces is more likely to be part-time, these traditional group structures are similar in that their membership is designed to be stable. Turnover does occur naturally over the lifespan of such groups but personnel changes are not an explicit strategic design feature.

In contrast, several new variations on cross-functional task design utilize temporary changes in group composition to make intergroup collaborations more efficient. In these group structures, membership is dynamic by design. Dynamic-composition workgroups are composed of a relatively small group of permanent core members and intermittently include peripheral members who either import or export knowledge on demand at specific times (for examples of specific designs see Ancona & Caldwell, 1998; Mohrman et al., 1995; Nahavandi & Aranda, 1994). Presumably, such changes in group composition provide the kind of culture shock that stimulates active thinking about group practices (Arrow & McGrath, 1993; Kiesler & Sproull, 1982; Louis & Sutton, 1991). In addition, the purported benefits of including temporary, peripheral group members include the exchange of best practices across groups with similar functions, providing core members with the alternative perspectives and dissent necessary to optimize group decision making (Nahavandi & Aranda, 1994) and developing the political capital necessary to implement those decisions within the organization (Ancona & Caldwell, 1998).

Theoretical discussions of membership change are relatively rare (for a recent review, see Arrow & McGrath, 1995). However, several scholars have noted that the process and performance of groups with closed boundaries and stable composition differ in important ways from those with open boundaries and unstable composition (Altman, Vinsel, & Brown, 1981; Arrow, 1997; Arrow & McGrath, 1993; Ziller, 1965). An important aspect of dynamic groups is that their functioning depends on interactions between newcomers and oldtimers (Moreland & Levine, 1989). Theoretically, knowledge and influence flow in both directions between newcomers and oldtimers (Levine & Moreland, 1991). When members change groups, newcomers assimilate, adopting the beliefs and norms of oldtimers, and oldtimers accommodate, adjusting their beliefs and norms in response to newcomers.

However, these outcomes are not equally likely in dynamic–composition work groups. In such groups, newcomers are typically outnumbered by oldtimers, which means they are also minority members. As such, they will be more susceptible to direct influence by the majority (i.e., oldtimers) than vice versa (for a review, see Wood et al., 1994). In addition, because newcomers in such groups are visitors who are expected to function as temporary, peripheral members and will subsequently return to their group of origin, they may experience role conflict and uncertainty about how to manage their commitments to new and old groups (Katz & Kahn, 1978). Newcomers in this context are not transfers, replacements, or recruits, who have been chosen by oldtimers, nor are they expected to become permanent, core members. In this context, the motivation for oldtimers to engage fully in accommodating newcomers should be substantially lower than it might be when such changes are willingly initiated by group members themselves (c.f., Sutton & Louis, 1987). Under these circumstances, the pressure for newcomers to assimilate should be greater than the pressure for oldtimers to accommodate.

This difference has important consequences for the transfer of tacit knowledge between groups. Specifically, the pressure to assimilate should increase awareness of group practices and active thinking about them in newcomers (Louis, 1980); hence, tacit knowledge is more likely to become explicit for newcomers than oldtimers. The switch from automatic to conscious thought occurs when individuals experience change, encounter surprise, and are motivated to make sense of discrepant events (Louis & Sutton, 1991). These conditions are characteristic of role transitions in general (Langer, 1989) and of newcomers' experiences in particular (Louis, 1980). Newcomers learn about their new environment through cognitive contrasts with prior experience, which lead to the emergence of a perceptual field whose features distinguish the new from old setting. The tension created by this discrepancy compels newcomers to revisit assumptions about the right way to do things and to generate explanations that make sense of the differences discovered (see also Van Maanen, 1977).

In contrast, the changes experienced by oldtimers should require less adjustment. Newcomers are expected to conform to oldtimers' behavioral standards and, typically, they do (Moreland & Levine, 1989). If they do not adopt the norms and behaviors of oldtimers, newcomers are often passive and withdrawn during group activity because they experience role ambiguity (Van Sell, Brief, & Schuler, 1981). As a result, the novelty, contrast, and surprise that could accompany a newcomer's arrival may be diminished by the newcomer's attempts to assimilate. Even if newcomers are inclined to comment on group practices or share their observations with oldtimers, such unique knowledge is likely to receive less attention than members' common knowledge (Gigone & Hastie, 1993; Stasser & Titus, 1985; Wittenbaum & Stasser, 1996). Moreover, oldtimers are more likely to favor their own opinions than to accept and agree with the opinions of newcomers, especially when those newcomers are smaller in number and have lower status than oldtimers (Levine, 1989; Levine & Russo, 1987; Wood et al., 1994). In sum, the use of dynamically composed groups to facilitate knowledge transfer seems unlikely to have the intended effects.

STUDY OVERVIEW

The research reported here examined this hypothesis in a longitudinal study of 22 continuing workgroups. Groups worked independently on a variety of organizational tasks and were asked after each work session to write essays reflecting on their performance. After 10 weeks of stable membership, groups were recomposed by rotating a single randomly selected member from each group into a new group. This manipulation created the presence of newcomers and oldtimers. Newcomers spent 2 weeks in the new group, returning to their original group for the final week of the study. To measure changes in awareness and active thinking about group process and performance, members' essays were scored for (a) recognition of multiple perspectives and (b) consideration of the trade-offs among perspectives, using the integrative complexity coding system (Baker-Brown, Ballard, Bluck, de Vries, Suedfeld, & Tetlock, 1992; Suedfeld, Tetlock, & Streufert, 1992). To measure information sharing and influence by newcomers and oldtimers, the ideas generated by individuals working independently were compared with those used in a collaborative group product.

HYPOTHESES

Membership Change and Integrative Complexity. Integrative complexity is a characteristic of cognitive style that reflects the breadth and depth of decision-makers' thoughts. Specifically, it is indicated by two cognitive components: *cognitive differentiation*, which corresponds to recognition of multiple perspectives, and *cognitive integration*, which corresponds to recognition of trade-offs among alternatives. High integrative complexity reflects active thinking in that it involves thoughtful cost-benefit comparisons of alternatives, whereas low integrative complexity is more characteristic of automatic processing in that it reflects a lack of awareness of alternatives and a more mindless reliance on a single perspective as a basis for judgment (for a review see Suedfeld, Tetlock, & Streufert, 1992). For example, the statement "Conflict had a negative impact on group performance" is less integratively complex than the statement "Conflict strained member relationships, but improved understanding of members' interests."

Prior research has not examined how membership change affects integrative complexity. As noted earlier, surprise and sense-making by newcomers could explain variations in their styles of reasoning after changing groups (Louis, 1980). When newcomers encounter the unique culture and norms of the new group, their awareness of important dimensions of group process should be heightened through cognitive contrasts between past and present experiences. This recognition of alternative approaches to group process should lead to an increase in cognitive differentiation. In addition, attempts to resolve the tension created by recognition of alternative viewpoints could lead to cognitive integration. To the extent that newcomers attempt to make sense of the differences they perceive by, for example, considering the costs and benefits of each, or the conditions under which each should enhance performance, cognitive integration should be increased.

Conceptual integration requires greater cognitive and emotional resources than simply choosing among alternatives (Streufert & Swezey, 1986). Hence, it is only likely to occur when decision makers are motivated to preserve the validity of competing perspectives (Tetlock, 1992). This state of mind is known as *value pluralism* and has been linked empirically to integrative reasoning in members of natural work groups (Tetlock, 1986; Tetlock, Peterson, & Lerner, 1996).

Newcomers in dynamic-composition work groups, who must contribute to their new group but will eventually return to their group of origin, are likely to experience this psychological state. When the values associated with membership in both groups are equally important and social acceptance in both groups is equally desired, newcomers will be motivated to remain cognizant of and committed to the distinct values associated with membership in each of the groups they span. In contrast, oldtimers are embedded in a single group whose norms and behavioral standards are relatively stable and likely to remain unchallenged. Oldtimers may notice the alternatives presented by newcomers but are unlikely to feel beholden to the newcomers' standards of behavior. Hence, oldtimers are less likely to experience value pluralism than newcomers.

These considerations suggest that membership change should have a greater impact on the integrative complexity of newcomers than oldtimers. Because the cognitive contrast experienced by newcomers is likely to be greater than that experienced by oldtimers, they are more likely to notice differences in group cultures and to attempt to understand them. Hence, newcomers should exhibit greater integrative complexity after the membership change than beforehand (H1). Moreover, because newcomers in dynamic-composition groups span the boundary between a standing group to which they remain committed, an acting group to which they must contribute, they are more likely to experience value pluralism than oldtimers, who are embedded in a single, albeit changing, group. This suggests that newcomers should exhibit greater integrative complexity after the membership change than oldtimers (H2).

Membership Change and Influence.   The fact that oldtimers are apparently unlikely to experience cognitive growth themselves in response to membership change does not preclude the possibility that they will learn secondhand from newcomers' insights. As noted earlier, the successful transfer of this type of knowledge will depend on two factors: (a) communication of that knowledge by the newcomer and (b) acceptance of that knowledge by oldtimers. Research on social influence indicates that both factors are likely to present challenges (for a review see Levine, Resnick, & Higgins, 1993).

Some of the challenges associated with communication of unique insights in groups have already been discussed. In addition to these factors, newcomers in this study are unlikely to influence oldtimers' beliefs for several reasons. One is that newcomers are more passive, quieter, and less involved in group activities with oldtimers than their counterparts (for a review, see Moreland & Levine, 1989). When they do interact, they are more dependent on oldtimers and are more likely to imitate them, ask for advice and help, ingratiate themselves, avoid disagreement, and to adopt the group's perspective than oldtimers.

Newcomers who are also boundary spanners may experience role conflict in addition to pressure to conform (Katz & Kahn, 1978). This is particularly likely when the behaviors they must perform are incompatible with the needs, values, or capacities associated with other aspects of their professional or personal identities (Bell, 1990; Jackson, Thoits, & Taylor, 1995). Such role conflicts are psychologically disturbing because the individuals who enact them often lose credibility and become marginalized in each of the groups they link (Adams, 1976) and their sense of integrity can suffer as well. These effects can lead to low job satisfaction, low confidence in the organization, and a high degree of job related tension (Kahn, Wolfe, Quinn, Snoek, & Rosenthal, 1964). To cope with these feelings, boundary spanners often withdraw altogether from interaction, which obviously reduces their contributions to knowledge-sharing activities (Van Sell, Brief, & Schuler, 1981). In contrast, participation by oldtimers is likely to increase in response to membership change as they take action to display their superior status, demonstrate important norms and customs, and show newcomers the ropes (Levine & Moreland, 1991; Sutton & Louis, 1987).

In sum, the same psychological experiences that stimulate active thinking in newcomers are likely to inhibit their active participation in group activities. Newcomers are inhibited in groups; they exhibit less activity in general than oldtimers. When they participate in group activities, newcomers are more likely to act in ways that are consistent with oldtimers' beliefs and routines than to act in ways that disrupt or challenge cultural customs. To the extent that this occurs, oldtimers will remain unaware of the contrasts experienced by newcomers. When newcomers do convey their unique insights, their contributions are less likely to influence others' beliefs than are those made by oldtimers. Newcomers are often the targets of out-group bias and discrimination by oldtimers (Moreland, 1985; Moreland & Levine, 1989). Those who are outnumbered by oldtimers also face the challenges associated with minority influence (Levine, 1989; Moscovici, 1985).

In addition, recent research has documented that integratively complex thinkers fall prey to a host of impression management liabilities—regardless of their status—that can interfere with their ability to influence others who might benefit from their insights. For example, decision makers who discuss alternatives in terms of trade-offs can appear indecisive and unprincipled (Suedfeld, 1985), which compromises their credibility. Considering that consistency is the key to effective minority influence (Moscovici, 1985), an integratively complex style could be a fatal flaw for a minority influence attempt. In addition, the tendency for integratively complex group members to raise alternatives just as consensus is emerging can also lead others to judge them as antagonistic and narcissistic (Tetlock, Peterson, & Berry, 1993). These considerations suggest that because of their integratively complex ideas, newcomers who have minority status are unlikely to influence the content of majority members' thoughts and, presumably, the content of group products on which oldtimers and newcomers collaborate.

These considerations suggest that communication and influence by newcomers and oldtimers should be affected by the membership change. First, participation by newcomers and acceptance of their ideas should decrease after the membership change. This implies that newcomers' ideas will be less influential after they change groups than prior to the membership change (H3). Second, participation by oldtimers should increase after the membership change and they should be more receptive to one another's contributions than to those provided by a single, integratively complex newcomer. This implies that newcomers' ideas will be less influential than oldtimers' ideas after the membership change (H4).

DESIGN

The research involved a longitudinal study of continuing workgroups composed of students in an advanced undergraduate course on the social psychology of organizations at a Midwestern university. Students were randomly assigned to permanent workgroups that met once a week outside of lecture (the workshop section of the course) to work on a variety of simulated organizational consulting tasks. The study lasted an entire semester (13 weeks). After 10 weeks, one member of each group was arbitrarily removed from his or her permanent group and assigned to a new group for a 2-week period. Original groups were restored for the final week of the course.

TASKS

The premise for the weekly workshops was that participants were to act as consultant teams whose job was to solve organizational behavior problems for a variety of clients. In each workshop, the team was required to generate a group product that would be evaluated for its effectiveness as a solution to the problem of the week. Tasks ranged from evaluating leadership effectiveness to designing a grievance system, to choosing among interventions for changing employee behavior. Each week, after the task was completed, group members also wrote essays describing their group's activities that week using theoretical concepts from the course. The first essay was written by individual group members working alone. Afterward, group members drew on the contents of their individual essays to compose a single group essay. Both individual and group essays were graded. These essays provided the data for the study.

PARTICIPANTS

Eighty undergraduate psychology students enrolled in this course. Although it fulfilled an area requirement for psychology majors, it was not required for the major and enrollment was voluntary. Attrition for this study was only 7.5%, with 74 out of 80 participants completing all 14 weeks of the course. The subjects met twice a week: once for a 2-hour lecture (with the entire class) and once for a 2-hour workshop (in four separate 20-person sections). Participants were randomly assigned to permanent 3- or 4-person workgroups within each of the four workshop sections, for a total of 22 workgroups.

MANIPULATION

To create newcomers and oldtimers, after week 10, one member from each group was selected to leave his or her original workgroup and to join another team (within the same section) for weeks 11 and 12. Prior to week 11, participants were aware that a membership change manipulation would occur but they received no information about who would be selected to move. In fact, roles were assigned at random and group members were informed of this procedure. Subjects were transplanted in a round-robin so that there were never two groups that simply exchanged members. Task types in the weeks immediately before and after the change were also held constant, to avoid confounding the effects of the change with those of task type.

DATA COLLECTION AND ANALYSIS

Essay Production.   Essays consisted of participants' 1 to 2 page responses to the question, "How did this week's workshop activity relate to the materials and concepts of the course?" Participants were allowed to answer this question in regards to either the task, the group's interaction during the activity, or both task and interaction. They were allotted 15 minutes to complete the individual essay and were not allowed to communicate with one another until afterward. Then, the team collaborated for 15 minutes to answer the same question in a single group essay. Although they were not required to interact or to share one another's individual products, team members were allowed to freely converse during the writing of the group essay. Teams were allowed to choose scribes in any way they saw fit. Essays were graded on the extent to which they demonstrated subjects' knowledge of course content and ability to critically analyze workshop events. These grades counted toward subjects' course grades, with individual and group essays contributing equally to the final grade. To assess the impact of the membership change manipulation, data were systematically sampled to include all individual and group essays written for the 2 weeks prior to the change and for the 2 weeks during the change. There were 273 individual essays and 86 group essays included in the final data set.

Integrative Complexity Coding. Essays were coded in their entirety by one of three trained raters using the Integrative Complexity Coding Manual (Baker-Brown et al., 1992). Raters worked independently and were unaware of the nature of hypotheses and the experimental conditions under which the rationales were generated. Essays from weeks 10 and 12 were selected for reliability coding. Interrater agreement (Kendall's W) was .91 ($p < .01$). Discrepancies were resolved by a third rater.

The integrative complexity coding system provides rules for inferring levels of differentiation (recognition of multiple dimensions or aspects of an issue) and integration (recognition of conceptual relations among differentiated dimensions). The following illustrations of different integrative complexity levels are paraphrased excerpts of participants' essays.

- Score of 1 (no differentiation, no integration):

The addition of a guest to our group shattered our group norms. We found that our performance, satisfaction and motivation was (sic) decreased when the new member brought his new attitudes, which conflicted with our norms, into our group. He didn't seem to care if we did well or if he fit in so we didn't care either. Everything fell apart today just because of one new member.

- Score of 3 (differentiation, no integration):

The old member returning had a strong effect on the dynamics and performance of the group. The group returned to the status quo, which was characterized by a lack of motivation and doing the least amount of work possible. However, to have all members together once again increased cohesiveness, and we all shared more ideas than usual on this essay.

- Score of 5 (differentiation, simple integration):

Since we had received our grades before the task started, the motivation for doing a quality job was almost non-existent. Most of our time was spent socializing. I think this is very productive however. Since we had completed our task we no longer need to spend time on this. If this were a continuing group we would need to remain cohesive in order to do well on our next assignment. Also we would need to reflect on what we had done over the semester to determine what would need to be changed if we were to continue.

- Score of 7 (differentiation, complex integration):

Two important things happened today. Our old member returned and we evaluated a proposal for using computer mediation and Stellar advertising. Based on our two weeks working via computer, we had decided that it made performance much more difficult. However, our member who just spent two weeks with a new group told us how inhibited she felt and how computer mediation would have made it easier for her to jump in and participate. . . . So we decided to recommend that Stellar evaluate both the type of tasks computers would be used for, and the dynamics of the groups that would use them, before making their decision.

Scores of 2, 4, and 6 represent transition points between adjacent levels. They are assigned when there is evidence of implicit differentiation (information seeking, qualification to an absolute rule) or implicit integration (hints of recognition of interactions and trade-offs).

Ideas and Influence. To assess the number and nature of ideas produced by individuals working independently and the origin of ideas used by the group, all of the essays in the sample were deconstructed into a set of distinct ideas, which were counted. The ideas presented in individual essays were also compared across group members, to determine whether they were *redundant* (i.e., produced by more than a single group member, working independently) or *unique* (i.e., produced by only one group member, working independently).[1] The ideas presented in individual essays were then compared against those presented in group essays to determine whose ideas were included in the group product.

RESULTS

To compare the integrative complexity scores assigned to essays written by newcomers and oldtimers, data were analyzed at the group level using

---

[1]The incidence of *emergent* ideas (i.e., ideas presented in the group essays that were not observed in any individual essay) were also assessed. The scarcity of emergent ideas precluded the use of statistical tests; hence, they were excluded from further analysis.

a MANOVA with two within-subjects factors: (a) role (oldtimer vs. newcomer) and (b) time (pre- vs. post-membership change).

Integrative Complexity

To insure that group members arbitrarily selected to change groups (i.e., to become newcomers) did not differ in integrative complexity from those selected to remain in their original groups (i.e., to become oldtimers) prior to the change manipulation, the scores of these individuals prior to the change were compared. Cell means are displayed in Table 11.1. As expected, there was no significant difference between the integrative complexity exhibited by individuals who would become newcomers ($M = 1.67$), and those who would become oldtimers ($M = 1.75$), prior to the change manipulation ($F < 1.0$, ns).

After the change however, the expected differences were observed. As predicted by Hypothesis 1, participants who became newcomers by changing groups experienced a significant increase in integrative complexity ($M_{change} = +.67$; $F (1, 21) = 15.34$, $p \le .001$). However, the integrative complexity of oldtimers did not change significantly ($M_{change} = +.10$; $F < 1.0$, ns) in response to the presence of a visitor in the group. As a result, participants who changed groups and became newcomers exhibited greater integrative complexity ($M = 2.34$) than those who remained in their original groups and became oldtimers ($M = 1.85$). This difference was statistically significant ($F (1, 21) = 7.32$, $p \le .01$), which supports Hypothesis 2. Moreover, the integrative complexity exhibited in the group essay, on which oldtimers and newcomers collaborated, was not affected by the change in membership. During the 2-week membership change, the integrative complexity of group essays ($M = 2.48$) was not significantly greater than that displayed in the 2 weeks prior to the change ($M = 2.25$; $F (1, 21) = 1.45$, $p \ge .10$).

Ideas and Influence

To assess whether group members arbitrarily selected to change groups (i.e., to become newcomers) differed in productivity from those selected to remain in their original groups (i.e., to become oldtimers) prior to the change manipulation, the number of ideas produced by these individuals

TABLE 11.1
Integrative Complexity Scores for Individual Essays of Newcomers
and Oldtimers Written Pre- and Postmembership Change

	Prechange	Postchange
Newcomer	1.67	2.34
Oldtimer	1.75	1.85

TABLE 11.2
Average Number of Ideas Produced by Newcomers and Oldtimers,
and Used in Group Essay, Pre- and Postmembership Change

	Newcomer		Oldtimer	
	Prechange	Postchange	Prechange	Postchange
Ideas Produced				
Unique	1.64	1.77	1.77	2.06
Redundant	.68	.69	1.01	.91
Total	2.32	2.46	2.78	2.97
Ideas Used				
Unique	.84	.84	.86	1.25
Redundant	.62	.55	.83	.75
Total	1.46	1.39	1.69	2.00

prior to the change were compared. Cell means are displayed in Table 11.2. Although subjects were randomly assigned to oldtimer and newcomer conditions, individuals in these two conditions differed in their idea productivity prior to the membership change. Those individuals who would become oldtimers inexplicably generated a greater number of total ideas ($M = 2.78$) than did individuals who would become newcomers ($M = 2.32$; $F(1, 21) = 5.62$, $p \leq .03$), prior to the change manipulation. However, regardless of their future status, participants' independently generated ideas were equally likely to be included in the before-change group product ($M = 1.46$ and $M = 1.69$, for future newcomers and future oldtimers respectively, $F(1, 21) = 1.68$, $p \geq .10$).

After the membership change, neither oldtimers nor newcomers became more or less productive in terms of the total numbers of ideas generated ($M_{change} = +.19$, $M_{change} = +.14$, respectively; both $Fs < 1.0$, ns). In addition, there were no significant changes in the number or proportion of unique and redundant ideas produced by newcomers and oldtimers (see Table 11.2). However, consistent with Hypotheses 3 and 4, newcomers had less influence on the group product. Hypothesis 3 predicted that newcomers' ideas would be less influential after they changed groups than prior to the membership change. After the change, the ideas of subjects who became newcomers were used less often in the group essay ($M = 1.39$) than they were in original groups, prior to the change ($M = 1.46$), but this difference was not statistically significant ($F < 1.0$, ns). In addition, the ideas of subjects who became newcomers were significantly less likely to appear in the group essay than the ideas of subjects who became oldtimers, which supports Hypothesis 4. After the change, group essays included fewer total ideas produced by newcomers ($M = 1.39$) than ideas produced by oldtimers ($M = 2.00$; $F(1, 21) = 5.69$, $p \leq .03$).

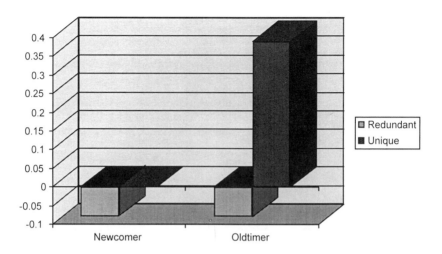

FIG. 11.1. Difference in average number of newcomers' and oldtimers' ideas appearing in prechange and postchange group essays.

Figure 11.1 depicts the nature of this result more clearly. Although new-comers' ideas are slightly less likely to appear in the group essays of their pre- and post-change groups ($M = 1.46$ and $M = 1.39$ for pre- and post-change groups, respectively; $M_{change} = -.07$), oldtimers' ideas are slightly more likely to appear in the group essay in the postchange group ($M = 2.00$) than in the prechange group ($M = 1.69$; $M_{change} = .31$). A comparison of changes in the use of unique and redundant ideas helps explain this pattern. After the membership change, the redundant ideas of both newcomers and oldtimers were used slightly less often ($M_{change} = -.08$ for both newcomers and oldtimers). However, unique ideas produced by oldtimers were significantly more likely to appear in the group essay after the change ($M = 1.25$) than they were prior to the change ($M = .86$). This increase is statistically significant ($M_{change} = .39$; $F(1, 21) = 5.64$, $p \leq .03$).

DISCUSSION

The results of this study are largely consistent with our predictions. When groups were re-composed after 10 weeks by exchanging a single member, subjects who became newcomers displayed greater integrative complexity in their essays about group functioning than they did prior to enacting that role. They also exhibited greater integrative complexity than subjects who did not change groups and therefore had oldtimer status. However, new-comers were also less influential in their new groups than in their old groups because oldtimers used a greater number of their own ideas after newcomers arrived than beforehand.

These findings provide empirical evidence for the argument that newcomers experience cognitive growth in response to their new environment (Louis, 1980). The fact that newcomers exhibited greater integrative complexity after changing groups is consistent with the notion that newcomers experience surprise and engage in sense-making on entering a new group. Cognitive contrast, in which newcomers notice differences between their new and old groups, should increase cognitive differentiation, which refers to recognition of alternative perspectives and stimulus dimensions. Sense-making, in which newcomers attempt to find meaning in the differences they observe, could correspond to cognitive integration, which refers to consideration of trade-offs among alternatives. Hence, it can be argued on the basis of these findings that surprise and sense-making in newcomers corresponds to increased integrative complexity.

However, prior discussions of membership change have assumed that insiders should also learn from the same events. For example, it has been argued that planning to recruit and interview newcomers engages oldtimers in organizational scanning and open-systems planning (Sutton & Louis, 1987) and provides opportunities for oldtimers to revisit their own values, practices, and shared identity (Levine & Moreland, 1991; Moreland & Levine, 1989). It is important to recognize that these descriptions refer to conditions in which insiders willingly engaged in recruiting and socializing new members. When groups are strategically recomposed by importing temporary visitors, without members' active participation, these motivations will be absent. This might occur in organizations when membership changes are imposed by a manager or executive without group-member involvement. It was also the case in the study reported here. Newcomers were chosen and moved using a logic that satisfied the interests of experimenters rather than those of the groups affected by the changes. As noted by Arrow & McGrath (1993), the impetus for membership change matters.

These findings have important implications for the widely documented assumptions and prescriptive advice of organizational practitioners who recommend rotating group members to transfer knowledge about group practices. Prior conceptions about the utility of using newcomers as conduits for knowledge transfer have assumed that individuals who span group boundaries are equally likely to import knowledge from and export knowledge to their groups of origin. Our results suggest that this is not necessarily the case. Newcomers, who differed from oldtimers only in their prior experience with outside groups, were more likely to notice and think integratively about alternative approaches to group process in the groups they visited than they were prior to changing groups. They also exhibited greater integrative complexity than oldtimers after the membership change. Yet there is no evidence that the insights generated by newcomers affected oldtimers' thinking. Newcomers' observations were documented in their individual essays, which served as the knowledge base for collaborative group work. However, a greater proportion of oldtimers' ideas and a smaller proportion of newcomers' ideas appeared in group essays written after the membership change.

In workgroups, where alternative perspectives are hard to come by (cf. Janis, 1972) and often necessary for effective performance, it is easy to see how the insights of an integratively complex newcomer could be a valuable asset. The problem, however, as revealed in this study, is that such members are also uniquely noninfluential. Groups in this study made little use of their new members' complex ideas. Consistent with the integrative complexity literature, this could be because the newcomers were perceived as indecisive or antagonistic; consistent with the research on minority influence, it could be that the newcomer's credibility was compromised by his or her failure to advocate a consistent position. It is also possible that newcomers were less assertive than oldtimers in conveying and advocating their ideas during collaborative work on the group essay (Moreland & Levine, 1989) and that oldtimers were simply less receptive to newcomers' ideas and opinions than they were to their own (Levine, 1989; Moscovici, 1985; Tetlock, Peterson, & Berry, 1993). The relative weight of these factors will be an important issue for future research.

Implications for Group Performance

Whatever the reason for it, group members' collective failure to utilize newcomers' integratively complex ideas is especially interesting, given the potential benefits of doing so. Although members' essays were scored for integrative complexity and graded independently by a set of researchers on the one hand and a set of graders on the other, there was a positive correlation between grades and integrative complexity (Gruenfeld & Hollingshead, 1993). In light of robust evidence that integrative complexity can improve decision analysis and judgment quality (Pruitt & Lewis, 1975; Streufert & Swezey, 1986; Tetlock, 1992), this is not surprising. At the time of the membership change manipulation, group members had been writing and receiving feedback on their essays for a period of 10 weeks. Hence, attentive and ambitious group members might have detected the relationship between complex ideas and high grades. Yet on average, groups failed to recognize the potential performance benefit presented by the newcomers' complex observations.

Integrative complexity has been linked to superior judgment and problem solving in a variety of domains (for a review see Suedfeld, 1992). In prior research, integratively complex explanations for group process were associated with superior group performance (Gruenfeld & Hollingshead, 1993). Hence, newcomers in this study were uniquely endowed with specialized wisdom that could, if applied, have enhanced the performance of the group. This finding shows the potential contribution of deviant members to group performance in a new light. In studies of minority influence, the value of deviates' contributions was conceived solely in terms of their impact on the quality of majority members' thoughts (Janis, 1972; Nemeth, 1986). The assumption that majorities converge around the truth implies that deviant proposals are more likely to be wrong, hence less likely to be useful, than those presented by majority members. However, in this study, newcomers' (i.e., minority members') explanations for group performance were potentially more valuable than those provided by oldtimers (i.e., majority members) due to their increased integrative complexity. Majority members in this study were less inclined to analyze their performance from multiple viewpoints and were less aware of the trade-offs associated with their activities than minority members were. Therefore, contrary to prior assumptions, the knowledge possessed by newcomers was actually more useful, potentially, than the knowledge possessed by oldtimers. By widening the lens through which social structures are viewed, these previously unobserved psychological phenomena were revealed.

Newcomers' complexity levels are also surprising given the well-established finding that minority members experience cognitive constraint in response to awareness of their social distinctiveness. Demographic minorities, for example, often experience heightened social awareness (Frabel, Blackstone, & Scherbaum, 1990; Saenz, 1994) and evaluation apprehension (Steele, 1997) in social contexts where their status is salient, which can interfere with their performance on tasks that require focused attention. Minority members have been previously found to be less apt to consider multiple perspectives (Nemeth, 1986), are less integrative in their thinking (Peterson & Nemeth, 1996), and therefore exhibit lower integrative complexity than majority members (Gruenfeld, 1995; Gruenfeld, et al., 1996; Tetlock, Bernzweig, & Gallant, 1985; Tetlock, Hannum, & Micheletti, 1984).

In light of the findings reported here, there is more to the status-complexity relationship than prior research has revealed. Theoretically, these findings suggest that when newcomer status is enacted through spanning the boundary between two groups—one in which a member is typical, and one in which he or she is not—newcomers can develop a unique awareness of the trade-offs associated with membership in each and exhibit increased integrative complexity as a result. In part, the conclusions based on psychological research might not map onto evidence from natural social systems because they reflect and are limited by the temporal constraints of the experimental paradigm (Kelly & McGrath, 1988). In experiments about reactions to majorities and minorities, status is defined solely by the single experimental group to which subjects are assigned; power and social standing are treated as fixed, unidimensional variables. In contrast, status in more natural and complex social systems (such as the one used in this research) tends to emerge in ways that involve simultaneous, multiple-group memberships and fluidity among them.

This perspective raises an additional possibility that could not be evaluated here. To the extent that temporary newcomers must manage their commitments to multiple groups, they are likely to maintain stronger bonds to their groups of origin than to the new groups they visit. If this is true, it might explain why newcomers are more thoughtful but less influential in new groups than old ones. Newcomers might see visits to new groups as an opportunity to gather information that will increase their status in groups that are more important to them. It would be interesting to know, for example, whether newcomers are more influential when they return to their old groups than they were before leaving, either because they are more likely to pitch their ideas or because their status and credibility are enhanced by virtue of their travel. Another possibility is that organization members use opportunities to become newcomers as a means of building their own social and intellectual capital rather than to improve the performance of groups to which they currently belong. If this were the case, it would suggest that strategic rotation of members between groups is a more useful method for training individuals than for improving group performance.

ACKNOWLEDGMENTS

We are grateful to Jennifer Berdahl, Jennifer Chatman, Marika Lindholm, John Levine, Richard Moreland, and Melissa Thomas-Hunt for their contributions to the conceptual development of this research; to Holly Arrow, Andrea Hollingshead, Joselito Lualhati, Joseph E. McGrath, and Kathleen O'Connor for help collecting and managing the data; and to an anonymous reviewer for helpful comments on an earlier version of this manuscript.

REFERENCES

Adams, J. S. (1976). The structure and dynamics of behavior in organizational boundary roles. In M. D. Dunnette (Ed.), *Handbook of industrial and organizational psychology* (pp. 1175–1199). Chicago: Rand McNally.

Altman, I., Vinsel, A., & Brown, B. B. (1981). Dialectical conception in social psychology: An application to social penetration and privacy regulation. In L. Berkowitz (Ed.), *Advances in experimental social psychology* (pp. 107–160). New York: Academic Press.

Ancona, D. G., & Caldwell, D. F. (1998). Rethinking team composition from the outside in. In M. A. Neale, E. A. Mannix, & D. H. Gruenfeld (Eds.), *Research on Managing Groups and Teams* (Vol. 1, pp. 21–37). Greenwich, CT: JAI Press.

Argote, L., Gruenfeld, D. H., & Naquin, C. (in press). Group learning in organizations. In M. Turner (Ed.), *Groups at work: Advances in theory and research*. Mahwah, NJ: Lawrence Erlbaum Associates.

Argyris, C., & Schon, D. A. (1978). *Organizational learning: A theory of action perspective*. Reading, MA: Addison-Wesley.

Arrow, H. (1997). Stability, bistability and instability in small group influence patterns. *Journal of Personality and Social Psychology, 72*(1), 75–85.

Arrow, H., & McGrath, J. E. (1993). Membership Matters: How member change and continuity affect small group structure, process and performance. *Small Group Research, 24*(3), 334–361.

Arrow, H., & McGrath, J. E. (1995). Membership dynamics in groups at work: A theoretical framework. *Research in Organizational Behavior, 17*, 373–311.

Baker-Brown, G., Ballard, E. J., Bluck, S., de Vries, B., Suedfeld, P., & Tetlock, P. E. (1992). The conceptual/integrative complexity scoring manual. In C. P. Smith (Ed.), *Motivation and personality: Handbook of thematic content analysis* (pp. 401–418). New York: Cambridge University Press.

Bell, E. L. (1990). The bicultural life experience of career-oriented black women. *Journal of Organizational Behavior, 11*, 459–477.

Berry, D. C., & Broadbent, D. E. (1987). The combination of explicit and implicit learning processes in task control. *Psychological Research, 49*, 7–15.

Frabel, D. E. S., Blackstone, T., & Scherbaum, C. (1990). Marginal and mindful: Deviants in social interactions. *Journal of Personality and Social Psychology, 59*, 140–149.

Friedman, R. A., & Podolny, J. (1992). Differentiation of boundary spanning roles: Labor negotiations and implications for role conflict. *Administrative Science Quarterly, 37*(1), 28–47.

Galbraith, C. S. (1990). Transferring core manufacturing technologies in high-technology firms. *California Management Review, 32*, 56–70.

Gigone, D., & Hastie, R. (1993). The common knowledge effect: Information sharing and group judgment. *Journal of Personality and Social Psychology, 65*, 959–974.

Gruenfeld, D. H. (1995). Status, ideology, and integrative complexity on the U.S. Supreme Court: Rethinking the politics of political decision making. *Journal of Personality and Social Psychology, 68*(1), 5–20.

Gruenfeld, D. H., & Hollingshead, A. B. (1993). Sociocognition in work groups: The evolution of group integrative complexity and its relation to task performance. *Small Group Research, 24*(3), 383–406.

Gruenfeld, D. H., Mannix, E. A., Williams, K. Y., & Neale, M. A. (1996). Group composition and decision making: How member familiarity and information distribution affect process and performance. *Organizational Behavior and Human Decision Processes, 67*(1), 1–15.

Jackson, P. B., Thoits, P. A., & Taylor, H. F. (1995). Composition of the workplace and psychological well-being: The effects of tokenism on America's Black elite. *Social Forces, 74*(2), 543–557.

Janis, I. (1972). *Victims of groupthink*. Boston: Houghton Mifflin.

Kahn, R., Wolfe, D., Quinn, D., Snoek, R., & Rosenthal, R. (1964). *Organizational stress: Studies in role conflict and ambiguity*. New York: Wiley.

Katz, D., & Kahn, R. L. (1978). The taking of organizational roles. In D. Katz & R. L. Kahn (Eds.), *The social psychology of organizations* (2nd ed., pp. 171–198). New York: Wiley.

Kelly, J. R., & McGrath, J. E. (1988). *On time and method*. Newbury Park, CA: Sage.

Kiesler, S., & Sproull, L. (1982). Managerial response to changing environments: Perspectives on problem sensing from social cognition. *Administrative Science Quarterly, 27*, 548–570.

Langer, E. J. (1989). Minding matters: The consequences of mindlessness/mindfulness. In L. Berkowitz (Ed.), *Advances in experimental social psychology* (Vol. 22, pp. 137–173). San Diego, CA: Academic Press.

Levine, J. M. (1989). Reactions to opinion deviance in small groups. In P. B. Paulus, (Ed.), *Psychology of group influence* (2nd ed., pp. 187–231). Hillsdale, NJ: Lawrence Erlbaum Associates.

Levine, J. M., & Moreland, R. L. (1991). Culture and socialization in work groups. In L. B. Resnick, J. M. Levine, & S. D. Teasly (Eds.), *Perspectives on socially shared cognition* (pp. 257–279). Washington, DC: American Psychological Association.

Levine, J. M., Resnick, L. B., & Higgins, E. T. (1993). Social foundations of cognition. *Annual Review of Psychology, 44*, 585–612.

Levine, J. M., & Russo, E. M. (1987). Majority and minority influence. In C. Hendrick (Ed.), *Review of personality and social psychology* (pp. 13–54). Beverly Hills, CA: Sage.

Louis, M. R. (1980). Surprise and sense making: What newcomers experience in entering unfamiliar organizational settings. *Administrative Science Quarterly, 25*, 226–251.

Louis, M. R. (1981, April). *The emperor has no clothes: The effect of newcomers on work group culture.* Paper presented at the Western Academy of Management Meetings, Monterey, CA.

Louis, M. R., & Sutton, R. I. (1991). Switching cognitive gears from habits of mind to active thinking. *Human Relations, 44*(1), 55–76.

Mohrman, S. A., Cohen, S. G., & Mohrman, A. M., Jr. (1995). *Designing team-based organizations: New forms of knowledge work.* San Francisco: Jossey Bass.

Moreland, R. L. (1985). Social categorization and the assimilation of "new" group members. *Journal of Personality and Social Psychology, 48*(5), 1173–1190.

Moreland, R. L., & Levine, J. M. (1989). Newcomers and oldtimers in small groups. In P. Paulus (Ed.), *Psychology or group influence* (2nd ed., pp. 143–186). Hillsdale, NJ: Lawrence Erlbaum Associates.

Moscovici, S. (1985). Social influence and conformity In G. Lindzey & E. Aronson (Eds.), *The Handbook of Social Psychology* (vol. 2, 3rd Ed., pp. 347–412). New York: Random House.

Nahavandi, A., & Aranda, E. (1994). Restructuring teams for the re-engineered organization. *Academy of Management Executive, 8*(4), 58–68.

Nemeth, C. J. (1986). Differential contributions of majority and minority influence. *Psychological Review, 93*, 23–32.

Nonaka, I., & Takeuchi, H. (1995). *The knowledge-creating company.* New York: Oxford University Press.

Peterson, R. S., & Nemeth, C. J. (1996). Focus versus flexibility: Majority and minority influence can both improve performance. *Personality and Social Psychology Bulletin, 22*(1), 14–23.

Pruitt, D., & Lewis, S. (1975). Development of integrative solutions in bilateral negotiations. *Journal of Personality and Social Psychology, 31*(4), 621–633.

Rousseau, D. M. (1993). Teamwork inside and out. *Business Week ADVANCE Executive Brief, 3*, 1–22.

Saenz, D. S. (1994). Token status and problem-solving deficits: Detrimental effects of distinctiveness and performance monitoring. *Social Cognition, 12*(1), 61–74.

Stasser, G., & Titus, W. (1985). Pooling of unshared information in group decision making: Biased information sampling during discussion. *Journal of Personality and Social Psychology, 48*, 1467–1478.

Steele, C. M. (1997). A threat in the air: How stereotypes shape intellectual identity and performance. *American Psychologist, 52*, 613–629.

Streufert, S., & Swezey, R. W. (1986). *Complexity, managers and organizations.* New York: Academic Press.

Suedfeld, P. (1985). APA presidential addresses: The relation of integrative complexity to historical professional, and personal factors. *Journal of Personality and Social Psychology, 49*, 1643–1651.

Suedfeld, P. (1992). Cognitive managers and their critics. *Political Psychology, 13*(3), 435–454.

Suedfeld, P., Tetlock, P. E., & Streufert, S. (1992). Conceptual/integrative complexity. In C. P. Smith (Ed.), *Motivation and personality: Handbook of thematic content analysis* (pp. 393–400). New York: Cambridge University Press.

Sutton, R. I., & Louis, M. R. (1987). How selecting and socializing newcomers influences insiders. *Human Resource Management, 226*(3), 347–361.

Szulanski, G. (1994). Unpacking stickiness: An empirical investigation of the barriers to transfer best practice inside the firm. Unpublished manuscript.

Tetlock, P. E. (1986). A value pluralism model of ideological reasoning. *Journal of Personality and Social Psychology, 50*(4), 819–827.

Tetlock, P. E. (1992). The impact of accountability on judgment and choice: Toward a social contingency model. In M. Zanna (Ed.), *Advances in experimental social psychology* (Vol. 25, pp. 331–376). New York: Academic Press.

Tetlock, P. E., Bernzweig, J., & Gallant, J. L. (1985). Supreme Court decision making: Cognitive style as a predictor of ideological consistency of voting. *Journal of Personality and Social Psychology, 48*, 1127–1239.

Tetlock, P. E., Hannum, K. A., & Micheletti, P. M. (1984). Stability and change in the complexity of senatorial debate: Testing the cognitive versus rhetorical style hypotheses. *Journal of Personality and Social Psychology, 46*(5), 979–990.

Tetlock, P. E., Peterson, R. S., & Berry, J. M. (1993). Flattering and unflattering personality portraits of integratively simple and complex managers. *Journal of Personality and Social Psychology, 64*(3), 500–511.

Tetlock, P. E., Peterson, R. S., & Lerner, J. S. (1996). Revising the value pluralism model: Incorporating social content and context postulates. In C. Seligman, J. M. Olson, & M. P. Zanna (Eds.), *The psychology of values: The Ontario Symposium* (Vol. 8, pp. 25–51). Mahwah, NJ: Lawrence Erlbaum Associates.

Trice, H. M., & Beyer, J. M. (1993). *The cultures of work organizations.* Upper Saddle River, NJ: Prentice-Hall.

Van Maanen, J. (1977). Experiencing organization: Notes on the meaning of career and socialization. In J. Van Maanen (Ed.), *Organizational careers: Some new perspectives* (pp. 15–45). New York: Wiley.

Van Sell, M., Brief, A. P., & Schuler, R. S. (1981). Role conflict and role ambiguity: Integration of the literature and directions for future research. *Human Relations, 34*, 43–71.

Williams, K. Y., Mannix, E. A., Neale, M. A., & Gruenfeld, D. H. (1998, August). *Sharing unique perspectives: The process of knowledge exchange in social and informational coalitions.* Paper presented at the Academy of Management Annual Meeting, Boston, MA.

Wittenbaum, G. M., & Stasser, G. (1996). Management of information in small groups. In J. L. Nye & A. M. Brower (Eds.), *What's social about social cognition? Research on socially shared cognition in small groups* (pp. 3–28). Thousand Oaks, CA: Sage.

Wood, W. Lundgren, S., Ouellette, J. A., Busceme, S., & Blackstone, T. (1994). Minority influence: A meta-analytic review of social influence processes. *Psychological Bulletin, 115*, 323–245.

Wood, W., Pool, G. J., Leck, K., & Purvis, D. (1996). Self-definition, defensive processing, and influence: The normative impact of majority and minority groups. *Journal of Personality and Social Psychology, 71*(6), 1181–1193.

Ziller, R. C. (1965). Toward a theory of open and closed groups. *Psychological Bulletin, 64*, 164–182.

12

Knowledge Transmission in Work Groups: Helping Newcomers to Succeed

John M. Levine
Richard L. Moreland
University of Pittsburgh

The traditional view of human cognition is highly individualistic, focusing on how solitary people acquire, store, and retrieve information and engage in various forms of thinking, including reasoning and problem solving. Recently, however, a number of studies have examined the impact of social factors on the content of cognition and the processes underlying cognitive activity (see Levine, Resnick, & Higgins, 1993; Nye & Brower, 1996; Resnick, Levine, & Teasley, 1991). Much of this work has focused on how social factors affect individual cognition via such processes as social loafing (Harkins & Petty, 1982), role playing (Anderson & Pichert, 1978), the activation of social identities (Charters & Newcomb, 1952), preparation for anticipated interaction (Levine, Bogart, & Zdaniuk, 1996), apprenticeship (Rogoff, 1990), sociocognitive conflict (Doise & Mugny, 1984), and majority–minority influence (Nemeth, 1995).

Other work has gone further, examining the processes by which two or more people develop shared cognitions and the consequences of these shared cognitions for the group and its members. Sherif's (1935) research on norm formation in groups provides an early example of this approach (see also Jacobs & Campbell, 1961; MacNeil & Sherif, 1976; Weick & Gilfillan, 1971). And many examples of more recent work can be cited, including Wegner's (1987, 1995) analysis of transactive memory; Hardin and Higgins's (1996) discussion of shared reality; Bar-Tal's (1990) analysis of group beliefs; Larson and Christensen's (1993) discussion of group problem solving; and Hinsz, Tindale, and Vollrath's (1997) analysis of groups as information processors.

One setting in which shared cognitions are especially important is the workplace. As people labor together on common tasks, they often develop similar understandings of the nature of their tasks and the skills required to master them. These understandings, sometimes called shared mental models (Cannon-Bowers, Salas, & Converse, 1993), have received substantial attention from researchers interested in group performance in organizational settings (see Klimoski & Mohammed, 1994). Although all workgroups probably evolve shared mental models of some kind, such models are more likely to be created (and to affect group processes and outcomes) under some conditions than others. Thus, we would expect shared mental models to form more quickly, to contain more information, and to exhibit greater coherence and integration when (a) the same people work together over a long period of time; (b) the group task is complex and requires a high degree of response coordination; and (c) important outcomes, such as money or status, are contingent on group performance. Given that workgroups in organizational settings often have these features (Ilgen, Major, Hollenbeck, & Sego, 1993), shared mental models are probably common in such groups.

THE CONTENT OF SHARED MENTAL MODELS

As Klimoski and Mohammed (1994) indicated, many terms have been used to describe shared cognition in workgroups, including group belief structure, collective interpretation, shared meaning, group situation awareness, core teamwork schemas, collective mind, and shared mental models (the term we use in this chapter). This list is notable not only for its length but also for its lack of precision. In describing the literature on shared mental models, which they call team mental models, Klimoski and Mohammed (1994) noted that few researchers clearly define or even explicitly describe what is meant by their terminology (p. 407). In an effort to bring some clarity to this literature, Klimoski and Mohammed made several useful points. For example, in discussing the content of shared mental models, they differentiated knowledge about task demands from knowledge about behavioral responses to these demands. In discussing the functions these models serve, they identified negative (e.g., groupthink) as well as positive (e.g., sensemaking) effects. And in discussing what it means to share a mental model, they distinguished between identical and overlapping cognitive representations and between observers' and participants' perceptions of sharing.

To illustrate how different theorists think about shared mental models, three perspectives on the content of those models are described. These are Levine and Moreland's (1991) analysis of workgroup culture; Cannon-Bowers, Tannenbaum, Salas, and Volpe's (1995) analysis of team competencies; and Chao, O'Leary-Kelly, Wolf, Klein, and Gardner's (1994) analysis of the content of organizational socialization.

According to Levine and Moreland (1991), a workgroup's culture embodies the task and social knowledge that group members must share in order to function effectively together. This culture plays a critical role in worker socialization because newcomers cannot participate fully in the life of the group until they acquire the cultural knowledge that oldtimers already possess. Borrowing from previous theories of culture (e.g., Fine, 1979; Rentsch, 1990; Schein, 1990; Trice & Beyer, 1984; Van Maanen & Barley, 1985), Levine and Moreland suggested that culture has two primary components, one cognitive and one behavioral.

The cognitive component of culture is shared knowledge, which helps group members understand and adapt to their environment and provides a common interpretive framework for their experiences (cf. Gundry & Rousseau, 1994; Stohl, 1986). Cultural knowledge can focus on the group as a whole, its members, or the work they perform. Knowledge about the group as a whole might involve reasons why the group is unique, historical forces that shaped the group, and evaluations of the group's performance. Knowledge about members might involve characteristics of people who belong to the group, the kinds of relationships they have with one another, and appropriate ways of interpreting their behavior. Finally, knowledge about the work the group performs might involve task demands, performance criteria, and working conditions.

The behavioral component of workgroup culture is customs, which embody, communicate, and reinforce the knowledge that workers share. Customs include routines (Gersick & Hackman, 1990), accounts (Orr, 1990), jargon (Truzzi & Easto, 1972), rituals (Vaught & Smith, 1980), and symbols (Riemer, 1977). Routines are everyday procedures that workgroups follow, including habits and traditions. Accounts are verbal descriptions or explanations of events that group members find interesting, including stories workers tell and superstitions they share. Jargon involves unusual words, phrases, or gestures that are meaningful to group members but meaningless to outsiders. Rituals are ceremonies that groups carry out to mark major events, including victory celebrations, anniversaries, and entry rites for new members. Finally, symbols are material objects that are unique to the group and carry special meaning for members, such as special tools, insignia, and uniforms.

Like Levine and Moreland (1991), Cannon-Bowers et al. (1995) analyzed shared mental models in small workgroups, or teams. To clarify the competencies necessary for successful team performance, Cannon-Bowers and her colleagues distinguished among knowledge, skills, and attitudes. They argued that these competencies vary as function of whether they are (a) specific to a particular team versus generic across teams and (b) specific to a particular task versus generic across tasks. Crossing these two dimensions yields a four-fold model of competencies: team-specific and task-specific (or context-driven); team-specific and task-generic (or team-contingent); team-generic and task-specific (or task-contingent); and team-generic and task-generic (or transportable).

Cannon-Bowers and her colleagues went on to suggest that different knowledge, skills, and attitudes may be necessary for team success in the four cells of the model. They argued, for example, that in the team-contingent cell, group members must share knowledge about teammate characteristics (e.g., general abilities and preferences); the team's mission, objectives, norms, and resources; and the team's relationship to the larger organization. In contrast, in the task-contingent cell, group members must have accurate models of the task and must share knowledge about task-specific role responsibilities; requirements for task sequencing; team role-interaction patterns; procedures for task accomplishment; and boundary-spanning roles. This analysis, then, suggests that the utility of different types of shared mental models depends on both how long group members work together and what kinds of tasks they face.

Rather than focusing on small work groups, Chao et al. (1994) turned their attention to organizations. Defining organizational socialization as "learning" on the part of the individual who is adjusting to a new or changed role within the organization (p. 731), Chao and her colleagues proposed a multidimensional framework for analyzing the content of socialization. They asked engineers and managers to complete a questionnaire assessing their organizational knowledge (e.g., "I know the organization's long-held traditions," "I know who the most influential people are in my organization"). Through factor analyses of respondents' answers, Chao et al. identified six dimensions of socialization—performance proficiency, politics, language, people, organizational goals and values, and history. Performance proficiency involves performing the tasks associated with a particular job. Politics refers to understanding formal and informal work relationships and power structures in the organization. Language involves knowing the technical terms, as well as the slang and jargon, used in the organization. People refers to establishing effective and satisfying work relationships with other employees. Organizational goals and values involves accepting the moral framework that ostensibly underlies organizational activity. Finally, history involves knowing the organization's traditions, customs, myths, and rituals. Each of these dimensions reflects shared knowledge of one sort or another.

SOCIALIZATION IN ORGANIZATIONS AND WORK GROUPS

These analyses of shared mental models suggest two related reasons why socialization may be challenging to newcomers. First, group members need substantial knowledge in multiple domains in order to function effectively.

These domains include the equipment the team uses (e.g., operating procedures, likely failures), the team's task (e.g., procedures, environmental constraints), the characteristics of team members (e.g., knowledge, skills), and the team interaction process (e.g., roles and responsibilities, communication channels; Cannon-Bowers et al., 1993). Second, much (perhaps most) of this knowledge is group-specific, which means that newcomers do not possess it when they enter the group and hence must acquire it after they join.

It would not be surprising, then, if newcomers found group entry quite unsettling. In fact, the evidence indicates that people who have recently joined a group often experience a good deal of anxiety and confusion (cf. Katz, 1985; Louis, 1980; Nelson, 1987; Wanous, 1992). Although these negative reactions may be due to several factors, including the group's failure to meet new members' expectations (Wanous, 1992) and paranoid cognitions on the part of new members (Kramer, 1994; Moreland, 1986), the fact that new members lack knowledge that others share is presumably a major contributor.

Although learning shared mental models can be a difficult task, it is not an impossible one. This is because ongoing groups develop mechanisms for ensuring that newcomers acquire the knowledge they need to become productive members. This is particularly true of large organizations, such as corporations and the military, that must continually absorb many new members and provide them with the knowledge they need to function in complex task and social environments (Ziller, 1965). Much is known about socialization in organizations (Ashford & Taylor, 1990; Fisher, 1986; Saks & Ashforth, 1997; Van Maanen & Schein, 1979; Wanous & Colella, 1989), but little attention has been paid to the contexts in which organizational socialization occurs. In particular, theorists and researchers have neglected the role that small groups play in the socialization process. This state of affairs may be changing, however, in light of recent arguments for the importance, and even the primacy, of socialization at the work group level (e.g., Anderson & Thomas, 1996; Feldman, 1989; Jablin, 1987; Major, Kozlowski, Chao, & Gardner, 1995).

We agree that the socialization process occurs mainly in work groups, which control what organizations and employees learn about one another and how they acquire this information (Moreland & Levine, in press). Moreover, we believe that work group socialization typically has more impact on employees than does organizational socialization. In light of these beliefs, our analysis of how newcomers acquire shared mental models focuses on work groups rather than the organizations in which they are embedded. Work group socialization begins with the role transition of entry, when a person ceases being a prospective member of the group and becomes a newcomer, and ends with the role transition of acceptance, when the person becomes a full member. During socialization, the group tries to change the individual so that he or she contributes more to the achievement of group goals and the individual tries to change the group so that it better satisfies his or her personal needs. To the extent these activities are successful, the individual experiences assimilation and the group experiences accommodation (see Levine & Moreland, 1994; Moreland & Levine, 1982).

Work group socialization can thus be viewed as a struggle between newcomers and oldtimers regarding the relative amount of assimilation and accommodation that will occur. Our analysis in this chapter focuses on newcomer assimilation (for discussions of oldtimer accommodation, see Feldman, 1994; Levine & Moreland, 1985; Sutton & Louis, 1987). We assume that the likelihood of newcomers acquiring shared mental models from oldtimers is determined by four general factors—newcomers' qualities, newcomers' tactics, oldtimers' qualities, and oldtimers' tactics (Levine & Moreland, 1991; Moreland & Levine, 1989).

Newcomers' Qualities

Newcomers do not enter work groups as blank slates. Instead, they possess a variety of personal qualities that can affect their motivation and ability to learn shared mental models. One such quality is familiarity with the group prior to entering it (cf. Adkins, 1995; Bauer & Green, 1994; Decker & Cornelius, 1979; Premack & Wanous, 1985; Suszko & Breaugh, 1986). Familiarity can derive from a variety of sources, including stereotypes about work groups of the type one is joining, prior memberships in similar groups, previous interaction with the group (as prospective member, client, or opponent), and contact with current and previous group members. To the extent prospective members have accurate information about a group prior to entry, their socialization is likely to proceed more smoothly.

Another newcomer quality that can facilitate socialization is adaptability, which refers to a set of personality characteristics that can enhance adjustment to new environments (cf. Black & Ashford, 1995; Church, 1982; Jones, 1983, 1986; Morrison & Brantner, 1992; Reichers, 1987; Saks, 1995). These characteristics seem to affect socialization in three ways. Some characteristics, such as desire for feedback, internal locus of control, and self-efficacy, may facilitate socialization because they prompt newcomers to gather information about the group. Other characteristics, such as cognitive complexity, may help newcomers make sense of whatever information they obtain. And still other characteristics—such as self-esteem, tolerance of ambiguity, and low anxiety—may help newcomers manage stress during the socialization process.

Finally, commitment to the group is clearly a newcomer quality relevant to socialization. In general, such commitment should increase newcomers' motivation to gain acceptance from oldtimers by allowing more assimilation and demanding less accommodation. Although a great deal of work has been done on organizational commitment (see reviews by Mathieu & Zajac,

1990; Morrow, 1993; and Randall, 1990), the relevance of this research to socialization in work groups is open to question. For one thing, organizational commitment is quite complex (Moreland & Levine, in press). It has multiple components, or dimensions, each of which has separate consequences; individuals are not simply committed to the organization as a whole but also to various social entities within and around the organization (e.g., work groups, supervisors, unions); and commitment changes in important ways over time. For another thing, organizational and work group commitment are not always correlated, and people frequently feel more committed to their work group than to the larger organization (e.g., Becker, 1992; Zaccaro & Dobbins, 1989). Thus, in trying to predict socialization in a work group, it is wiser to focus on newcomers' commitment to that group than on their commitment to the organization in which it is embedded.

In trying to explain commitment, theorists have given more attention to situational than to personality factors, but both are probably important. Regarding situational factors, there is widespread agreement that the rewards and costs associated with group membership are critical determinants of commitment. According to Moreland and Levine (1982; Levine & Moreland, 1994), for example, newcomers feel committed to a group to the extent that (a) their present relationship with the group is perceived to be more rewarding than other current alternative relationships and (b) their future relationship with the group is expected to be more rewarding than other future alternative relationships (see also Rusbult & Farrell, 1983). Regarding personality factors, a variety of individual differences may predispose people to become highly committed to groups. These include dispositional group loyalty (James & Cropanzano, 1994), commitment propensity (Lee, Ashford, Walsh, & Mowday, 1992), and biodata indices, such as a general preference for group attachments (Mael & Ashforth, 1995). Dependency may be important as well. According to Bornstein (1992), people who are highly dependent want to obtain and maintain nurturant, supportive relationships, which causes them to engage in behaviors such as affiliation. People high in dependency may thus develop stronger group commitment than people low in dependency.

Of course, newcomer socialization cannot succeed without the active cooperation of oldtimers, and this cooperation depends on their commitment to the newcomer. Thus, any newcomer qualities that affect oldtimers' commitment will affect their socialization behavior—specifically, how much assimilation oldtimers demand and how much accommodation they allow. To the extent a newcomer seems to possess task and social skills that can facilitate the attainment of group goals, that person will elicit high commitment from oldtimers. This commitment, in turn, will cause oldtimers to demand relatively little assimilation from the newcomer and to exhibit relatively high accommodation toward him or her. Other newcomer characteristics, such as sex, race, and personality traits, may also affect oldtimers' commitment to a newcomer and hence their treatment of that person (cf. Fairhurst & Snavely, 1983; Putallaz & Wasserman, 1989).

Newcomers' Tactics

It is often assumed that newcomers exert little or no intentional control over the socialization process, but this is not true (Ashford & Black, 1996; Comer, 1991; Feldman & Brett, 1983; Miller & Jablin, 1991). In fact, newcomers can be quite active in shaping what happens during socialization, employing a variety of tactics to influence assimilation and accommodation. We highlight three of these tactics here—information acquisition, participation in mentoring, and collaboration with other newcomers.

Information acquisition can be either passive or active (Ashford & Cummings, 1983; Comer, 1991; Morrison, 1993; Ostroff & Kozlowski, 1992). In the former case, newcomers simply observe people and events in the work group. Through this surveillance, newcomers can gain valuable information about many aspects of group life, including role and status systems, leader–follower relations, accepted work practices and social interaction patterns, and relations with other groups. Surveillance also allows newcomers to engage in social comparison with others, a process that can provide valuable information about their abilities and outcomes (Festinger, 1954; Levine & Moreland, 1987). Because surveillance involves silent observation, it allows newcomers to acquire information about the group without making explicit just how ignorant they are. More active forms of information acquisition are also possible. Feedback seeking, for example, involves asking direct questions about the group and one's place in it. Miller and Jablin (1991) argued that these questions are generally of three types: referent (What does it take to succeed in the group?), appraisal (Am I succeeding?), and relational (Am I accepted?). Although feedback seeking is often an efficient means of obtaining group-relevant knowledge, it has some drawbacks (Ashford & Cummings, 1983; Morrison & Bies, 1991). For example, as previously suggested, merely asking certain questions can make one seem ignorant and insecure, and receiving certain answers (e.g., You are doing terribly and no one likes you) can be disheartening. Sometimes these costs can be reduced by asking group members indirect questions or by consulting outsiders who are familiar with the group (Miller & Jablin, 1991).

Another tactic that newcomers can use during socialization is participation in mentoring relationships with older group members. Evidence from organizational settings indicates that mentors can help their proteges in several ways, for example by providing training on group tasks, revealing hidden information about the group, interpreting ambiguous work experiences, acting as advocates, and offering emotional support (Kram, 1988;

Whitely & Coetsier, 1993). To the extent new workers are aware of these potential benefits, it would be sensible for them to identify potential mentors in the group and establish relationships with them. Although suggestions have been offered for how organizations should set up mentoring programs (e.g., Lawrie, 1987; Zey, 1985), little is known about how new members of organizations (or work groups) initiate mentoring relationships with more senior members (Kram, 1983). A potentially useful perspective on the development of mentoring relationships is leader–member exchange theory (Dienesch & Liden, 1986; Scandura & Schriesheim, 1994). Studies derived from this theory have shown that leaders are more likely to develop ingroup relationships (which resemble mentoring) with followers who seem competent, likeable, and similar (Deluga & Perry, 1994; Liden, Wayne, & Stilwell, 1993). Extrapolating from these findings, a critical determinant of a newcomer's ability to establish a mentoring relationship may be his or her ability to make a favorable impression on potential mentors.

Finally, newcomers can collaborate with one another during the socialization process. Through such collaboration, they often develop a peer group that provides them with various forms of assistance, including information, encouragement, and protection. This collaboration can occur spontaneously because newcomers view one another as similar and hence want to affiliate (Becker, Geer, Hughes, & Strauss, 1961; Van Maanen, 1975). Alternatively, it can be encouraged by the group on the assumption that treating newcomers as a subgroup gives them a special identity that promotes assimilation (Rohlen, 1973) and increases the likelihood that they will all learn the same things (Van Maanen & Schein, 1979). To the extent that newcomers collaborate during socialization, they can function as mentors for one another, particularly if oldtimers are unwilling or unable to assume this role (Kram & Isabella, 1985; Ostroff & Kozlowski, 1993). Although newcomer collaboration is often tolerated or encouraged by the group because of the assumption that it facilitates assimilation, it can just as easily inhibit assimilation and promote accommodation. This happens when newcomers band together to express dissatisfaction with the group and demand that it do better at meeting their needs (Becker, 1964; Dunham & Barrett, 1996; Van Maanen, 1984). Of course, because socialization can occur through group accommodation as well as newcomer assimilation, collaboration that elicits compliance from the group can facilitate socialization as much as collaboration that involves capitulation to the group.

Oldtimers' Qualities

Just as newcomers possess personal qualities that affect their motivation and ability to learn shared mental models, so oldtimers possess qualities that affect their motivation and ability to transmit these models. Oldtimers' motivation can be affected by several factors, including the group's current success at achieving its goals and the newcomers' perceived likelihood of contributing to future goal attainment. Thus, if a group does not have enough members to accomplish its goals or its members lack necessary skills, oldtimers should feel more committed to newcomers and be more motivated to transmit shared mental models to them (Cini, Moreland, & Levine, 1993). And, as suggested earlier, this commitment and motivation should be particularly strong if the newcomers possess skills that the group needs. This is not to say, of course, that oldtimers' commitment to newcomers always motivates them to transmit shared mental models. In some cases, oldtimers may have other motives that lead them to withhold information (cf. Dandridge, Mitroff, & Joyce, 1980; Martin, 1982). For example, oldtimers might desire to maintain their status and power by possessing unique information, fear that newcomers will leak privileged information to outsiders, or want newcomers to have the satisfaction of acquiring information on their own. In any case, if oldtimers do not have the motivation to transmit shared mental models to newcomers, they will not do so even if they have the ability.

Oldtimers' ability to transmit shared mental models can also be affected by several factors, including their knowledge of these models and their familiarity with newcomers. The greater oldtimers' knowledge of shared mental models, the greater their ability to transmit these models. Knowledge of shared mental models may be limited because the models are tacit, in the sense that oldtimers are not fully aware of what they know (cf. Gregory, 1983; Van Maanen, 1980; Wilkins & Ouchi, 1983). The contents of shared mental models may have been originally acquired via implicit learning so they were never consciously accessible, or they may have been initially accessible but later forgotten or repressed. Oldtimers may also lack knowledge of shared mental models because these models are dynamic, in the sense that they change in subtle (and not-so-subtle) ways as a function of fluctuating environmental factors, such as turnover in membership and variation in the group task (cf. Fine, 1979; Gregory, 1983; Van Maanen, 1977).

The greater oldtimers' familiarity with newcomers, the greater their ability to transmit shared mental models. Familiarity is important because it affects oldtimers' knowledge of what newcomers already know and how they are likely to respond to new information. Low familiarity occurs when oldtimers have no knowledge about either the newcomers themselves or newcomers in general. The latter kind of ignorance happens when groups are closed and do not have a history of recruiting new members (Ziller, 1965). Moderate familiarity occurs when oldtimers have some information about the newcomers from formal applications, recommendations of third parties, and so on. And high familiarity occurs when oldtimers have substantial knowledge about the newcomers from personal contacts prior to their entry into the group.

Oldtimers' Tactics

Oldtimers can use several tactics to transmit shared mental models to newcomers. To the extent these tactics are successful, newcomers will learn the models quickly and accurately (cf. Saks, 1996). One such tactic is initiation ceremonies, which are used to mark the newcomer's transition from prospective member to new member. In some cases, initiation ceremonies involve positive experiences, such as parties, gifts, and offers of advice (Lewicki, 1981; Schein, 1968), which elicit gratitude toward the group and attraction toward its members. In other cases, initiation ceremonies involve negative experiences, such as harassment and degrading rituals (Haas, 1972; Vaught & Smith, 1980). The latter initiations elicit commitment to the group through cognitive dissonance as well as other mechanisms (Aronson & Mills, 1959; but see Feldman, 1977; Hautaluoma, Enge, Mitchell, & Rittwager, 1991; Lodewijkx & Syroit, 1997). Both kinds of initiation ceremonies are assumed to increase newcomers' motivation to learn about the group and their attentiveness to information provided by oldtimers.

After they are initiated, newcomers are often subjected to other socialization tactics by oldtimers. Two such tactics are encapsulation within the group and feedback. In the case of encapsulation, efforts are made to separate newcomers (both physically and psychologically) from old groups or relationships and to integrate them into the new group (Kanter, 1968; Reichers, 1987). Integration involves maximizing the frequency and positivity of newcomers' interactions with oldtimers on the assumption that these experiences will increase newcomers' motivation and ability to learn to shared mental models. Encapsulation can be carried out both on and off the job. During working hours, oldtimers often try to decrease the amount of time newcomers spend alone or with outsiders (e.g., by forbidding private telephone calls) and to increase the amount of time they spend with reliable group members. After working hours, oldtimers often try to spend leisure time with newcomers, using these informal social interactions to monitor how well newcomers understand the shared mental models that the group is trying to impart.

When oldtimers perceive that newcomers are having difficulty learning shared mental models, they may provide feedback designed to ameliorate this problem. In some cases, this feedback is indirect, as when oldtimers offer advice in an offhand manner or express nonverbal approval or disapproval of newcomers' comments. Indirect feedback may also involve informally testing newcomers, such as tempting them to violate group norms or observing their reactions to inside jokes. In other cases, feedback is direct, as when oldtimers give newcomers explicit advice or information and formally evaluate their knowledge in simulated or real work situations. Whether indirect or direct, feedback is most effective when it is consistent within and across newcomers (Adler & Shuval, 1978; Van Maanen & Schein, 1979; Zurcher, 1967). The likelihood of consistent feedback is increased if socialization is formalized, in the sense that the group has clear goals and procedures for training newcomers, and if the oldtimers responsible for carrying out socialization (e.g., mentors or trainers) feel accountable for the subsequent performance of their charges.

IMPROVING GROUP SOCIALIZATION THROUGH SELECTION AND TRAINING

What if organizations tried harder to manage the socialization process in work groups so that newcomers could learn shared mental models more quickly and efficiently? Two major organizational strategies for accomplishing this goal are *selection*, which involves recruiting particular types of new members for work groups, and *training*, which involves helping new members obtain the information and skills they need to perform effectively. In the case of selection, the goal is to obtain new members who require relatively little socialization and who are likely to benefit from whatever socialization they receive. In the case of training, the goal is to provide new members with experiences that will facilitate their adjustment to the groups they are joining. Although a great deal of attention has been devoted to selection and training at the organizational level, little work has focused on how organizations use these two mechanisms to facilitate newcomers' socialization into work groups.

Selection and Socialization

Regarding selection, organizations can facilitate work group recruiting by helping these groups identify and evaluate prospective members and then persuade the most attractive ones to join (Moreland & Levine, 1982). As mentioned earlier, several newcomer qualities are likely to make socialization faster and easier. These include familiarity with the group prior to entering it; personality traits associated with adaptability (internal locus of control, self-efficacy, cognitive complexity, tolerance for ambiguity, self-esteem, low anxiety); commitment to the group; and task and social skills that will help the group attain its goals. To the extent organizations can assist work groups in locating prospective group members who possess these qualities, the time and energy required for socialization should be reduced (cf. Klimoski & Jones, 1995; Morgan & Lassiter, 1992; Prieto, 1993).

Familiarity with a new work group can be gained from prior experience in other groups, and this can be either general or specific. General familiarity is obtained through experience as a newcomer in any kind of group. That general familiarity can facilitate socialization is suggested by evidence that newcomers who have had more experience joining small groups require less socialization, perhaps because they have learned how to recognize and respond to changing group norms (Brett, 1980; Fellin & Litwak, 1963; Van Maanen, 1984). In contrast, specific familiarity is obtained through previous membership in groups that are similar to the group the person is joining, and evidence indicates that this kind of experience is particularly likely to facilitate socialization (Bell & Price, 1975; Hopper, 1977; Nicholson, 1984).

One way organizations can increase the likelihood that newcomers to a work group have had previous experience in similar groups is to selectively recruit such people. These people might be current members of the organization or outsiders. In the former case, the organization might create new work teams using members of old teams that previously performed the same or similar tasks. In the latter case, the organization might try to lure away members of other organizations who are currently working on teams similar to the one that is being staffed. In either case, the better the organization is at identifying prospective members who are familiar with the group that is being staffed, the easier it should be to socialize these people if they later join.

There are two major reasons why prior experience in similar groups facilitates socialization. First, compared to inexperienced prospective members, experienced members have a better understanding of the demands of the new work group and hence are less likely to be disappointed after they enter. This idea is consistent with research on realistic job previews, which suggests that new employees are less likely to feel dissatisfied and angry about their working conditions if they are informed about the negative as well as positive features of an organization prior to joining it (Wanous, 1992; but see Wanous, Poland, Premack, & Davis, 1992). A similar point has been made regarding responses to group therapy. Several authors have suggested that clients are more likely to benefit from such therapy if they undergo pretraining prior to entry (Kaul & Bednar, 1994; Nichols, 1976). Second, prior experience in similar groups may facilitate socialization because it increases the likelihood that newcomers possess personality traits associated with adaptability, feel committed to the group, and have task and social skills that the group needs. If newcomers have been successful in similar groups, then they are likely to have most if not all of the personal qualities that the new work group will demand.

Of course, in trying to recruit prospective members who possess adaptive personalities, commitment to the group, and valuable skills, organizations can do more than simply identify people with prior experience in similar groups. They can also spend time and money to acquire detailed information about prospective members' personal qualities. Good sources of such information are informal recruiting agents, such as family members and friends, who are familiar with both the prospective member and the work group (Rynes, 1991; Wanous, 1992; Wanous & Colella, 1989). Because these people know what it takes to succeed in the group, they are in a good position to recommend prospective members who have the personal qualities needed for success and thus require relatively little socialization. Moreover, if these prospective members join the group, they are likely to be satisfied with membership, work hard to achieve group goals, and want to stay. Besides providing information to the group about prospective members, informal recruiting agents can also provide information to prospective members about the group. To the extent this information helps prospective members identify groups for which they are suited, they will require relatively little socialization after they join.

In addition to using informal recruiting agents, organizations can employ a variety of other, more formal, methods to obtain information about prospective members' personal qualities. These include inviting the members to participate in group activities and observing their behavior, obtaining evaluations of their performance in previous jobs (e.g., through letters of recommendation), and requiring them to provide personal information via questionnaires, personality tests, face-to-face interviews, and even biological samples (e.g., EKG responses on lie detector tests, blood and urine samples). Of course, if prospective members view these methods as unnecessarily intrusive, they may produce hostility toward the organization and reduce the likelihood that any offer of employment will be accepted.

The solicitors and/or recipients of information about prospective members may or may not be members of the work group that requires staffing. In many cases, organizational members (e.g., personnel officers) who have little or no contact with the work group solicit and evaluate information and make a hiring decision on their own. Although these decisions sometimes produce good matches between group needs and individual qualities, a potentially more effective approach involves asking members of the work group that the person might join, or other similar groups in the organization, to evaluate the prospective member's suitability for membership (Martin, 1998; Zellner, 1994). This evaluation could be based on reading information about the prospective member, meeting the person outside the job setting, or interacting with the person inside the job setting. Because of their intimate knowledge of work group practices, people who belong to the group may be better judges of a prospective member's fit than are people from other parts of the organization, including recruitment specialists from the personnel department.

Not only may such specialists be insensitive to the subtle social and task demands of a work group, but they may be motivated to achieve special staffing goals that have negative consequences for how the group operates. One such goal is diversity, defined as variability among members on demographic characteristics such as race, sex, or age (Jackson, May, & Whitney, 1995; Milliken & Martins, 1996). Although diversity can improve group performance (Bantel & Jackson, 1989; Wood, 1987), it can also impede the social integration of new members (Jackson, Stone, & Alvarez, 1993) and produce conflicts that weaken group cohesion and increase the likelihood that oldtimers will leave (Jackson et al., 1991; Maznevski, 1994). Because the risks of diversity sometimes outweigh its benefits (Moreland, Levine, & Wingert, 1996), recruitment specialists who strive for diversity may end up selecting new members who create problems for the groups they join.

Once the organization has identified and evaluated prospective members and decided which ones are suitable for a given work group, it must persuade these people to join. As Levine, Moreland, and Ryan (1998) noted, this process can be more or less difficult, depending on whether prospective members currently belong to another work group. If they do not, the organization has only one task, namely to convince them that group membership will be sufficiently rewarding to justify their entry. This can be accomplished by raising prospective members' commitment to the group and/or lowering their entry criteria for membership. There are several ways in which organizations might raise prospective members' commitment to a work group. These include providing information about attractive qualities of the group, such as working conditions or opportunities for advancement; encouraging the group to make changes that increase its attractiveness to prospective members, such as altering its work practices to accommodate prospective members' skills; and involving prospective members in pleasant group activities. There are also several ways in which organizations might lower prospective members' entry criteria for group membership. These include claiming that people who joined the group in the past and had low entry criteria were later quite successful and indicating that the group will lose interest in prospective members if they hold an unreasonably high standard for joining.

If prospective members belong to another work group, the organization must do more than increase their commitment to the new work group and/or reduce their entry criteria for that group. It must also convince them to leave their current group, which will only happen if their commitment to that group falls far enough (i.e., to their exit criteria). In this case, the organization has the additional task of decreasing prospective members' commitment to their current group and/or raising their exit criteria for that group. An obvious way to reduce commitment is to transmit negative information about the group. But because prospective members are often suspicious of blatant attempts to denigrate their current group, the organization may have to use subtle techniques that disguise its true intentions. Such techniques include damning with faint praise (i.e., extolling the group's trivial virtues while ignoring its important ones); persuading prospective members that the dimensions on which the new group seems better are the most important criteria for evaluating the groups; and using disgruntled ex-members of the current group to provide information about its weaknesses. To raise prospective members' exit criteria for their current group, the organization might claim that ex-members of the group who had high exit criteria, and hence left when their commitment was still relatively strong, were later happier than ex-members who had low exit criteria, and hence remained in the group despite relatively weak commitment. Or the organization might imply that external forces will cause the group to dissolve in the near future, regardless of members' commitment levels or exit criteria.

These strategies for reducing prospective members' commitment to their current work group and/or raising their exit criteria for that group will be more effective in some circumstances than in others. In particular, they are more likely to succeed when the current and new work groups are embedded in different organizations than in the same organization. This is because prospective members may feel betrayed by negative statements about their work group from organizational insiders, but not by equally harsh comments from organizational outsiders. Organizations also run more serious risks in bad-mouthing their own work groups than those of other organizations. Compared to groups outside the organization, those inside are more likely to hear about the negative information and feel angry about it, and they are in a better position to retaliate and perhaps damage the organization.

Training and Socialization

As noted earlier, the goal of training is to provide new members with experiences that will facilitate their adjustment to the work groups they are joining. Although many organizations devote substantial time and energy to training new workers, most American workers receive no formal training (U.S. Department of Labor, 1992), and the training they do get typically focuses on individual skills and ignores the group context in which workers must perform. Moreover, even training programs that explicitly focus on work in groups are often based on two faulty assumptions (Moreland, Argote, & Krishnan, 1998). First, most worker competencies are assumed to be generic qualities that affect group performance similarly across diverse settings. Second, learning to do a specific job and learning to work with others are assumed to be largely independent processes.

Regarding the first assumption, Cannon-Bowers and her colleagues (1995), in a publication mentioned earlier, argued that specific as well as generic competencies can contribute to team effectiveness and that the particular mix of competencies required in a given situation depends on several factors. These include the level of interdependence among team members, the stability of the team's environment, the degree of turnover in the team, and whether team members hold memberships in multiple teams and interact across diverse tasks. Thus, in many team situations, specific competencies may be as or more important than generic competencies.

Regarding the second assumption, several observers, including Brown and Duguid (1991), Levine and Moreland (1991), and Darrah (1992, 1994), have argued that many work groups develop their own unique operating procedures. New members must therefore learn to do their jobs in a manner that is compatible with the working styles of the groups they are entering. This reasoning suggests that, rather than being independent, learning to do a specific job and learning to work with others are interdependent and perhaps inseparable processes.

There are several ways in which organizations might employ training to facilitate the socialization of new members into work groups. Some of these efforts focus on generic competencies that are presumably instrumental to success across a wide range of groups. A provisional list of these competencies can be found in McIntyre and Salas' (1995) analysis of teamwork behaviors. According to McIntyre and Salas, there are four essential teamwork behaviors (performance monitoring, feedback, closed-loop communication, and backing-up behavior) and two enabling conditions for these behaviors (members' collective perception of themselves as a group and their feeling of mutual interdependence). If these behaviors and enabling conditions are indeed generic, then organizations that use training procedures to instill them in new group members will facilitate their socialization. What might those training procedures look like? According to Cannon-Bowers et al. (1995), the training techniques needed to impart generic competencies are less involving and complicated than those needed to impart specific competencies. Thus, in the case of transportable competencies, which are generic in relation to both the task and the team, Cannon-Bowers et al. argued that training can be directed toward the individual (rather than the group) and can involve passive techniques such as lectures and demonstrations.

These kinds of training techniques may also be useful for transmitting general information about the content and process of group socialization, which organizational newcomers should find valuable regardless of which work group they are joining. Content information might involve the origins of work group cultures, the cognitive and behavioral components of these cultures, and the functions such cultures serve. Process information might involve the challenges that newcomers typically face in acquiring cultural knowledge, the techniques that newcomers can use to learn group culture, and the difficulties that newcomers often encounter in becoming full group members.

Although training procedures designed to impart generic competencies for group work and general knowledge about group socialization can be quite useful, as suggested previously, these procedures are unlikely to be sufficient in and of themselves. New group members also need to acquire specific competencies and knowledge. According to Cannon-Bowers et al. (1995), different training techniques are needed to impart different specific competencies. For example, when team-specific competencies are required, training in intact teams should be conducted. In contrast, when task-specific competencies are needed, teams should be allowed to practice in the actual task environment (or a realistic simulation) and should receive information about the roles and responsibilities of each member. To the extent an organization can tailor a work group's training to the specific competencies its new members need, their socialization should be facilitated.

Consistent with this analysis, there has been much recent interest in training members of newly formed work groups together on the kinds of tasks they will later encounter (e.g., Andrews, Waag, & Bell, 1992; Hackman, 1993; Prince, Chidester, Bowers, & Cannon-Bowers, 1992). Although such team training has certain disadvantages, such as information and coordination loss arising from subsequent member turnover, it also has some distinct advantages. In particular, training members of newly formed work groups together increases the likelihood that they will acquire the specific (as well as generic) competencies they need to work together in the future. Moreover, such training may also increase members' commitment to the group and strengthen group cohesion and potency, which can have positive effects on group performance (Griffith, 1989; Guzzo, Yost, Campbell, & Shea, 1993; Moreland, 1987; Mullen & Copper, 1994).

Wegner's (1987, 1995) analysis of transactive memory provides a useful framework for understanding the effectiveness of team training. According to Wegner, transactive memory is a socially shared system for encoding, storing, and retrieving information, which develops as group members interact over time. A functioning transactive memory system has two basic components: (a) the individual memory systems of the group members and (b) the communication processes these people use in handling information. In order to communicate effectively, of course, group members must have a shared awareness of who knows what. It seems likely that team training is helpful in large part because it facilitates the development of transactive memory within a group. To the extent that group members know which workers possess particular knowledge and how to elicit that knowledge from them, they are likely to assign tasks sensibly, react appropriately to unexpected problems (Moreland & Levine, 1992), and anticipate others' behavior rather than merely react to it (Wittenbaum, Vaughan, & Stasser, 1998).

Several lines of work are consistent with the idea that transactive memory systems facilitate group performance. Indirect evidence for the benefits of transactive memory is provided by studies indicating that increased familiarity among work group members (Argote, 1993; Foushee, Lauber, Baetge, & Acomb, 1986; Larson, Foster-Fishman, & Keys, 1994; Watson, Kumar, & Michaelsen, 1993) and increased recognition of expertise by group members (Henry, 1995; Littlepage & Silbiger, 1992; Stasser, Stewart, & Wittenbaum, 1995; Yetton & Bottger, 1982) are associated with better group performance. More direct evidence for the benefits of transactive memory is provided by studies conducted by Moreland, Argote, and their colleagues (Liang, Moreland, & Argote, 1995; Moreland, Argote, & Krishnan, 1996, in press). Using laboratory experiments in which small groups were trained to perform complex tasks, these researchers assessed the impact of various types of individual and group training on group performance. Their findings indicated that groups performed better when their members were trained together rather than apart and that the benefits of group training depended heavily on the operation of transactive memory systems. It would seem, then, that organizational training aimed at increasing transactive memory in newly formed work groups can pay big dividends in terms of group performance (see Moreland, chap. 1, this volume).

Of course, people do not always join new groups in which their coworkers are all inexperienced newcomers like themselves. Instead, people often join intact groups in which many of their coworkers are experienced oldtimers, and these oldtimers can have a substantial impact on the socialization process (Chao, 1988; Feldman, 1989). Organizations can do much to increase the likelihood that new members of existing groups will acquire the specific competencies and knowledge they need. An important technique for achieving this goal is on-the-job training, in which newcomers learn job skills by watching and talking to oldtimers (Lave & Wenger, 1991; Scribner & Sachs, 1990). The more involved newcomers are in this training, the more effective their socialization is likely to be (cf. Bauer & Green, 1994).

An organization might increase the effectiveness of on-the-job training in several ways. For example, oldtimers could be encouraged to encapsulate new members in the group by spending leisure time with them. In addition, oldtimers could be asked to act as mentors for new members and to respond to their requests for feedback in a supportive manner. The organization could also increase oldtimers' ability to communicate the group's shared mental models by providing refresher courses on group culture. And it could strengthen their motivation to communicate these models by providing information about newcomers' positive qualities and the group benefits that will accrue if newcomers are adequately socialized. The organization could also try to increase oldtimers' empathy for newcomers, on the assumption that this will increase their understanding of newcomers' informational needs. For example, oldtimers could be encouraged to recall their own experiences as new members of work groups, or they could be asked to play the role of newcomers in simulated groups that are culturally different from their own. Thus, in cases where people join intact work groups, organizational training efforts directed toward oldtimers in those groups can be as or more effective in facilitating socialization than training efforts directed toward newcomers themselves.

CONCLUSIONS

In this chapter, we argued that a critical task for newcomers entering work groups is learning the shared mental models that oldtimers possess (or, in the case of people joining new groups, helping to create such models). Moreover, we suggested that whether newcomers joining intact groups acquire shared mental models during socialization depends on four factors—newcomers' qualities (e.g., familiarity with the group, adaptability, commitment to the group); newcomers' tactics (e.g., information acquisition, participation in mentoring, collaboration with other newcomers); oldtimers' qualities (e.g., perceptions of the group's needs and the newcomers' skills, knowledge of shared mental models, familiarity with newcomers); and oldtimers' tactics (e.g., initiation ceremonies, encapsulation within the group, feedback). Finally, we suggested several ways in which organizations might improve work groups' ability to transmit shared mental models to newcomers by (a) bringing certain types of people into the groups (member selection) and (b) helping these people acquire the general and specific competencies they need to function effectively (member training).

Although acquiring shared mental models is helpful for newcomers in many group settings, some caveats are worth noting (Cannon-Bowers et al., 1993; Klimoski & Mohammed, 1994; Levine & Moreland, 1991). In spite of the burgeoning interest in shared mental models by organizational and social psychologists, team performance research provides very little direct evidence for either the existence or operation of these models. Instead, the concept of shared mental models is often merely invoked post hoc to help describe and interpret team phenomena (Klimoski & Mohammed, 1994). In addition, even if we assume that most groups develop shared mental models, it is not clear that they are always beneficial for the group as a whole or its members, including newcomers.

If a group's environment is changing rapidly, for example, then its shared mental models may become obsolete, in which case continuing to rely on them and encouraging newcomers to learn them would be mistakes. In addition, even in the absence of rapid environmental change, shared mental models may contain elements that are harmful to the internal integration or external adaptation of the group. For example, sports teams that attach too much importance to losing a single game may become despondent and perform poorly in later games (Fine, 1985). And shared (but incorrect) notions about how ability is distributed in a group may lead to suboptimal work assignments and reduced group performance (Ridgeway, 1984). In these examples, it is assumed that shared mental models are problematic because they contain incorrect information, which, if relied on, will undermine group performance. But, rather than simply being wrong, shared mental models may be problematic for another reason, namely because they reflect too much overlap in members' knowledge and beliefs.

Although many observers have suggested that groups function best if their members share a common perspective (Argote, 1989; Cummings, 1981; Mackie & Goethals, 1987; Stasser & Titus, 1985), several lines of research suggest that maximally shared information and opinions can sometimes inhibit group (and individual) performance. For example, research on majority influence and groupthink indicates that shared opinions can produce pressures to uniformity that reduce attention to novel alternatives and lead to poor decisions (Janis, 1982; Levine & Thompson, 1996; Nemeth, 1995). In addition, research on communication in groups indicates that too much information sharing can overload members' processing capacities and thereby inhibit their performance (Foushee, 1984; Goodman, Ravlin, & Argote, 1986). Finally, knowledge differences across group members can enhance their performance by increasing the availability of needed information and decreasing the cognitive responsibilities of individual workers (Hackman, 1987; Wegner, 1987).

Clearly, then, there is reason to believe that shared mental models can inhibit as well as enhance group performance. The conditions leading to these two outcomes are not well understood, but several candidates are plausible. For example, it may be that broadly distributed knowledge is more beneficial than narrowly distributed knowledge when (a) the group's task is unitary (all members have the same responsibilities) rather than divisible (different members have different responsibilities); (b) status differences among members are small rather than large; (c) the likelihood of member loss is high rather than low; (d) communication and coordination opportunities are low rather than high; and (e) the total amount and diversity of knowledge are small rather than large. Research on these and other determinants of the efficacy of shared mental models would be useful in clarifying how organizations can facilitate newcomer socialization into work groups.

REFERENCES

Adkins, C. L. (1995). Previous work experience and organizational socialization: A longitudinal examination. *Academy of Management Journal, 38*, 839–862.

Adler, I., & Shuval, J. (1978). Cross pressures during socialization for medicine. *American Sociological Review, 43*, 693–704.

Anderson, A., & Thomas, H. D. C. (1996). Work group socialization. In M. A. West (Ed.), *Handbook of work group psychology* (pp. 423–450). Chichester, England: Wiley.

Anderson, R. C., & Pichert, J. W. (1978). Recall of previously unrecallable information following a shift in perspective. *Journal of Verbal Learning and Verbal Behavior, 17*, 1–12.

Andrews, D. H., Waag, W. L., & Bell, H. H. (1992). Training technologies applied to team training: Military examples. In R. W. Swezey & E. Salas (Eds.), *Teams: Their training and performance* (pp. 283–327). Norwood, NJ: Ablex.

Argote, L. (1989). Agreement about norms and work-unit effectiveness: Evidence from the field. *Basic and Applied Social Psychology, 10*, 131–140.

Argote, L. (1993). Group and organizational learning curves: Individual, system, and environmental components. *British Journal of Social Psychology, 32*, 31–51.

Aronson, E., & Mills, J. (1959). The effect of severity of initiation on liking for a group. *Journal of Abnormal and Social Psychology, 59*, 177–181.

Ashford, S. J., & Black, J. S. (1996). Proactivity during organizational entry: The role of desire for control. *Journal of Applied Psychology, 81*, 199–214.

Ashford, S. J., & Cummings, L. L. (1983). Feedback as an individual resource: Personal strategies of creating information. *Organizational Behavior and Human Performance, 32*, 370–398.

Ashford, S. J., & Taylor, M. S. (1990). Adaptation to work transitions: An integrative approach. In G. R. Ferris & K. M. Rowland (Eds.), *Research in personnel and human resources management* (Vol. 8, pp. 1–39). Greenwich, CT: JAI.

Bantel, K. A., & Jackson, S. E. (1989). Top management and innovations in banking: Does the composition of the top team make a difference? *Strategic Management Journal, 10*, 107–124.

Bar-Tal, D. (1990). *Group beliefs: A conception for analyzing group structure, processes, and behavior.* New York: Springer-Verlag.

Bauer, T. N., & Green, S. G. (1994). Effects of newcomer involvement in work-related activities: A longitudinal study of socialization. *Journal of Applied Psychology, 79*, 211–223.

Becker, H. S. (1964). Personal changes in adult life. *Sociometry, 27*, 40–53.

Becker, H. S., Geer, B., Hughes, E. C., & Strauss, A. L. (1961). *Boys in white: Student culture in medical school.* New Brunswick, NJ: Transaction Books.

Becker, T. E. (1992). Foci and bases of commitment: Are they distinctions worth making? *Academy of Management Journal, 35*, 232–244.

Bell, C. G., & Price, C. M. (1975). *The first term: A study of legislative socialization.* Beverly Hills, CA: Sage.

Black, J. S., & Ashford, S. J. (1995). Fitting in or making jobs fit: Factors affecting mode of adjustment for new hires. *Human Relations, 48*, 421–437.

Bornstein, R. F. (1992). The dependent personality: Developmental, social, and clinical perspectives. *Psychological Bulletin, 11*, 2–23.

Brett, J. M. (1980). The effect of job transfer on employees and their families. In C. L. Cooper & R. Payne (Eds.), *Current concerns in occupational stress* (pp. 99–136). Chichester, England: Wiley.

Brown, J. S., & Duguid, P. (1991). Organizational learning and communities of practice: Toward a unified view of working, learning, and innovation. *Organization Science, 2*, 40–57.

Cannon-Bowers, J. A., Salas, E., & Converse, S. (1993). Shared mental models in expert team decision making. In N. J. Castellan (Ed.), *Individual and group decision making* (pp. 221–246). Hillsdale, NJ: Lawrence Erlbaum Associates.

Cannon-Bowers, J. A., Tannenbaum, S. I., Salas, E., & Volpe, C. E. (1995). Defining competencies and establishing team training requirements. In R. Guzzo & E. Salas (Eds.), *Team effectiveness and decision making in organizations* (pp. 333–380). San Francisco: Jossey-Bass.

Chao, G. T. (1988). The socialization process: Building newcomer commitment. In M. London & E. Mone (Eds.), *Career growth and human resource strategies* (pp. 31–47). Westport, CT: Quorum Press.

Chao, G. T., O'Leary-Kelly, A. M., Wolf, S., Klein, H. J., & Gardner, P. D. (1994). Organizational socialization: Its content and consequences. *Journal of Applied Psychology, 79*, 730–743.

Charters, W. W., & Newcomb, T. M. (1952). Some attitudinal effects of experimentally increased salience of a membership group. In G. E. Swanson, T. M. Newcomb, & E. L. Hartley (Eds.), *Readings in social psychology* (2nd ed., pp. 415–420). New York: Holt, Rinehart & Winston.

Church, A. T. (1982). Sojourner adjustment. *Psychological Bulletin, 91*, 587–597.

Cini, M., Moreland, R. L., & Levine, J. M. (1993). Group staffing levels and responses to prospective and new group members. *Journal of Personality and Social Psychology, 65*, 723–734.

Comer, D. R. (1991). Organizational newcomers' acquisition of information from peers. *Management Communication Quarterly, 5*, 64–89.

Cummings, T. G. (1981). Designing effective work groups. In P. C. Nystrom & W. H. Starbuck (Eds.), *Handbook of organizational design* (Vol. 2, pp. 250–271). Oxford, England: Oxford University Press.

Dandridge, T. C., Mitroff, I., & Joyce, W. F. (1980). Organizational symbolism: A topic to expand organizational analysis. *Academy of Management Review, 5*, 77–82.

Darrah, C. (1992). Workplace skills in context. *Human Organization, 51*, 264–273.

Darrah, C. (1994). Skill requirements at work: Rhetoric versus reality. *Work and Occupations, 21*, 64–84.

Decker, P. J., & Cornelius, E. T. (1979). A note on recruiting sources and job survival rates. *Journal of Applied Psychology, 64*, 463–464.

Deluga, R. J., & Perry, J. T. (1994). The role of subordinate performance and ingratiation in leader-member exchanges. *Group and Organization Management, 19*, 67–86.

Dienesch, R. M., & Liden, R. C. (1986). Leader-member exchange model of leadership: A critique and further development. *Academy of Management Review, 11*, 618–634.

Doise, W., & Mugny, G. (1984). *The social development of the intellect.* Oxford, England: Pergamon.

Dunham, R. S., & Barrett, A. (1996, January 29). The house freshmen. *Business Week*, 24–31.

Fairhurst, G. T., & Snavely, B. K. (1983). Majority and token minority group relationships: Power acquisition and communication. *Academy of Management Review, 8*, 292–300.

Feldman, D. C. (1977). The role of initiation activities in socialization. *Human Relations, 11*, 977–990.

Feldman, D. C. (1989). Socialization, resocialization, and training: Reframing the research agenda. In I. L. Goldstein (Ed.), *Training and development in organizations* (pp. 376–416). San Francisco: Jossey-Bass.

Feldman, D. C. (1994). Who's socializing whom? The impact of socializing newcomers on insiders, work groups, and organizations. *Human Resource Management Review, 4*, 213–233.

Feldman, D. C., & Brett, J. M. (1983). Coping with new jobs: A comparative study of new job hires and job changers. *Academy of Management Journal, 26*, 258–272.

Fellin, P., & Litwak, E. (1963). Neighborhood cohesion under conditions of mobility. *American Sociological Review, 28*, 364–376.

Festinger, L. (1954). A theory of social comparison processes. *Human Relations, 7*, 117–140.

Fine, G. A. (1979). Small groups and culture creation: The idioculture of Little League Baseball teams. *American Sociological Review, 44*, 733–745.

Fine, G. A. (1985). Team sports, seasonal histories, and significant events: Little League Baseball and the creation of collective meaning. *Sociology of Sport Journal, 2*, 299–313.

Fisher, C. D. (1986). Organizational socialization: An integrative review. In G. R. Ferris & K. M. Rowland (Eds.), *Research in personnel and human resources management* (Vol. 4, pp. 101–145). Greenwich, CT: JAI.

Foushee, H. C. (1984). Dyads and triads at 35,000 feet: Factors affecting group process and aircrew performance. *American Psychologist, 39*, 885–893.

Foushee, H. C., Lauber, J. K., Baetge, M. M., & Acomb, D. B. (1986). *Crew factors in flight operations: The operational significance of exposure to short-haul transport operations* (Number 88342). Moffett Field, CA: NASA Ames Research Center.

Gersick, C. J., & Hackman, J. R. (1990). Habitual routines in task-performing groups. *Organizational Behavior and Human Decision Processes, 47*, 65–97.

Goodman, P. S., Ravlin, E. C., & Argote, L. (1986). Current thinking about groups: Setting the stage for new ideas. In P. S. Goodman (Ed.), *Designing effective work groups* (pp. 1–33). San Francisco: Jossey-Bass.

Gregory, K. L. (1983). Native-view paradigms: Multiple cultures and culture conflicts in organizations. *Administrative Science Quarterly, 28,* 359–376.

Griffith, J. (1989). The Army's new unit personnel replacement system and its relationship to unit cohesion and social support. *Military Psychology, 1,* 17–34.

Gundry, L. K., & Rousseau, D. M. (1994). Critical incidents in communicating culture to newcomers: The meaning is the message. *Human Relations, 47,* 1063–1088.

Guzzo, R. A., Yost, P. R., Campbell, R. J., & Shea, G. P. (1993). Potency in groups: Articulating a construct. *British Journal of Social Psychology, 32,* 87–106.

Haas, J. (1972). Binging: Educational control among high steel iron workers. *American Behavioral Scientist, 16,* 27–34.

Hackman, J. R. (1987). The design of work teams. In J. Lorsch (Ed.), *Handbook of organizational behavior* (pp. 315–342). Englewood Cliffs, NJ: Prentice-Hall.

Hackman, J. R. (1993). Teams, leaders, and organizations: New directions for crew-oriented flight training. In E. L. Weiner, B. G. Kanki, & R. L. Helmreich (Eds.), *Cockpit resource management* (pp. 47–69). New York: Academic Press.

Hardin, C. D., & Higgins, E. T. (1996). Shared reality: How social verification makes the subjective objective. In R. M. Sorrentino & E. T. Higgins (Eds.), *Handbook of motivation and cognition* (Vol. 3, pp. 28–84). New York: Guilford.

Harkins, S. G., & Petty, R. E. (1982). Effects of task difficulty and task uniqueness on social loafing. *Journal of Personality and Social Psychology, 43,* 1214–1229.

Hautaluoma, J. E., Enge, R. S., Mitchell, T. M., & Rittwager, F. J. (1991). Early socialization into a work group: Severity of initiations revisited. *Journal of Social Behavior and Personality, 6,* 725–748.

Henry, R. A. (1995). Improving group judgment accuracy: Information sharing and determining the best members. *Organizational Behavior and Human Decision Processes, 62,* 190–197.

Hinsz, V. B., Tindale, R. S., & Vollrath, D. A. (1997). The emerging conceptualization of groups as information processors. *Psychological Bulletin, 121,* 43–64.

Hopper, M. (1977). Becoming a policeman: Socialization of cadets in a police academy. *Urban Life, 6,* 149–170.

Ilgen, D. R., Major, D. A., Hollenbeck, J. R., & Sego, D. J. (1993). Team research in the 1990s. In M. M. Chemers & R. Ayman (Eds.), *Leadership theory and research: Perspectives and directions* (pp. 245–270). New York: Academic Press.

Jablin, F. M. (1987). Organizational entry, assimilation, and exit. In G. M. Goldhaber & G. A. Barnett (Eds.), *Handbook of organizational communication* (pp. 679–740). Norwood, NJ: Ablex.

Jackson, S. E., Brett, J. F., Sessa, V. I., Cooper, D. M., Julia, J. A., & Peyronnin, K. (1991). Some differences make a difference: Individual dissimilarity and group heterogeneity as correlates of recruitment, promotions, and turnover. *Journal of Applied Psychology, 76,* 675–689.

Jackson, S. E., May, K. E., & Whitney, K. (1995). Understanding the dynamics of diversity in decision-making teams. In R. A. Guzzo & E. Salas (Eds.), *Team effectiveness and decision making in organizations* (pp. 204–260). San Francisco: Jossey-Bass.

Jackson, S. E., Stone, V. K., & Alvarez, E. B. (1993). Socialization amidst diversity: The impact of demographics on work team oldtimers and newcomers. In L. L. Cummings & B. M. Staw (Eds.), *Research in organizational behavior* (Vol. 15, pp. 45–109). Greenwich, CT: JAI.

Jacobs, R. C., & Campbell, D. T. (1961). The perpetuation of an arbitrary tradition through several generations of a laboratory microculture. *Journal of Abnormal Social Psychology, 62,* 649–658.

James, K., & Cropanzano, R. (1994). Dispositional group loyalty and individual action for the benefit of an ingroup: Experimental and correlational evidence. *Organizational Behavior and Human Decision Processes, 60,* 179–205.

Janis, I. L. (1982). Counteracting the adverse effects of concurrence-seeking in policy-planning groups: Theory and research perspectives. In H. Brandstatter, J. H. Davis, & G. Stocker-Kriechgauer (Eds.), *Group decision making* (pp. 477–501). London: Academic Press.

Jones, G. R. (1983). Psychological orientation and the process of organizational socialization: An interactionist perspective. *Academy of Management Review, 8*, 464–474.

Jones, G. R. (1986). Socialization tactics, self-efficacy, and newcomers' adjustment to organizations. *Academy of Management Journal, 29*, 262–279.

Kanter, R. M. (1968). Commitment and social organization: A study of commitment mechanisms in utopian communities. *American Sociological Review, 33*, 499–517.

Katz, R. (1985). Organizational stress and early socialization experiences. In T. Beehr & R. Bhagat (Eds.), *Human stress and cognition in organizations: An integrative perspective* (pp. 117–139). New York: Wiley.

Kaul, T. J., & Bednar, R. L. (1994). Pretraining and structure: Parallel lines yet to meet. In A. Fuhriman & G. M. Burlingame (Eds.), *Handbook of group psychotherapy: An empirical and clinical synthesis* (pp. 155–188). New York: Wiley.

Klimoski, R., & Jones, R. G. (1995). Staffing for effective group decision making: Key issues in matching people and teams. In R. A. Guzzo & E. Salas (Eds.), *Team effectiveness and decision making in organizations* (pp. 291–332). San Francisco: Jossey-Bass.

Klimoski, R., & Mohammed, S. (1994). Team mental model: Construct or metaphor? *Journal of Management, 20*, 403–437.

Kram, K. E. (1983). Phases of the mentor relationship. *Academy of Management Journal, 26*, 608–625.

Kram, K. E. (1988). *Mentoring at work: Developmental relationships in organizational life*. Lanham, MD: University Press of America.

Kram, K. E., & Isabella, L. A. (1985). Mentoring alternatives: The role of peer relationships in career development. *Academy of Management Journal, 28*, 110–132.

Kramer, R. M. (1994). The sinister attribution error: Paranoid cognition and collective distrust in organizations. *Motivation and Emotion, 18*, 199–230.

Larson, J. R., Jr., & Christensen, C. (1993). Groups as problem-solving units: Toward a new meaning of social cognition. *British Journal of Social Psychology, 32*, 5–30.

Larson, J. R., Foster-Fishman, P. G., & Keys, C. B. (1994). Discussion of shared and unshared information in decision-making groups. *Journal of Personality and Social Psychology, 67*, 446–461.

Lave, J., & Wenger, E. (1991). *Situated learning: Legitimate peripheral participation*. New York: Cambridge University Press.

Lawrie, J. (1987). How to establish a mentoring program. *Training and Development Journal, 41*, 25–27.

Lee, T. W., Ashford, S. J., Walsh, J. P., & Mowday, R. T. (1992). Commitment propensity, organizational commitment, and voluntary turnover: A longitudinal study of organizational entry processes. *Journal of Management, 18*, 15–32.

Levine, J. M., Bogart, L. M., & Zdaniuk, B. (1996). Impact of anticipated group membership on cognition. In R. M. Sorrentino & E. T. Higgins (Eds.), *Handbook of motivation and cognition: The interpersonal context* (Vol. 3, pp. 531–569). New York: Guilford.

Levine, J. M., & Moreland, R. L. (1985). Innovation and socialization in small groups. In S. Moscovici, G. Mugny, & E. Van Avermaet (Eds.), *Perspectives on minority influence* (pp. 143–169). Cambridge, England: Cambridge University Press.

Levine, J. M., & Moreland, R. L. (1987). Social comparison and outcome evaluation in group contexts. In J. C. Masters & W. P. Smith (Eds.), *Social comparison, social justice, and relative deprivation: Theoretical, empirical, and policy perspectives* (pp. 105–127). Hillsdale, NJ: Lawrence Erlbaum Associates.

Levine, J. M., & Moreland, R. L. (1991). Culture and socialization in work groups. In L. B. Resnick, J. M. Levine, & S. D. Teasley (Eds.), *Perspectives on socially shared cognition* (pp. 257–279). Washington, DC: American Psychological Association.

Levine, J. M., & Moreland, R. L. (1994). Group socialization: Theory and research. In W. Stroebe & M. Hewstone (Eds.), *European review of social psychology* (Vol. 5, pp. 305–336). Chichester, England: Wiley.

Levine, J. M., Moreland, R. L., & Ryan, C. S. (1998). Group socialization and intergroup relations. In C. Sedikides, J. Schopler, & C. A. Insko (Eds.), *Intergroup cognition and intergroup behavior* (pp. 283–308). Mahwah, NJ: Lawrence Erlbaum Associates.

Levine, J. M., Resnick, L. B., & Higgins, E. T. (1993). Social foundations of cognition. *Annual Review of Psychology, 44*, 585–612.

Levine, J. M., & Thompson, L. (1996). Conflict in groups. In E. T. Higgins & A. W. Kruglanski (Eds.), *Social psychology: Handbook of basic principles* (pp. 745–776). New York: Guilford.

Lewicki, R. J. (1981). Organizational seduction: Building commitment to organizations. *Organizational Dynamics, 10*, 4–21.

Liang, D. W., Moreland, R. L., & Argote, L. (1995). Group versus individual training and group performance: The mediating role of transactive memory. *Personality and Social Psychology Bulletin, 21*, 384–393.

Liden, R. C., Wayne, S. J., & Stilwell, D. (1993). A longitudinal study on the early development of leader-member exchanges. *Journal of Applied Psychology, 78*, 662–674.

Littlepage, G. E., & Silbiger, H. (1992). Recognition of expertise in decision-making groups: Effects of group size and participation patterns. *Small Group Research, 23*, 344–355.

Lodewijkx, H. F., & Syroit, J. E. M. M. (1997). Severity of initiation revisited: Does severity of initiation increase attractiveness in real groups? *European Journal of Social Psychology, 27*, 275–300.

Louis, M. R. (1980). Surprise and sense-making: What newcomers experience in entering unfamiliar organizational settings. *Administrative Science Quarterly, 25*, 226–251.

Mackie, D. M., & Goethals, G. R. (1987). Individual and group goals. In C. Hendrick (Ed.), *Group processes: Review of personality and social psychology* (Vol. 8, pp. 144–166). Newbury Park, CA: Sage.

MacNeil, M. K., & Sherif, M. (1976). Norm change over subject generations as a function of arbitrariness of prescribed norms. *Journal of Personality and Social Psychology, 34*, 762–773.

Mael, F. A., & Ashforth, B. E. (1995). Loyal from day one: Biodata, organizational identification, and turnover among newcomers. *Personnel Psychology, 48*, 309–333.

Major, D. A., Kozlowski, S. W. J., Chao, G. T., & Gardner, P. D. (1995). A longitudinal investigation of newcomer expectations, early socialization outcomes, and the moderating effects of role development factors. *Journal of Applied Psychology, 80*, 418–431.

Martin, J. (1982). Stories and scripts in organizational settings. In A. Hastorf & A. Isen (Eds.), *Cognitive social psychology* (pp. 255–305). New York: Elsevier.

Martin, J. (1998, January 12). So, you want to work for the best. . . . *Fortune*, Vol. 137, No. 1, 77–78.

Mathieu, J. E., & Zajac, D. M. (1990). A review and meta-analysis of the antecedents, correlates, and consequences of organizational commitment. *Psychological Bulletin, 108*, 171–194.

Maznevski, M. L. (1994). Understanding our differences: Performance in decision-making groups with diverse members. *Human Relations, 47*, 531–552.

McIntyre, R. M., & Salas, E. (1995). Measuring and managing for team performance: Lessons from complex environments. In R. A. Guzzo & E. Salas (Eds.), *Team effectiveness and decision making in organizations* (pp. 9–45). San Francisco: Jossey-Bass.

Miller, V. D., & Jablin, F. M. (1991). Information seeking during organizational entry: Influences, tactics, and a model of the process. *Academy of Management Review, 16*, 92–120.

Milliken, F. J., & Martins, L. L. (1996). Searching for common threads: Understanding the multiple effects of diversity in organizational groups. *Academy of Management Review, 21*, 402–433.

Moreland, R. L. (1986). Social categorization and the assimilation of "new" group members. *Journal of Personality and Social Psychology, 48*, 1173–1190.

Moreland, R. L. (1987). The formation of small groups. In C. Hendrick (Ed.), *Review of personality and social psychology: Group processes* (Vol. 8, pp. 80–110). Newbury Park, CA: Sage.

Moreland, R. L., Argote, L., & Krishnan, R. (1996). Socially shared cognition at work: Transactive memory and group performance. In J. L. Nye & A. M. Brower (Eds.), *What's social about social cognition? Research on socially shared cognition in small groups* (pp. 57–84). Thousand Oaks, CA: Sage.

Moreland, R. L., Argote, L., & Krishnan, R. (1998). Training people to work in groups. In R. S. Tindale, L. Heath, J. Edwards, E. J. Posavac, F. B. Bryant, Y. Suarez-Balcazar, E. Henderson-King, & J. Myers (Eds.), *Theory and research on small groups* (pp. 37–60). New York: Plenum.

Moreland, R. L., & Levine, J. M. (1982). Group socialization: Temporal changes in individual-group relations. In L. Berkowitz (Ed.), *Advances in experimental social psychology* (Vol. 15, pp. 137–192). New York: Academic Press.

Moreland, R. L., & Levine, J. M. (1989). Newcomers and oldtimers in small groups. In P. Paulus (Ed.), *Psychology of group influence* (pp. 143–186). Hillsdale, NJ: Lawrence Erlbaum Associates.

Moreland, R. L., & Levine, J. M. (1992). Problem identification by groups. In S. Worchel, W. Wood, & J. A. Simpson (Eds.), *Group process and productivity* (pp. 17–47). Newbury Park, CA: Sage.

Moreland, R. L., & Levine, J. M. (in press). Socialization in organizations and work groups. In M. Turner (Ed.), *Groups at work: Advances in theory and research*. Mahwah, NJ: Lawrence Erlbaum Associates.

Moreland, R. L., Levine, J. M., & Wingert, M. L. (1996). Creating the ideal group: Composition effects at work. In E. H. Witte & J. H. Davis (Eds.), *Understanding group behavior: Small group processes and interpersonal relations* (Vol. 2, pp. 11–35). Mahwah, NJ: Lawrence Erlbaum Associates.

Morgan, B. B., Jr., & Lassiter, D. (1992). Team composition and staffing. In R. Swezey & E. Salas (Eds.), *Teams: Their training and performance* (pp. 75–100). Norwood, NJ: Ablex.

Morrison, E. W. (1993). Newcomer information seeking: Exploring types, modes, sources, and outcomes. *Academy of Management Journal, 36,* 557–589.

Morrison, E. W., & Bies, R. J. (1991). Impression management in the feedback seeking process: A literature review and research agenda. *Academy of Management Review, 16,* 522–541.

Morrison, R. F., & Brantner, T. M. (1992). What enhances or inhibits learning a new job? A basic career issue. *Journal of Applied Psychology, 77,* 926–940.

Morrow, P. C. (1993). *The theory and measurement of work commitment.* Greenwich, CT: JAI.

Mullen, B., & Copper, C. (1994). The relation between group cohesiveness and performance: An integration. *Psychological Bulletin, 115,* 210–227.

Nelson, D. L. (1987). Organizational socialization: A stress perspective. *Journal of Organizational Behavior, 8,* 311–324.

Nemeth, C. J. (1995). Dissent as driving cognition, attitudes, and judgments. *Social Cognition, 13,* 273–291.

Nichols, K. A. (1976). Preparation for membership in a group. *Bulletin of the British Psychological Society, 29,* 353–359.

Nicholson, N. (1984). A theory of work role transitions. *Administrative Science Quarterly, 29,* 172–191.

Nye, J. L., & Brower, A. M. (1996). *What's social about social cognition?* Thousand Oaks, CA: Sage.

Orr, J. E. (1990). Sharing knowledge, celebrating identity: War stories and community memory among service technicians. In D. S. Middleton & D. Edwards (Eds.), *Collective remembering: Memory in society* (pp. 169–189). Newbury Park, CA: Sage.

Ostroff, C., & Kozlowski, S. W. (1992). Organizational socialization as a learning process: The role of information acquisition. *Personnel Psychology, 45,* 849–874.

Ostroff, C., & Kozlowski, S. W. (1993). The role of mentoring in the information-gathering processes of newcomers during early organizational socialization. *Journal of Vocational Behavior, 42,* 170–183.

Premack, S. L., & Wanous, J. P. (1985). A meta-analysis of realistic job preview experiments. *Journal of Applied Psychology, 70,* 706–718.

Prieto, J. M. (1993). The team perspective in selection and assessment. In H. Schuler, J. L. Farr, & M. Smith (Eds.), *Personnel selection and assessment: Individual and organizational perspectives* (pp. 221–234). Hillsdale, NJ: Lawrence Erlbaum Associates.

Prince, C., Chidester, T. R., Bowers, C., & Cannon-Bowers, J. (1992). Aircrew coordination: Achieving teamwork in the cockpit. In R. W. Swezey & E. Salas (Eds.), *Teams: Their training and performance* (pp. 329–353). Norwood, NJ: Ablex.

Putallaz, M., & Wasserman, A. (1989). Children's naturalistic entry behavior and sociometric status: A developmental perspective. *Developmental Psychology, 25,* 297–305.

Randall, D. M. (1990). The consequences of organizational commitment: A methodological investigation. *Journal of Organizational Behavior, 11,* 361–378.

Reichers, A. E. (1987). An interactionist perspective on newcomer socialization rates. *Academy of Management Review, 12,* 278–287.

Rentsch, J. R. (1990). Climate and culture: Interaction and qualitative differences in organizational meanings. *Journal of Applied Psychology, 75,* 668–681.

Resnick, L., Levine, J., & Teasley, S. (Eds.). (1991). *Perspectives on socially shared cognition.* Washington, DC: American Psychological Association.

Ridgeway, C. L. (1984). Dominance, performance, and status in groups: A theoretical analysis. In E. Lawler (Ed.), *Advances in group processes* (Vol. 1, pp. 59–93). Greenwich, CT: JAI.

Riemer, J. W. (1977). Becoming a journeyman electrician: Some implicit indicators in the apprenticeship process. *Sociology of Work and Occupations, 4,* 87–98.

Rogoff, B. (1990). *Apprenticeship in thinking.* New York: Oxford University Press.

Rohlen, T. P. (1973). "Spiritual education" in a Japanese bank. *American Anthropologist, 75,* 1542–1562.

Rusbult, C. E., & Farrell, D. (1983). A longitudinal test of the investment model: The impact on job satisfaction, job commitment, and turnover of variations in rewards, costs, alternatives, and investments. *Journal of Applied Psychology, 68,* 429–438.

Rynes, S. L. (1991). Recruitment, job choice, and post-hire consequences: A call for new research directions. In M. Dunnette & M. Hough (Eds.), *Handbook of industrial and organizational psychology* (Vol. 2, pp. 399–444). Palo Alto, CA: Consulting Psychologists' Press.

Saks, A. M. (1995). Longitudinal investigation of the moderating and mediating effects of self-efficacy on the relationship between training and newcomer adjustment. *Journal of Applied Psychology, 80,* 211–225.

Saks, A. M. (1996). The relationship between the amount and helpfulness of entry training and work outcomes. *Human Relations, 49,* 429–451.

Saks, A. M., & Ashforth, B. E. (1997). Organizational socialization: Making sense of the past and present as a prologue for the future. *Journal of Vocational Behavior, 51,* 234–279.

Scandura, T. A., & Schriesheim, C. A. (1994). Leader-member exchange and supervisor career mentoring as complementary constructs in leadership research. *Academy of Management Journal, 37,* 1588–1602.

Schein, E. H. (1968). Organizational socialization and the profession of management. *Industrial Management Review, 9,* 1–15.

Schein, E. H. (1990). Organizational culture. *American Psychologist, 45,* 109–119.

Scribner, S., & Sachs, P. (1990, February). *A study of on-the-job training* (Number 13). New York: National Center on Education and Employment.

Sherif, M. (1935). A study of some social factors in perception. *Psychological Archives,* No. 187.

Stasser, G., Stewart, D. D., & Wittenbaum, G. M. (1995). Expert roles and information exchange during discussion: The importance of knowing who knows what. *Journal of Experimental Social Psychology, 31,* 244–265.

Stasser, G., & Titus, W. (1985). Pooling of unshared information in group decision making: Biased information sampling during discussion. *Journal of Personality and Social Psychology, 48,* 1467–1478.

Stohl, C. (1986). The role of memorable messages in the process of organizational socialization. *Communication Quarterly, 34,* 231–249.

Suszko, M. K., & Breaugh, J. A. (1986). The effects of realistic job previews on applicant self-selection and employee turnover, satisfaction, and coping ability. *Journal of Management, 12,* 513–523.

Sutton, R. I., & Louis, M. R. (1987). How selecting and socializing newcomers influences insiders. *Human Resource Management, 26,* 347–361.

Trice, H. M., & Beyer, J. M. (1984). Studying organizational cultures through rites and ceremonials. *Academy of Management Review, 9,* 653–669.

Truzzi, M., & Easto, P. (1972). Carnivals, road shows, and freaks. *Trans-Action, 9,* 26–34.

U. S. Department of Labor. (1992, August). *How workers get their training: A 1991 update* (Number 2407). Washington, DC: Bureau of Labor Statistics.

Van Maanen, J. (1975). Police socialization: A longitudinal examination of job attitudes in an urban police department. *Administrative Science Quarterly, 20,* 207–228.

Van Maanen, J. (1977). Toward a theory of the career. In J. Van Maanen (Ed.), *Organizational careers: Some new perspectives* (pp. 67–130). New York: Wiley.

Van Maanen, J. (1980). Career goals: Organizational rules of play. In C. B. Derr (Ed.), *Work, family, and the career* (pp. 111–143). New York: Praeger.

Van Maanen, J. (1984). Doing new things in old ways: The chains of socialization. In J. L. Bess (Ed.), *College and university organizations* (pp. 211–246). New York: New York University Press.

Van Maanen, J., & Barley, S. R. (1985). Cultural organization: Fragments of a theory. In P. J. Frost, L. F. Moore, M. R. Louis, C. C. Lundberg, & J. Martin (Eds.), *Organizational culture* (pp. 31–53). Beverly Hills, CA: Sage.

Van Maanen, J., & Schein, E. (1979). Toward a theory of organizational socialization. In B. M. Staw (Ed.), *Research in organizational behavior* (Vol. 1, pp. 209–264). Greenwich, CT: JAI.

Vaught, C., & Smith, D. L. (1980). Incorporation and mechanical solidarity in an underground coal mine. *Sociology of Work and Occupations, 7,* 159–187.

Wanous, J. P. (1992). *Organizational entry: Recruitment, selection, orientation, and socialization of newcomers.* Reading, MA: Addison-Wesley.

Wanous, J. P., & Colella, A. (1989). Organizational entry research: Current status and future research directions. In K. M. Rowland & G. R. Ferris (Eds.), *Research in personnel and human resources management* (Vol. 7, pp. 59–120). Greenwich, CT: JAI.

Wanous, J. P., Poland, T. D., Premack, S. L., & Davis, K. S. (1992). The effects of met expectations on newcomer attitudes and behaviors: A review and meta-analysis. *Journal of Applied Psychology, 77,* 288–297.

Watson, W. E., Kumar, K., & Michaelsen, L. K. (1993). Cultural diversity's impact on interaction process and performance: Comparing homogeneous and diverse task groups. *Academy of Management Journal, 36,* 590–602.

Wegner, D. M. (1987). Transactive memory: A contemporary analysis of the group mind. In B. Mullen & G. R. Goethals (Eds.), *Theories of group behavior* (pp. 185–205). New York: Springer-Verlag.

Wegner, D. M. (1995). A computer network model of human transactive memory. *Social Cognition, 13,* 319–339.

Weick, K. E., & Gilfillan, D. P. (1971). Fate of arbitrary traditions in a laboratory microculture. *Journal of Personality and Social Psychology, 17,* 179–191.

Whitely, W. T., & Coetsier, P. (1993). The relationship of career mentoring to early career outcomes. *Organization Studies, 14,* 419–441.

Wilkins, A. L., & Ouchi, W. G. (1983). Efficient culture: Exploring the relationship between culture and organizational performance. *Administrative Science Quarterly, 28,* 468–481.

Wittenbaum, G. M., Vaughan, S. I., & Stasser, G. (1998). Coordination in task-performing groups. In R. S. Tindale, L. Heath, J. Edwards, E. J. Posavac, F. B. Bryant, Y. Suarez-Balcazar, E.

Henderson-King, & J. Myers (Eds.), *Theory and research on small groups* (pp. 177–204). New York: Plenum.

Wood, W. (1987). Meta-analytic review of sex differences in group performance. *Psychological Bulletin, 102*, 53–71.

Yetton, P. W., & Bottger, P. C. (1982). Individual versus group problem solving: An empirical test of a best-member strategy. *Organizational Behavior and Human Performance, 29*, 307–321.

Zaccaro, S. J., & Dobbins, G. H. (1989). Contrasting group and organizational commitment: Evidence for differences among multilevel attachments. *Journal of Organizational Behavior, 10*, 267–273.

Zellner, W. (1994, October 17). Teamplayer: No more "same-ol'-same-ol.' " *Business Week*, 95–96.

Zey, M. G. (1985). Mentor programs: Making the right moves. *Personnel Journal, 64*, 53–57.

Ziller, R. C. (1965). Toward a theory of open and closed groups. *Psychological Bulletin, 64*, 164–182.

Zurcher, L. A. (1967). The Naval Recruit Training Center: A study of role assimilation in a total institution. *Sociological Inquiry, 37*, 85–98.

13

Organizational Learning and New Product Development: CORE Processes

Fernando Olivera
Linda Argote
Carnegie Mellon University

An organization's ability to generate commercially successful new products is central to its competitive advantage. Companies need to find ways that enable them to develop products that meet customer needs better, faster, and more efficiently than competitors (Leonard-Barton, Bowen, Clark, Holloway, & Wheelwright, 1994). Product development requires translating data on market and technological opportunities into assets for commercial production (Clark & Fujimoto, 1991).

Product development is a group activity. Developing a new product requires the involvement of individuals with different types of expertise and typically from multiple functional areas in the organization. Researchers have argued that the management and organization of the product development process affects a product's ultimate success or failure in the marketplace (Clark & Fujimoto, 1991). Thus, understanding the functioning of product development teams can be critical for understanding organizational performance. It is worth noting that product development is a complex process and most companies have great difficulties in managing their product innovation efforts.

Despite the important role of product development groups in organizations, the literature has not yet produced adequate frameworks for analyzing their functioning and performance. A recent review points out that the literature is largely fragmented and that it is challenging to understand the findings of the empirical research (Brown & Eisenhardt, 1995).

This chapter advances our understanding of the product development process by: (a) providing a theoretical framework for analyzing the performance of product development teams based on the CORE model of group processes (Argote & McGrath, 1993) and (b) using the framework to analyze the case of the development of a new product. This analysis provides insights about the processes of new product development and about how to manage those processes effectively.

In the next section we present a definition of product development that highlights the critical role of linking the various constituents and processes that constitute a development project. In the following sections we develop aspects of new product development in the context of the CORE model of group processes. We begin by describing the CORE model of group processes. We then apply the model to analyze the case of the development of a personal computer. We conclude with insights gained from this analysis about the process of new product development.

PRODUCT INNOVATION

Clark and Fujimoto (1991) defined product development as "a process by which an organization transforms data on market opportunities and technical possibilities into information assets for commercial production" (p. 20). Dougherty and Heller (1994) argued that the activities that constitute product innovation can be grouped into three sets of linkages. The first linkage is the one that innovators make between market and technological possibilities. Successful products incorporate customer needs in a technically sound design. The second set of linkages are among the expertise of different functions or departments [such as marketing, manufacturing, and research and development (R&D)] within the organization. The third linkage is between the product and the firm's strategy and resources.

The management of these linkages demands a continuous flow of information and social interaction between the product development team and customers (Leonard-Barton, 1993; von Hippel, 1988), other functional areas within the organization (Dougherty, 1992), and top management (Ancona & Caldwell, 1992a). In the development process, knowledge is continuously created, transferred, combined, stored, and, ultimately, embodied in product and process designs (Clark & Fujimoto, 1991; Nonaka & Takeuchi, 1995). The success of a product development effort depends to a large extent on the effective management of these linkages and the appropriate sharing of knowledge (Dougherty & Heller, 1994; Nonaka & Takeuchi, 1995).

THE CORE MODEL OF GROUP PROCESSES

The focus of the CORE model of group processes is on acting groups in organizational contexts. Acting groups are sets of people who are engaged in interdependent activities, such as the design of a new product. Acting groups in organizational contexts are composed of three components: people, tools, and purposes (Argote & McGrath, 1993). People are the human component, tools are the technological component, and purposes, or intentions, are the motivational component.

Multiple criteria of success exist for an acting group in an organizational context. For new product development teams, these criteria might include time to market, sales revenue generated by the product, market share, adherence to budget, product quality, ease of manufacture, customer satisfaction, technical innovation, ability to resolve conflicts, and contribution of the product development effort to the firm's capabilities. These criteria are related to one another in complex and, at times, conflicting ways. Further, the relative importance attached to these criteria may vary across constituencies. For example, marketing may place more weight on customer satisfaction, manufacturing may highly value ease of assembly, and management may place a high premium on adherence to budget.

According to the CORE model of group processes (Argote & McGrath, 1993), groups in organizations accomplish their work through recurring cycles of four major sets of processes. Groups come into being through construction (C) processes. They do their work via operations (O) processes. Reconstruction (R) processes are those by which groups modify themselves and learn through experience. Groups stay interconnected with, have effects on, and are affected by other parts of the organization or larger environment through external relations (E) processes.

These CORE processes are not conceived as a series of stages that unfold in a fixed sequence over a group's life span. Instead the processes represent different aspects of a group's patterns of activity, with some temporal ordering but with much overlap and recycling. For example, a group has to be set up (the Construction process) before it can do its work (the Operations process). After the group operates for a while, however, it may recycle back to the Construction process by bringing in new members and training and socializing them. Thus, the processes in the CORE model are not a series of developmental stages but rather recurring patterns of activity that occur in a group.

CONSTRUCTION

Construction processes refer to activities involved in the initial establishment of a work group. Construction entails both the acquisition of members, purposes, and tools to form the group and their adaptation to one another. Acquisition involves the selection and recruitment of people, the establishment of purposes, and the appropriation of tools from the larger organization. Adaptation refers to the processes by which a social unit brings about changes in the people, tools, and purposes of which it is composed so that those people can use those tools to attain those purposes. Members are socialized or trained. Technologies are implemented, and often modified in the process. Purposes are elaborated into plans and specified in terms of tasks, steps, schedules, and assignments. Adaptation is related to what DeSanctis and Poole (1994) referred to as "adaptive structuration."

OPERATIONS

Operations processes refer to the activities of the group as it carries out its purposes. Operations processes involve technical problem solving, conflict resolution, and task execution (McGrath, 1991). *Technical problem solving* involves forming representations of the problem and its potential solutions and acquiring, sharing, and combining information effectively. *Conflict resolution* involves recognition of differing perspectives, values, and interests and the operation of consensus-building mechanisms (see McGrath, 1984). *Task execution* processes often involve coordination of activities of interdependent group members. Operations processes also include internal control of group activity. This entails monitoring and managing the coordination required for effective task performance, managing the conflicts that arise among group members, and monitoring the quality of the group's products.

RECONSTRUCTION

Reconstruction processes involve changes the group makes in itself as a result of experience. Thus, we distinguish here, on the one hand, between modifications of the members, tools, and purposes in order to do a project properly (i.e., the construction processes already described) and, on the other hand, modifications of the people, tools, and purposes as a consequence of having done a project (i.e., the reconstruction processes considered here). Reconstruction processes refer to how the group uses its own activities and experience as a basis for modifying itself.

The reconstruction processes include aspects of what has been referred to as organizational learning (Argote & Epple, 1990; Levitt & March, 1988) or knowledge-embedding processes. Knowledge can be embedded in (a) the people who compose the group, (b) its tools, and (c) its project plan or structure. These knowledge-embedding processes become apparent when one is dealing with a group that has some meaningful history and continuation over time.

EXTERNAL RELATIONS

These processes refer to how the group relates to the organizational and environmental context within which it is embedded. External relations processes involve monitoring the external environment with respect to members, tools, and purposes and managing potential changes in relations between the group and those aspects of its environment. A group's performance and success is affected by its relations with many individuals and groups both inside and outside the organization (Ancona, 1990). The ability to learn from and transfer knowledge from other groups plays a major role in a group's success (Darr, Argote, & Epple, 1995). External relations refer to the group's reaching out and learning from external sources. These processes become important when one is dealing with natural groups that exist in context.

CONTRIBUTION OF THE CORE MODEL

The CORE model of group processes includes processes that previous work has shown to be important contributors to group effectiveness. One key difference between the CORE model and previous influential models of group performance (e.g., Hackman & Morris, 1975) is that the CORE model includes the dynamics of group performance over time. Focusing on group performance over time sharpens our understanding of important phenomena that change as groups gain experience. For example, group members may learn who is good at which tasks and how to distribute work to take advantage of members' expertise and skills (Liang, Moreland, & Argote, 1995). Group members may become more adept at sharing information (Larson, Christensen, Abbott, & Franz, 1996) and their decisions may become more sophisticated (Gruenfeld & Hollingshead, 1993) as members gain experience working together. Focusing on group performance over time enables us to see these important changes that occur in groups as they gain experience.

A second key difference between the CORE model and previous models of group effectiveness is the prominence CORE attaches to a focal group's relationship to other groups in its context. Some past work has examined how groups manage their relationships with other groups in their environment (e.g., Ancona & Caldwell, 1992a). In addition to managing relationships with other groups, the CORE model includes how groups learn from and modify themselves as a result of their interactions with other groups. For example, a group may import a more effective procedure or innovation that another group developed (Darr, Argote, & Epple, 1995; Hargadon & Sutton, 1997). This ability to learn from and transfer knowledge from other groups is critical to a group's success. The ability to transfer knowledge is very important for acting groups in context, the focus of the CORE model.

OVERVIEW OF CASE

In the sections that follow, we use the CORE framework to analyze the case of the development of a personal computer, the XC. The XC was developed by COMPCO,[1] a large, multinational corporation in the computer industry. COMPCO assigned the task to a small development team (of five members) that designed the product and coordinated the work of several subsystem teams located on three continents. The computer was developed in a period of 11 months (from concept definition to market release), which, at the time, was a remarkably short development time for COMPCO. The XC was an innovative product. It exceeds the low-power requirements of the Energy Star program.[2] It incorporates several technologies that were new to the market when the product was released,[3] including a low-power digital Liquid Crystal Display (LCD), the use of PCMCIA (Personal Computer Memory Card International Association) cards,[4] silent operation (the computer does not use a fan), small size and light footprint, and a newly designed keyboard. The XC was also innovative in incorporating several attributes that reflect an awareness for the natural environment, such as the use of recycled plastics, a design for easy disassembly and recyclability, and use of recycled paper in packaging and documentation.

The product received excellent reviews from popular computer magazines, customers, and the Environmental Protection Agency (EPA) and other groups concerned with the environment. It also received a best computer system award from a famous computer magazine.

In spite of the favorable press and recognition it received, the XC was not a market success. Sales were so disappointing that production of the machine stopped a year after it was announced. Members of the development team attribute the low sales to several factors, including a high initial cost, concerns with expandability, inadequate marketing, and being too innovative.

We interviewed most members of the XC development team as well as the member of the marketing department who was in charge of the publicity for the XC. We used open-ended questions about the origin of the product, the development process, and the results of the project. We obtained further data about this case from publications in magazines and journals, product specifications, internal publications, and marketing materials for the product.

We conducted the interviews after the product had been released and the results of the project were known. We recognize that retrospective data have several limitations, including forgetting, the possibility of attribution bias, and the difficulty of verifying the episodes recalled (Dougherty, 1992). Unless otherwise indicated, the episodes we present here were consistently recalled by more than one of the interviewees and–or are consistent with actual features of the product and published materials (cf. Eisenhardt, 1989; Yin, 1994).

In the following sections, we use the CORE framework to analyze the development of the XC. It is worth noting that, although the XC is, like all development projects, a unique case, it is a project that shares several features with other development projects both within and outside the computer industry. Some of these features are inherent in the current nature of product development. For example, the use of multifunctional teams is a widespread practice in development projects.

The XC also shares several current trends in development practices with projects in different companies. For example, product development projects are increasingly done by geographically dispersed teams. The globalization of organizations and markets, coupled with advances in communication technologies, are largely responsible for this trend. Several researchers have documented development projects that involve developers from several countries (e.g., Datar, Jordan, Kekre, Rajiv, & Srinivasan, 1996; Leonard-Barton, 1995). Other trends include the use of small development teams and industry-driven shorter development cycles (e.g., Clark & Fujimoto, 1991).

The case of the XC development is, thus, useful for analyzing key aspects of product development in general. As we discuss later this chapter, however, further research is needed to systematically examine the role of different factors on product development effectiveness. Although we present the current state of knowledge in the literature, there are still many questions that remain unanswered about the factors that drive development efforts to success (Brown & Eisenhardt, 1995).

The following sections review processes related to the CORE model of group process. Table 13.1 is an outline of the specific processes relevant to product development that we analyze in this chapter.

CONSTRUCTION

Construction processes involve the acquisition of team members, purposes and tools, and their adaptation to each other. Construction processes include activities associated with team formation, composition, and structure, with member socialization and training and with planning. Each of these activities is now discussed in the context of our new product development team.

TEAM FORMATION

The product development literature has paid limited attention to how new product development teams are formed. We know little about the processes by which individuals are selected into these teams, purposes are established, and technologies appropriated. To our knowledge, the literature has

TABLE 13.1
CORE Processes in New Product Development

Construction	Operation	Reconstruction	External Relations
Team Formation Composition Structure	Communication & Coordination	Embedding Knowledge Individuals Documents Structure Products	Communication with Users
Socialization	Problem Solving & Decision Making		Transfer of Knowledge
Planning		Learning	

not yet produced an integrated picture of how new product development teams are formed. We agree with Moreland (1987) in his suggestion that team formation should be analyzed as a process (as opposed to an event that marks the transformation from a nongroup into a group). The forming of the XC team is a good illustration of this process.

The formation of the XC team had several stages. Initially, a senior product planner at COMPCO sold to senior management the idea of developing a desktop computer that was small and energy efficient. COMPCO was interested in entering the market for users with limited desk space (e.g., banks and hospitals) and in producing energy efficient products that would satisfy or exceed requirements recently set by the EPA. A few weeks later, a second product planner who had experience and interest in developing small desktop computers learned about this project and contacted the first planner. They realized there was a great potential for synergy in their ideas and together they defined the XC.

Once the product was almost fully defined, a project team was assigned. The basis for assigning this project team was availability—the team had just finished working on another product. The core project team consisted of the two product planners, a project manager, a systems engineer, and an electrical engineer. The team was in charge of coordinating the development and integration of the various subsystems that form the final product. The XC used several components that had been developed for other products, such as portable computers. But several components were designed specifically for this product by subsystem teams, such as the power supply, mechanical design, keyboard, engineering software, and some PCMCIA technologies. These subsystem teams were located at sites in the United States, Europe, and Asia and were assigned to this project on the basis of their availability and experience. In cases where more than one team was available to design a particular component, cost was taken into consideration through a bidding process. In one case, a subsystem team was selected

305

because the planner felt that they understood the product better than a competing team.

This case illustrates that the forming of a product development team is a process with several stages that can take several weeks. Also, it shows that there are several reasons why individuals are assigned to a team: some are happenstance (e.g., availability), some planned (e.g., experience), and some negotiated (through bids and assessments of fit).

Finally, it is worth noting that determining the size of a product development team is not a straightforward task. Membership can be defined in many ways. We have used the term *core team* to refer to the few individuals who were in charge of defining and managing the integration of the product's components (five individuals in this case). A looser definition of team membership would include the liaisons with the subsystem teams, manufacturing, marketing, health and safety, materials, and management, among others. An even looser definition would include the members of all the subsystem teams, marketing representatives, manufacturing teams, individuals involved in the development of earlier subcomponents, and so on (which would add up to over 100 people). In this chapter, we generally use the more selective membership definition when referring to the development team, consistent with the way the members defined themselves.

TEAM COMPOSITION

Developing new products requires linking the capabilities of several functional areas in the organization. Development teams are typically diverse. The development of a personal computer, for example, will involve individuals from engineering, manufacturing, marketing, health and safety, R&D, and legal departments. The use of cross-functional teams has been viewed by many organizations as a means for improving the quality of products and speed of development. Some researchers have concluded that, indeed, the use of cross-functional teams results in superior process performance (Brown & Eisenhardt, 1995; Clark & Fujimoto, 1991). This improved performance is attributed to several factors, including the variety of information available to the team and the possibility of anticipating downstream problems in the production process (Brown & Eisenhardt, 1995).

Using cross-functional teams, however, poses several challenges that can offset their benefits. Although functional diversity can increase the amount of information and mix of skills the team has available, it can also hinder the team's internal processes by, for example, complicating internal communication (Ancona & Caldwell, 1992b). Dougherty (1992), for example, argued that departments in an organization develop "thought worlds" that affect how individuals understand a product. Although team members may share the same goals, their thought worlds interfere with their ability to see the product in similar ways and to collaborate. Organized collective action requires developing some consensus among individuals' different interpretations (Fiol, 1994).

The difficulties faced by the development team of the XC to incorporate silent operation in the product is a good example of the challenges involved in sharing knowledge across functions. The XC, as mentioned earlier, is a low-power computer. As such, it is also a machine that produces little heat. The product planners realized early in the development process that the machine would not require a fan as a cooling system. Doing without a fan would allow for silent operation, an attribute that both developers wanted to incorporate in the machine. Manufacturing engineers, however, were resistant to the idea of building a computer without a fan. In their view, the fan was a necessary component that could not be excluded from the design.

Manufacturing is the department that becomes responsible for any malfunctioning equipment that is returned by customers. Given that responsibility, they were not willing to risk shipping a machine that they believed would surely malfunction. Although multiple tests showed that the machine would not need a fan, manufacturing engineers were never convinced and agreed to manufacture the computer only if a space were provided for installing a fan in case the machines overheated. The space was provided and one year after the product was released to the market, no machine had been returned due to overheating problems.

Differences in how to conceptualize the product also existed between the product planners and marketing. Although the product planners felt the distinctive features of the product were its small size, appealing looks, and silent operation, marketing thought that its distinctive feature was its energy efficiency and that should be emphasized in order to attract buyers. Marketing decided to go for an environmentally friendly image for the product. This image was not only inconsistent with the one the product planners had in mind but also forced them to compromise some of the features they thought the machine should have. For example, planners thought of including several plastic stripes with different colors to fit around the machine. Buyers could use these stripes to decorate the machine to match its surroundings. Providing these plastic stripes, however, was inconsistent with the environmental message in that the unused stripes would probably be discarded by the user and go to waste. Marketing decided to use a green stripe on all the machines.

The use of multifunctional teams presents a paradox. Diversity is valuable for producing innovative products but, at the same time, can be a barrier to collective action. The XC project gave two planners the opportunity to synergistically combine their ideas but also presented several challenges. As one of the planners mentioned in an interview, "Part of the difficulty in managing a product development process is knowing how to communicate with people from different functions. When talking to marketing, you need to be very general. For engineers, you need to be very specific." A critical task of the core development team is to bridge across these different thought worlds.

TEAM STRUCTURE

New product development teams vary widely in size and structure. Size, as mentioned earlier, largely depends on how team membership is defined. It also depends on the product's complexity. Clearly, there is an order of magnitude difference in the number of people involved in designing an airplane compared to a personal computer.

Clark and Wheelwright (1992) classified the structures of product development teams into four categories: functional, lightweight, heavyweight, and autonomous. These structures differ in how members from each functional area are involved in the project, the role of project managers, how resources are allocated, and how members are evaluated.

The functional team structure mirrors the functional organization of many large firms. Individuals in these teams are grouped by functional area (e.g., manufacturing, engineering, and marketing) and work almost independently on activities specified at the outset of the project. Functional managers are in charge of controlling, coordinating, and evaluating the activities of these individuals.

Lightweight teams differ from functional teams in that each functional area assigns a liaison person as a representative in a coordinating committee. The representatives work with a project manager who coordinates the activities of the different functions. Project managers for lightweight teams are generally middle- or junior-level, do not have influence on resource allocation, and do not have direct control over the team members.

Heavyweight teams have a structure similar to lightweight but differ in that project managers are senior-level, have an influence on the allocation of resources, and directly supervise the work of team members. Often the core team members are physically colocated with the project manager. Heavyweight team leaders affect team members' performance evaluations but career development decisions remain with the functional managers.

In an autonomous team structure, members are separated from their functional areas and fully dedicated to the project. As in the heavyweight teams, a senior-level person serves as project leader. This person has full control over the allocation of resources and is also responsible for the evaluation of team members. These teams are given a great amount of freedom in the development process.

Clark and Wheelwright (1992) also discussed the strengths and weaknesses of these structures. For example, functional and lightweight team structures serve to capture experience within a functional area and give opportunities to apply the resulting knowledge to other projects. These structures, however, pose coordination difficulties and can interfere with developing innovative, systemic views of a product. Heavyweight and autonomous teams have the advantage of creating a sense of ownership and commitment that can motivate team members to make the project succeed. But these teams, particularly autonomous ones, can suffer from being separated from the organization's functional areas and have difficulty managing their relationships with the rest of the organization.

These categories are a useful starting point to characterize a development team's structure. Often, however, project teams do not fall neatly into any of these categories. The XC development team, for example, has elements of more than one structure in Clark and Wheelwright's scheme. The XC team included senior-level individuals who had access to resources from the organization, a characteristic of heavyweight teams. The relationship with members of subsystem teams, however, resembled a functional structure where the liaisons remained in their functional areas. Although none of the structure categories fully describes the XC team, the classification scheme is useful for understanding the implications of structural features on development processes. For example, as we explain later this chapter, the functional elements of the XC team's structure played a critical role in the communication between the core and subsystem teams.

SOCIALIZATION

Product development projects provide a setting for team members' socialization. Working together gives individuals the opportunity to acquire task knowledge about how to do the job and social knowledge about the team's culture, norms, history, capabilities, and so on (Levine & Moreland, 1991). Product development teams that share task and social knowledge are likely to function better than teams that do not share this knowledge. Research has shown, for example, that shared goals, norms, information about other members' skills, and task information can all result in superior group performance (see Argote, 1989; Levine & Moreland, 1991).

There are several means by which team members can acquire task and social knowledge. Training, for example, gives individuals task knowledge that is necessary to do the job. Group training can serve the additional function of helping team members learn about each others' skills (Moreland, Argote, & Krishnan, 1998). Group members also acquire task and social knowledge through interaction. Brown and Duguid (1991) illustrated some of the mechanisms by which individuals learn about their jobs in communities-of-practice. These authors observed, for example, that telling stories and collaborating play a critical role in the development of individuals' role identity.

Members of the XC core team were physically colocated, which gave them opportunities to develop shared task and social knowledge. Furthermore, three of the members had worked together on other projects. There were less opportunities, however, to share task and social knowledge with members of subsystem teams who were in other locations. Some of these subsystem team members met face-to-face with the core team only once and some did not meet at all. Communication technologies are unlikely to serve as a substitute for physical interaction in the socialization and knowledge-sharing process. We explore later in this chapter some of the negative consequences of team members who do not develop shared understandings about a product.

PLANNING

Planning can be a key determinant of a product development project's success. Planning involves determining what activities need to be done and by whom, developing strategies for coordinating these activities, how subtasks should be delegated, the timing of subtasks, and their integration (e.g., Weingart, 1992). Several researchers have argued that planning can help to reduce the time it takes to bring a product to market, reduce development costs, and allow for simultaneous execution of development processes (e.g., Bacon, Beckman, Mowery, & Wilson, 1994; Clark & Fujimoto, 1991; Gupta & Wilemon, 1990).

The effects of planning on product development, however, have not yet been examined extensively and may largely depend on the nature of the product being developed, as well as other contingencies (Brown & Eisenhardt, 1995). In rapidly changing industries, such as personal computers, where there is high uncertainty, initial planning may not be particularly beneficial (Eisenhardt & Tabrizi, 1995). Teams often need to engage in online planning in response to changing task demands that result, for example, from changes in the product's definition. In uncertain environments, therefore, improvisation and learning may have a stronger effect on development performance than initial planning (Eisenhardt & Tabrizi, 1995).

OPERATIONS

Operations processes refer to the activities of the group as it carries out its purposes. These activities include communication, coordination, problem solving and decision making. These major activities in the operations area are now analyzed for new product development teams.

COMMUNICATION AND COORDINATION

Communication has been a central theme in research on product development teams and R&D groups. This research explores the relationship between project teams' communication patterns, particularly with outsiders,
and performance (e.g., Allen, 1977, Katz & Tushman, 1981). Ancona and
Caldwell (1992a), for example, identified and categorized a variety of external activities of product development teams. They classified these activities
into three categories: (a) ambassadorial, which are activities aimed at acquiring and securing resources, promoting and protecting the team; (b)
task-coordinator, which are horizontal communications aimed at getting
feedback on the product and coordinating with outsiders; and (c) scouting
activities that involve scanning for information and ideas about the competition, market, or technologies. These authors found that the pattern of
external communication activities was a better predictor of performance
than the mere frequency of external communication.

We have already discussed some of the challenges posed by communication across functional areas. A second, related aspect is communication
between geographically dispersed team members. Organizations increasingly use development teams with team members or subsystem teams
located in several sites of the organization. Often these sites are located in
different countries.

Information technologies have made it possible for individuals to collaborate while working at different sites. The use of electronic mail, computer-
aided design systems, and groupware facilitate communication and collaboration for distributed development teams. We have, however, limited
understanding of the implications and challenges of distributed work
groups in general and of how technology can support the task of product
development teams in particular (Ancona & Caldwell, 1990).

The XC team was notable for its ability to coordinate the efforts of teams
dispersed across several locations in the United States, Europe, and Asia.
The development team and some of the subsystems liaisons met face-to-
face for the first time after working virtually for the initial three months of
the project. In this meeting, they successfully assembled for the first time
the prototypes that would, a few hours later, receive a Best System award
at a computer fair.

Communication across countries, however, was not always successful in
the XC project. A subsystem team based in Europe in charge of developing
the monitor's power supply failed to understand the product's concept.
This team developed a sharp-looking power supply designed to stand on
the desk next to the monitor. This notion was inconsistent with the design
concept of saving desk space and by the time the error was noticed, it was
too late to design a new power supply. The product was shipped with this

inadequate component. One of the product planners regrets not having visited the power supply team to make sure they understood what the product was about.

The product development team was able to effectively communicate complex design information but had difficulty transferring the concept behind the product's design. There are several possible explanations for why it was difficult to communicate the product's concept effectively. As already mentioned, individuals from different functional areas develop different ideas about a product. Similarly, individuals who are located in different social settings may conceptualize the same product in different ways. Being physically separated reduces the opportunities for team members to develop a shared understanding of the product. Knowledge about the product's concept derived from discussions at one location may likely remain in the heads of the individuals who participated in these discussions. Furthermore, the product's concept may become tacit for the product planners and hard to articulate (Polanyi, 1966). Thus, the concept may be hard to convey, especially without frequent interaction and opportunities for observation (cf. Nonaka, 1994).

PROBLEM SOLVING AND DECISION MAKING

Along with communicating and coordinating, problem solving and decision making form the core of the product development team's operations activities. New products incorporate elements that have not been created before, or combine existing elements in new ways (Hargadon & Sutton, 1997). The development team conceptualizes the new product, generates solutions for meeting the product's requirements, and integrates the work of subsystem teams. These tasks involve continuous problem solving and decision making.

The development of the XC, an innovative product in many respects, required solving several difficult problems that the company and team had not faced before, such as developing a security system for PCMCIA cards, an analog interface for an LCD display, providing silent operation, using new recyclable materials, and fitting all the components in a small mechanical package.

The development process is often made up of unanticipated difficulties, changes in the product's features and requirements, and other novel situations (Eisenhardt & Tabrizi, 1995). Although most of the key product features are decided on when the project begins, changes are made as a result of feedback from users, senior management, marketing, and subsystem teams. As mentioned earlier, online planning and improvisation can play a critical role in a project's success.

Some researchers have argued that product innovation is largely an adaptive learning process where innovators deal with ambiguity and uncertainty (Van de Ven & Polley, 1992). Product development teams engage in a variety of learning activities, including trial-and-error experimentation, assessment of technological possibilities, development of prototypes, testing, and so on. Research by Polley and Van de Ven (1996) suggests that innovators use different learning activities at different stages of the innovation process. For example, the initial stages are characterized by discovery activities that help innovators identify necessary knowledge, whereas later stages involve trial-and-error learning. How development teams react to uncertainty and adversity is likely to be affected by factors such as the team's cohesiveness, structure, and stage of group development (see Argote, Gruenfeld, & Naquin, in press).

RECONSTRUCTION

Reconstruction processes involve modifications in group members, tools, and purposes that result from experience. In this section, we describe how the new product development team modified itself and what the team learned from its experience.

EMBEDDING KNOWLEDGE

A product embodies a great amount of knowledge generated during the development process. By itself, however, the product does not capture all the knowledge that was required in order to build it. Some of this knowledge will remain, for example, in prototypes, design plans, schedules, manufacturing processes, and the heads of the development team members. This section explores the means by which knowledge derived from product development is retained in the organization.

Individuals. Perhaps the most efficient way to learn about what happened during the development of a new product is to ask the individuals who were involved in it. These individuals are likely to remember the history of how the product was developed and the rationale behind many of the decisions made. A great amount of the knowledge generated during the development of a product is embedded in the individuals who participated in it. Other researchers have stressed the role of people as a form of organizational memory (Engeström, Brown, Engeström, & Koistinen, 1990; Simon, 1991; Walsh & Ungson, 1991). Walsh and Ungson (1991), for example, pointed out that people are able to store different types of knowledge, such as knowing what, where, when, who, how, and, in particular, why.

Individuals' ability to store knowledge about why decisions were made is of particular importance. Although the product itself may capture the "what" of a decision, it may not be able to capture the "why." As one of the XC team members pointed out, the rationale behind many decisions goes undocumented. For example, the story of why the XC includes a green band around it (explained earlier) was not captured in any document and probably remains only in the memories of those in the development team.

When knowledge remains in the heads of individuals, it runs the risk of being lost when these individuals leave the team or the organization. Engeström et al. (1990) provided a good example of a medical clinic where knowledge that is possessed by an administrator is likely to be lost when he retires. Recent research has shown that the effects of turnover on a group will depend on how the group is structured (Carley, 1992; Devadas & Argote, 1995) and the complexity of the task they perform (Argote, Insko, Yovetich, & Romero, 1995). Devadas and Argote (1995) found that turnover affected the performance of groups that are high in structure less than that of groups low in structure. This finding suggests that the effect of turnover on product development teams will depend on how they are structured.

Argote et al. (1995) found that turnover had a reduced impact on complex tasks in comparison to its effect on simple tasks. They explain this finding by observing that groups working on complex tasks produced more innovations, which may make the previous knowledge obsolete. Thus, the departure of members may not be costly because much of their knowledge may no longer be relevant. This finding suggests that the effects of turnover on development teams are likely to depend not only on their structure but also on the nature of the project they are working on. The cost of losing a team member may be offset by the benefits of bringing in members with new ideas (cf. Virany, Tushman, & Romanelli, 1992).

Another consequence of turnover is that individuals who leave a development team can serve as a means for transferring knowledge to other development teams. Recent research on transfer of learning suggests that individuals who have worked in groups can learn problem-solving strategies that affect their subsequent performance (Olivera & Straus, 1997; Stasson, Kameda, Parks, Zimmerman, & Davis, 1991). This finding suggests that individuals who have worked in development teams are likely to learn development strategies that can be used in other projects. We further discuss transfer of knowledge in the external relations section.

Documents. The documents generated during the development of a product capture a great amount of knowledge about the product and its development process. Development schedules, designs and CAD files, technical reports, memorandums, and press releases all serve to document the history of a product.

Messages sent through electronic means among team members also capture knowledge about the development process. This communication can take the form of electronic mail and discussion databases or newsgroups where individuals can post questions, replies, or announcements (e.g., Constant, Sproull, & Kiesler, 1996; Finholt, in press; Orlikowski, Yates, Okamura, & Fujimoto, 1995). Electronic mail records are usually accessible only to those involved in the communication but discussion databases can be accessible to all team members or people outside the team.

COMPCO provides such communication systems for development teams, and they were used by the XC team primarily to coordinate the efforts of the various subsystem teams. The internal electronic network was also heavily used to transfer design files. Databases for frequently asked questions were also available but rarely used.

Electronic networks can be a powerful means for capturing the development process, but there are several challenges for making them effective. These systems are rarely designed with the explicit purpose of supporting the specific tasks these teams perform (Ancona & Caldwell, 1990). Also, organizations rarely provide incentives for contributing to knowledge databases. Individuals who contribute to these systems are often motivated because they find satisfaction in doing so or because they appreciate being recognized as experts by their peers (Constant et al., 1996; Orlikowski, 1996). Finally, the complex and fast-paced nature of product development may be a strong barrier to capturing knowledge about why and how critical decisions were made. Developers rarely take the time to document these subtle, but critical, aspects of the development process (cf. Barkan, 1992).

Structure. Knowledge about a product is also captured in the processes and patterns of interactions that emerge during and as a consequence of the development process. Several parts of the organization can be affected as a result of the development team's innovations, coordination, negotiation, and decision making. For example, the interactions between manufacturing and development departments will be affected by the production of a new product. These interactions may be guided by the existing organizational structure or modified to fit particular needs of a product. The interactions between departments capture knowledge about the development process and product itself.

The concept of architectural knowledge (Henderson, 1992; Henderson & Clark, 1990) captures the idea that products reflect aspects of the organizational structure and vice-versa. Architectural knowledge is embedded in the way the firm is organized. It refers to the ways in which components are linked and integrated and is therefore reflected in and reflects how different departments in the organization communicate, filter information, and make decisions. Similarly, architectural innovation refers to making changes in the architecture of a product or to the relationship between its components. This type of innovation requires changes in communication, information filtering, and problem-solving strategies in the organization.

The patterns of interaction among team members are also likely to be affected by the team's activities. In particular, a team's transactive memory, or knowledge about who is good at doing what (Wegner, 1986), will change as a consequence of working together in a development project. Recent research shows that transactive memory systems are likely to develop in work groups. Transactive memory involves developing an understanding of what knowledge others possess that allows group members to access a wider pool of information than each possesses individually. Groups of individuals who have a history of working together exhibit greater role differentiation, trust, and better coordination than groups formed of individuals who had not worked together before (Liang et al., 1995; Moreland, Argote, & Krishnan, 1996).

Product development teams are likely to develop transactive memory systems. Team members can learn about each others' skills and experience as a result of working together. We would expect teams where members have more opportunities to interact, such as autonomous or heavyweight teams, to be more likely to develop a strong transactive memory than teams with less opportunities to interact. Similarly, being physically colocated would aid in the development of transactive memory.

Information technology can be an alternative to interaction for acquiring knowledge about who in the organization is good at doing what. Databases of individuals' skills profiles and electronic discussion groups can serve to identify the areas of expertise of people in the organization. Moreland, in chapter 1 of this volume, describes systems that are currently being used in organizations to document the expertise of their members.

Products. Products can be viewed as a collection of ideas and solutions to design concepts. A great amount of knowledge generated during the development of a new product is embedded in the product itself (Nonaka & Takeuchi, 1995). The final product is evidence of the decisions and innovations made by the development team as well as the technologies used to produce it. The product can also reflect assumptions about its intended use and the concept and values behind its design. The practice of reverse engineering products is evidence of the vast amount of knowledge that is embedded in them.

Sutton and Hargadon (1996) described how existing products are used as sources of ideas in brainstorming sessions at a product development firm. These objects not only provide ideas that can be creatively recombined in new products but also support the organization's memory by storing the ideas of previously designed products.

Products contain knowledge in their components, architecture, physical appearance, functions, and so on. All these factors reflect solutions to design problems. How accessible this knowledge is to team members or others in the organization will likely depend on several factors, including the complexity of the product and the prior knowledge of the individual who is trying to access the knowledge (cf. Cohen & Levinthal, 1990).

It is likely, however, that a large portion of knowledge about the development process, such as the logic behind some of the design choices, will not be accessible from the product itself. As mentioned earlier, much of this knowledge is likely to remain in the heads of the development team members. Members of the XC mentioned that they get frequent phone calls and messages from other designers in the firm asking questions about some of the product's features. Although the product does not contain all this knowledge, it does serve as a signal to members in the design community about the existence and, to a certain extent, the location of this expertise in the firm.

LEARNING

New product development projects provide an opportunity for organizational learning (Bowen, Clark, Holloway, & Wheelwright, 1994; Leonard-Barton, 1992; McKee, 1992; Nonaka & Takeuchi, 1995). The innovation that results from the development process can strengthen the capabilities of the development team and the organization. However, learning from product development experience is usually difficult for organizations. Managers often fail to recognize that the capabilities that result from a product's development may be as important as the product itself. Postmortem meetings often focus on sales and lead time as key indicators of a project's success while de-emphasizing other capabilities that may have resulted from the development process. Furthermore, as mentioned earlier, it is very hard to capture the complex knowledge generated in the development process.

Several researchers have pointed out that learning from experience is, in general, difficult for organizations (e.g., Argyris, 1993; Levinthal & March, 1993; Levitt & March, 1988). Superstitious learning, overlooking failures, giving privilege to the short over the long run, and lacking a systemic view of issues are some of the common errors in interpreting experience.

The XC case is useful for illustrating the difficulties an organization or development team can have in learning from its experience. Although the XC received awards and general praise from customers and the engineering community, sales were disappointing. The project was evaluated as being a technical success and a commercial failure. Management was able to recognize that low sales could be attributed to its high initial price and inadequate marketing. In spite of this recognition, the company decided to move away from designing products with attributes that had made the XC unique. For example, team members mentioned that it would be very hard to sell management the idea of developing another computer with certain features the XC had. A product planner commented that although other engineers recognized the XC was a machine ahead of its time, they would want to stay away from following in its footsteps.

A critical aspect in the evaluation of a product development project is considering multiple performance criteria. As mentioned earlier, projects are evaluated on a number of dimensions, including budget adherence, technical innovations, market share, sales, and so on. Often times, doing well in some of these dimensions compromises the results in others. A challenge for organizations is to understand the relationships between these dimensions in their assessments of lessons learned from a development effort.

EXTERNAL RELATIONS

New product development teams are embedded in larger social systems. How the teams manage relationships with their external environment, especially their customers, and how knowledge is transferred to and from the organizational context are the subjects of this section.

COMMUNICATION WITH USERS

A strong market orientation, which entails close and effective interaction between innovators and customers, can be a key driver of product performance (Cooper, 1994). There are two reasons why user involvement can lead to successful products. First, the product's quality may be improved by incorporating users' knowledge of needs and preferences (Urban & von Hippel, 1988; von Hippel, 1988). Von Hippel (1988) identified a number of cases in which innovations were developed by users and later adopted by manufacturers. Second, users may be more receptive to a product if they contributed to its design (Leonard-Barton, 1993). An example of successful customer involvement in product development is the case of Hewlett Packard's DeskJet printer project. During this project, marketing representatives and, later, design engineers conducted studies in shopping malls and identified and implemented several valuable suggestions made by potential customers (Leonard-Barton et al., 1994).

However, in spite of the apparent advantages of customer involvement, there is mixed evidence about its benefits (Ives & Olson, 1984). The relationship between user involvement and product success or user satisfaction may not be linear (Leonard-Barton, 1993). Extensive user involvement may actually be detrimental in some development projects (Datar et al., 1996).

The level and timing of involvement may be important determinants of its impact. The XC case is a useful illustration of how customer involvement can have both positive and negative effects.

The development of the XC computer was strongly driven by customers. The product planners interacted continuously with over 100 potential customers both in the United States and Europe. At one of COMPCO's facilities, one of the product planners met two or three times a week with customers and got their input regarding features the computer should have. Features like silent operation, the use of PCMCIA technology, and the use of a flat, high-tech looking LCD monitor were all incorporated in the XC because customers were interested in them.

Interacting with customers was critical in identifying aspects of the XC that designers needed to address to have a successful product. An example of the benefits of interacting with customers is the inclusion of a dormant state for the computer's hard drive and, subsequently, the use of a small light to indicate that the computer is turned on. A customer pointed out to a product planner that there seemed to be something wrong with the computer's hard drive because it was making a loud noise. The drive, however, was not defective and the sound it emitted was the regular sound that most hard drives emit when operating. In most machines, the noise of the hard drive is masked by the noise of the fan. The XC did not use a fan and, although the noise level was consequently lower than other machines, the sound of the hard drive became noticeable, giving the impression of malfunction. To solve this problem, the XC incorporated a hard drive management system that set it to a dormant state when not in use. The hard drive did not emit noise when in dormant state. A problem that resulted from this change was that when the hard drive entered the dormant state, users could not tell whether the computer was on or off. This problem was due not only to the fact that the machine was silent but also to the fact that the power management system made the screen dim when in dormant state. Designers decided to include a small light on the front panel of the computer to indicate whether the machine was on or off. These two innovations, which had not been originally conceived by the designers, contributed to the users' satisfaction with the product.

Relying on user involvement can also have negative consequences for a product development effort. Trying to incorporate the requirements of users can slow and complicate the development process. Making continuous changes to a design takes time, requires coordination, and can result in high costs. Once the development process has started, changes to the product's definition should be carefully managed (Bacon et al., 1994). These changes can be dysfunctional not only because they can cause dissatisfaction and stress for the developers but also because they increase costs of coordination and, potentially, production.

TRANSFER OF KNOWLEDGE

Through their external activities, product development teams can transfer knowledge to and from other parts of the organization. Transfer of knowledge is an important component of organizational learning and has recently received attention in the literature. Recent research has found evidence for transfer of knowledge across shifts in a manufacturing facility (Epple, Argote, & Murphy, 1996), across pizza stores in the same franchise (Darr et al., 1995), and across units of hotel chains (Ingram & Baum, 1997). These studies have also uncovered some of the mechanisms through which knowledge has been transferred. Argote and Darr (in press), for example, found that embedding knowledge in structures and production technology facilitated transfer of innovations between pizza stores.

There are several means by which existing organizational knowledge can transfer into the development team and, conversely, knowledge generated by the team can transfer to the organization. First, products and their components serve as knowledge carriers. Products serve to preserve knowledge and to make this knowledge available to others in the organization (e.g., Sutton & Hargadon, 1996). The XC, for example, benefitted from the firm's experience by incorporating components that had been developed for other products. Similarly, other developers at COMPCO have used, in new products, features that were developed for the XC, such as the power management system.

A second means to transfer product knowledge is through internal publications. COMPCO, like other large organizations, generates periodical publications and technical reports that document the development of new technologies. These publications are distributed throughout the firm. An internal newsletter at COMPCO, for example, published a report about the development of the XC. Some of the innovative features of the XC were also documented in technical reports.

Individuals are also a means for transferring knowledge. Team members bring their own experience to the project and can subsequently transfer their knowledge to other projects. The senior planners in the XC development team, for example, brought to the XC project their experience with low power and small mechanical systems. This knowledge was critical in the development of the XC. Similarly, knowledge generated during the development of the XC can transfer through the team members to other projects at COMPCO.

Finally, the organization's structure and routines can serve to transfer knowledge. We have discussed the relationship between product characteristics and structure and argued that a product's architecture may reflect the organization's structure and vice-versa (Henderson & Clark, 1990). Development projects that cause changes to the organization's structure or routines are likely to affect projects that operate over this structure in the future. Argote and Darr (in press) and Darr et al. (1995), for example, illustrated how production innovations generated at pizza stores were embedded in routines that later transferred to other stores.

CONCLUSION

Product development is central to an organization's effectiveness. How product development teams operate is critical for the successful development of new products. In this chapter we presented a framework for analyzing product development team processes and used the case of the development of a personal computer to illustrate the importance of these processes. The CORE framework has several advantages for analyzing this type of work group. First, it considers processes that groups engage in when operating in an organizational context. Understanding product teams requires analyzing how the organization affects and is affected by their functioning and performance. Processes related to the acquisition of resources, communication across groups, and knowledge transfer are important for new product development and are strongly tied to the organizational context. These processes are brought to the fore by considering the external relations processes of the CORE framework.

Second, the CORE framework highlights the relevance of learning processes in product development. Learning and knowledge-embedding processes are critical in the development of an organization's core capabilities. Other researchers have acknowledged that the knowledge generated by a product development project is of great importance to the firm (e.g. Bowen et al., 1994). Our framework identifies specific mechanisms through which this knowledge is embedded and transferred in the organization. By explicitly considering the reconstruction processes specified in the CORE framework, one arrives at a deeper understanding of the learning and knowledge-embedding aspects of new product development.

The CORE framework helped us to identify interesting tensions or trade-offs that need to be managed effectively in the product development process. These tensions are suggested by current findings. Further research, however, is needed to understand them more deeply. One tension is between diversity and consensus. Product development teams require diverse membership to capture all the skills, departmental affiliations, and functional backgrounds that are needed to create a new product. Yet the teams also require sharing knowledge and developing common understandings about product characteristics and features. How teams manage the tension between constructing themselves of diverse members and operating so as to achieve consensus is an important question that would benefit from future research.

Another tension is between planning in advance and learning by doing as the team performs. There are benefits to planning. But in fast-paced environments, plans may be inadequate or even harmful. Taking action, learning from the effect of the actions, and modifying the team accordingly will be more adapted to the context and likely more effective in rapidly changing contexts. How teams manage the tension between planning in advance and learning as they perform and the conditions under which they should favor one over the other is an interesting topic for future research.

Another interesting tension suggested by the CORE analysis that would benefit from future research is the trade-off between promoting learning at the level of the team versus promoting learning at the level of the organization by transferring knowledge across teams. Providing new product development teams with autonomy will enhance their internal processes but may make it difficult for them to learn from and transfer knowledge to external teams. When is it most beneficial to emphasize the team's internal processes and when is it appropriate to emphasize their external relations with other groups? This is an important question that we believe is worthy of future research.

The development of the XC is useful to illustrate how sociocognitive processes can have a strong impact on the development of a new product. This case highlights, for example, the importance of developing a shared understanding of the product's concept. Not having this shared understanding resulted in the development and production of a power supply that was inconsistent with the overall product concept. The XC case also illustrates how different thought worlds can be a barrier to communication and innovation. Manufacturing's resistance to produce a machine without a fan shows how difficult it can be for product developers to implement their innovations in new products.

Understanding the performance of product development teams is challenging. Given the importance of product development in organizations, it is critical to learn how these teams work and how their actions relate to various criteria of success. Existing research suggests that the relationship between product development processes and success outcomes is complex. In this chapter, we have derived some conclusions based on our own observations of a product development project and on studies reported by other researchers. Clearly, further research is needed to understand how product development team activities affect the multiple criteria that reflect the success of a development project.

NOTES

1. The names of product and company were altered to preserve their anonymity.
2. In mid-1992, the EPA announced an initiative to encourage manufacturers to design low-power personal computers. The goal of the Energy Star program was the development of

computers and peripherals that enter a low-power state (of 30W or less, which is a large reduction compared to the 300W average power consumption of regular computers) when the unit is inactive.

3. Note that the product was released in the early 1990s.
4. PCMCIAs (Personal Computer Memory Card International Association) are credit-card-size devices that contain software or data. Originally introduced for laptop computers, these cards can be thought of as a portable hard disk. They can be removed from one computer and inserted into another.

ACKNOWLEDGMENT

This research was supported by Grant III-9319731 from the National Science Foundation.

REFERENCES

Allen, T. J. (1977). *Managing the flow of technology: Technology transfer and the dissemination of technological information within the R&D organization.* Cambridge, MA: MIT Press.

Ancona, D. G. (1990). Outward bound: Strategies for team survival in an organization. *Academy of Management Journal, 33,* 334–365.

Ancona, D. G., & Caldwell, D. F. (1990). Information technology and work groups: The case of new product teams. In J. Galegher, R. E. Kraut, & C. Egido (Eds.), *Intellectual teamwork: Social and technological foundations of cooperative work* (pp. 173–190). Hillsdale, NJ: Lawrence Erlbaum Associates.

Ancona, D. G., & Caldwell, D. F. (1992a). Bridging the boundary: External activity and performance in organizational teams. *Administrative Science Quarterly, 37,* 634–665.

Ancona, D. G., & Caldwell, D. F. (1992b). Cross-functional teams: Blessing or curse for new product development? In T. A. Kochan & M. Useem (Eds.), *Transforming organizations* (pp. 154–166). New York: Oxford University Press.

Argote, L. (1989). Agreement about norms and work unit effectiveness: Evidence from the field. *Basic and Applied Social Psychology, 10,* 131–140.

Argote, L., & Darr, E. (in press). Repositories of knowledge in franchise organizations: Individual, structural and technological. In G. Dosi, R. Nelson, & S. Winter (Eds.), *Nature and dynamics of organizational capabilities.*

Argote, L., & Epple, D. (1990). Learning curves in manufacturing. *Science, 247,* 920–924.

Argote, L., Gruenfeld, D., & Naquin, C. (in press). Group learning in organizations. In M. E. Turner (Ed.), *Groups at work: Advances in theory and research.* Mahwah, NJ: Lawrence Erlbaum Associates.

Argote, L., Insko, C. A., Yovetich, N., & Romero, A. A. (1995). Group learning curves: The effects of turnover and task complexity on group performance. *Journal of Applied Social Psychology, 25,* 512–529.

Argote, L., & McGrath, J. E. (1993). Group processes in organizations: Continuity and change. *International Review of Industrial and Organizational Psychology, 8,* 333–389.

Argyris, C. (1993). *On organizational learning.* Oxford, England: Blackwell Business.

Bacon, G., Beckman, S., Mowery, D., & Wilson, E. (1994). Managing product definition in high-technology industries: A pilot study. *California Management Review, 36*(3), 32–56.

Barkan, P. (1992). Productivity in the process of product development: An engineering perspective. In G. I. Susman (Ed.), *Integrating design and manufacturing for competitive advantage* (pp. 56–68). New York: Oxford University Press.

Bowen, H. K., Clark, K. B., Holloway, C. H., & Wheelwright, S. C. (1994). Development projects: The engine of renewal. *Harvard Business Review, 72*(5), 110–120.

Brown, J. S., & Duguid, P. (1991). Organizational learning and communities of practice: Toward a unified view of working, learning, and innovation. *Organization Science, 2,* 40–57.

Brown, S. L., & Eisenhardt, K. M. (1995). Product development: Past research, present findings, and future directions. *Academy of Management Review, 20,* 343–378.

Carley, K. (1992). Organizational learning and personnel turnover. *Organization Science, 3,* 20–46.

Clark, K. B., & Fujimoto, T. (1991). *Product development performance: Strategy, organization, and management in the world auto industry.* Cambridge: Harvard Business School Press.

Clark, K. B., & Wheelwright, S. C. (1992). Organizing and leading "heavyweight" development teams. *California Management Review, 34* (3), 9–28.

Cohen, W. M., & Levinthal, D. A. (1990). Absorptive capacity: A new perspective on learning and innovation. *Administrative Science Quarterly, 35,* 128–152.

Constant, D., Sproull, L., & Kiesler, S. (1996). The kindness of strangers: The usefulness of weak ties for technical advice. *Organization Science, 7,* 119–135.

Cooper, R. G. (1994). New products: The factors that drive success. *International Marketing Review, 11*(1), 60–76.

Darr, E., Argote, L., & Epple, D. (1995). The acquisition, transfer and depreciation of knowledge in service organizations: Productivity in franchises. *Management Science, 41,* 1750–1762.

Datar, S., Jordan, C., Kekre, S., Rajiv, S., & Srinivasan, K. (1996). New product development structures: The effect of customer overload on post-concept time to market. *Journal of Product Innovation Management, 13,* 325–333.

DeSanctis, G., & Poole, M. S. (1994). Capturing the complexity in advanced technology use: Adaptive structuration theory. *Organization Science, 5,* 121–147.

Devadas, R., & Argote, L. (1995, May). *Collective learning and forgetting: The effects of turnover and group structure.* Paper presented at the Midwestern Academy of Management Meetings, Chicago.

Dougherty, D. (1992). Interpretive barriers to successful product innovations in large firms. *Organization Science, 3,* 179–202.

Dougherty, D., & Heller, T. (1994). The illegitimacy of successful product innovation in established firms. *Organization Science, 5,* 200–218.

Eisenhardt, K. M. (1989). Building theories from case study research. *Academy of Management Review, 14,* 532–550.

Eisenhardt, K. M., & Tabrizi, B. N. (1995). Accelerating adaptive processes: Product innovation in the global computer industry. *Administrative Science Quarterly, 40,* 84–110.

Engeström, Y., Brown, K., Engeström, R., & Koistinen, K. (1990). Organizational forgetting: An activity-theoretical perspective. In D. Middleton & D. Edwards (Eds.), *Collective remembering* (pp. 139–168). London, Newbury Park, CA: Sage.

Epple, D., Argote, L., & Murphy, K. (1996). An empirical investigation of the micro structure of knowledge acquisition and transfer through learning by doing. *Operations Research, 44,* 77–86.

Finholt, T. A. (in press). Outsiders on the inside: Sharing know-how through computer message archives. *Management Information Systems Quarterly.*

Fiol, C. M. (1994). Consensus, diversity, and learning in organizations. *Organization Science, 5,* 403–420.

Gruenfeld, D. H., & Hollingshead, A. B. (1993). Sociocognition in work groups: The evolution of group integrative complexity and its relation to small group performance. *Small Group Research, 24,* 383–405.

Gupta, A. K., & Wilemon, D. L. (1990). Accelerating the development of technology-based new products. *California Management Review, 32,* 24–44.

Hackman, J. R., & Morris, C. G. (1975). Group tasks, group interaction processes and group performance effectiveness: A review and proposed integration. In L. Berkowitz (Ed.), *Advances in Experimental Social Psychology* (Vol. 8, pp. 44–99). New York: Academic Press.

Hargadon, A., & Sutton, R. I. (1997). Technology brokering and innovation: Evidence from a product design firm. *Administrative Science Quarterly, 42,* 716–749.

Henderson, R. M. (1992). Technological change and the management of architectural knowledge. In T. A. Kochan & M. Useem (Eds.), *Transforming organizations* (pp. 119–131). New York: Oxford University Press.

Henderson, R. M., & Clark, K. B. (1990). Architectural innovation: The reconfiguration of existing product technology and the failure of established firms. *Administrative Science Quarterly, 35,* 9–30.

Ingram, P., & Baum, J. A. C. (1997). Chain affiliation and the failure of Manhattan hotels, 1898–1980. *Administrative Science Quarterly, 42,* 68–102.

Ives, B., & Olson, M. H. (1984). User involvement and MIS success: A review of the research. *Management Science, 30,* 586–603.

Katz, R., & Tushman, M. L. (1981). An investigation into the managerial roles and career paths of gatekeepers and project supervisors in a major R&D facility. *R&D Management, 11,* 103–110.

Larson, J. R., Jr., Christensen, C., Abbott, A. S., & Franz, T. M. (1996). Diagnosing groups: Charting the flow of information in medical decision-making teams. *Journal of Personality and Social Psychology, 71,* 315–330.

Leonard-Barton, D. (1992). Core capabilities and core rigidities: A paradox in managing new product development. *Strategic Management Journal, 13,* 111–125.

Leonard-Barton, D. (1993). Developer-user interaction and user satisfaction in internal technology transfer. *Academy of Management Journal, 36,* 1125–1139.

Leonard-Barton, D. (1995). *Wellsprings of knowledge: Building and sustaining the sources of innovation.* Cambridge, MA: Harvard Business School Press.

Leonard-Barton, D., Bowen, H. K., Clark, K. B., Holloway, C. H., & Wheelwright, S. C. (1994). How to integrate work and deepen expertise. *Harvard Business Review, 72*(5), 121–130.

Levine, J. M., & Moreland, R. L. (1991). Culture and socialization in work groups. In L. B. Resnik, J. M. Levine, & S. D. Teasley (Eds.), *Perspectives on socially shared cognition* (pp. 257–279). Washington, DC: American Psychological Association.

Levinthal, D. A., & March, J. G. (1993). The myopia of learning. *Strategic Management Journal, 14,* 95–112.

Levitt, B., & March, J. G. (1988). Organizational learning. *Annual Review of Sociology, 14,* 319–340.

Liang, D. W., Moreland, R., & Argote, L. (1995). Group versus individual training and group performance: The mediating role of transactive memory. *Personality and Social Psychology Bulletin, 21,* 384–393.

McGrath, J. E. (1984). *Groups: Interaction and performance.* Englewood Cliffs, NJ: Prentice-Hall.

McGrath, J. E. (1991). Time, interaction and performance (TIP): A theory of small groups. *Small Group Research, 22,* 147–174.

McKee, D. (1992). An organizational learning approach to product innovation. *Journal of Product Innovation Management, 9,* 232–245.

Moreland, R., Argote, L., & Krishnan, R. (1996). Socially shared cognition at work: Transactive memory and group performance. In J. L. Nye & A. M. Brower (Eds.), *What's so social about social cognition? Social cognition research in small groups* (pp. 57–84). Newbury Park, CA: Sage.

Moreland, R., Argote, L., & Krishnan, R. (1998). Training people to work in groups. In R. S. Tindale, L. Heath, J. Edwards, E. J. Posavac, F. B. Bryant, Y. Suarez-Balcazar, E. Henderson-King, & J. Myers (Eds.), *Theory and research on small groups* (pp. 37–60). New York: Plenum.

Moreland, R. L. (1987). The formation of small groups. In C. Hendrick (Ed.), *Review of Personality and Social Psychology* (pp. 80–110). Newbury Park, CA: Sage.

Nonaka, I. (1994). A dynamic theory of organizational knowledge creation. *Organization Science, 5,* 14–37.

Nonaka, I., & Takeuchi, H. (1995). *The knowledge-creating company: How Japanese companies create the dynamics of innovation.* New York: Oxford University Press.

Olivera, F., & Straus, S. G. (1997, April). *Group-to-individual transfer of learning: Cognitive and social factors.* Paper presented at meeting of the Society for Industrial and Organizational Psychology, St. Louis, MO.

Orlikowski, W. J. (1996). Improvising organizational transformation over time: A situated change perspective. *Information Systems Research, 7,* 63–92.

Orlikowski, W. J., Yates, J., Okamura, K., & Fujimoto, M. (1995). Shaping electronic communication: The metastructuring of technology in the context of use. *Organization Science, 6,* 423–444.

Polanyi, M. (1966). *The tacit dimension.* London: Routledge & Kegan Paul.

Polley, D., & Van de Ven, A. H. (1996). Learning by discovering during innovation development. *International Journal of Technology Management, 11,* 871–882.

Simon, H. A. (1991). Bounded rationality and organizational learning. *Organization Science, 2,* 125–134.

Stasson, M. F., Kameda, T., Parks, C. D., Zimmerman, S. K., & Davis, J. H. (1991). Effects of assigned group consensus requirements on group problem solving and group member's learning. *Social Psychology Quarterly, 54,* 25–35.

Sutton, R. I., & Hargadon, A. (1996). Brainstorming groups in context: Effectiveness in a product design firm. *Administrative Science Quarterly, 41,* 685–718.

Urban, G. L., & von Hippel, E. (1988). Lead user analyses for the development of new industrial products. *Management Science, 34,* 569–582.

Van de Ven, A. H., & Polley, D. (1992). Learning while innovating. *Organization Science, 3,* 92–116.

Virany, B., Tushman, M. L., & Romanelli, E. (1992). Executive succession and organization outcomes in turbulent environments: An organizational learning approach. *Organization Science, 3,* 72–91.

von Hippel, E. (1988). *The sources of innovation.* New York: Oxford University Press.

Walsh, J. P., & Ungson, G. R. (1991). Organizational memory. *Academy of Management Review, 16,* 57–90.

Wegner, D. M. (1986). Transactive memory: A contemporary analysis of the group mind. In B. Mullen & G. R. Goethals (Eds.), *Theories of group behavior* (pp. 185–208). New York: Springer-Verlag.

Weingart, L. R. (1992). Impact of group goals, task component complexity, effort, and planning on group performance. *Journal of Applied Psychology, 77,* 682–693.

Yin, R. (1994). *Case study research* (3rd ed.). Beverly Hills, CA: Sage.

14

Themes and Variations in *Shared Cognition in Organizations*

Terry L. Boles
University of Iowa

The preceding chapters reflect the variety of themes and perspectives that emerge when multidisciplinary scholars examine the concept of shared knowledge. Indeed, one's interpretation of the concept is likely to be discipline-specific. Those with a social cognitive perspective, for example, may focus on how individuals' perceptions and beliefs about what knowledge is shared with group members in turn affects their own information processing and resultant beliefs. Social psychologists, on the other hand, may conceptualize shared knowledge in terms of social norms and focus on their effects on behavior, or they may examine how one's majority or minority status and position in the social structure affects what information is shared or attended to. Organizational psychologists may explore shared knowledge as a function of the power structures inherent in organizations and examine how these structures lead to differences in status among members and affect beliefs about who can be trusted with knowledge. Industrial/Organizational psychologists may care about shared knowledge because to the extent that interdependent workers understand "who knows what," organizational performance is likely to be enhanced. Sociologists tend to take a network systems approach and examine, for example, the value that accrues to individuals who strategically position themselves at the intersection of multiple networks and, thus, benefit from sharing multiple knowledge structures. Ethicists may be more concerned with organizational knowledge that is not shared, especially when society may suffer from this concealment. Thus, the multidisciplinary contributions to this volume ensure the reader is exposed to rich and multiple perspectives on shared knowledge in organizations.

To one given the opportunity to summarize the chapters in this volume, this multiplicity provides a considerable challenge. There are many ways to slice this multifaceted pie. My approach will be to identify the major emergent themes and orientations the authors have taken on the topic of shared knowledge. I have classified these as: (a) the differences in the levels of analysis of shared knowledge; (b) the effect of norms as shared knowledge; (c) the effect of status and trust on knowledge sharing; (d) third parties and social validation—the pros of cons of creating shared reality; (e) the downside of not sharing knowledge; and (f) a consideration of the extent to which the cognitive processes related to shared knowledge are automatic or motivated.

The organization of this chapter follows these themes and highlights specific contributions to the various perspectives. I conclude with thoughts about what questions remain as regards shared knowledge in organizations and consider areas ripe for future research.

LEVELS OF ANALYSIS IN SHARED KNOWLEDGE

How does one study and measure shared knowledge? One approach is to study individuals and how differences in their moods, cognitions, and belief systems affect the nature of the knowledge they share. Another route is to examine the relationship between individuals and the primary groups to which they belong and investigate how that relationship affects knowledge sharing. A third avenue is to examine the effects of shared knowledge on the group or organization. Thus, the analysis of shared knowledge can be at the micro, meso, or macro levels, and all are present in the current volume.

Individual Level of Analysis

Jost, Kruglanski, and Simon (chap. 5, this volume) examine individual differences in cognitive style and study in particular the "need for cognitive closure." In his theory of lay epistemics, Kruglanski (1989) suggested individuals differ in their motivation to seek knowledge that is secure and stable. Some tend to be open to new and novel information and others prefer to preserve the status quo. Those high on the need for closure have a tendency to "seize and freeze" on existing knowledge structures and by doing so, they contribute to the stability of existing social structures (the status quo; Kruglanski & Webster, 1996). Such adherence to the status quo may not always be a good thing—especially if individuals with this tendency are in organizations in the process of change. When one adheres to knowledge structures which advocate applying tried-and-true solutions to new organizational challenges, the organization and those within it may suffer.

Although Webster and Kruglanski (1994) developed an individual difference measure that captures the need for cognitive closure, Jost et al. (chap. 5, this volume) demonstrate that this need can also be situationally induced. In their experiments, increasing levels of environmental noise were found to increase individuals' need for closure, which in turn increased their reliance on chronically accessible ideological attitudes. Jost et al. suggest any factor that increases cognitive and motivational needs to make up one's mind quickly may tend to shorten informational searches and, thus, strengthen normative and ideological adherence to the status quo. If one extrapolates these research findings to organizational settings where environmental noise and cognitive pressures are normative, one might speculate that individuals in such organizations would be less likely to embrace change and be resistant to novel problem-solving approaches. Thus, situations that heighten the need for closure tend to preserve the status quo and, as such, might inhibit organizational learning.

In a theoretical piece that cites prior empirical work on negotiation, Thompson, Nadler, and Kim (chap. 7, this volume) consider the role negotiator affect has on negotiator cognition and effectiveness. Negotiators in positive moods are found to be more confident, trusting, and more likely to use collaborative strategies. They also have an increased expectation of cooperation by their negotiation counterparts. Further, positive-mood negotiators achieve better individual and better joint outcomes than do neutral or negative-mood negotiators (see Carnevale & Isen, 1986; Kramer, Newton, & Pommerenke, 1993). These findings may lead one to speculate that the reason positive-affect negotiators achieve better outcomes may be because they are more willing to share knowledge (information) with their counterparts and by doing so induce their counterparts to do the same. Its possible shared knowledge may be an important moderator of the relationship between negotiator mood and outcome. Because most negotiation research tends to examine negotiation outcomes as the primary dependent variable rather than the information exchange process, this question awaits empirical validation.

Most of the work in this volume investigates the effects of shared knowledge in terms of its interaction between individuals and the groups to which they belong. Although individual cognitive processes are considered, these are more often examined in the context of how group membership interacts with these cognitive processes. It is to this intersection between the individual and group level of analysis that we now turn.

Intersection of Individual and Group Level of Analysis

This volume's contributions by Burt (chap. 10), Gruenfeld and Fan (chap. 11), Higgins (chap. 2), Stasser (chap. 3), Tetlock (chap. 6), and Thompson et al. (chap. 7) describe theoretical and empirical work that explores the interaction between individuals and the groups with whom they share knowledge. They further consider the consequences, both to the individual and the group, of doing so.

In a longitudinal study of ongoing work groups, Gruenfeld and Fan (chap. 11, this volume) found that individuals who span the boundaries between groups (in their study, this was operationalized by requiring individuals to move from groups where they had been long-time members to groups in which they became minority members) demonstrate more integrative complexity in their cognitive style (a concept introduced by Tetlock, 1986) than do members who remain in the same group. These boundary-spanning individuals consequently have the capacity to benefit new groups with whom they interact by sharing their more differentiated thinking and insights. The groups in the Gruenfeld and Fan study did not, however, benefit from the integrative complexity that minority members brought to the group. Their findings imply that although individuals may receive cognitive benefits from the knowledge they accrue from multiple groups, groups themselves may not benefit from the knowledge these boundary-spanning individuals bring. This finding perhaps should not be overgeneralized, as the failure of individual knowledge to benefit group knowledge may have occurred because these boundary-spanners were not necessarily welcomed by the group. That is, their cross-group membership was experimentally imposed and possibly disrupted once-cohesive groups. One might ask (and study) whether groups who openly welcome boundary spanners would be more likely to benefit from the knowledge they share.

Burt (chap. 10, this volume) also examines how knowledge and strategic benefits accrue to individuals who position themselves at the intersections of multiple groups or social networks relative to those who are embedded in one strong network. The latter, Burt argues, are more likely to share in group knowledge that is potentially biased due to in-group cohesion (which Burt refers to as a form of "structural arthritis"). Those who share knowledge with multiple groups, on the other hand, are more likely to be exposed to variable interpretations of events and thus be more accurate in their judgments about the trustworthiness and validity of the information they receive. Burt suggests that not only do individuals benefit from the knowledge they attain from filling the structural holes between groups that are not otherwise connected, but groups themselves also benefit from the unique value-added information the individual brings.

Higgins and Tetlock (chaps. 2 and 6, this volume) examine the ways groups affect what individuals say and believe. Higgins asserts an individual's attitudes and beliefs are shaped by the audience these attitudes and beliefs are being presented to and finds this shaping is more likely to occur when the audience is perceived to be an in- rather than out-group. This finding is consistent with Burt's arguments (chap. 10, this volume) that cohesive groups narrow individual focus. Tetlock believes it is the level of accountability that individuals feel toward various constituents and groups that shapes individual behavior. He argues this accountability affects not only what people think but how they think. Thus, Burt, Higgins, and Tetlock appear to agree that cohesive in-groups, particularly those to which individuals feel accountable, affect individual attitudes and beliefs about reality and shape behavior toward those beliefs shared by the group. Because this shaping process often leads individuals to say what groups want to hear—or already believe—one can question what, if any, intellectual or cognitive benefits accrue to either the individual or the group when these processes occur. Still, there are likely to be psychological and emotional benefits associated with this process that provide both groups and individuals with a sense of validation and security.

At the interpersonal level of analysis, Thompson et al. (chap. 7, this volume) focus on the potential costs and benefits of shared emotion (which might be thought of as a form of shared knowledge). They suggest an emotional social-facilitation effect occurs that causes individuals to experience their own emotions more intensely when they are in the presence of others. Happiness, for example, is better shared than experienced alone. Further, they suggest that emotions may be contagious and this contagion is a result of several processes (mimicry, "catching," and emotional tuning). Like Higgins (chap. 2, this volume), who suggests that individuals do "audience tuning" to understand the beliefs and expectations of relevant others, Thompson et al. suggest that a form of "emotional tuning" occurs as part of the emotional contagion process. Obviously there will be costs associated with such contagion if the emotional germ being shared is negative— anger leading to tit-for-tat behavior, for example. Thompson et al. prefer to focus instead on the benefits of emotional contagion for both groups and individuals. They cite, as an example, the work of George (1990), who showed positive affect workgroups had fewer sick days than negative affect groups. At the individual level, Thompson et al. suggest an emotionally skilled negotiator should have more accurate perceptions of other parties (due to emotional tuning); be able to infect negotiation opponents in a positive way, and be able to use an emotional system with both opponents and teammates to their advantage. These assertions, although compelling, await empirical validation.

The theoretical and empirical work discussed to this point has examined the interactions between individual and groups in knowledge-sharing and has focused primarily on the effects such sharing has on individuals. We turn now to research that acknowledges the role of individual behavior and cognition but focuses primarily on group and organizational processes and outcomes as a function of knowledge sharing.

Group and Organizational Level of Analysis

A number of contributors to this volume (Stasser, chap. 3; Moreland, chap. 1; Levine & Moreland, chap. 12; Olivera & Argote, chap. 13) consider the consequences for group and organizational processes and outcomes when the knowledge individuals possess is or is not shared with others. In a number of studies, Stasser demonstrated that when individuals in decision-making groups each possess both unique (unshared) and common (shared) information, the common information is more likely to be discussed and recalled by group members. Part of this bias for sharing common, rather than unique, information can be accounted for by collective information sampling theory (see Stasser, Taylor, & Hanna, 1989; Stasser & Titus, 1987), which demonstrates there is a higher probability of sampling common information than unique information. It has been shown (Larson, Christensen, Abbott, & Franz, 1996) that when discussion is prolonged, unique information does eventually surface once common information is exhausted, but Stasser argues that pressures on the group (for early consensus, time pressures, etc.) often prevent them from exhausting common information. Thus, unique information never surfaces. The reason it matters is that in Stasser's paradigms, it is essential for unique information to be shared in order for optimal decisions to be made.

All is not lost, however, as some procedural interventions have been shown to reduce this sampling bias. When Hollingshead (1996) asked groups in a decision-making task to rank options rather than decide which option was best, group members were more likely to sample and discuss unique (unshared) information. Similarly, Stasser and Stewart (1992) showed when a decision is framed such that the task is to solve (find the one right answer), more unique information is shared than when it is framed as a judgment (evaluation) task. Also, Stewart and Stasser (1995) found that when individuals in a group are told some members are experts, the groups not only sample more information overall but sample much more unique information than when groups are not told that some individuals are experts. The term metaknowledge, coined by Larson & Christensen (1993), is used to describe the collective knowledge a group possesses about how task-relevant resources are distributed among members. Stasser argues that in order to pool unshared knowledge effectively, members have to possess not only the same, but also reasonably accurate, meta-knowledge.

The concept of metaknowledge is closely linked to Moreland's (chap. 1, this volume) construct of *transactive memory systems.* Moreland finds that individuals who are trained together on a production task perform better as a team than do individuals who are trained alone and then perform the task on a team with other individuals who also received individual training. In a series of studies, Moreland demonstrates it is not group training per se that leads to performance improvement but rather that individuals trained together develop transactive memory systems. These systems are the groups' shared understanding of what each person in the group knows and what unique skills each possess. Moreland finds that when a work group whose members share complex and accurate knowledge about one another's skills work together on a group task, they perform significantly better than do groups who do not have this shared knowledge. Although one might assume transactive memory is the result of individuals spending time together, communicating with one another, and observing one another in joint training, recent experiments by Moreland find that individuals trained alone who then receive accurate written feedback about the skills and knowledge of other potential group members perform just as well on team tasks as do groups who are trained together. Although there may be social benefits to team training, Moreland's findings imply that new team members can be brought on board and perform equally well as a team member as long as they receive the necessary knowledge beforehand about the skills and abilities of other team members. These findings have implications for the performance of teams whose members may be physically remote from one another. They suggest as long as each understands what the other knows and the group is able to capitalize on this knowledge, group performance will be enhanced.

Metaknowledge and transactional memory systems might be thought of as subcategories of a larger concept that Levine and Moreland (chap. 12, this volume) call shared mental models. In this theoretical chapter, Levine and Moreland propose that a critical task for organizational newcomers is to learn the shared mental models held by current members (who they refer to as oldtimers). They assert that such learning is an important part of acculturation into the organization and that it includes both a cognitive component (the knowledge that is shared with newcomers) and a behavioral component (learned customs, routines, rituals, and symbols). Levine and Moreland believe the socialization that occurs at the work group level has a greater impact on the development of shared mental models than does organizational socialization. They propose and discuss four factors that will determine whether or not newcomers who join intact groups will come to acquire the mental models held by the group. These include: *newcomer qualities* (how familiar they are with the group, how adaptable they are, how committed they are to the group); *newcomer tactics* (how they acquire information, whether they seek mentoring with oldtimers, and whether they collaborate with other newcomers); *oldtimer qualities* (do they desire and welcome new members, do they understand the mental models and are they able to communicate them to others, and how familiar are they with the newcomers); *oldtimer tactics* (initiations, socialization, feedback). Levine and Moreland further suggest that newcomers will be more likely to learn and share the group's mental models if they are carefully selected by the organization and if they receive specific training with intact teams. An implicit assumption of the value of shared mental models is that work groups who posses them will be less likely to experience conflict and more likely to be productive. These assumptions, although compelling, have to date received little empirical support.

Olivera and Argote (chap. 13, this volume) also examine shared knowledge at the organizational level. Specifically, they apply the CORE process model (Argote & McGrath, 1993) to analyze how organizational learning occurs in new product development. The CORE model is an acronym for Construction (the process by which groups come into being), Operations (the work the group does), Reconstruction (the ways in which groups collectively modify their work group experience), and External relations (the connection between the group with the larger environment). Olivera and Argote analyzed team process using the CORE model by interviewing cross-functional team members after the product was completed and (not very successfully) marketed. One thing they learned from this analysis was that although cross-functional teams increase diversity and ideas as regards product development, individual members, due to their specific knowledge and training, often inhabit different "thought worlds" that can be barriers to collective action. Valuable knowledge distributed among team members that could be usefully shared in product development is often not shared or not understood or valued when it is shared and thus, is lost. A tension exists between the diversity that cross-functional teams possess and their ability to achieve consensus about what is important in product development and how to pursue the task.

When examining how knowledge from product development is retained in organizations, Olivera and Argote again find that considerable knowledge is lost, often due to organizational structures that inhibit organizational learning. Many individuals may possess specific knowledge about aspects of the development process, but no one may possess it all. If individuals leave the organization, the knowledge often departs with them. Although organizational learning from product development can be captured with good documentation, Olivera and Argote suggest many subtle but critical aspects of information are exchanged in informal discussions or over e-mail and are not documented.

The research in this volume focusing on the effects of knowledge sharing at the group and organizational level suggests that organizational structures and norms need to be in place to facilitate the knowledge-sharing process. Moreover, organizations need to find ways to capture the metaknowledge that groups possess so that such information is retained at the organizational level and not lost when individuals exit the system.

NORMS AS SHARED KNOWLEDGE

Norms are perhaps the most striking example of shared knowledge in groups, organizations, communities, and cultures. Although norms are rarely documented in any formal way, practically any member of the constituencies named previously would, if asked, be able to articulate the norms of the groups to which they belong. The work of Tetlock and Cialdini, Bator, and Guadagno (chaps. 6 and 9, this volume) addresses the effect group norms have on individual knowledge and behavior.

In his meso-level accountability theory, Tetlock argues that the central function of individual judgment and choice is to protect one's social identity in the eyes of key constituencies. When considering possible response options, people act as intuitive politicians by assessing how justifiable certain responses may be given the institutional norms. Tetlock addresses situations under which individuals are likely to adopt the norms and cognitions of organizations and institutions, by considering identity-defining choices that arise in accountability dilemmas. His empirical work (Tetlock, 1997) suggests individuals are more likely to internalize organizational norms when there are economic necessities that require it, when the norms are perceived to be procedurally fair, and when the norms are attainable with available resources.

Tetlock's belief that accountability to institutional norms affects not only what people think but also how they think is a phenomenon not unlike Higgins' (chap. 2, this volume) audience-tuning principle. Higgins finds that communicators spontaneously tune their messages to suit what they know about their audience's knowledge and evaluation of the message topic. This audience turning in turn affects the communicators' own knowledge and evaluation of the topic. Thus, group norms and desires to be accepted by the group affect individual cognition and behavior.

Cialdini, Bator, and Guadagno (chap. 9, this volume) distinguish between two kinds of social norms: descriptive and injunctive. Descriptive norms develop from observable patterns of behavior in situations. Cialdini et al. find when descriptive norms are made particularly salient (when one piece of litter is placed in an otherwise clean environment, for example), individuals are more likely to follow normative behavior. Injunctive norms, on the other hand, are those that describe behaviors others approve or disapprove of in certain situations. In empirical studies (Cialdini, Kallgren, & Reno, 1991) that compared descriptive and injunctive norms (what is done versus what is approved), injunctive norms were found to be the stronger of the two in influencing behavior. Cialdini et al. suggest organizational climate encompasses the descriptive norms of organizations, whereas organizational culture is more likely to provide injunctive norm information. When one considers the two types of norms in light of Tetlock's (chap. 6, this volume) accountability theory, it appears that injunctive norms are more likely to be the ones that lead individuals to experience accountability dilemmas, which in turn leads them to engage in coping strategies to justify nonnormative behavior.

EFFECTS OF STATUS AND TRUST ON KNOWLEDGE SHARING

Several contributors to this volume (Cialdini et al., Higgins, and Gruenfeld & Fan) illuminate the ways in which an individual's status in the group or organization affects knowledge sharing and willingness to adapt to group norms. Others (particularly Kramer and Burt) examine the role trust plays in the willingness to share knowledge.

Status Effects on Knowledge Sharing

Higgins (chap. 2, this volume) finds the effects of audience tuning varies as a function of the audience's status and whether the communicator is high or low on the trait of authoritarianism. When communicators addressed an equal-status audience, both high and low authoritarian communicators tuned equally. When the audience had high status, those high on authoritarianism tuned more to the audience than did those low on authoritarianism. Thus, Higgins' work suggests the status of an audience or group with which an individual is communicating affects the messages the individual produces and, in turn, the individual's own evaluation of the topic. Moreover, this tuning effect is more pronounced when individuals have greater concerns with status (are high on authoritarianism).

Whereas Higgins examines effects of audience status on individual thoughts and behavior, Cialdini et al. (chap. 9, this volume) consider how status of the individual affects groups' willingness to allow deviation from group norms. Cialdini et al. find group norms are more likely to be adhered to when the norms are crystallized and intense and when the group is highly cohesive. Yet, even under these conditions, high-status group members are allowed more latitude in deviating from group norms than are lower status members (see e.g., Hackman, 1992).

Stasser (chap. 2, this volume) also highlights the effect status has on information sharing. Because unique, rather than common, information tends to be dismissed or undervalued in group discussion and decision making, Stasser believes individuals may be reluctant to share the unique information they possess unless they have some social standing in a group. Leaders and other high-status group members, on the other hand, can risk sharing unique information because, due to their status, they are less vulnerable to criticism. Larson et al. (1996) confirmed status difference in the willingness to discuss unique information. They found resident physicians, who were part of three-person groups that included an intern and a third-year medical student, were more likely to repeat and discuss information that was not held in common than were lower status group members.

One can conclude that status, both of groups themselves and of individuals in their relationship to the group, affects the extent to which individuals will adopt and be shaped by group norms and knowledge.

Trust and Knowledge Sharing

Kramer (chap. 8, this volume) conceptualizes groups and organizations as knowledge communities whose main goal is often the development and promulgation of collective knowledge. Both formal and informal mechanisms are assumed to facilitate the exchange of knowledge within knowledge communities and the success of these communities in accumulating shared knowledge depends largely on the cooperation of group members. For such cooperation to occur, collective trust must develop within the community. Kramer considers the barriers to the development of collective trust in knowledge communities as a type of social dilemma that he terms "trust dilemmas." When collective trust is high, individuals can share information with the community without risk; however, when collective trust is lacking, individuals may be suspicious of others and be unwilling to put themselves at risk by sharing valuable information with the community. Hence, when trust is low, collective paranoia develops and the knowledge community suffers.

Kramer examines the role individual cognitive processes play in the development of collective paranoia. His empirical work suggests that when concerns about trust are high, the more individuals will ruminate about others' motives and intentions and the greater will be their distrust and suspicion. Further, due to the time individuals spend ruminating, the more confident they will be in their judgments that others are untrustworthy. He suggests these processes occur because paying attention to interdependent others increases one's own perception of self-as-target. This heightened state of self-consciousness leads to biased interpretations of others' behavior as untrustworthy.

The picture for developing collective trust may not be as dim as it appears. Kramer suggests the cognitive processes that lead to distrust can go both ways. That is, if trust within the collective is already high, the rumination process could lead to heightened positive evaluations of others' behavior. Moreover, when trust is high, collective trust becomes institutionalized (at the collective level) and internalized (at the individual level) and the likelihood for suspicion and biased interpretation of other's behavior will be diminished. Lastly, Kramer suggests that the development of "collective discourse" within knowledge communities increases trust. Collective discourse is the language used when talking about and framing the nature of the relationships that exist in the knowledge community. Such language captures the mutual expectations and perceived obligations that exist between members of the community. To the extent that collective discourse embodies the positive and benign nature of the knowledge community, trust and cooperation will increase.

Burt (chap. 10, this volume) also agrees the anticipation of cooperation among others in a social network is essential for trust to develop. He uses Coleman's (1990) definition of trust as "committing to an exchange before knowing how the other person will behave" and argues trust is more likely to develop when individuals are embedded in a network of friends and acquaintances. Embeddedness leads to increased density in network connections. Burt hypothesizes that the greater the density of indirect connections in a network, the greater will be the trust and cohesion among members.

In an empirical study examining the effects of strong indirect network connections, Burt finds support for these hypotheses but also finds the distrust, likely to develop when relationships among members is weak, is amplified when indirect connections within a social network are strong. This effect is even more pronounced for distrust than it is for trust. That is, indirect network connections amplify the distrust associated with weak relations more than it amplifies trust within strong relations. Burt concludes that cohesion's primary effect is rigidity—it enhances trust between people who are already close and increases the distrust between people who are not close.

Although Kramer and Burt differ in their approaches to studying the development of trust in organizations—Kramer focusing on individual cognitive process and Burt emphasizing social networks—both suggest that the initial relationships between group members have a powerful influence on the development of trust. Both agree the downside—the development of distrust—has the more powerful effects, both on the individual and on the networked communities in which they are embedded.

The relationship between trust and knowledge sharing appears to be reciprocal. To the extent that knowledge is shared within a network or group, trust will develop among its members, and to the extent trusts exists in groups, individuals will be willing to share the knowledge they possess.

THIRD PARTIES AND SOCIAL VALIDATION—THE PROS AND CONS OF CREATING SHARED REALITY

One might reason the primary value of shared knowledge is that it provides social validation for individual beliefs and creates socially shared realities. To the extent that others believe what we believe, we can be more confident in our judgments, decisions, and predictions. We can feel safe in otherwise uncertain worlds. It is not surprising, then, that individuals seek social validation of their own knowledge and beliefs from the groups and organizations to which they belong. A theme running through the various contributions to this volume is that although shared realities foster trust and cohesion, they can also bias cognitive processing and lead to skewed views of the world. Thus, there are both benefits and burdens to shared reality.

For example, Gruenfeld and Fan (chap. 11, this volume) find that boundary-spanning individuals, who possess integrative complex knowledge that arises from multiple group membership, have the potential to enlighten and enhance the knowledge of majority group members. Yet, because boundary-spanners are likely to be viewed as minority rather than majority group members, their views and knowledge are often not acknowledged or sought by majority members. Further, even when boundary-spanners' views are expressed, they usually have little influence on majority decision making. One could hypothesize that boundary-spanners threaten the socially shared reality of majority group members and that to protect this shared reality, majority members are willing to exclude potentially valuable information. Thus, groups intent on maintaining a shared reality often pay a price in the form of loss of intellectual capital from their potential knowledge bank.

Even though their methodologies are quite different, Stasser's findings (chap. 3, this volume) are in line with those of Gruenfeld and Fan. Whereas Gruenfeld and Fan examine the impact of a minority member's viewpoint on group processing and outcome, Stasser examines the impact of minority information (in the form of unique unshared information that each member of a discussion or decision-making group possesses) on group process and outcomes. He finds that although discussion groups may be responsive to unique information that is unshared by all group members, that unique information receives relatively little weight in their deliberations. Stasser suggests that when unique information counters an emerging group consensus groups tend to ignore it because it interferes with what members experience as progress toward a group goal. This process occurs even when the unique information is vital to the decision task.

Jost et al. (chap. 5, this volume) suggest that one role shared reality serves is to protect the status quo. Social systems require and gain stability through the power of socially shared cognitions and Jost et al. argue that individuals who benefit from the status quo will go to great lengths to preserve it by amassing materials and resources to bolster their subjective sense that present arrangements are fair and just. Such system-justifying attitudes and beliefs are maintained by ignoring or dismissing potentially valuable (but system-threatening) information.

Similarly, Levine and Moreland (chap. 12, this volume) caution about the potential downside of shared mental models in organizations. If, for example, the mental models workgroup members share are inaccurate or become outdated, they could actually inhibit group performance. Moreover, to the extent that organizations select individuals to fit a strong group culture, they are likely to reject competent individuals who hold different and potentially valuable perspectives. Such a process may reduce the quality of decision making within the group by increasing the likelihood of a "groupthink" (Janis, 1972) decision process, to say nothing of the effect of reducing diversity within the organization.

Because shared reality turns subjective experience into objective reality, Higgins (chap. 2, this volume) suggests that individuals will seek out social validation for their beliefs, especially in ambiguous situations. By seeking out others who share one's view of the world, one is able to believe one's own uncertain views are now reliable, valid, generalizable, and predictive. The enigma, however, is that this need for social validation often leads to a biased search for confirming evidence at the expense of equally plausible evidence to the contrary.

Burt (chap. 10, this volume) agrees with this view and submits that when individuals are seeking information, they often select as third parties individuals who are like themselves. This tendency to select similar others leads to biased information processing in two ways. First, there is a selection bias in the third-party information that is obtained and second, there is a selection bias in the information that third parties choose to share. Burt refers to the result of this process as gossip, clearly a negative view of the process. Moreover, he argues that managers embedded in one strong social network are more likely to receive biased third-party views, are less likely to be exposed to variable interpretations of events and, thus, are more likely to be biased by third-party gossip than are individuals who are not embedded in social networks. Those who instead have multiple network connections are more likely to be exposed to more variable (and less biased) information. The knowledge such individuals accrue is a form of social capital, a commodity that can be brokered. Brokers, who are less likely to be influenced by third-party gossip, may make more accurate judgments about the trustworthiness of information shared. Burt's concept of brokers is not unlike the concept of "boundary-spanners" discussed by Gruenfeld and Fan. They are similar in that both assume the boundary-spanning or brokering individual possesses valuable or "integratively complex" knowledge due to their multiple-group memberships. Yet Gruenfeld and Fan's work suggests groups that boundary-spanners span many not necessarily benefit from the knowledge they bring, whereas Burt suggests brokers benefit from their cross-group knowledge because of their ability to broker the knowledge to others.[1]

WHEN KNOWLEDGE IS NOT SHARED

The prior section focused on the pros and cons of knowledge sharing for individuals and the groups and organizations to which they belong. I now consider the reasons for and consequences of not sharing knowledge.

The social cognitive processes and biases discussed earlier are not the only reasons why information may not be shared. Stasser (chap. 3, this volume) argues that a number of structural barriers also prohibit the sharing of unique information. One, discussed earlier, is a simple sampling barrier—there is less unique information to sample from in the pool of information. Second, communication structures exist within groups that dictate who talks to whom, which may also prevent information sharing. Third, there are often role structures within groups such that there are shared behavioral expectations for group members regarding the information they are believed to possess. These expectations may or may not be accurate, and if they are not, important information may be lost because individuals who have information may not be asked to share it. Although Stasser focuses on why unique information is not shared, the clear implication from his work is that group outcomes would be superior if information were shared. He finds groups whose members do not share relevant information perform more poorly on decision tasks than do groups whose members share their knowledge.

Thompson et al. (chap. 7, this volume) also offer structural barriers as an example of the ways organizations control emotions. Individual displays of emotion are often thought to be disruptive to organizational life and, hence, functioning organizations are structured in ways to neutralize, buff-

---

[1]This difference between Burt's beliefs of the value of brokers and Gruenfeld and Fan's findings may be partially explained by the methodology used in the Gruenfeld and Fan study. The boundary-spanning individuals they studied had their minority membership "imposed" on pre-existing groups, thus disrupting group cohesion and norms. Burt's concept of brokers, on the other hand, suggests that brokers possess unique information other groups would value and desire. The broker does not impose him- or herself on a group but rather accrues value by his or her ability to fill structural informational holes in the group's knowledge.

er, and normalize emotions. The shared cognitions within organizations about appropriate levels of emotion might be thought of as organizational "emotional norms." Although on the surface it may appear that emotional controls facilitate smoother organizational functioning, one can speculate that rumbling occurs under the surface, which will eventually erupt if there are no outlets for emotional expression. Organizations exerting excessive control over employee opportunities to express emotions may suffer not only because employees may resist and react to such controls but also because they may be missing the benefits of capturing and utilizing the energy behind emotions, especially positive ones, for the organizational good.

Olivera and Argote (chap. 13, this volume) also consider the structural barriers within organizations that inhibit knowledge sharing. The structure of cross-functional teams often leads to teams that are not well knit, especially in the development stage, and Olivera and Argote suggest this lack of a common understanding between team members may inhibit the innovation necessary to succeed. Product development often occurs in uncertain and novel environments (unstructured) and planning often occurs online rather than through formal channels. Further, because cross-functional team members are often not at the same physical location and no face-to-face interaction occurs, product development suffers due to poorer communication about concepts. Physical separation decreases opportunities to develop shared understanding. Product development is an adaptive process requiring continuous learning and because shared knowledge and experience is vital to this process, organizations that are involved in new product development need to remove structural barriers to insure that opportunities for knowledge sharing will occur. Otherwise, organizational outcomes will be less than optimal.

Messick (chap. 4, this volume) takes an even more macro approach in considering the potential downside to constituents and communities when organizations purposely conceal relevant information from them. In particular, he focuses on the U.S. tobacco industry and the strategies and tactics they have used to effectively conceal information and data about the harmfulness of their products. Messick refers to such concealment as "dirty secrets" and suggests that once the concealment process begins, it grows exponentially as each act of concealment then needs to be concealed. This concealment occurs not only between the organization and those who consume its products but also within the organizational walls. Messick suggests specific knowledge about harmful products may not be shared within organizational units in order to protect and insulate high-ranking officials and spokespersons from blame and responsibility.

Messick examines two general strategies organizations use to conceal dirty secrets. He refers to them as "knowledge shields" and "smoke screens." Knowledge shields include the requirement and enforcement of confidentiality agreements, personal attacks on and discrediting of individuals who blow the whistle on organizational misconduct, and "patterned amnesia," a form of strategic retrieval failure that includes destruction of documents and other incriminating evidence. Smoke screens include the development of procedures, strategies, and institutions whose specific purpose is to create doubt, suspicion, and uncertainty about any allegations that would reveal or imply the existence of dirty secrets. These smoke screens include: sham objectivity, such as creating institutions like the Tobacco Industry Research Committee that appear to be independent and objective but are in actuality outlets for organizational propaganda; creating an illusion of controversy by suggesting experts disagree about product harmfulness or by critically scrutinizing all unfavorable research; or shifting responsibility to divert attention away from organizational knowledge of product harm.

The consequences of unshared knowledge, when such knowledge is purposely concealed in order to protect organizations from taking responsibility for the harm their products may cause, are immense and far reaching. They are likely to effect employees of the organization, their customers, and the organization itself. One can only imagine the psychological and moral toll that employees who work in an environment of concealment must pay. An organization engaged in concealment on a grand scale must create a culture where there is little trust and much suspicion. Although the organization may profit financially from the concealment, it is likely to suffer in the long run from the culture it fosters. Considerable energy must be expended on the concealment process that could be directed toward much more creative and productive organizational pursuits. Unfortunately, it is the consumer and general public that pays the ultimate price for organizational concealment, and it is understandable how those addicted to a harmful product will be easily swayed by the misinformation that organizational smoke screens provide.

SHARING KNOWLEDGE: AN AUTOMATIC OR MOTIVATED PROCESS?

One way to conceptualize the process of knowledge sharing is to consider the extent to which, or the conditions under which, it occurs automatically as a natural process requiring little cognitive effort or if and when it results from motivated cognition; that is, by choice. I first consider automatic processes related to knowledge sharing.

When Shared Knowledge Is an Automatic Process

The "seize and freeze" tendency to rely on chronically accessible knowledge structures exhibited by individuals who are high on the need-for-closure trait appears to be automatic process (Jost et al., chap. 5, this volume). Moreover, that this tendency can be situationally induced by environmental noise suggests individuals engage in this process with little cognitive awareness. People may be aware of the content of their chronically accessible knowledge structures but are likely unaware that they engage in the type of heuristic processing that excludes knowledge inconsistent with those structures. Thus, some individuals—and, under certain environmental conditions, most individuals—will limit the amount of information they utilize and will for the most part be unaware of this exclusion process.

The process of audience tuning (Higgins, chap. 2, this volume) appears to be a combination of automatic and motivated processing. The initial tuning of communicators to an audience is a form of ultrasensitivity to audience members' beliefs and attitudes. This tuning is likely a motivated process because communicators need to understand audience beliefs in order to deliver messages effectively. The processes that follow from this tuning (saying is believing effects, the correspondence bias) however, appear to be automatic ones. Thus, even though communicators may initially choose the knowledge they will share with others as a function of what they know about the others, communicators are unaware of the effect this tuning process has on their own subsequent beliefs and evaluations.

Similarly, the process of seeking social validation from similar others described by both Burt and Kramer (chaps. 10 and 8, this volume) suggest a combination of motivated and automatic processing. Individuals may be aware they are choosing to share information with and obtain information from in-group members. They tend to be unaware, however, that the information they obtain is likely to be biased and, in turn, biases their own information processing.

The same mix of processing appears to hold for the effects of norms on behavior. Norms are perhaps the best example of shared knowledge within a community, even though they are often implicit. Cialdini et al. (chap. 9, this volume) suggest that in new and uncertain situations, people are particularly attentive to what others do in order to understand what is normative behavior for the situation; yet, once the norms are assimilated, individuals behave in normative ways without really thinking about them. Thus, conformation to norms becomes an automatic process. In many instances, people often are unaware that norms are operating until one is violated, thus making it salient.

Thompson et al.'s (chap. 7, this volume) description of "the social facilitation of emotion" and "emotional contagion" suggests these processes also occur automatically. People are generally not aware, for example, that their emotions are more intense when experienced in the presence of others. And, even though people are usually aware of their own happy or sad feelings that result from emotional contagion, they are likely unaware of the processes of mimicry, catching, and emotional tuning that occur in spreading emotion.

When Shared Knowledge Is a Motivated Process

Many of the processes described in this volume are examples of motivated decision processes that individuals use in deciding whether and what knowledge to share with constituent groups. Tetlock (chap. 6, this volume), for example, describes a number of "identity-defining choices" that individuals must make when facing accountability dilemmas. Because individuals feel accountable to groups, a number of situations arise where they must choose to either accommodate their attitudes toward group norms or remain true to themselves, to use preemptive self-criticism or to self justify, to avoid or to enter into controversy, or to implement or resist the collective mission. Tetlock discusses the conditions under which individuals will make one choice or the other, but key in this decision process is the underlying motivation of the individual. The cognitive processes Tetlock describes are clearly motivated ones.

Although information, communication, and role structures are shown to affect what information individuals share in decision-making groups, Stasser (chap. 3, this volume) also acknowledges that individuals often choose not to disclose the unique information they possess. They may, for example, be concerned about being outliers, that they are keeping groups from reaching consensus, or that they do not have enough status or expertise to offer information. Regardless of the reasons, the decision to share information or not is usually motivated.

The development of transactional memory systems in work groups (Moreland, chap. 1, this volume; Olivera & Argote; chap. 13, this volume) also implies motivated learning. Individuals learn what others know in order to facilitate production success. Although Moreland suggests that some of this learning may come about as a result of group members spending time together, the fact that individuals are aware of who knows what implies motivated processing of information.

In his work on the development of collective trust, Kramer (chap. 8, this volume) characterizes individuals as intuitive social auditors who maintain a strict accounting of past exchanges and transactions with interdependent others in order to determine who is trustworthy. Although he goes on to illustrate the many ways that cognitive processes can go astray and lead to incorrect decisions about trustworthiness, the initial decision to audit is, again, motivated.

Similarly, Burt's (chap. 10, this volume) concept of brokers implies that in filling "structural information holes" between loosely connected social networks, individuals are doing so strategically. That is, these individuals realize that by obtaining knowledge from multiple networks, they acquire social capital and can position themselves where they can broker the information as a commodity, a process that is clearly motivated.

Lastly, decisions not to share, or to specifically conceal, information about harmful products (Messick, chap. 4, this volume) could be said to be motivated in the extreme. Thus, the studies in this volume lead one to conclude that a range of cognitive processes, from purely automatic to highly motivated, affect what people come to know about their social worlds, what they believe is true, what information they choose to share, and what they ultimately do.

LIMITATIONS AND FUTURE DIRECTIONS

The introduction to this chapter hinted at the variety of perspectives the various contributors to this volume have taken on the concept of shared knowledge in organizations. They are as diverse as the many disciplines represented. Yet, as I have tried to illuminate, there are many connections as well. Several contributions are very complementary and others bring completely new perspectives. Taken together, they provide considerable insights into the topic of knowledge sharing at the individual, the group, and to a lesser extent, the organizational level.

It is at the organizational level that there is still much to be learned. Because individuals and small groups are so much more accessible and easier to study, it is perhaps not surprising that most of the work presented here is done at that level. The organization as a whole is a bulky, nearly unmanageable, behemoth. Yet it is difficult to describe and understand the whole when we only examine its parts. It is like the story of several blindfolded individuals each touching only one part of an elephant (the foot, the trunk, the ear, the tail): Each can only describe the part they experience and will make inferences about the whole based on that experience, yet none correctly perceives or understands the entire being.

To understand the impact of shared and unshared knowledge on organizational processes and outcomes, more research attention needs to be focused at the organizational level. We need to better understand, for example, the effect organizational structure has on how and with whom knowledge is shared. The field of communication could likely inform such questions and network analysis appears to be useful methodology for this pursuit.

The call for more research at the organizational level in no way diminishes the value of the research presented here. This volume illuminates the cognitive and emotional processes that occur at the individual level when individuals interact with relevant groups. It highlights the ways individual knowledge is shared and becomes part of collective knowledge. It reveals how individual beliefs about what those in collectives know in turn affect individual cognition. It shows how memory systems develop among interactive groups and how such memory enhances group performance. Last, it demonstrates the downside to group and organizational decision making when information is not shared. A challenge for future research on shared knowledge in organizations will be to determine the extent to which the interactive processes described above will pertain at the organizational level.

REFERENCES

Argote, L., & McGrath, J. E. (1993). Group processes in organizations: Continuity and change. *International Review of Industrial and Organizational Psychology, 8*, 333–389.

Carnevale, P. J., & Isen, A. M. (1986). The influence of positive affect and visual access on the discovery of integrative solutions in bilateral negotiation. *Organizational Behavior and Human Decision Processes, 37*, 1–13.

Cialdini, R. B., Kallgren, C. A., & Reno, R. R. (1991). A focus theory of normative conduct: Recycling the concept of norms to reduce littering in public places. *Journal of Personality and Social Psychology, 58*, 1015–1026.

Coleman, J. S. (1990). *Foundations of social theory.* Cambridge, MA: Harvard University Press.

George, J. M. (1990). Personality, affect and behavior in groups. *Journal of Applied Psychology, 75*, 107–116.

Hackman, J. R. (1992). Group influences on individuals in organizations. In M. C. Dunette & L. M. Hough (Eds.), *Handbook of industrial and organizational psychology* (Vol. 3, pp. 199–268). Palo Alto, CA: Consulting Psychologists Press.

Hollingshead, A. B. (1996). The rank order effect in group decision making. *Organizational Behavior and Human Decision Processes, 68*, 181–193.

Janis, I. L. (1972). *Victims of groupthink.* Boston: Houghton Mifflin.

Kramer, R. M., Newton, E., & Pommerenke, P. L. (1993). Self-enhancement biases and negotiator judgment: Effects of self-esteem and mood. *Organizational Behavior and Human Decision Processes, 56*, 110–133.

Kruglanski, A. W. (1989). *Lay epistemics and human knowledge: Cognitive and motivational bases.* New York: Plenum.

Kruglanski, A. W., & Webster, D. W. (1996). Motivated closing of the mind: "Seizing" and "freezing". *Psychological Review, 103*, 263–283.

Larson, J. R., Jr., & Christensen, C. (1993). Groups as problem-solving units: Toward a new meaning of social cognition. *British Journal of Social Psychology, 32*, 5–30.

Larson, J. R., Jr., Christensen, C., Abbott, A. S., & Franz, T. M. (1996). Diagnosing groups: Charting the flow of information in medical decision making teams. *Journal of Personality and Social Psychology, 71*, 315–330.

Stasser G., & Stewart, D. (1992). Discovery of hidden profiles by decision-making groups: Solving a problem versus making a judgment. *Journal of Personality and Social Psychology, 63*, 426–434.

Stasser, G., Taylor, L. A., & Hanna, C. (1989). Information sampling in structured and unstructured discussion of three-and six-person groups. *Journal of Personality and Social Psychology, 57*, 67–78.

Stasser, G., & Titus, W. (1987). Effects of information load and percentage of shared information on the dissemination of unshared information during group discussion. *Journal of Personality and Social Psychology, 53,* 81–93.

Stewart, D. D., & Stasser, G. (1995). Expert role assignment and information sampling during collective recall and decision-making. *Journal of Personality and Social Psychology, 69,* 619–628.

Tetlock, P. E. (1986). A value pluralism model of ideological reasoning. *Journal of Personality and Social Psychology, 50,* 819–827.

Tetlock, P. E. (1997). Accountability: *Who must answer to whom?* Unpublished manuscript. Ohio State University, Columbus, OH.

Webster, D. M., & Kruglanski, A. W. (1994). Individual differences in need for cognitive closure. *Journal of Personality and Social Psychology, 67,* 1047–1062.

Author Index

Subject Index